ARCHITECTURE:
In Fashion

EDITED BY

Deborah Fausch

Paulette Singley

Rodolphe El-Khoury

Zvi Efrat

PRINCETON ARCHITECTURAL PRESS

This publication grew out of a conference by the same name, held in April 1991 under the auspices of the Princeton University School of Architecture. Neither conference nor book would have been possible without the generous financial contributions of the Princeton University School of Architecture, the Andrew W. Mellon Foundation for the Visual Arts and Humanities and the Graham Foundation for Advanced Study in Fine Arts. It is equally indebted to the contributions of professors, colleagues and staff at Princeton who helped with everything from small but numerous administrative tasks to encouraging our efforts while offering welcome criticism. Finally, we would especially like to thank Kevin Lippert for his consistent willingness to support new avenues of architectural discussion, and Seonaidh Davenport for her generous and thoughtful editorial assistance.

Published by
Princeton Architectural Press
37 East 7th Street
New York, NY 10003
ISBN 1–878271–99–7

Printed and bound in the United States by Edwards Brothers, Inc.

Associate Editor
Seonaidh Davenport

Book Design
Allison Saltzman

Special editorial assistance:
Jesse Easley

Special thanks to:
Caroline Green, Clare Jacobson, Kevin Lippert,
Bill Monaghan, and Ann Urban

Library of Congress Cataloging-in-Publication Data
Architecture: In Fashion / edited by Deborah Fausch.
          p.   cm.
     A collection of essays and projects resulting from a symposium
organized by graduate students of Princeton University School of
Architecture in April 1991.
     ISBN 1-878271-99-7 (pbk.) : $17.95
     1. Signs and symbols in architecture—Congresses.
2. Architecture, Postmodern—Congresses. 3. Deconstructivism
(Architecture)—Congresses. I. Fausch, Deborah, 1950–
II. Princeton University. School of Architecture.
NA682.P67A73   1994
724'.6—dc20
94–7730
CIP

Contents

In

PAULETTE SINGLEY
DEBORAH FAUSCH

The statuesque woman, provocatively draped in white fabric and carefully posed among the columns of a classical temple, establishes an archetypal site for focusing the sartorial gaze onto the petrified facade (Fig. 1).[1] But while the body in the temple has yielded rich rewards to those peering into the depths

WHAT IS ARCHITECTURE: IN FASHION?

of its oppositions—monument and maiden, edifice and ornament, architecture and anatomy—lingering instead on the surface of this image allows us to isolate a paradox constituted of two received but apparently conflicting equations between fashion and architecture: 1) the transitory: architecture, unlike fashion's system of rapid

duction

change, is static; 2) the vestimentary: architecture, like fashion's garment, clothes the body. The antimony between these transitory and ves-

timentary syllogisms suggests that architecture remains at once "in" and "out of" fashion.

Although artificially constructed, both of these equations are naturally motivated: one recalls the near identity between the column's flutes and the fabric draped over the matron's body, while the

IS IT NATURAL OR SYNTHETIC?

other depends upon fashion's rapid cycle of consumption to define architecture as fashion's "other."[2] This latter cleavage between durable edifice and ephemeral textile motivates not only advertising's use of architecture as a sign for resistance to change, but also fashion's desire to acquire an aura of classic timelessness through a metonymical relationship with the edifice. To locate the intersti(t)c(h)es between these two ostensibly natural paradigms is one of the central intentions of this publication.

FIG. 1 *Advertisement, Henri Bendel Department Store. Reprinted with permission from Henri Bendel*

In the woodcut "The Draftsman and the Reclining Woman" (1538), Albrecht Dürer's drawing machine mediates between spectacle and spectator. Its components include a frame—with which a view is bounded, a needle—through which one perceives, and a thread—by which the line of sight is marked.

The history of the drawing machine reflects an increased dependency on the mathematical eye and a decreased concern for the body. Substitutions: Where Dürer's drawing machine analyzes and produces a homogeneous grid of similarities, the speculum dilates and mirrors, and the sewing machine connects disparate materials and produces seams that bind and divide.

The Complete Woodcuts of Albrecht Dürer *(Mineola, N.Y.: Dover Publications, 1963), Marcel Duchamp,* Salt Seller *(New York: Oxford University Press, 1973). Chihiro Yokochi,* Photographic Anatomy of the Human Body *(Tokyo: Igaku-Shoin, 1989). Photographs of Sewing Machine and Vanity Mirror courtesy of Christine Magar.*

FIG. 2 Speculations, *Christine S. E. Magar, 1993*

But our concern is also to pick out other, more unnatural threads contaminating architectural theory with fashion's discursive apparatus. To slip into a pocket, to hang on a rack, to hide in a closet, to occupy a storefront, is to locate the body in the spaces of fashion. Yet unraveling the fabric that makes up architecture's apparel only to discover that the body is its central lack, that the body dwells within the surface, is to challenge architecture's apprehension of fashion's whims. From Georges Seurat's umbrellas to Albrecht Durer's "sewing machine," the operations of this heterogeneous couple intersect on the architect's table (Fig. 2).

WHAT OCCURS IN THE SPACE BETWEEN FABRIC AND SKIN? ARE SKIN AND BONES BUILDINGS MISSING CLOTHING OR FLESH?

In addition to Gottfried Semper's weaving of text, context, texture and textile, a lexicon of commonplaces—curtain wall, window dressing, skirt board, outskirts, underpinning, foundation, dress, coat, uniform, formal, margin, border, facing, fringe, fabric, fabricate, fashion, fold, bias, tack, cut, alter, pin, pattern, patch—suggests the extent of overlap between the discipline of architecture and the tailor's quotidian craft. Jennifer Bloomer augments this relationship between sewing and architecture with her own practice of patching: stitching together diverse remnants to bind architecture and literature. Quoting Gilles Deleuze and Felix Guattari, Bloomer identifies the theoretical affiliations of her architectural raiment:

> Patchwork, for its part, may display equivalents to themes, symmetries, and resonances that approximate it to embroidery. But the fact remains that its space is not at all constituted in the same way: there is no center; its basic motif ("block") is composed of a single element: the recurrence of this element frees uniquely rhythmic values distinct from the harmonies of embroidery (in particular, in "crazy" patchwork, which fits together pieces of varying size, shape, and color, and plays on the *texture* of the fabrics).[3]

Likewise, we have assembled these essays into a patchwork of sundry notions and diverse scraps, cut, trimmed, and pinned together to form a garment which, by its very design, remains open and unconstructed.

This patchwork is the product of a series of seminars held at the Princeton University School of Architecture, sponsored by the Andrew W. Mellon Foundation for the Arts and Humanities as well as the Graham Foundation for Advanced Study in Fine Arts. It also emerges from an uncertain moment at the school, when diverse and often conflicting interests

WHO IS INVITED? WHAT IS THE ATTIRE?

focused, for a brief period, on questioning the connections binding architecture and fashion. During the fall of 1990, Mary McLeod presented a preliminary version of the paper published here, sparked by a workshop which she and Leila Kinney held at Barnard's Feminist Art History Conference in October 1990. At about the same time, Mark Wigley was theorizing the structure of ornament in his graduate seminar. In addition, Beatriz Colomina had raised the issue of architecture and fashion in her paper for the conference "Sexuality and Space," held at Princeton in March 1990.[4] The work of this constellation of figures, in combination with Val Warke's 1987 seminar on fashion at Cornell University and our own desire to discuss the mechanisms of fashion as they operate within an institution such as Princeton University, encouraged us to organize a conference during the spring of 1991 entitled "Architecture: In Fashion."[5] Recognizing that any discussion of architecture and fashion would be incomplete without engaging the polemics of architecture's postmodern apparel, in the fall of 1991 we invited Robert Venturi and Denise Scott Brown to speak to us about their work. We have also included an essay by Erin Mackie, then at Princeton's English department, on the treatment of fashion in early eighteenth-century London. We introduce this collection more or less in order of appearance, with the addition of projects by Machado and Silvetti and Diller + Scofidio that raise issues of architecture and fashion.

[J. I.] Grandville, "Die Mode," Eine Andere Welt (Zurich: Diogenes Verlag, **FIG. 3**
1979 [1844]), 276.

In "Undressing Architecture: Fashion, Gender, and Modernity," Mary McLeod exposes the profound ambivalence of modern architecture towards both femininity and fashion, an apprehension belied by its preoccupation with dress. McLeod contrasts Charles

DOES FASHION'S PRE-HISTORY IN THE SPACE OF CARNIVAL OR SPECTACLE ALLOW MODERN ARCHITECTURE TO CONSTRUCT IT AS A FLIMSY ADVERSARY TO MODERN ARCHITECTURE?

Baudelaire's somewhat contemptuous equation of modern beauty and ephemeral female fashion with Gottfried Semper's attempt to "delineate the slow, rather tedious route that architecture takes to construct meaning." She traces the vicissitudes of Semper's belief in a structural truth behind the ornamental surface in the fulminations of Otto Wagner, Adolf Loos, and Le Corbusier against the fleeting appearances of feminine fashions.

For Semper, the "principle of cladding" found its embodiment in temporary scaffolding ornamented with carnival decoration. But his conception of the wall as "dressing" became, in the theories of his followers, a more literal concern with male clothing as a model for modern architecture—an attempt to halt the ever-accelerating revolutions of fashion's wheel with the universal lines of English tailoring (Fig. 3). The attempt to pin down a styleless form of building led architects to define "the style representative of our times" in terms of a nude, white, male edifice. While they rejected

"FASHION IS THE ETERNAL RECURRENCE OF THE NEW. ARE THERE NEVERTHELESS MOTIFS OF REDEMPTION PRECISELY IN FASHION?"[6]

Semper's analogy between building and fabric, their entanglement with its implications manifests itself in their fixation, not just on the metaphor of suitable clothing, but also on its design and designers.

McLeod's outline of these developments in actual practices of clothing design reveals not only the extent of modern architects' clothing addiction, but also their bias toward the universal, permanent, and timelessly modern. However, as Val Warke writes, in the carnival of late modern life, fashion itself provides an aura of "facile contemporariness" for both animate and inanimate wearers. Warke's essay, "'In' Architecture: Observing the Mechanisms of Fashion," uses Mikhail Bakhtin's "allure of a carnivalized present, in which everything participates in a jolly relativity," as a metaphor for the devolution of *haute couture* onto "ready-to-wear." Warke analyzes the "quasi-rules" and formal systems of clothing design in the last stages of fashion's evacuation of content and progressive domestication of the new. He applies this analysis to the operations of architectural fashion in the academy, the journal, and the museum. Noting that fashion and consumer capitalism each require the other's operations, he asserts the futility of architecture's attempts to evade complicity with the fashion parade. Indeed, according to Warke, the all-perva-

"WHY WOULD ARCHITECTURE BE CONSTRUED AS BEING IMMUNE TO THE VICISSITUDES OF FASHION?"[7]

sive mechanisms of fashion replace modernism's pursuit of a universal *Zeitgeist* with Walter Benjamin's concept of an ever-changing *jetztzeit*, a present continuously created from the shifting fragments of the past. (Ironically, it is the specter of Benjamin, and his analyses of nineteenth-century Paris, that haunts many of these essays as the fashionable spirit of *our* age.)

Warke identifies the art museum, an important locus for the operations of the fashion machine, as an instrument for transmutating the elite negations of the avant-garde into more mainstream "radical charm." From Hitchcock and Johnson's 1932 "International Style" show to Wigley and Johnson's 1988 exhibit of "Deconstructivist

IS THIS FROM PARIS? IS RADICAL EVER REALLY CHIC?

Architecture," the Museum of Modern Art's showcasing of hand-picked architects as "current" provides a significant instance of this process.

Perhaps this very waning of radical aura underlies Wigley's charges (in an extended preface to his conference talk) that deconstruction in architecture still remains under attack; despite (or because of) its rapid dissemination, its status as " fashionable" subjects it to hostile criticism. Such criticism—that this type of theory remains on the surface of the architectural text—further censures it as fashionable clothing, hastily discarded from season to season. Instead, Wigley's own strategy of surface reading, which delineates this distaste for the "superficial," actually penetrates architecture's fear of what we may term the "transvestimentary"—its apprehension of contemporary theory as a transitory vestment. In his essay, "White-Out: Fashioning the Modern," which follows a series of published articles on this topic, Wigley's continuing fascination with the naked or painted surfaces of modernism—now expanded to include a panoply of modern figures, from Semper and Alois Riegl to Walter Gropius and Le Corbusier—demonstrates deconstruction's ability to sustain lasting discourse and its importance to the architectural canon.

HOW CAN WE DISTINGUISH BETWEEN AN ORIGINAL AND A "KNOCK-OFF?"

Wigley's exhaustive reading of these texts exposes architects, on all sides of modernism's debates, disavowing fashion as the necessary adversary of their own practices. In particular, Sigfried Giedion's constructed history of modernism, in which the architectural clothing of the nineteenth century serves as a defense against the unrefined structural truths lurking underneath, fabricates a psychology of buildings which places the historian in the privileged position of analyst. But Wigley's own analysis reveals that historians themselves employ their disavowal of fashion as a cover-up for the equivocal status of their own ideas within theoretical fashion.

Radical or *arrière garde*, architectural *haute couture*, like clothing design, relies upon the designer's unmistakable and presumably inimitable signature or style to guarantee its authenticity. From the architect's incised name to the "signature building," Hélène Lipstadt explored the role of the designer's signature in marking construction as architecture in her conference talk, "The Signature on the Building: Propositions for a Method of

WHAT IS THE LABEL? CAN I HAVE IT MONOGRAPHED?

Comparison of Architecture and Fashion Using Pierre Bourdieu's analysis of the *Griffe*." Applying Bourdieu's concept of "symbolic magic," Lipstadt argued that fashion can be understood as a "field" in which symbolic transformation or social alchemy occurs through the imposition of the signature, or *griffe*.[8] The *griffe*, a designer's label, originally referrred to the mark of an animal's claw. It acts as both site and instrument of a transubstantiation which, without changing the physical quality of an object, radically alters its social role. By thus engaging in the production of value the *griffe*, whether outright signature or identifiable style, is what creates architecture as such.[9]

Like Roland Barthes, Bourdieu considers fashion to be of special value for study because it releases the rules that all fields obey. Lipstadt investigated the homologies between the architecture profession and *haute couture*; she noted that both are situated between economic and symbolic/artistic fields, that they have similar conditions of production—team work, use of a model, etc.—and similar conditions of consumption, in which the distinctiveness of the original product is wasted away through diffusion. The use of prominent designers to promote clothing can be seen as an extension of the process by which the signature of the architect acts to guarantee legal responsibility, intellectual property, or artistic status. Rather than appropriating the building's aura, these advertisements borrow the fashionable architect's "name," which radiates into the garment, distorting or exaggerating the action of the commodity fetish. Although we are unable to reproduce Lipstadt's talk in this volume, we hope that the "symbolic magic" of our summary here will lead to its eventual publication.

To copy a design is to forge a signature; to alter one's appearance through clothing is to "forge" an appearance. In "Fashion and Figuration in Modern Life Painting," Leila Kinney describes nineteenth-century Parisians' apprehension of fashion's ability to dissimulate identities. Through her discussion of modern life painting, in particular Seurat's *Un dimanche à la Grande Jatte*, Kinney delineates the time and space of leisure within the domain of commodity fetishism. She traces the rhythmic sequence of changing appearances and daily activities that distinguish the man or woman of leisure—who might not even go out on Sunday—from the working class, for whom Sunday is work's only respite.

"WHO ARE THESE STIFF PEOPLE, THESE WOODEN DOLLS...?" [10] **HOW DO CLOTHING AND ARCHITECTURE DISCIPLINE THE BODY?**

Kinney identifies the department store, the museum, and the park as the most prominent arenas for the public's diurnal routine of shopping and promenading *en masse*. Extending Marcel Mauss's observation that "techniques of the body"—standing, sitting, eating, and even giving birth—are acquired rather than innate, Kinney argues that clothing inculcates class behaviors. The new democratization of luxury within which appearance formed "both a barrier and a bridge to social mobility" allowed the fluctuations of fashion to create an unstable system of signification, undermining the "physiognomic" classification systems—typologies and taxonomies—that had organized legible hierarchies within architecture and painting. It became increasingly clear that "the operation of fashion interferes with clothing's ability to function as an index." Kinney describes a persistent desire for coded hierarchies of form and content on the part of the Parisian bourgeoisie, hinting at the more pernicious social polemic lurking behind the anti-fashion rhetoric of functionalism.

"WHEN DID FASHION BEGIN?" HAVE WE REALLY MOVED THE DIS-CUSSION VERY FAR BEYOND ARCHI-TECTURE'S DEBATE OVER ARBITRARY AND ABSOLUTE VALUES? [11]

Locating this fashion anxiety a century earlier, in the rise of stylish shops, museums and other curiosity collections, Erin Mackie focuses on the fashion debates published by Joseph Addison and Richard Steele in *The Tatler* and *The Spectator*. In her essay, "Fashion in the Museum: An Eighteenth-Century Project," Mackie argues that the problem of clothing in eighteenth-century society was also one of "reference"—the disturbing ability of apparel to "forge identities." She reads a parallel between this emerging consumer environment and the world within the eighteenth-century viewer's brain, where "the thing holds sway over the psyche, the commodity displaces identity and the non-sense of fashion colonizes the interior locus of rationality." She examines *The Spectator*'s response to this disorderly milieu of unruly objects—a fashion museum in the form of a "sphinx," a startling representation of the ruthless mechanism of consumption. Half woman and half beast, the sphinx allegorizes fashion as a monstrous feminine edifice that consumes the shopper who cannot answer fashion's riddle.

WHAT PRICE ARE YOU WILLING TO PAY?

The act of interring fashion within the monumental taxonomic structure of a museum effectively embalms it in antiquarian dust. But by adorning the sphinx's facade with the ribbons, bows, and powder-puffs of contemporary clothing, Steele contaminates architecture's eternal classicism with fashion's ephemeral garb, thereby undermining the building's "natural" resistance to fashion's transitory whims. Indeed, as a repository for artifacts that can be disinterred periodically in order to affect or reflect shifting sensibilities of taste, the sphinx implicates all museums equally as museums of fashion. Likewise, *Architecture: In Fashion*—publication date, jacket design, epistemological assumptions, theoretical language, and list of contributors—is an artifact of the fashion museum. Inescapably, and like the building process itself, this publication emerges from a torpid cycle of production that can never match fashion's rapid rhythm of consumption. Always, already *passé*. Rather than attempt to evade this fading fashionability by embracing the surrealist notion of the outmoded, seeking to divine an ensuing trend, or presuming to initiate a new style, we accept and even relish the position of fashion victim.

In so doing, however, we also assume the greater risk of consigning the architectural projects presented here to the fashion heap. The work of each of these designers engages with the metaphor of architecture as fabric or clothing as well as with architecture's more ambiguous relationship to fashion's emphemerality. Each has effectively taken up a strategic position from which to negotiate the architect's precarious indebtedness to fashion's capricious appetites. In other words, each architect is fashionable in both senses of the word. We could assign them heuristically to three different spaces in a fashion matrix: whereas Venturi and Scott Brown appear to remain outside of fashion's consumptive mechanisms, Machado and Silvetti work within architectural fashion in order to cultivate transgressions against its strictures, and Diller + Scofidio, conspicuously located in fashion's spotlight, operate on its innermost organs. Bourdieu's description of poststructuralist philosophers' self-positioning on the "margins of philosophy" applies equally well to the three spaces of this matrix: each can be reduced to the single strategy of objectifying the practices and traditions of one's own institution, transforming this "commentary" into avant-garde production:

> By means of this semi-objectification one can situate oneself simultaneously inside and outside, in the game and on the touchline, i.e., on the margin, at the frontier, in the regions which, like the "frame," *parergon*, are so many limits,...points from which one can be as distant as possible from the interior without falling into the exterior, into outer darkness, that is, into the vulgarity of the non-philosophical [or non-fashionable]...where one can combine the profits of transgression with the profits of membership by producing the discourse that is simultaneously closest to an exemplary performance of philosophical discourse and to the exposure of the objective truth of this discourse.[12]

Thus, within the boundaries of the discipline, each of these architects is simultaneously performing on the periphery and in the center—both "in" and "out" of fashion.

Adopting a position that appears to be entirely exterior to fashion's imperatives, Venturi and Scott Brown maintain that their work is misapprehended from all sides of current discourse—the critics endorsing either classical or neo-radical styles dismiss their intentional manipulations of the formal territories of architecture. But to accept their self-analysis would be to misread their success at negotiating architecture's fashion system. While the award of the Pritzker Prize assigns Venturi's work to a comfortable orthodoxy within the architectural establishment, the private symposium at MoMA in April 1990 devoted to a discussion of their theories and practice, sponsored by Philip Johnson, also marks them as theoretically chic.[13] Thus, by their self-positioning outside of the mainstream of architectural debate, they have enhanced their role as fashionably radical other.[14]

IS IT COMING BACK IN STYLE? WAS IT EVER OUT OF STYLE? IS IT INTERNATIONAL STYLE?

In the conversation included in this volume, Venturi and Scott Brown's examination of architecture through the idiom of clothing places them within modern theory's tradition of fashion fixation. Tracing the shifting exaggerations of women's silhouettes throughout the ages allows them to distinguish between fashion and style, "hype" and decorum. They situate their own work within eighteenth-century notions of propriety in order to extend an on-going meditation on the role of convention—like fashion, "a way of doing things at a time." Underlying their discussion of suits, ties, and thrift-shop chic, however, is a reconciliation of apparent historicisms in the notion that classical decorum found its natural conclusion in the modernist problematic of fabric on frame.

Venturi and Scott Brown comment on the fancy-dress ball of architecture, proposing to replace the quick-changes of the neo-avant-garde with the *bienséance* of architectural "designer jeans." In the addition to the Bard College Library, the hyperbolic signage which characterizes their earlier work is succeeded by an abstract essay on the idea of the curtain wall that, in its flamboyant coloration and drapery, flatters the Roman temple which is at once overshadowed and set on center stage. Here Venturi and Scott Brown's ability to embellish modernism's strict codes of dressing introduces a discomfiting tension between structure and facade that, paradoxically, manifests their commitment to the ideology of structural truth.

Likewise, in a period when momentary flashes of the avant-garde are recycled in quick succession, that Machado and Silvetti's work cannot be reduced to a glossy signifier of such radical nostalgia guarantees its position as institutionally *en vogue*. The firm pins together the menacing, yet enticing, uniform of monumental architecture—often identified with totalizing political regimes—and the fragmentary, allusive accessories of technology—frequently associated with the politics of subversion. They create a meticulously tailored urban montage, veiled in propriety and the "discreet charm of the bourgeoisie." But behind this curtain of normalcy is the staged pathology of deviance which marks their work as razor-sharp and leather-bound. Between the erotic allure of the austere, even banal facades of the Vienna *Nordbahnhofgelände* project and the libertine effluvium of carnal pleasure located in the adult playgrounds of its outdoor theater and the funicular station, there lies a space of libidinal equivocation. The project delineates strict zones of public and private behavior, while encouraging the transgression of these very boundaries. Their pleasure in the perversion of order manifests itself in the plan for Vienna as a literal fabric, tightly stretched to its very limit, pulling on the city's historical and cultural biases. Machado and Silvetti arrive at an architectural discourse of pleasure and pain that marks the building as a sensual body and the city as a repository for hidden desire. They enhance this desire with the rhetoric of disguise, negotiating their position in fashion wearing the costume of decorum.

WHO IS WEARING THE CARNIVAL MASK? WHO IS LOST IN THE CROWD? WHO IS DRESSED TO KILL?

In contradistinction to Machado and Silvetti's careful shearing and tailoring of architectural apparel, Diller + Scofidio operate directly upon the epidermal layer of the anatomized object. Theirs is less the voyeur's pleasure in the veil of lingerie than the hypochondriac's delight in the hospital gown. By clinically examining the anesthetized sublimity of surgical eroticism, they dangle hazardously on fashion's sheer precipice.[15] Herbert Muschamp, who considers Diller + Scofidio to be among the most "elevated" thinkers in architecture today, describes the screen image of an open mouth which they projected into the vestibule of the Rialto Theater on 42nd Street for "Soft Sell" street interventions: "Though scarlet lips flirt with porn-shop imagery...the mouth speaks for the entire city: for Madison Avenue, for Wall Street, for the garment district, for an infernal machine that manufactures desire for people who have no patience with satisfactions."[16] Muschamp's succinct definition of fashion places their work in the very center of its infernal machine.

The approbation of institutions such as *The New York Times*, as Warke notes, reduces the radical to the commonplace, the daring to the tame.[17] Yet Diller + Scofidio's balancing on the edge of complete consumption marks their work as risky, and therefore *risqué*. As much as the *content*, *technique*, or even *theory* they employ, it is their audacity in returning fashion's sphinxlike gaze directly, unmasked, which characterizes their ability to manipulate the fashion system.

HOW CAN WE PROJECT OURSELVES INTO SUCH INDICES OF THE BODY'S FLUCTUATING EROGENOUS ZONES?

This is not, however, to discount the relevance of the object itself in their tactics of the market-place. In the project reproduced here, the *technique* of meticulously starching and folding a series of white dress shirts evacuates the body's *contents* from its habitable space and, in so doing, expounds a *theory* of the voided subject.[18] Thus, Diller + Scofidio prevent the inhabitation of fashion's space; the pocket, the rack, the closet, and the storefront are all inaccessible. That this project concerns clothing is, in fact, almost negligible with regard to its fashionable status: the fashion, as well as the architecture, consists in the fold as much as in the shirt.[19]

However, it is also the status of the object itself that fashion calls into question.

> Henceforth, oh living matter, you are nothing more
> Than the fixed heart of chaos, soft horror's granite core,
> Than a forgotten Sphinx that in some desert stands,
> Drowsing beneath the heat, half-hidden by the sands,
> Unmarked on any map,—whose rude and sullen frown
>
> Lights up a moment only when the sun goes down.[20]

IN WHAT WAYS DOES THE SPHINX'S BODY SERVE ARCHITECTURAL FASHIONS EMBLEMATICALLY AND ICONOGRAPHICALLY? HOW DOES THIS EMBLEM SPEAK TO THE ESSENTIALIZING AND CONTRADICTORY CATEGORIES OF FEMALE AS MATTER, MALE AS IDEA, FEMALE AS NATURE, MALE AS CULTURE, WOMAN AS CHANGEABLE, MAN AS ABSOLUTE, FEMININE AS ORIENT, MASCULINE AS OCCIDENT? [22]

From Steele's description of a dolled-up riddle museum to Baudelaire's slumbering metaphor for out-of-fashion, forgotten materiality, the sphinx's hybrid body offers a tangible image of modernity's fear of and resistance to contamination from physical impurity—the monstrous and horrifying, the unnatural, the feminine, the oriental, the arbitrary, the irrelevant and forgotten, the inscrutable, irrational, or even incomprehensible. [21]

Steele depicts the sphinx as an oriental feminine mystery that conflates the fashionable with the exotic, the temptations of the seraglio with the addictions of tea, coffee, and opium: fashion as sensuous luxury and moral turpitude. And in Deleuze and Guattari's *Anti-Oedipus*—whose title implies as its unstated reverse the possibility of *Pro-Sphinx*—the sphinx represents the undifferentiated other of Oedipus' egotistical and exclusive rationality. [23] But aside from her voracious appetite, the sphinx—like the Greek temple—does not offer a satisfying emblem of the transvestimentary—few monuments are more eternal than her colossal heap. [24] Thus the riddle posed by Steele's sphinx is her suitability as a metaphor for fashion, gender, and modernity. Nonetheless, we conclude by returning to her stony body, both as an allegory for the artifactual nature of this collection and because we have yet to subject this discussion to her implacable interrogations. Perhaps the sphinx of fashion—in her specifically feminine guise—can offer some answers to our initial queries concerning architecture and gender. Unlike the statuesque woman who, as ornamental appendage, is distinct from the temple, the

TO WHAT CONUNDRUMS DOES THIS OBDURATE SPHINX DEMAND AN ANSWER?

"I FORGET THE QUESTION." [25]

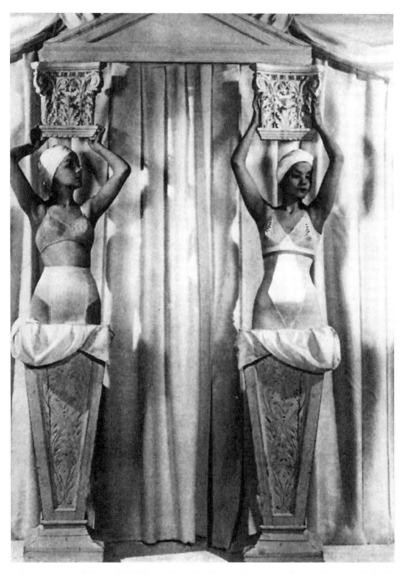

Advertisement in Vogue, *1939. From Christina Probert,* Lingerie in Vogue *Since   **FIG. 4**
1910 (London: Thames and Hudson, 1981), 38.*

sphinx constitutes an animate edifice which confounds in its mis-cegenation these rigid oppositions. The sphinx returns our gaze with a distinctively feminine one, challenging any univocally male

HOW DOES THE FEAR OF THE TRANSVESTIMENTARY CONDITION MOD-ERN ARCHITECTURE'S SELF-FASHIONING?

model of modernism. And indeed, as both McLeod and Wigley demonstrate, modern architecture's manifest critique of feminine fashion—the fear of the arbitrarily motivat-ed, the artificially natural, the temporarily permanent—all too readily slips into latent alliance with it. Fashion as psychosis.

It is in this sense that Henri LeFebvre describes modernity as char-acterized by crisis and change.[26] Perhaps, for modernity, fashion is simply the figure of instability which, by its reification, is constituted as the "other" of the desire for an originary, and supposedly stable, premodern past. Thus the transvestimentary

DOES INCITING A "CRISIS" INITIATE A FASHION?

constellates the fear of losing an underlying authenticity (Fig. 4). And perhaps what Roland Barthes depicts as a semiotic struc-ture—the endless circulation of signifiers reinforcing the system they make up, the denial of depth or underlying meaning—is in modernity emblemized as crisis, and in modern architecture deni-grated as the "battle of the Styles."

WHAT EXACTLY ARE THE CONSEQUENCES OF EMBEDDING FASHION WITHIN MODERNISM? IS IT FASHION'S STARK ENGAGEMENT IN THE COMMODITY RELATIONSHIP WHICH MAKES IT SUCH AN APPOSITE METAPHOR FOR MODERNITY?

For Baudelaire, "the transitory, fleeting beauty of our present life, the character of what the reader has permitted us to call *modernism*," constitutes an important characteristic of mod-ern art: "A constant, unchangeable element...and a relative, limited element coop-erates [sic] to produce beauty. The latter ele-ment is supplied by the epoch, by fashion, by morality, and the passions."[27]

Embellishing this lamination of the fleeting onto the permanent as modernity's *griffe*, Benjamin notes: "This illusion of novelty is reflected, like one mirror in another, in the illusion of infinite sameness."[28] Fashion as *mise-en-abyme*.

DOES YOKING FASHION TO FETISHISM IGNORE THE PREMODERN CONDITION OF ARISTOCRATIC TASTE, THE ELABORATIONS OF CODES, ARTIFICE AND ART? IS IT POSSIBLE TO THEORIZE THE ARCHITECTURE OF FASHION EXCLUSIVE OF MODERNITY'S "FLOUNDERING BETWEEN MARX AND FREUD?" [29]

DOES FEAR OF FASHION REALLY EXPRESS THE ALARM FELT BY 19TH-CENTURY OBSERVERS AT RAPID CHANGE? OR IS THE TRANSITORY NATURE OF FASHION A METAPHOR FOR THE PROGRESSIVE DESTABILIZATION OF WESTERN SOCIETY'S MOVEMENT TOWARDS A COMMUNITY OF STRANGERS, OF LAW INSTEAD OF CUSTOM, OF *GESELLSCHAFT* REPLACING *GEMEINSCHAFT*? ARE WE BASING OURSELVES UPON THEORIES OF RUPTURE THAT CREATE FALSE EPISTEMOLOGIES?

"HOW DOES ONE EXPLAIN THE PARADOX BY WHICH MODERN ARCHITECTS PARTICIPATED IN A CYCLE OF RAPID STYLISTIC CHANGE, YET DENIED THE TEMPORALITY OF FASHION AS A FORCE OR MODEL?" [31]

While Benjamin insists that transitoriness is merely illusion, Georg Simmel describes fashion's activity as at once characteristic of modern democratic bourgeois society and riddled with shifting imperatives that disrupt the economies of production and consumption: "The element of feverish change is so essential here that fashion stands, as it were, in a logical contrast to the tendencies for development in modern economics."[30] Fashion as paralysis.

The preoccupation of these authors with fashion conceals a more fundamental concern with the destabilizing assaults of rapid change.

"BUT CAN ONE SUGGEST HERE THAT ANY INQUIRY INTO FASHION MUST REFORM OR DEFLECT THE MODES OF INQUIRY, IF NOT TEASE THE LIMITS OF A DISCIPLINE THAT CONSTITUTES ITSELF BY OSTENSIBLY REJECT-ING FASHION, WHETHER THAT DISCIPLINE BE THAT OF ARCHITECTURE OR SCHOLARLY ARGUMENT IN GENERAL, WITHOUT HAV-ING THAT VERY SUGGES-TION EITHER UNCRITICAL-LY EMBRACED BY CERTAIN WELL-DEFINED GROUPS OF READERS OR UNCRITICALLY CENSORED BY OTHER GROUPS AS TOO FASHIONABLE? ...AND WOULDN'T A RIGOROUS INTERROGA-TION OF FASHION, WHATEVER THAT MIGHT MEAN, BE RIGOROUS ONLY INSOFAR AS IT CONFUSED THE DISTINCTION BETWEEN SUCH GROUPS?" [33]

And although modern archi-tecture tries to resist fash-ion's chimerical whims by proposing a style to end all styles, the demon of change slips in through the meta-phor of dress.[32] Fashion as sleight-of-hand.

WHAT IS THE HIDDEN THREAD OF ELITISM WHICH GATHERS THEORY INTO FASHION'S HEM? WHAT HAPPENS WHEN WE PULL AT IT?

DOES PURE FORM, IN WHICH THE "WHAT" IS LESS IMPORTANT THAN THE "HOW"—ART FOR ART'S SAKE, THEORY VS. PRACTICE, *HAUTE COU-TURE*—OCCUR ONLY WITH-IN SEGMENTS OF SOCIETY

Thus modernity constitutes fashion as one of its theore-tical topoi, which we can grasp only by means of the same defining vision—the sexual/commodity fetish, class and libidinal econo-mies, circulation of meta-phors and money.

DISTANCED FROM NECESSITY—ACADEMIC INSTITUTIONS AND COURT SOCIETIES FOR EXAMPLE? OR ARE SUCH GROUPS FORCED TO RENEW THEMSELVES BY RETURNING TO THE EXIGENCIES AND IMPROPRIETIES OF THE MARKET-FAIRE, BY FEEDING OFF OF THE REBELLION OF NEED AS THE SOURCE OF FASHION? IS FASHION "A VORTEX OF EFFECTS WHICH SUCKS A VACUUM INTO ITS OWN CORE"?[34] IS FASHION DEATH'S SISTER?[35] DOES THEORY ESCAPE

If these conceptual tools are in fact tautolgogical, fashion's "engine of distinction" also propagates hermetic, self-referential, ostensibly universalized codes of style—mannerism, "pure" theory, the escape into practice, anti-intellectualism—stylized modes of behavior and closed systems of otiosity not unique to modernity. Fashion as solipsism.

INTO THE REALM OF THE UNMOTIVATED OR IMMATERIAL IN ORDER TO EVADE THE CIRCUMSTANCES OF ITS OWN FASHIONABLE HISTORY? AND DOES HISTORY LIKEWISE ATTEMPT TO ESCAPE ANY THEORETICAL RISK THAT MARKS IT AS UNFASHIONABLE IN TODAY'S ACADEMIC MARKET? AND TOMORROW, WHAT WILL BE ON SALE?

IS IT POSSIBLE—AS WARKE AND KINNEY BEGIN TO SUGGEST—TO CONSTRUCT A COGNITIVE MAP OF ARCHITECTURAL FASHION WITHIN FASHION'S OWN SHIFTING SYSTEM OF SIGNIFICATION? WHAT SITES MIGHT THIS MAP CONTAIN WITHIN ITS DIACHRONIC AND SYNCHRONIC BOUNDARIES?

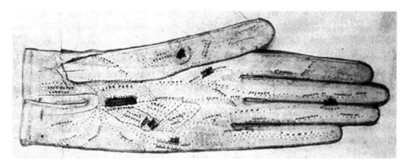

FIG. 5 *Map glove, souvenir of the Great Exhibition of London in 1851, registered by George Shore of New Oxford Street. From Sarah Levitt,* Victorians Unbuttoned *(London: George Allen & Unwin, 1986), 23.*

Returning to our initial question, we conclude by inquiring instead: "Where is Architecture in Fashion?"

Steele and Baudelaire left fashion's sphinx "unmarked on any map," abandoning her an existence solely within the space of the mind ("furniture" for the "empty cabinet" of the mind, as Locke puts it in *An Essay Concerning Human Understanding*).[36]

Perhaps this equivocal location suggests, to our poststructural apprehension, a teleological progression away from fashion's operation within the traditional spheres of the market, the arcade, the department store, the mall, towards the "private" domain of video shopping and a process of endlessly recycling the past in a post-modern mirage of urbanity that conflates high and low, orthodox and mannered, evolving and decadent, public and private, ad infinitum.

Perhaps it marks the city's frenzied sites of fashionable consumption in the club, the real estate market, the museum, the bookstore, the boutique, the cafe, or the salon. Or perhaps fashion exists in the extra-urban, extra-architectural space of the media, delineating a network of changes determined by the fluctuating successes of publications in the virtual realm of computer networks, and television. Superimposed upon one another, these speculative cartographies offer palpable, yet ephemeral, sites for *Architecture: In Fashion* (Fig. 5).

NOTES

1   We have taken the idea of the "sartorial gaze" from Joan Copjec's "The Sartorial Superego," *October* 50 (Fall 1989), 56–95. In her analysis of the obsessive photographs of Moroccan women entirely covered in the robes typical of Arab dress, taken by the French psychiatrist G. G. de Clérambault, Copjec emphasizes Clérambault's influence on the architects of his day. In 1923, the year in which Le Corbusier published *Vers une architecture*, he delivered a series of lectures on drapery at the École des Beaux Arts. Simultaneously, the Grand Prix competition was a residence for the representative of France in Morocco. At this time, the École favored a classical style for colonial architecture which "euphemized the brutal process of the erasure of the colonies' own beginnings." Copjec continues: "Nor is there any doubt that Clérambault's lectures and photographs assisted in this process. Moroccan drapery was not merely being used to reinterpret classical sculpture, classical sculpture was also being used to reinterpret Moroccan drapery—to reinvent it for the West." (65) Copjec also notes that, between Jacques-Francois Blondel's *Cours d'Architecture*..., published in the late eighteenth century (1771–1777), and J. N. L. Durand's *Recueil et Parallèle*..., published in 1799, there was a shift toward identifying building types by function, and thus a nascent move towards modernism. "It is at this point that style and ornament began to be considered precisely as *clothing*; their connection to the building, in other words, was taken as arbitrary rather than necessary, and they were viewed for the first time as the wrapping or covering of an otherwise nude building." (67) This early reconceptualization of buildings found its destination in Le Corbusier's reconceptualization of man: "While the designer of 'machines for living' was arguing that buildings must be tailored for man's use, he was simultaneously saying that man himself could be tailored by buildings." (74)

2   There is, we should recall, another relationship between clothing and columns: both also function as the parerga of Kant's third *Critique*. They are extrinsic yet integral forms of ornamentation that frame the body and the building. See Jacques Derrida, *The Truth in Painting*, trans. Geoff Bennington and Ian McLeod (Chicago: University of Chicago Press, 1987), 52–53.

3   Gilles Deleuze and Félix Guattari, *Thousand Plateaus: Capitalism and Schizophrenia*, trans. Brian Massumi (Minneapolis: University of Minnesota Press, 1987), 476, cited in Jennifer Bloomer, *Architecture and the Text: The (S)crypts of Joyce and Piranesi* (New Haven: Yale University Press, 1993), 175.

4   See for example Beatriz Colomina, "The Split Wall: Domestic Voyeurism," in *Sexuality and Space* (New York: Princeton Architectural Press, 1992), 73–130.

5   The speakers were Val Warke, Mark Wigley, Hélène Lipstadt, and Leila Kinney. The organizers were Michael Djordjevitch, Zvi Efrat, Rodolphe El-Khoury, Deborah Fausch, Louis Martin, Detlef Mertins, Daniel Monk, Eric Mumford, and Paulette Singley. The conference was sponsored by the Andrew W. Mellon Foundation for the Visual Arts Arts and Humanities in a grant to Princeton University School of Architecture's Ph.D. program in History, Theory and Criticism of Architecture, and Princeton University School of Architecture.

6   Walter Benjamin, *One Way Street and Other Writings*, trans. Edmund Jephcott and Kingsley Shorter (London: NLB, 1979), 46.

7   See Warke, this volume, 125.

8   See Pierre Bourdieu and Yvette Delsaut, "Le Couturier et sa griffe: contribution à un theorie de la magie, *Actes de la Recherche en Sciences Sociales* 1 (January–February 1975), 7–36.

9   Bourdieu, in contradistinction to Barthes, believes this production of value to be not a function of the power of words themselves, but rather the conditions which, by producing collective beliefs, empower words. Bourdieu and Delsaut, "La Couturier et sa griffe," 2, cited in Lipstadt's talk.

10   See Kinney, this volume, 292.

11   In the preface to *Ordonnance de Cinq Espéces de Colonnes* (1683), Claude Perrault notes that "habit...like that which causes a fashionable dress to please by its proportions" is the determination of arbitrary beauty. Positive beauty is self-evident; arbitrary beauty, on the other hand, depends on inclination, which is that "which makes us like fashionable things, and the ways of speaking which fashion has fixed at court." Arbitrary beauty is, however, the most important kind in architecture: "it is certain that the knowledge of arbitrary beauties is more proper to the formation of what is called taste, and that it is this which alone distinguishes the true architects from those who are not so; since to know most positive beauty, it is enough to have common sense...." Cited in Joseph Rykwert, *The First Moderns* (Cambridge, Mass.: MIT Press, 1983), 36–37.

12   Pierre Bourdieu, *Distinction: A Social Critique of the Judgment of Taste* (Cambridge, Mass.: Harvard University Press, 1984 [1979]), 496–97.

13   The entire event was a private showing of *haute couture* for the theorists with the most recent intellectual currency, but without their object of desire. Once again locating himself outside of the most fashionable architectural discourse, Robert Venturi declined the invitation to be present. John Whiteman, who attended the conference, summarized Venturi's position in a statement that is not entirely sympathetic to our own: "Wisely he stays away, for the more he knows about architecture, the more likely he is to lose in a game where the stakes have more to do with the mobilization for publicity than with the difficulties of architecture. Yet, ironically, he will be mistaken always for a master of

publicity...." Given that Whiteman finds himself in the position of publicizing an architect so supposedly unskilled at the techniques of self-promotion, the only irony here is the conference tone, which casts Robert Venturi and Denise Scott Brown as *idiots savants* or wild savages brought home by the "civilized world" and displayed as its new acquisition. For the speakers' summaries of this event see "The Rebirth of Theory: Reconstructing Venturi at MoMA," *Newsline*, May 1990.

14   See for example "'Leading from the Rear': Reply to Martin Pawley," in which Denise Scott Brown characterizes the firm as having then (in 1970) engaged in "nine years of almost unsuccessful practice." In Robert Venturi and Denise Scott Brown, *The View from the Campidiglio: Selected Essays 1953–1984* (New York: Harper and Row, 1984), 24.

15   Indeed, Georges Teyssot, in describing Diller's work as a consultant to the exhibition *Intimate Architecture: Contemporary Clothing Design*, at the Hayden Gallery in 1982, states that "the starting point is not fashion, but the very nature of the mechanical array, the eroticism of the apparel, the message provided by any attire, the layers of the mask and the artificial skin." "Erasure and Disembodiment: Dialogues with Diller and Scofidio," *Ottagono* 96 (*Prostheses*), September 1990, 57.

16   Herbert Muschamp, "A Highbrow Peep Show on 42nd Street," "Arts and Entertainment" section, *The New York Times* (Sunday, August 1, 1993), 34.

17   For example, in 1993, *The New York Times* "Styles of the Times" section devoted a full page cover to describing "deconstructivism" in clothing design. But, as Val Warke notes in his essay in this volume, this not only exemplifies poststructuralism's complete commodification by mainstream discourse but also the loss of elitism necessary for maintaining a fashionable status. There is no more sure fire way to kill a fashion than to publish it as fashionable. See Amy M. Spindler, "Coming Apart," "Styles of the Times," *The New York Times*, Sunday, 25 July 1993, 1. Spindler identifies the major proponents of "deconstructionism" in fashion as Comme des Garçons, Rei Kawakubo, Jean-Paul Gaultier, Martin Margiela, and Yohji Yamamoto. Defining deconstruction, she states: "The term first described a movement in literary analysis in the mid-20th century, founded by the French philosopher Jacques Derrida. It was a backlash against staid literary analysis, arguing that no work can have a fixed meaning, based on the complexity of language and usage." She explains the relationship of deconstructivism to fashion thus: "So not only does it mean that jacket linings, for example, can be on the outside or sleeves detached, but the function of the piece is re-imagined. The term as applied to fashion was first coined by Bill Cunningham in *Details* magazine in 1989, and, he said, it stuck." In this connection, Wim Wenders's and Yohji Yamamoto's film for the Centre Georges Pompidou entitled "Notebook on Cities and Clothes" (Santa Monica,

Calif.: Connoisseur Video, 1993), which treats the ways cities, like clothes and cinema, reshape our perceptions of our lives, is of particular interest.

18   Speaking of nineteenth-century men's dress, Baudelaire says: "And haven't the folds in the material, which make grimaces and drape themselves around mortified flesh like snakes, their secret charm?" *Salon de 1845*, 134, cited in Walter Benjamin, *Charles Baudelaire: A Lyric Poet in the Era of High Capitalism* (London: Verso, 1983 [1938]), 77.

19   See Gilles Deleuze, *The Fold: Leibniz and the Baroque*, foreword and trans., Tom Conley (Minneapolis: University of Minnesota Press, 1993), 121. originally published as *Le Pli: Leibniz et la baroque* (Paris: Editions de Minuit, 1988). As Deleuze explains:

> If the Baroque is defined by the fold that goes out to infinity, how can it be recognized in its most simple form? The fold can be recognized first of all in the textile model of the kind of implied garments: fabric or clothing has to free its own folds from its usual subordination to the finite body it covers. If there is an inherently Baroque costume, it is broad, in distending waves, billowing and flaring, surrounding the body with its independent folds, ever-multiplying, never betraying those of the body beneath: a system like *rhingrave-canons*— ample breeches bedecked with ribbons—but also vested doublets, flowing cloaks, enormous flaps, overflowing shirts, everything that forms the great contribution to clothing of the seventeenth century.

See also Peter Eisenman, "Unfolding Events," in Jonathan Crary and Sanford Kwinter, eds., *Incorporations* (*Zone* 6) (New York: Zone Publications, 1992), 424. Discussing the fold, Eisenman explains, "What is needed is the possibility of reading figure/object and ground within another frame of reference. Such a new reading might reveal other conditions that may always have been immanent or repressed in the urban *fabric* [italics added]. Such a reframing would perhaps allow for the possibilities of new urban structures and for existing structures to be seen in a way that they too are refined. In such a displacement, the new, rather than being understood as fundamentally different from the old, would instead be seen as slightly out of focus in relation to what exists. This out-of-focus condition, then, would permit a blurring or displacing of the whole, which is both old and new. One such possibility of displacement can be found in the form of the *fold*."

20   Charles Baudelaire, *Paris Spleen*, 86, cited in Benjamin, *Charles Baudelaire*, 55.

21   Benjamin identifies this materiality with the left-over objects of capital-

ist production, noting that Baudelaire's empathy with inorganic things allows him to speak the part of the commodity, or "the fetish itself." Ibid, 55–56.

22   Sherry Ortner, "Is Female to Male as Nature is to Culture?" in *Woman, Culture, and Society*, Michelle Zimbalist Rosaldo and Louise Lamphere, eds. (Stanford: Stanford University Press, 1974).

23   Gilles Deleuze and Félix Guattari, *Anti-Oedipus: Capitalism and Schizophrenia*, trans. Robert Hurley, Mark Seem and Helen R. Lane (Minneapolis: University of Minnesota Press, 1983, rpt. 1990), 311. Deleuze and Guattari write:

> Destroy, destroy. The task of schizoanalysis goes by way of destruction—a whole scouring of the unconscious, a complete curettage. Destroy Oedipus, the illusion of the ego, the puppet of the superego, guilt, the law, castration. It is not a matter of pious destructions, such as those performed by psychoanalysis under the benevolent neutral eye of the analyst. For these are Hegel-style destructions, ways of conserving. How is it that the celebrated neutrality, and what psychoanalysis calls—dares to call—the disappearance or dissolution of the Oedipus complex, do not make us burst into laughter? We are told that Oedipus is indispensable, that it is the source of every possible differentiation, and that it saves us from the terrible nondifferentiated mother. But this terrible mother, the sphinx, is herself part Oedipus; her nondifferentiation is merely the reverse of the exclusive differentiations created by Oedipus, she herself created Oedipus: Oedipus necessarily operates in the form of this double impasse.

24   Mark Jarzombek, in "Ready-made Traces in the Sand," suggests an analysis of the sphinx that sets her apart architecturally and institutionally as fashion's other. Interpreting Flaubert's fable of the meeting of the sphinx and the chimera as an allegory for the meeting of the universal and the original in architectural theory, Jarzombek labels various architectural theorists and practitioners as one creature or the other: "The archetypal problematic at the core of these oppositional debates was ingeniously dramatized by Gustav Flaubert in his masterpiece of 1874, *The Temptation of Saint Anthony*, toward the end of which a stony Sphinx and a multi-headed, many-limbed Chimera confront one another in the desert. Each is repulsed by the other, yet secretly longs for the other's attributes....The Sphinx suffers from a stifling aridity and timeless immobility, the Chimera from the emptiness of endless innovation. The Sphinx embodies everything conventional, doctrinaire, inflexible, and totalitarian, the Chimera everything disruptive, facile, fleeting, and vapid." Mark Jarzombek, "Ready-made Traces in the Sand: The Sphinx, the Chimera, and Other Discontents in the Practice of Theory," *Assemblage* 19 (December 1992), 74–5. Jarzombek ends by delivering a critique

of the position he terms the "liberation topos of contemporary architects," for example Peter Eisenman and Daniel Libeskind, who prefer the disordered fragment to the ordered whole. These theorists favor the fashionable chimera over the architectural sphinx to the degree that "the Sphinx-witch must be burned on the altar of a post-structuralist liberation." Jarzombeck, "Readymade Traces," 87.

25   Georges Bataille, in Denis Hollier, *Against Architecture: The Writings of Georges Bataille*, trans. Betsy Wang (Cambridge, Mass: MIT Press), 85, writes "The sphinx, with its numerous and huge examples, is of major importance to Egyptian sculpture. The figure is composed of an animal body and a human (feminine) face.

> "On the road to Thebes, Oedipus meets a sphinx who asks him a riddle: what animal walks on four feet in the morning, on two at midday, and on three at night? He is the first to figure out the answer ("man"), and he causes the death of the Sphinx.
>
> "(But, asks Bataille, "would not the answer be: 'I forget the question'?)
>
> "In the *Aesthetics* Hegel interprets this episode and this answer as an allegory for the birth of Greece: man is the Greek answer to the riddle, an answer that eliminates any trace of animality...
>
> "Bataille does not go along with either Oedipus or Hegel. He "prefers" the Sphinx. He refuses to have man be the answer. Instead he transforms man into a sphinx, into the riddle of his own contamination by animality."

26   Modernity, according to Lefebvre, is "something that, strictly speaking, has not changed at all for some centuries but that is accentuated by the present 'crisis.' This one cannot be confused with all the others because it seems to be total and permanent. Total, in that it throws into question values and norms as much as socioeconomic structures. Permanent, in that it is not making for some solution to the crisis, but seems rather to constitute the very mode of existence of 'modern' societies. Should we not recognize, in all the sensational annunciations of newness, as much a symptom of the crisis as any prediction based on knowledge? Crisis is a concept that affects all aspects of modernity: art, literature, philosophical truth, everyday life, the priority of the visual in both practice and conscience, etc.... Strangely enough, it is always accompanied by a retrogressive—even an archaeological—mode, or by a confusion between the ancient and the modern." Henri Lefebvre, "Modernity and Modernism," in *Modernism and Modernity*, Benjamin H. D. Buchloh, Serge Guilbaut, and David Solkin, eds. (Halifax, Nova Scotia: The Press of the Nova Scotia College of Art and Design, 1983), 2.

27   Charles Baudelaire, *The Painter of Modern Life*, 337, 363. Cited in Benjamin, *Charles Baudelaire*, 82–83.

28   "Novelty is a quality which does not depend on the use-value of the commodity. It is the source of the illusion which belongs inalienably to the images which the collective unconscious engenders. It is the quintessence of false consciousness, of which fashion is the tireless agent." Benjamin, *Charles Baudelaire*, 172.

29   Deleuze and Guattari, *Anti-Oedipus*, 63. As Foucault says, in his preface to Anti-Oedipus, in Europe between 1945 and 1965 "there was a certain way of thinking correctly....One had to be on familiar terms with Marx, not let one's dreams stray too far from Freud. And one had to treat sign-systems—the signi-fier—with the greatest respect." (xi) As Wigley notes in "Theoretical Slippage: the Architecture of the Fetish," the distinction of false front and real referent is common to all of these discourses. Mark Wigley, "Theoretical Slippage: the Architecture of the Fetish," in *Fetish* (*The Princeton Architectural Journal* 4) (New York: Princeton Architectural Press, 1992), 92ff. Structuralism, in its attempt to elucidate the nature of this relationship, only succeeded in prob-lematizing it irrevocably.

30   Georg Simmel's classic essay on fashion describes the contradictions between fashion and the market economy: "It has been noticed, especially in the older branches of modern productive industry, that the speculative element grad-ually ceases to play an influential *rôle*. The movements of the market can be bet-ter overlooked, requirements can be better foreseen and production can be more accurately regulated than before, so that the rationalization of production makes greater and greater inroads on chance conjunctures, on the aimless vacillation of supply and demand. Only pure articles of fashion seem to prove an exception. The polar oscillations, which modern economics in many instances knows how to avoid and from which it is visibly striving towards entirely new economic orders and forms, still hold sway in the field immediately subject to fashion. The ele-ment of feverish change is so essential here that fashion stands, as it were, in a logical contrast to the tendencies for development in modern economics." Georg Simmel, "Fashion," *On Individuality and Social Forms: Selected Writings*, ed. Donald N. Levine (Chicago: University of Chicago Press, 1971 [1904]), 319.
Simmel also notes that fashion is especially characteristic of middle class society: "On the one hand the lower classes are difficult to put in motion and they develop slowly....The highest classes, as everyone knows, are the most conser-vative, and frequently enough they are even archaic. They dread every motion and change, not because they have an antipathy for the contents or because the latter are inju-rious to them, but simply because it is change and because they regard every modification of the whole as suspicious and dangerous. No change can bring them

additional power, and every change can give them something to fear, but nothing to hope for. The real variability of historical life is therefore vested in the middle classes, and for this reason the history of social and cultural movements has fallen into an entirely different pace since the *tiers état* assumed control. For this reason fashion, which represents the variable and contrasting forms of life, has since then become much broader and more animated." Simmel, "Fashion," 317–18.

31   See McLeod, this volume, 40.

32   Many of these writers also muse, however, on the possibility that fashion is in some way "natural" to human society. Simmel avers that fashion is a natural characteristic of our species: "We cannot claim that all fashion is unnatural, because the existence of fashion itself seems perfectly natural to us as social beings, yet we can say, conversely, that absolutely unnatural forms may at least for a time bear the stamp of fashion." Simmel, "Fashion," 322. And in "Project for a Glossary of the Twentieth Century," J. G. Ballard includes this entry on fashion: "A recognition that nature has endowed us with one skin too few, and that a fully sentient being should wear its nervous system externally." J. G. Ballard, "Project for a Glossary of the Twentieth Century," in *Incorporations* (*Zone* 6) (New York: Zone Publications, 1992), 275.

33   See Wigley, this volume, 171.

34   Victor Burgin, "The End of Art Theory," *The End of Art Theory: Criticism and Postmodernism* (London: MacMillan, 1986), 174.

35   According to Giacomo Leopardi, the answer is yes:

> Death: ...So as you were born from the body of my mother, it would be right and proper for you to help me in some way with my business.

> Fashion: I have already done so in the past, more than you imagine. In the first place, I who continually annul or distort all other customs, have never allowed the practice of dying to fall anywhere into disuse, and you can see this is why it has universally endured to this day ever since the beginning of time.

> Death: Wonderful, that you haven't done what you couldn't have done anyway!

> Fashion: Why couldn't I? You just show you don't know the power of Fashion

From Giacomo Leopardi, *Giacomo Leopardi: The Moral Essays*, trans. Patrick Creagh (New York: Columbia University Press, 1983), 52. Originally published as *Operette morali* (Milan: Antonio Fortunato Stella, 1827).

36   John Locke, *An Essay Concerning Human Understanding*, ed. Peter H. Nidditch (Oxford: Clarendon Press, 1975), 55, Bk. 1, Chptr. 2, para. 15.

PART ONE
essays

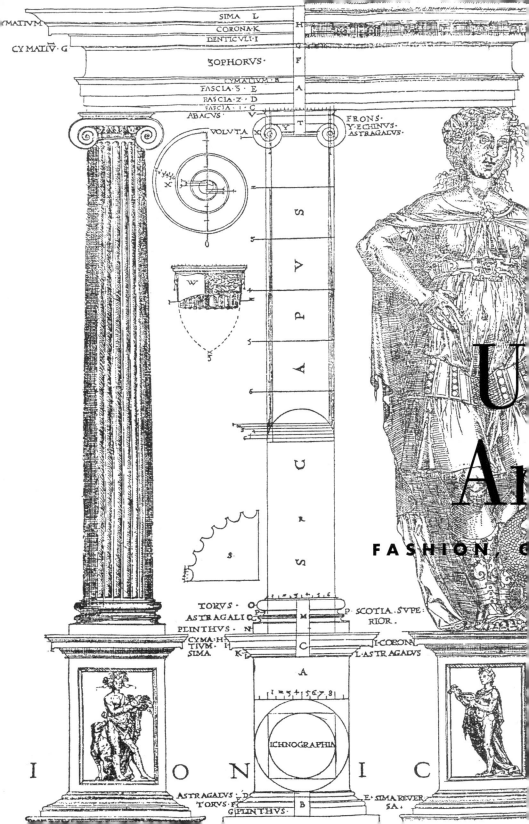

MATIVM

CYMATIV·G

SIMA L

CORONA·K

DENTICVLI·I

ZOPHORVS·

CYMATIVM·B

FASCIA·3·E

FASCIA·2·D

FASCIA·1·C

ABACVS·   V

VOLVTA X

FRONS·

Y·ECHINVS·

ASTRAGALVS·

H

G

F

A

T

Y

C

A

P

V

S

C

V

R

S

V

S

W

S

X

Z

S

TORVS· O

ASTRAGALI·Q

PLINTHVS·N

CYMA·H

TIVM·I

SIMA

K·L

P

M

P·SCOTIA·SVPE-

RIOR·

C

I·COROM

L·ASTRAGALVS

A

ICHNOGRAPHIA

B

ASTRAGALVS·D

TORVS·F

G·PLINTHVS·

E·SIMA·REVER-

SA·

I   O   N   I   C

U

An

FASHION, G

MARY MCLEOD

"...What we wished to express in art was the Universal and
Permanent and to throw to the dogs the Vacillating and the
Fashionable."

—Amédée Ozenfant, *Foundations of Modern Art*, 1931[1]

This revulsion that Ozenfant felt against fashion was typical of the
Modern Movement in architecture. From the late nineteenth century
to the outbreak of World War II architects shunned the transient and
commercial qualities of fashion, associating it with the superficiality
of ornament, they viewed fashion, especially women's fashion, as
frivolous, unfunctional, and wasteful, the antithesis of rationality and
simplicity. The spoken and unspoken assumption was that it was
feminine or effeminate. Paradoxically, it also played another role.

ressing
itecture
, AND MODERNITY

Fashion—primarily
men's fashion—was a
symbol of the functional-
ism, timelessness, and
internationalism that
architects sought in their
own designs. Adolf Loos
wrote extensively about
contemporary fashions;
Peter Behrens, Henry van
de Velde, and Frank
Lloyd Wright designed
women's clothes. As
metaphor, model, and
arena of practice, fashion became a fundamental component of the
struggle to define modernity in architecture.

This powerful bond, however fraught, between fashion and modernity
was well acknowledged by contemporary architects and critics. In

FIG. 1 *The Ionic order as depicted in John Shute's treatise,* The First and
Chief Groundes of Architecture *(London: Ihon Shute, 1563), Folio 8. Courtesy
Avery Library, Columbia University.*

his 1902 treatise *Stilarchitektur und Baukunst* Hermann Muthesius noted, with disdain, the association of the German and French word *mode* to the modern, provoking Otto Wagner to change the title of his book *Moderne Architektur* in his last edition of 1914 to *Die Baukunst unserer Zeit* [The Architecture of Our Time].[2] But in 1910 Gropius was already applauding fashion, as opposed to national costume, for exemplifying the internationalization of modern culture, which architecture must inevitably follow.[3]

This contradictory relationship raises a series of questions that have been largely overlooked in architectural histories of the epoch. How does one explain the paradox in which modern architects participated in a cycle of rapid stylistic change, yet denied the temporality of fashion as a force or model? What are the differences among notions of modernity in architecture and art with regard to the question of truth versus fashion, eternal values versus ephemeral styles? And how does the association of fashion with the feminine relate to its acceptance or rejection in modern architecture or even its complete absence from contemporary architecture criticism?[4]

Fundamental to any investigation of these issues is the distinction between "fashion" and "clothes." "Fashion" derives from the Latin word *facere* [to make, to do] and still retains this sense, as in the verb "to fashion."[5] But since the sixteenth century it has also (and now, primarily) meant the spectrum of appearances acceptable at any one moment in time. Like the French and German word *Mode*, "fashion" connotes ephemerality and taste, implying a cycle of rapid stylistic change, however repetitive the process of novelty itself might become. Perhaps not coincidentally, *mode* has two genders in French and Italian. *Mode* (or *moda*) is feminine when it alludes to fashion and style; masculine when it refers to those meanings derived from the Latin, such as musical modes, philosophical forms, or other more technical usages. The words "clothes" and "clothing" have a more general use than "fashion." Of old English origin, and etymologically linked to the German word *Kleid*, "clothes" refers to the covering of the human body with cloth, and usually implies something more enduring and functionally based than fashion. Closely related in meaning are the words "costume" and "dress,"[6] which primarily designate types of clothing by a particular region, epoch, or circumstance. Here, changes in appearance or function are evolutionary, or so gradual as to be nearly invisible. Beyond this issue of temporality, which so distinguishes "fashion" from "clothes," "costume," and "dress," other, more connotative distinctions have variously followed: artifice/nature, internationalism/regionalism, commercial/noncommercial, superfluity/necessity, licentiousness/purity, and femininity/masculinity. Much of the tension associated with fashion and modernity in architecture stems from ambiguities surrounding these dichotomies.

Although these dichotomies did not become central issues in architecture until the late nineteenth century, discussions of gender and dress in architecture were certainly not new to modernism. Vitruvius himself gave us one of the earliest and most vivid associations of gender and clothes with architecture.[7] In the oft-cited example in Book Four of *The Ten Books*, he compared the Doric column (Dorus was the son of Helen) to "the strength and beauty of the body of a man"; Ionic was associated with a matron, and Corinthian with a young maiden. Discussing the founding of the Ionic order, the Roman architect wrote:

> Just so afterwards, when they desired to construct a temple to Diana in a new style of beauty, they translated these footprints into terms characteristic of the slenderness of women, and thus first made a column the thickness of which was only one eighth of its height, so that it might have a taller look. At the foot they substituted the base in place of a shoe; in the capital they placed the volutes, hanging down at the right and left like curly ringlets, and ornamented its front with cymatia and with festoons of fruit arranged in place of hair, while they brought the flutes down the whole shaft, falling like the folds in the robes worn by matrons. Thus in the invention of the two different kinds of columns, they borrowed manly beauty, naked and un-adorned, for the one, and for the other the delicacy, adornment, and proportions characteristic of women.[8]

In Vitruvius's description of the orders there is little to suggest an anti-feminine perspective; if anything, the account would appear to favor the influence of womanly beauty. Posterity, "having made progress in refinement and delicacy of feeling and finding pleasure in more slender proportions," thus made all the orders more slender. Nonetheless, we find here a juxtaposition that persisted into twentieth-century architectural rhetoric: that the male is associated with simplicity, nudity, and brute strength, and the female is associated with adornment and clothes.

The association of the orders with gender and sometimes with nudity and clothes became a refrain reiterated or reformulated by numerous theorists of classicism. Serlio tried to Christianize the orders, suggesting that Doric represented Christ the Redemptor, St. Paul, and St. George, who embodied some kind of virility; and that Corinthian represented the virgin and those saints "who led a virginal life."[9] Several centuries later, in the *Grammaire des arts du dessin* of 1867, academician Charles Blanc compared the Doric to an athlete flexing his muscles; and in a sequel treatise on adornment, published in 1875, he equated the three orders with *toilettes de genre*—austerity, elegance, and coquetry—and advised that women with Doric necks "should wear light collars and ruffs, to restore feminine characteristics to their manly proportions."[10] And as late as the 1920s, Paul Valery referred in *L'Eupalinos* to a "delicate temple" as the "mathematical image of a girl of Corinth, whom I once sweetly loved."[11]

Although many of these references to the orders are free of gender preferences, by the end of the seventeenth century, practitioners and critics began to discuss architecture together with gender and fashion (not just clothes) in a moralistic and judgmental tone. For instance, Christopher Wren in a letter from France in 1665 complained that "the Women, as they make here the Language and Fashions, and meddle with Politicks and Philosophy, so they sway also in Architecture;...but Building certainly ought to have the Attribute of eternal, and therefore the only Thing uncapable of new Fashions."[12]

To sort out all the historical and geograpical nuances (for instance, femininity sparks more fear in England and Germany than in France) would take too long to recount here. Whether praised or criticized, however, by the eighteenth century, femininity tended to be associated in European architectural discourse with change, fashion, capriciousness, play, artifice, frivolity, charm, delicacy, ornament, and masquerade.

MODERNITY AS WOMEN'S FASHION

These qualities were clearly anathema to most modern architects, who heralded the absolute rationality of the engineer as a paragon of modern life. But paradoxically, they are exactly the attributes that Charles Baudelaire praised in his essay "The Painter of Modern Life," written in 1859–60, and published in 1863 in the Parisian newspaper *Figaro*. Curiously, this text, which has been so fundamental in literary and art criticism for undermining long-standing notions of classical art, has been almost ignored in architecture writing. Extolling fashion as an artistic model, the essay provides a pointed contrast to notions of architectural modernity.

What was so innovative to nineteenth-century readers was Baudelaire's assertion that beauty and virtue have nothing to do with nature, but rather are the result of artifice and masquerade. Sardonically, he equated the statement "Simplicity embellishes beauty" with "Nothing embellishes something." "Virtue" is "artificial, super-natural....Good is always a product of some art."[13] After acknowledging a notion of constant, eternal beauty, he argued that modern art must free itself from ideas of classical essence or absolute truth. Beauty is historical, changing, and fleeting; only the superficial can lead us to the ideal, "the poetry within history."[14] Citing the journalistic sketches and paintings of Constantin Guys, Baudelaire claimed that women and fashion offer such an enticing "taste"—a means to understand the elusive nature of modern urban life. "Fashion," he continued, "should thus be considered...

FIG. 2 *"A terrible moment." A gentleman in peg-top trousers attempting to shake hands with a woman wearing a crinoline skirt, 1856. From C. Willet and Phillis Cunnington,* Handbook of English Costume in the Nineteenth Century *(London: Faber and Faber, 1959), pl. 190.*

a sublime deformation of Nature, or, rather, a permanent and repeated attempt at her reformation." Thus, he celebrated women's preoccupations with fashion and adornment.

> Woman is quite within her rights, indeed she is even accom-
> plishing a kind of duty, when she devotes herself to appearing
> magical and supernatural;...It matters but little that the arti-
> fice and trickery are known to all, so long as their success is
> assured and their effect always irresistible.[15]

In Baudelaire's view, it would seem, women epitomize the nature of "man" as self-invention, as fabrication.[16]

Perhaps not coincidentally, this model of woman as paragon is contemporaneous with the establishment of the modern fashion industry in France. While the nation had long been a leader in setting women's fashions, it was not until 1857 that the House of Worth (arguably the first modern couture firm) was founded, producing designs for rich clients, from the Empress Eugénie to the notorious English-born courtesan Cora Pearl.[17] The introduction of cotton in the 1830s, the wide-scale use of the sewing machine (patented in 1851), and the establishment of the department store permitted middle- and lower-class women as well to participate more fully in the cycle of changing styles. By the late 1850s, women's fashion had itself become highly assertive (Fig. 2), creating a marked contrast with the rather self-effacing, sentimental styles of the 1840s. Crinolines were now 5 1/2 to 6 yards in circumference; one evening dress of 1859 with four skirts required 1,100 yards of tulle![18] Baudelaire's paradigm was not a modest cloak but a forthright proclamation of women's artifice and public presence.[19]

For all of Baudelaire's admiration of women, and his striking equation of modernity with women and fashion, his argument rests on assumptions that many present-day women would shun: the insistence on woman's adornment, her primary role as seducer, and her position as muse and inspiration rather than artistic creator or even aristocratic dandy observer.[20] (Elsewhere, in his journal *Mon Coeur mis à nu*, Baudelaire retracted his praises of woman as artifice and condemned her as "natural, that is to say abominable...the contrary of the Dandy.")[21]

But in the context of architecture, what is so provocative in "The Painter of Modern Life" is the extent to which Baudelaire's notion of modernity—a fleeting temporal modernity, self-conscious in its artifice—depends on the notion of fashion. Although the word "fashion" appeared intermittently in writing on architecture from the late seventeenth century to the mid-nineteenth century, fashion was rarely the subject of extended investigation. By the end of the nineteenth century this changed dramatically, with fashion becoming both a persistent metaphor and an arena of actual practice. The attitudes that were expressed, however, differed considerably from Baudelaire's paradigm. While many architects of the Modern Movement shared with Baudelaire an appreciation of the *new*, of mass culture, and of historicism—the belief that each age has its own style—they consistently rejected all notions of feminine fashion, artifice, and masquerade in their search for a "truthful" architecture based on absolute values. It would appear that certain attributes of modern architecture—for instance, its emphasis on simplicity, functionalism, and structural rationalism, as well as its antipathy to the urban street—worked against a conception of modernity inspired by fashion, or by what is viewed so often in nineteenth- and early twentieth-century European society as "the feminine."

If in the history of European painting from the late eighteenth century to the mid-nineteenth century, as Leila Kinney has noted, there was a general evolution from the "nude" to the clothed, from the idealized to everyday life, one might—extending the analogy—inversely characterize the later search for modernity in architecture, from the mid-nineteenth century to the post-World War I period, as a movement from the clothed to the "nude": from Gottfried Semper's Dresden Opera to Le Corbusier's Villa Savoye.[22] This trajectory is especially apparent in what might be characterized as the classical strain of modern architecture—notably, the works of Otto Wagner, Adolf Loos, and Le Corbusier, which, in their latent stasis and assertion of eternal values, seem to resist the fugitive pleasures of Baudelaire's aesthetic of appearances.

DRESSING ARCHITECTURE

Gottfried Semper, the author of the great unfinished theoretical tract, *Der Stil*, was almost an exact contemporary of Baudelaire. Like Baudelaire, he sided with the democrats and revolutionaries in the events of 1848 (though with more consistent political convictions and at greater personal cost), and like Baudelaire, he endorsed "a rational, historical theory of beauty."[23] He also posited connections between clothing and art and granted women a role in artistic developments.[24] The differences, however, between these unlikely figures—the German architect, serious and academic, almost plodding in his search for a historical basis for architecture; and the French poet, a dandy and voyeur who focused almost entirely on the present—are readily apparent in Semper's two-volume magnum opus *Der Stil in den technischen und tektonischen Künsten, oder praktische Aesthetik* [Style in the Technical and Tectonic Arts, or Practical Aesthetics], published 1860–63. (The third volume on architecture was never finished.)

Semper's historicist position was a rejection of the static idealism of the Enlightenment primitive hut. Instead of Laugier's bare structural frame (which he described in his treatise as being erected by a mythic nude man), Semper proposed a more complex archetypal concept, which included four elements: the hearth, man's communal gathering place; the substructure or platform, which raised the hearth off the damp earth; the roof, which protected the fire against the rain; and finally, the enclosure, which sheltered man and hearth from wind and cold. He envisioned the latter as being composed of non-load-bearing filler, such as textiles, hides, or wattle, hung or stretched between the structural posts.[25] Semper found his system confirmed in a Caribbean cottage shown at the Great Exposition in London, which he published in *Der Stil*. His emphasis on textiles incorporated traditional domestic (i.e., female) crafts into architecture's foundation and evolution. Semper even began *Der Stil* with an examination of textiles, which he considered to be the origin of many ornamental types and symbols in architecture and design.[26]

It is in this section on textiles that Semper made connections between architecture and dress. Significantly, he also used the more neutral words "costume" and "dress" instead of "fashion," following his ethnographic predecessors C. A. Bottiger and Herman Weiss. "Almost all structure symbols...like those ornaments on Egyptian capitals" were "borrowed directly from the domain of costume and, in particular, from its finery!"[27] The connections between architecture and dress extended, however, beyond the figural to architecture's origins and its symbolic role.

Not only did Semper explain that the word *Wand* (wall, partition, screen) relates etymologically to *Gewand* (dress, garments, clothing), but he made *Bekleidung* (dressing or cladding), which relates to *Kleidung* (clothing), the focus of his investigation of style.[28] Semper considered adornment "the first and most significant step toward art"; it is what separates the human from the animal. In a section entitled "The Most Primitive Formal Principle in Architecture Based on the Concept of Space and Independent of Construction: The Masking of Reality in Art," he explained:

> I think that the *dressing* and the *mask* are as old as human civilization and the joy in both is identical with the joy in those things that drove men to be sculptors, painters, architects, poets, musicians, dramatists, in short, artists. Every artistic creation, every artistic pleasure presupposes a certain carnival spirit, or to express myself in a modern way—the haze of carnival candles is the true atmosphere of art. The denial of reality, of the material, is necessary if form is to emerge as a meaningful symbol.[29]

 Like Baudelaire, Semper celebrated that which covers nature. Artifice and masking were the very essence of man's civilization: his art. But Semper was not concerned with the fleeting and the ephemeral, despite his appreciation of the "carnival spirit."[30] Instead, he was attempting to delineate the slow, rather tedious route that architecture takes to construct meaning. He did not express the connections between costume and symbol in terms of modernity, although ultimately his goal was also to define the proper artistic forms for his age.[31] The differences between these two contemporaries are even more pronounced in another statement by Semper:

> Masking does not help, however, when *behind* the mask the thing is false or the mask is no good.[32]

This belief in the truth behind the mask and the goodness of the mask itself was fundamental to the subsequent evolution of architectural modernity. For Semper, adornment involved a moral imperative, divorced from the vagaries and superficiality of fashion. The "principle of dressing" architecture represented the structural/symbolic essence of a building; decoration and the "art form" were so intimately bound that to conceive either in isolation was impossible. In contrast to primitive buildings, such as Assyrian structures, where the support was subservient to decoration, mature works of art, such as those of fourth-century Greece, demonstrated that material realization and technique were requisite to adornment itself.[33] Only with "complete technical perfection, by judicious and proper treatment of the material according to its properties," could the artistic creation transcend the material for its larger social and cultural purpose. The "law of nature" implicit in construction was, in fact, that which permitted artistic symbolism.[34] Thus, Semper's rejection of static idealism was not a rejection of truth. The historicism of decoration demanded another kind of logic, true to the values and techniques of its time and place.

When Semper used the word "fashion," he did so pejoratively, linking it to marketing and the rapid circulation of nineteenth-century styles.[35] Here he recalls German architect Heinrich Hübsch, who in a publication of 1847 linked society's "unprecedented illness," embodied in the frenetic pace of fashion in both dress and surroundings, to the profit motives of industry.[36] For Semper, this constant change was a particularly French problem, encouraged by the fickleness and effeminacy of Parisian taste; the "flat and insipid affectations of the neo-Greek, the false coquettish [*falsche kokette*] romanticism of the neo-Gothic" were French styles that quickly went out of fashion.[37] In rejecting fashion, Semper drew a sharp distinction between novelty and originality: novelty, a product of market forces, resulted in decoration without "character or local color"; only an original symbolism resulting from a deep understanding of the present could become part of "our flesh and blood."[38] Ultimately, dress and body, decoration and structure, were seen as one.

Semper's interest in dress was hardly unique in nineteenth-century European architecture circles. In France, the impetus appears to

FIG. 3 *Jane Morris, posed by D. G. Rossetti, 1865. From Alison Gernsheim,* Fashion and Reality *(London: Faber and Faber, 1963), pl. 75.*

come less from ethnographic literature than from the sheer pervasiveness of fashion in French culture, and by the end of the Second Empire it even extended to academic discourse. Charles Blanc, the director of the École des Beaux Arts, whose aesthetic theories crystallized so much of academic teaching, devoted an entire book to aesthetic standards for clothing—*L'Art dans la parure et dans le vêtement* (1875), in which he enthusiastically cited Semper's lectures on the "ornamentation of the body" given at the Zurich Polytechnic.[39] And Charles Garnier, celebrating the very opulence that modernists would later decry, made numerous references to women's adornment in *Le Théâtre* (1871); he regarded their silks and jewels as being as much a part of the architecture of the Paris Opera as the building's own lavish ornamentation.[40] In an earlier, rhapsodic text, *À travers les Arts* (1867), he had imagined the day when "monuments will be decorated in marble and enamel, and mosaics will make the city vibrate with color....Once people have become accustomed to the city's marvelous, dazzling nuances, they will demand that our clothes be redesigned and brightened up as well, and the entire city will be harmoniously bathed in silks and golds."[41] Like Semper, Garnier associated adornment with collective festivity and theatricality; and by the 1870s, each of these architects had designed an opera house in a neo-Baroque style. But whereas the very exuberance and invention of Garnier's ornament—and the intuitive passion of his writing—irrevocably linked him to nineteenth-century ostentation and excess, Semper's sober commitment to tectonics, his reasoned principles of adornment, and the morality implicit in his stand marked him as a forefather of modern architecture.

Contemporaneously, William Morris and participants in the British Arts and Crafts Movement saw dress as one component of a more encompassing social transformation, dissolving boundaries between art and life, artist and producer, maker and user. Their aesthetic ideal joined simplicity and ornamentation, but more significant in this populist vision was "the joy of the worker." Craft—and consequently costume—attained the same stature as the traditional fine arts, leading Morris to ask: "How can this people expect to have good architecture when they wear such clothes?"[42] For Morris, so committed to living according to his precepts, this question was an issue of practice. He rejected conventional dress for blue workman's smocks; his wife Jane Burden wore flowing gowns, designed by Morris (Fig. 3), which she frequently embroidered herself.[43] Inspired in part by the Arts and Crafts circle, women of the Aesthetic Movement, and, later women of the Glasgow School, also wore loose, draping gowns, equating personal adornment with the simpler forms of their new residential interiors.[44] By the 1880s this "Artistic" style of dress had itself become fashionable, inspiring Worth and other Parisian couture houses.

MODERNITY AS MEN'S FASHION

Toward the end of the nineteenth century, references to clothing became especially current in architectural commentary in German and Austrian circles, where the moral resonances of Semper's legacy were strongest. But, in a clear departure from the writings of the man that almost all considered their mentor, the emphasis switched from clothing to fashion; and when they did discuss past connections between dress and architecture, it was merely to justify connections in the present. One of the first to draw parallels between contemporary fashion and architecture was the Viennese architect and teacher Otto Wagner. In his seminal text *Moderne Architektur* (1896), after citing a series of examples of court life in France from Louis XIII to XVI, he declared: "The pictures of style just evoked logically allow us to perceive the close and hitherto ignored relationship between taste, fashion, and style."[45]

In the urbane, cultivated circles of Viennese café society, Wagner's observation must have seemed as inevitable as Baudelaire's provocative comments in Parisian boulevard society. But it was undoubtedly Semper's commentary on dress, in conjunction with the burgeoning German literature on fashion, that inspired Wagner to correlate fashion and style in an academic treatise.[46] Wagner frequently admitted his debt to the German master and was regularly seen by his contemporaries as Semper's spiritual heir.[47] But the two architects also differed on important issues. Wagner rejected Semper's emphasis on cultural expression, and berated him for making "do with the symbolism of construction instead of designating construction itself as the germ cell of architecture."[48] In essence, it was Semper's dressing thesis that Wagner repudiated, however much his own buildings might yet be "masked." *Moderne Architektur* was unequivocal. "The style of our time" was simply an issue of new building materials and techniques: "NEW METHODS OF CONSTRUCTION MUST ALSO GIVE BIRTH TO NEW FORMS."[49]

Wagner's interest in construction was part of a larger project, one that seemed to elude Semper: to define an architecture whose "SOLE DEPARTURE POINT...CAN ONLY BE MODERN LIFE." His preoccupation with modernity, and the impact that it had on his contemporaries in architecture, must have paralleled that of Baudelaire's for an earlier generation of painters and writers. Both men were willing to dispense with the weight of historical tradition to capture their own present; history itself mandated discarding the past. And here fashion, as opposed to dress, gave one of the clearest indications of modernity. Like Baudelaire, he announced: "THINGS THAT HAVE THEIR SOURCE IN MODERN VIEWS CORRESPOND PERFECTLY TO OUR APPEARANCE."[50] But unlike the poet, who celebrated woman's appearance, and Semper, whose attention was equally divided between men and women,[51] Wagner proposed a model that was completely male. In a statement anticipating both Loos and Le Corbusier, he wrote:

> A man in a modern traveling suit, for example, fits in very well
> with the waiting room of a train station, with sleeping cars,
> with all our vehicles; yet would we not stare if we were to see
> someone dressed in clothing from the Louis XV period using
> such things?[52]

Reversing the equation, he continued:

> It is simply an artistic absurdity that men in evening attire, in
> lawn tennis or bicycling outfits, in uniform or checkered
> breeches should spend their life in interiors executed in the
> styles of past centuries.[53]

Wagner completely ignored women's dress, except for a comment added in the third edition of *Moderne Architektur*—a comment that is simultaneously disparaging and sympathetic—in which he stated that because of women's lack of proper artistic training, "the artistic contribution of half of mankind is frustrated achieving a result [in terms of fashion] that is no doubt unsatisfactory."[54] Clearly, it was the utility and honesty of modern (i.e., male) fashion, and not its attributes of masquerade and artifice, that Wagner applauded. What he did not acknowledge was that the functionalism of male fashion resembled conventional interpretations of "dress" as utilitarian and relatively static.[55]

When Wagner used the word "fashion" in an architectural context, he meant it to be derogatory like female fashion. In a vehement attack on historical styles, he wrote: "The matter has even gone so far that architectural styles almost change like fashions, and works of art are intentionally made 'old' in order to give them the appearance of dating from past centuries."[56] Fashion no longer represented the *Zeitgeist*; rather it was cheap, false, and expendable. Architecture required more enduring values. Wagner's notion of the *Zeitgeist*—like that later embraced by Loos and Le Corbusier—paradoxically embodied a vision of eternal truth. The truly modern was both timely and timeless.

Wagner's remarks on fashion suggest that he was either unaware of or chose to ignore the burgeoning reform movement in women's dress that had been slowly evolving since Mrs. Amelia Jenks

FIG. 4 *The American Dr. Mary Walker wearing "rational dress," c. 1865. From Gernsheim,* Fashion and Reality, *pl. 76.*

Bloomer of Seneca Falls, N.Y. appeared in 1849 in Turkish-style trousers tied at the ankle. If Mrs. Bloomer's initial efforts generated little more than sharp public ridicule, by the 1880s American and British woman, including such upper-class celebrities as Mrs. Oscar Wilde and the Viscountess Harberton, were actively engaged in a campaign for "rational dress" (Fig. 4). Besides fighting to abolish tight-lacing, hampering skirts, and high heels, one of the aims of their Rational Dress Society was "to recommend that the maximum weight of underclothing (without shoes) should not exceed 7 pounds"![57] Harberton herself wore black satin Turkish trousers and a velvet jacket when she lectured, lashing her riding whip to make points. There was an equivalent German movement, represented by Dr. Gustav Jäger, a professor of zoology and anthropology at Stuttgart Royal Polytechnic, who promoted his designs for woolen underwear, marketed as the Sanitary Woolen System ("Being animals," he asserted, "we should wear animal clothing"). The women's dress designs—"flour sacks," as more than one contemporary called them—lacked the flair of Harberton's exotic costume.

This campaign for dress reform, along with the quite separate aesthetic objectives of *Gesamtkunstwerk*, inspired Otto Wagner's followers and other contemporary architects to consider the problem of women's dress. Peter Behrens, Henry van de Velde, Josef Hoffmann, Richard Riemerschmid, Paul Schultze-Naumburg (who later became a Nazi propagandist), and even Frank Lloyd Wright were all involved in women's clothing design.[58] Like Wagner, they were unhappy with women's dress and wanted to "reform" it, advocating looser, more fluid lines. In the case of Schultze-Naumburg this involved anatomical studies and an insistence on naturalism (Fig. 5); but for most of these designers aesthetic objectives took precedence.[59] Proclaiming their women's clothes art, not fashion, they were concerned primarily with making beautiful clothes that allowed women to fit into their designed surroundings. In published photographs van de Velde's and Behren's dresses are shown only in interior settings (Fig. 6); any notion of women's freedom seems confined to this realm.[60] With the telling exception of August Endell—whose lyrical writings on women's fashion and the city recall Baudelaire's homage to modern life[61]—most Art Nouveau and Secessionist designers sought refuge from both urban commercialism and women's fashion, which by the late nineteenth century had become increasingly linked. Like their interiors, their dresses were usually one-off creations, and despite the high hopes placed on a major exhibition at Krefeld in 1900 displaying some of these new artistic efforts, the architect-designed clothes had little impact on public taste and consumption.[62]

Reform Dress, designed by Paul Shultze-Naumburg, c. 1900. From Max van Boehn, Bekleidung Kunst und Mode *(Munich: Delphin Verlag, 1918), pl. 85.*

FIG. 5

FIG. 6 *Frau Salomonsohn wearing a dress designed by Henry van de Velde, c. 1900. The photo was taken in van de Velde's home in Berlin. Frau Salomonsohn's husband was later a client of van de Velde. From Henry van de Velde, "Das neue Kunst = Prinzip in der modernen Frauen = Kleidung,"* Deutsche Kunst und Dekoration *9–10 (October 1901–March 1902), 379.*

ARCHITECTURE: *In Fashion*

THE ENGLISHMAN'S MASK

Certainly the Secessionist dress designs would not have pleased the movement's most sardonic critic, Adolf Loos. Like the Secessionists, Loos was deeply interested in fashion, and like the Secessionists, he was undoubtedly inspired by Otto Wagner,[63] but his own "modest" conception of the architect's role precluded designing dresses or the cigarette cases, umbrella stands, and tea services so popular with the Wiener Werkstätte group.[64] Loos's interests in everyday culture took another direction, focusing on the links between function and form. This concern he attributed to Semper, who in Loos's interpretation was a full-fledged materialist. Loos, in his essay "Glass and Clay" (a title that might have been taken straight from *Der Stil*), praised Semper for cutting "many an idealist to the quick."[65] In another essay, "The Principle of Dressing" [*Bekleidung*], Loos reiterated both Semper's historical chronology, in which cladding precedes structure, and Semper's insistence on the integrity of the mask—that the material dressed should never be mistaken for the dressing.[66]

Loos's rejection of total design did not preclude him from making moral—and aesthetic—pronouncements on nearly every aspect of daily life. In 1898 he wrote a series of articles for the Viennese paper *Neue Freie Presse* (the liberal newspaper of intellectuals and the commercial classes) on topics as diverse as plumbing, the decorative arts, and women's underwear. Several of these pieces were devoted to fashion, and his 1908 essay "Ornament and Crime" encapsulates, with even greater rhetorical flair, much of this earlier commentary.

In one of his earliest essays, "Men's Fashion," Loos addressed the issue of what it means to be well dressed. "It is," he declared, "a question of being dressed *in such a way that one stands out the least.*"

> A top hat stands out at the ice-skating rink. Consequently it is
> unmodern to wear a top hat while on the ice. In good society,
> to be conspicuous is bad manners.[67]

For Loos, like Wagner, the style of a man's dress signaled the proper architectural style for the modern age—the non-style. Loos considered this an English lesson: to be properly dressed meant to be properly dressed in London's Hyde Park, for that was "the center of Western civilization" (Figs. 7, 8). His anglophilia was shared by other Germans and Austrians struggling to create a modern style. In *Das englische Haus* of 1904–05, for instance, Muthesius echoed Loos:

> The richer a man is, the more restrained his behavior, the more modest and inconspicuous he is....What serious-minded man today would think of wearing bizarre clothes? Even artists in England are careful to avoid making themselves look different from others by the way their hair is cut or their choice of tie.[68]

Loos saw the situation in Germany and Austria as dramatically different. "No nation has so many dandies as the Germans....A dandy is a man whose clothes serve only to make him stand out from his surroundings." For Loos, this type of German dandy included both the back-to-nature hygienists, such as Dr. Jäger, and the aesthetes, "would-be-poets," who wear checkered suits, velvet collars, and Secession-style ties."[69] It was surely Olbrich's and Hoffmann's manner of dress that prompted this last complaint,[70] just as it may have been van de Velde's slippers that inspired his parable of the Poor Little Rich Man.[71] To Loos, both the dress reformers and the aesthetes represented a false modernity in fashion, for they stood out. Instead, his ideal is the anonymity of simple clothing slowly perfected over time;[72] men's fashion was, to borrow a Purist phrase, a kind of *objet type*. But this did not imply to Loos, as it would to Le Corbusier, mass production. It was the beautifully detailed and carefully tailored English clothing and accessories that Loos applauded. In his essay "Architecture" (1910), he noted that this clothing had changed very little over the course of a century.[73] Again, it would seem that genuinely modern fashion—men's fashion—was as timeless and traditional as "dress." Only now, tradition carried an internationalist mandate; "correct" fashion remained the same whether in New York, London, or Vienna.[74]

Both Loos and Baudelaire defined the dandy as someone who distinguishes himself from his peers; but whereas Baudelaire esteemed him, Loos condemned him. Paradoxically, these contrary views on men's fashion share a similar sensibility. Baudelaire's dandy gains his "distinction" through the perfection of his dress and grooming, which consists of absolute simplicity. When he could (which was not always), Baudelaire attempted to practice what he preached; legend has it that he ordered a dozen of the same black suit, while another anecdote claims that he sandpapered his suits so that they wouldn't look too new. Loos paid similar attention to his own dress, often accepting fine clothes in lieu of architectural fees from his clients such as Goldman and Salatsch or Knize.[75] More to the point, although Loos scorned the foppish ostentation of the *fin-de-siècle* dandy, he embraced Baudelaire's dandy. The modern man endorsed absolute austerity; and if Loos ambivalently alternated between ideals of democratic mass culture and aristocratic disdain, the latter placed him close to Baudelaire's "last aristocrat" in a time of decadence. In "Ornament and Crime" Loos stated, "I am preaching to the aristocrat, I mean the person who stands at the pinnacle of mankind and yet has the deepest understanding for the distress and want of those below."[76]

Perhaps the major difference between Loos and Baudelaire is that the democratization of culture that Baudelaire so regretted had become by the end of the century the inescapable norm. Although more than fifty percent of the senior officials in the Austro-Hungarian Empire were hereditary aristocrats at the turn of the century, the intense riots over nationalities in 1897 (occuring in Vienna, Gaz, and later, Prague) signaled the end of an epoch. In Loos's view, politics paralleled dress; both were a mess. Hence his embrace of an Anglo-Saxon utopia. If Loos and his liberal Viennese readers could no longer cling to remnants of an aristocratic presence, their only hope was a mass embrace of aristocratic values—an aristocracy of taste, not of blood or money.

As Jules Lubbock has argued, the model for both Loos and Baudelaire appears to be Beau Brummel, the original dandy, and the man whom Max Beerbohm described as the father of modern dress.[77] In England about 1800, Brummel reformed male dress; he invented the well-tailored, austere dark suit and starched white linen neckwear, believing that "the severest mortification a gentleman could incur was to attract observation in the street by his outward appearance."[78] It was the beginning of what the psychoanalyst John Carl Flugel described as "The Great Renunciation" in male dress.[79]

THE CRIME OF WOMEN'S FASHION

While Loos and Baudelaire shared convictions about the appropriate man's dress for the modern age, they differed sharply in their assessment of women's fashion. The artifice and masquerade, the self-conscious practices of seduction that Baudelaire so admired and enjoyed, were for Loos painful indications of woman's backwardness and man's "sickly sensuality." In the opening lines of his essay "Ladies' Fashion," Loos declared, "That which is noble in a woman knows only one desire: that she hold on to her place by the side of the big, strong man." But if she wins a man's love, she becomes man's subordinate. It was for Loos an "unnatural" love. "If it were natural, the woman would be able to approach man naked. But the naked woman is unattractive to the man."[80]

In his discussions of women as opposed to men, Loos embraced nature as a sensual and artistic ideal, an attitude that Baudelaire had tried to overturn. However, the two men agreed on the social mechanisms by which women's fashion operates. The man "that occupies the highest social position" established man's fashion, whereas the coquette, the prostitute, the *demimondaine* led the way in woman's dress.[81] For Loos, this lowly status provided evidence for his theories of social evolution: "The lower the culture, the more apparent the ornament. Ornament is something that must be overcome. The Papuan and the criminal ornament their skin."[82] The woman, the criminal, and the Papuan are thus all placed at the bottom of civilization, with the British male aristocrat at its top. While Semper had also associated ornament with primitive cultures, his historicism was not teleological or particularly judgmental. Loos's was, because in his view civilization was a universal objective. "In the twentieth century only *one culture* will dominate," he asserted.[83]

One source for Loos's association of ornament with degradation may have been literature on criminology. Another possible source was contemporary literature on criminology. Cesare Lombroso, an influential nineteenth-century criminologist, studied the use of tattoos on prostitutes and criminals (although Lombroso found only eight percent of all criminals tattooed, not the eighty percent that Loos claimed).[84] But Loos's general correlation of ornament with social barbarism most likely had British roots. Already in 1833, in his famous diatribe against the dandy, *Sartor Resartus*, Thomas Carlyle had equated tattooing and decoration with "barbarous man" and "the barbarous classes in civilized countries"; and sixteen years later, John Ruskin, that most eloquent spokesman for ornament, elaborated in a tone uncannily close to Loos's:

> There are many forms of so-called decoration in architecture,...the expense of which ought in truth to be set down in the architect's contract, as "For Monstrification." I believe that we regard these customary deformities with a savage complacency, as an Indian does his flesh patterns and paint.[85]

Other parallels with Loos's evolutionary model can be seen in the writings of the English Social Darwinist Herbert Spencer. Like Loos, Spencer placed England at the pinnacle of civilization in terms of dress and commerce, and thought that Germany, with its partiality to titles, military medals, and the trappings of social status, would be one of the last countries to attain such high stature.[86] Spencer also believed that female emancipation would automatically result in the eradication of distinctions between male and female costume.

Loos took the same position at the conclusion of "Ladies' Fashion." His positive examples of woman's new equality were, on the one

FIG. 7   *English dress, 1897, and blouse and shirt, 1899. From Willet and Cunnington,* Handbook of English Costume, *543.*

FIG. 8   *English top frock, 1898, and covert coat, 1899–1900. From Willet and Cunnington,* Handbook of English Costume, *330.*

hand, the woman's "tailor-made costume in England," (Fig. 9) where the sexes were permitted platonic love; and, on the other, "the pants of the female coal miner in the Belgium mines or the dairymaid in the Alps or the female shrimp-fisher in the North Sea."[87] The woman who earned her living wore pants. Paradoxically, sports (of the upper classes) would lead the way. Just as horseback riding had led to reforms in male dress, "the concession will be made to the twentieth-century female bicyclist to wear pants and clothing that leaves her feet free."[88] Loos concluded dramatically with the statement that has earned him the title of "protofeminist" from at least one woman critic:

> We are approaching a new and greater time. No longer by an appeal to sensuality, but rather by economic independence earned through work will the woman bring about her equal status with the man. The woman's value or lack of value will no longer fall or rise according to the fluctuation of sensuality. Then velvet and silk, flowers and ribbons, feathers and paints will fail to have their effect. They will disappear.[89]

Mrs. Weir, photo by F. Hoeffler, ca. 1893. From Gernsheim, Fashion and **FIG. 9**
Reality, *pl. 177.*

Adolf Loos and Elizabeth "Bessie" Bruce, his second "wife," 1913. From **FIG. 10**
Burkhard Rukschcio and Roland Schachel, Adolf Loos: Leben und Werk
(Salzburg and Vienna: Residenz Verlag, 1982), pl. 181.

Loos clearly linked modernity and woman's liberation. In 1896, when he first resettled in Vienna after his travels in the United States, he was an assistant in the building firm of Carl Mayreder, husband of Rosa Mayreder, the pioneer of the Austrian women's emancipation movement. Here, he was undoubtedly exposed to the most progressive feminist ideas of the day. His own personal experiences might suggest a more complicated perspective. He was known for being highly sympathetic to women and supportive professionally, but he was also a notorious womanizer, had four wives and numerous mistresses (including some liaisons with underage women), and frequently dictated the dress of his wives, much along the lines of Peter Behrens or Henry van de Velde—although it was usually a more conventional form of dress (Fig. 10).[90] Whether one considers such biographical details relevant or not, Loos's early writings reveal a more ambivalent attitude toward women and women's dress than his pro-equality proclamation might suggest. In brief, Loos saw women's emancipation as the abolition of all that was previously female. In contrast to both Baudelaire and Semper, he sought a purely functional, seemingly maskless modernity—a modernity that would transcend the frivolous swings of fashion and women's taste. It was a male modernity. Loos's liberated woman wore man's clothes.[91] In this respect, he appeared to understand less than the German sociologist Georg Simmel, who described the liberated woman in his essay "Fashion" (1904) as taking on both the best and the worst of what is male, and who also recognized that women dress not just to please men but to please themselves.[92] Yet, neither he nor Loos could acknowledge—perhaps because it was too difficult at the turn of the century—the extent to which successful professional women often seek and need a mask of femininity; it is this condition that the psychoanalyst Joan Riviere so perceptively described in her 1929 essay "Womanliness as a Masquerade."[93]

Loos's notion of women's liberation—and of modernity—was in some very important ways restrictive. Despite the irony, wit, and very human tone of his own writings, his reaction to the conspicuous consumption of Vienna's bourgeois's and to the aesthetic decadence of the avant-garde led him to formulate a vision of modernity that condemned play, fantasy, change, and even eroticism. Erotic dress was, in his view, degenerate or criminal, like the modern man who tattooed himself. This model is inherently paradoxical: the modern is that which reveals its underlying truth—a condition analogous to nudity—but the private, the world of interior truth, is never allowed to intrude in the public sphere. In other words, simplicity and functionalism themselves become a kind of mask, like the exquisitely simple clothes of Baudelaire's dandy.

BUTTONED-UP ARCHITECTURE

Do these ideas have any role in Loos's architecture? One of the most commonly noted observations made about his buildings is the dichotomy between the exterior and the interior, the public and the private spheres. More than one critic has compared the division to that of Simmel's metropolitan man—an exterior, a public persona whose behavior is objective, ordered, anonymous, and collective; and an interior or private persona whose nature is highly subjective and individual. The modern metropolis engendered this split, and whatever communities lost in human exchange, individuals gained in new personal freedom. Commenting on this division, Loos noted: "The house should seem reserved from the outside, but inside it should reveal all its richness."[94] In his essay "Architecture," he made the link to men's clothing:

> When it finally became my lot to build a house, I told myself, "The external appearance of a house can only have changed as much as the tailcoat, that is, not a great deal." And I looked at the old buildings, and saw how they emancipated themselves from ornamentation from century to century and year to year....had to become significantly less complicated in order to remain within the line of development. I had to replace the gold buttons with black ones. The house must look inconspicuous. Was it not I who had said, "He who is modernly dressed is always least conspicuous"?[95]

Discussing this schism between the exterior and the interior in Loos, Massimo Cacciari and, more recently, Beatriz Colomina, have proposed that it might be seen in gendered terms: as a male exterior of rationality and discipline, and a female interior of comfort, privacy, and subjectivity.[96] While there is undoubtedly a sharp division in Loos's architecture, his ambivalent attitude toward some of these last attributes in his discussion of women and fashion raises questions about this last equation.[97] Indeed, when we look at the interiors, the reading becomes more problematic (Fig. 11). His early interiors, especially the domestic ones, hardly evoke images of the feminine; more often they evoke the world of British men's clubs—leather club chairs, Chesterfield sofas, and wood beams and paneling. While masculine, the atmosphere is certainly not austere or formal. To make another analogy to clothing, it is akin not to black evening apparel but men's intimate apparel (silk smoking jackets, cravats, braces)—the luxurious simplicity of the accessories sold in the men's fashion houses that he

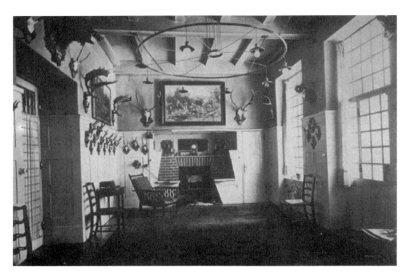

FIG. 11 *Adolf Loos, apartment of Rudolf Kraus, 1907. From Rukschcio and Schachel,* Adolf Loos: Leben und Werk, *pl. 107.*

designed (Ebenstein Fashion House, 1897; Goldman and Salatsch Men's Clothing Store, 1898; Goldman and Salatsch Store, 1910–11; Knize Store, Vienna, 1909–13; P. C. Leschka and Co., 1923–24; and Knize Store, Paris, 1927). It is a particularly male notion of comfort that appears to govern the home, however much Loos may have lauded, as he did in his early essay "Die Frau und das Haus" (1898), the role of American women, who try to free themselves from household drudgery to create attractive homes.[98]

When Loos did design explicitly gender-designated spaces, they conform to conventional gender stereotypes. The interior of a bank looks very much like a male arena of business (in which the level of comfort is minimal); and a bar looks like a traditional men's bar. The explicitly female spaces in his houses represent a distinct shift in vocabulary. In a 1903 issue of the magazine *Die Kunst*, two photographs of the bedroom of Loos's first wife, Lina, were described by the following caption: "Adolf Loos, my wife's bedroom, white walls, white curtains, white Angora sheepskin."[99] Twenty-seven

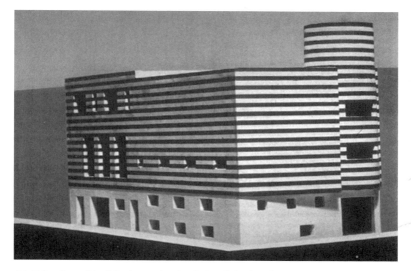

Adolf Loos's model of the house that he designed for Josephine Baker, 1927. **FIG. 12**
From Rukschcio and Schachel, Adolf Loos: Leben und Werk, *pl. 302.*

years later, when Loos was designing a woman's room in the Müller house, he chose yellow satinwood for the wood paneling and a delicate floral print to upholster the built-in sofa.[100]

Although Loos had very few single women clients—which makes it difficult to generalize—it does not seem accidental that his design in 1928 for the black, American-born entertainer, Josephine Baker, has a dramatically different exterior than his other houses. The zebra striping of the facade (Fig. 12) is as attention-getting as Baker's own dynamic and original presence. Most probably, this was not just an issue of "negritude," but one of sex. Benedetto Gravagnola called the project "gay," with a "refined and seductive character," a "toy"; and Ludwig Münz and Güstav Kunstler, of an older generation, alluded to its African qualities, describing the facade as "strange and exotic."[101] However sexist or biased these commentaries might be, they correctly suggest that Loos hadn't fulfilled his own predictions—women's and men's dress had not become the same. Perhaps coincidentally, the exterior of Loos's

FIG. 13 *Josephine Baker and her "husband" Pepito (Giuseppi Abatino) in the East Indian room of her house, Le Beau-Chêne, c. 1934. Baker was famous for spending outrageous sums on clothing. Two designers, Jeanne Beauvois and Marcel Rochas, each named dresses for her—"La Créole" and "Zouzou." There was also a mass-produced brown lizard skin shoe named after her.* From Lynn Haney, Naked at the Feast: A Biography of Josephine Baker, *(London: Robson Books, 1981), 170.*

FIG. 14 *Le Beau-Chêne, Josephine Baker's thirty-room, turn-of-the-century mansion, where she stayed from 1929 to 1947, in Le Vésinet.* From Haney, Naked at the Feast, *169.*

ARCHITECTURE: *In Fashion*

other project for a woman client, for the daughter of Dr. F. Müller, also displayed a marked horizontal striation, this time in wood.[102]

One could say that Loos proposed in these projects a modernity of "difference," but it might be closer to the truth—and to the thrust of most of his writings and interiors—to admit that the modern was still a male province. Baker, who loved extravagant clothes, rejected the house that Loos designed and bought an eclectic chateau in the Parisian suburbs, Le Beau-Chêne (Figs. 13, 14). Despite its decorative patterning, Loos's design may have been too nude, too male to suite her taste.[103] In 1910 Loos asserted, "By culture I mean that harmony of man's inner and outer life which can only be maintained by rational thought and action," leaving no doubt that he considered these last to be distinctly masculine qualities.[104]

TOWARDS A NUDE ARCHITECTURE

In the early 1920s Le Corbusier was clearly indebted to Loos in his attitudes toward fashion, decoration, and modernity. Not only did he republish Loos's famous diatribe "Ornament and Crime" in *L'Esprit Nouveau*, but he declared in one of his own articles, republished in *L'Art décoratif d'aujourd'hui* in 1925: "It seems justified to affirm: *the more cultivated a people becomes, the more decoration disappears.* (Surely it was Loos who put it so neatly)."[105] His description of Lenin, *un homme type*, appearing under a painting of Louis XIV by Rigaud, dramatically makes his point.

> Lenin is seated at the [Café] Rotonde on a cane chair; he has paid twenty *centimes* for his coffee, with a tip of one *sou*. He is drinking out of a small white porcelain cup. He is wearing a bowler hat and a smooth white collar....He is teaching himself to govern one hundred million people.[106]

On the facing page is a photo of Khai Dinh, the emperor of Annam, while the next page features Gaston Doumergue, President of the French Republic. Modernity is neither the exotic (which Le Corbusier had so enjoyed in his youth and would return

FIG. 15 *Advertisement for Jove couturier, run by Germaine Bongard. The drawing was done by painter Marie Laurencin. From* Esprit Nouveau, *nos. 11–12.*

FIG. 16 *Germaine Bongard, photo by Henri Manuel (no. 248), c. 1923. From Musée de la Mode et du Costume,* Paul Poiret et Nicole Grout: Maîtres de la Mode Art Déco, *exhibition catalog, Palais Galliera, Paris, 5 July–12 October 1986, 30.*

to in the 1930s) nor the past; rather, it is embodied in the crisp white collar and businessman's suit—the mode of dress Le Corbusier himself sported. The model is again British men's clothes, although the evidence is nearly all visual. The pages of *L'Esprit Nouveau* and Le Corbusier's books of the 1920s are brimming with hats, shoes, suitcases, and other male accessories. The last image of *Vers une architecture* is a briar pipe—an *objet type* slowly perfected over time.

In selecting his models, Le Corbusier was in a bit of a bind: "Trash [usually mass-produced] is always abundantly decorated; the luxury object [usually handcrafted] is well-made, neat and clean, pure and healthy, and its bareness reveals the quality of its manufacture."[107] Loos was seemingly content with these simple "luxury" goods. Le Corbusier's goal, however, was mass production. Fashion's purported

progenitor was not the aristocrat, but an *homme type*. Like the furnishings of the Pavilion of the Esprit Nouveau, his masculine accessories represented a seductive fiction: an image of future mass production using expensive, often traditional, handcrafted goods.
Women's fashion played no equivalent role. In the early 1920s it
was clearly outside of Le Corbusier's vision of aesthetic purity and
industrial production. Just as the Ville Contemporaine relegated
family dwellings to the outskirts (off the drawings), women and their
dress were restricted in the pages of *L'Esprit Nouveau* to marginal
allusions. Slipped among the ads for such male-oriented products
as Omega watches, *Monsieur* magazine, Briques Aéroscorie, Le
Thermidor, and "la plus robuste" Ford were discreet announce-
ments for Jove (Fig. 15), "le couturier de maintenant,"[108] while, in
later issues, ads for the Parisian fashion house Jenny joined the barrage of male, mechanistic publicity. Mme. Jenny was known for her
dresses' slim forms and decorated necklines.[109] Although both Jove
and Jenny appealed in their advertising copy to "modern" sensibilities, these establishments undoubtedly failed to project the image of
standardization and anonymity requisite to the Purists' vision.

Ozenfant's and Le Corbusier's personal involvement with women's
fashion was considerably greater than their public pronouncements
would seem to indicate. Jove, run by Mme. Germaine Bongard
(Fig. 16), Paul Poiret's sister and a close personal friend of
Ozenfant, doubled as Galerie Thomas, where the first Purist exhibition was held. In his *Mémoires*, written in the 1960s, Ozenfant
explained how his exposure to couture, which revealed to him the
"enormous difference" between *couture* and *mode*, inspired his
interest in constants and universals. For Ozenfant, *couture* stood
for self-conscious "constructed" dress, outside the "chance" of
fashion.[110] Le Corbusier may have had an even closer connection
to women's fashion. From 1921, he lived with Yvonne Gallis (Fig.
17), who reportedly worked as a fashion model.[111]

These connections with women's fashion did not significantly alter
L'Esprit Nouveau's Loosian indictment of women's taste. In *L'Art
decoratif*, decoration was clearly female, and clearly primitive:

FIG. 17 *Yvonne Gallis, Le Corbusier's wife and reportedly a fashion model, is wearing the dramatic hat. Other individuals (left to right) are August Klipstein (Le Corbusier's companion on the "Voyage to the Orient"), his wife Frieda Jäggi, Pierre Jeanneret, and Le Corbusier. Paris, 1927. Photograph courtesy of Alfred Roth.*

"Decoration: baubles, charming entertainment for a savage."[112] In a tirade against the goods in a department store, Le Corbusier complained:

> Decoration in all departments! Decoration, decoration yes indeed, in all departments; the department store became "the ladies' joy!"[113]

It was shop-girls who usually bought these cheap mass-produced goods, who were deceived by decoration's disguise. Le Corbusier wouldn't, however, mind "the pretty little shepherdess shop-girl in her flowery cretonne dress," if only her setting were different. As it was, she appeared like "a sickening apparition" from "the costume department in the ethnographic museum."[114] In other words, Le Corbusier would be willing to make women a charming exception to his strictures against decoration, if only they lived in whitewashed rooms, with Thonet chairs and a table from the Bazar de l'Hôtel de Ville.[115] Earlier, he had parenthetically remarked, "And

I do not deny that it is an excellent thing to keep an element of the savage alive in us—a small one."[116] An earthier, less snobbish sensibility than Loos's allowed Le Corbusier to entertain these notions; but women were merely a counterpoint, a delightful diversion, from the real tasks of modernity that lay ahead. In any case, women were not to be encouraged to enter the decorative arts; Le Corbusier decried the contribution of women to the field. Describing the situation at the turn of the century, he wrote:

> So young ladies became crazy about decorative art—poker-work, metal-work, embroidery. Girls' boarding schools made room for periods of Applied Art and the History of Art in their timetables.
>
> At this point it looked as if decorative art would founder among the young ladies, had not the exponents of the decorative ensemble wished to show...that male abilities were indispensable in this field: considerations of ensemble, organization, sense of unity, balance, proportion, harmony.
>
> There were germs of architecture in this....The *ensembliers* were right.[117]

Le Corbusier thus proclaimed the modern *Gesamtkunstwerk* an issue of male attributes.[118]

Limiting himself in his references to men's fashion to almost exclusively to visual images, Le Corbusier for the most part avoided discussing issues of temporality underlying nineteenth-century distinctions between costume and fashion. These themes emerged, however, in the more general aesthetic discourses of *L'Esprit Nouveau*. For example, the conclusion of Ozenfant and Le Corbusier's essay "Purism," published in 1921, underscores Purism's opposition to fashion:

> One could make an art of allusions, an art of fashion, based upon surprise and the conventions of the initiated. Purism strives for an art free of conventions which will utilize plastic constants and address itself above all to the universal properties of the senses and the mind.[119]

Earlier in the text Ozenfant and Le Corbusier distinguished between "those arts whose only ambition is to please" and those such as painting and architecture, whose ambition is "to put the spectator in a state of a mathematical quality." "Let us leave," they declared, "to the clothes-dyers the sensory jubilation of the paint tube." Purism was clearly on the side of "order," "economy," and "rationality," whereas fashion and dress (presumably here, female dress) were on the side of the senses. Purism—and that which transcended the vagaries of non-mathematical, sensual impressions—was the end product of a process of "mechanical selection," in which forms evolved according to the necessities of economic manufacture. Thus, time served to perfect goods, resulting in something close to "permanence."[120] This notion of "mechanical selection" translated one of Loos's underlying passions into aesthetic law: the modern strives for elimination of all superfluity and transitory sentiment; progress leads to the universal and constant. Again, the passage of time produces the truly timeless. The architect's role is simply to recognize this inevitable historical process, or else accept impotence.

Where Loos and Le Corbusier parted ways, however, was in their understanding of the nature of this historical time leading to modern "constants." For Loos, the modern was deeply embedded in tradition. Change was slow, almost indiscernible; the pace had not dramatically altered in the past one hundred years. But for Le Corbusier, fashion, not costume, was the paradigm for historical transformation. He embraced the Futurists' sense of urgency, celebrating "the rapid tempo of our time,"[121] and saw time itself as pushing us frenetically toward the future. He claimed that time had brought society to the point where the current "fashion" *was* simplicity and economy.[122] In other words, twentieth-century fashion accelerated "mechanical selection." Le Corbusier's relation to fashion thus becomes paradoxical: he endorsed fashion's temporal pace and its embodiment of the *Zeitgeist*; but he rejected its surface attributes and perpetual novelty. In "mechanical selection," it would seem, fashion obliterates itself.

Although fashion played a critical role in Le Corbusier's vision of modernity, his ultimate model appears to be nudity. "The naked man does not wear an embroidered waistcoat; he wishes to think. The naked man is a normally constituted being, who has no need of trinkets. His mechanism is founded on logic."[123] Le Corbusier cited as his model Diogenes, the Greek Cynic philosopher, who spent his last days living in a tub and who is said to have thrown away his last utensil, a cup, when he saw a peasant drink from his hands.[124] Like the philosopher's quest for an honest man, Le Corbusier's goal was a truthful architecture. His tone was explicitly moralistic: in the culminating section of *L'Art décoratif d'aujourd'hui*, "A Coat of Whitewash: The Law of Ripolin [enamel paint]," he declared: "A moral act: *to love purity*." After the white house, "then comes *inner* cleanness."[125] Le Corbusier regarded whitewash as the architectural equivalent of nudity, a perfected nakedness. This form of "dressing" inverts Semper's earlier principle. Instead of a building's tectonics permitting cultural expression, as in Greek polychromy, the dressing reveals the truth of the underlying body (its volume, its economy, its purposefulness). But Le Corbusier also granted whitewash another meaning, further distancing it from the Semperian position. Instead of covering, whitewash becomes a background, the base that permits us to think clearly and discard the superfluous. Although the Law of Ripolin applied to both the exterior and the interior, its application to the latter is significant in this treatise on the decorative arts. Surface was the foundation for a new purified interior that blurred distinctions between surface and essence, appearance and truth.

In many respects Le Corbusier's discussion of nudity seems remarkably gender-free (with the conspicuous exception of his use of the masculine pronoun). Like the abstraction of his own architectural forms, it dispenses with the trappings of earlier gender representations. A new generation was free to create new behaviors and new images that would break with nineteenth-century conventions. Yet, a cloak of masculinity still haunts this vision of nudity. After all, Le Corbusier's naked man was fed, housed, and clothed—and not in "flowery cretonne dresses." In *Vers une architecture*, it was the engineer who was "healthy and virile, active and useful."[126] And in his section on whitewash, it was the stadium and the bank that Le Corbusier upheld as settings that demanded "precision and clarity, speed and correctness," and whose backgrounds must be white. The distance, however, may not have been so far from Vitruvius's first order. At the conclusion of this passage on "whitewash," Le Corbusier described his new heroes as "men of vigor in an age of heroic reawakening from the powers of the spirit, in an epoch that rings out with a tragic thunder not far from Doric."[127] It was no accident that Le Corbusier chose the Parthenon, and not the Erechtheion, to compare to the modern automobile.

OTHER MODERNISMS

Numerous modern architects raised the model of nudity, and almost exclusively it was a male nudity, or alternatively, one dressed in men's clothes. Architects as diverse as Walter Gropius, Hugo Häring, and George Howe all alluded to men's fashion as a model of functional simplicity that architecture had yet to emulate.[128] Inversely, and just as frequently, avant-garde practitioners decried women's fashion and taste. For all their rhetoric advocating a synthesis of masculine and feminine attributes, De Stijl designers Theo van Doesburg and Cor van Eesteren demanded an "objective system" opposed to "subjective speculation," "animal spontaneity (lyricism),...complicated hair-styles, and elaborate cooking."[129] In *Modern Architecture* (1929) Bruno Taut invoked the zeitgeist argument equating clothes and architectural styles, and dismissed the "prettiness" of British workers' cottages as exemplifying flappers' taste.[130] And as late as 1934, Marcel Breuer explicitly denounced women's fashion as a model of temporality:

> The new in the Modern Movement must be considered simply
> a means to an end, not an end in itself, as in women's
> fashion....Novelty is not our aim. We seek what is definite and
> real, whether old or new.[131]

It would seem that there was little in women's fashion or indeed, in any other realm of women's restricted world that might be incorporated or given new stature in these visions of the new order.

Two architecture movements did escape the paradigm of masculine dress (i.e., dark suit, bowler hat, white shirt) as a model of modernity: Futurism and Constructivism. Both movements remained outside the classicizing axis of the Modern Movement, represented by Loos's and Le Corbusier's timeless modernity, which so dominated the evolution of modern architecture in the 1920s. Futurism presents a complicated scenario in terms of fashion and women. Although early photographs of the principal Futurist artists show them impeccably dressed in the Loosian mold, they decried the static, stultifying qualities of men's dress. In his 1913 manifesto on men's clothes, proto-Dadaist in tone, Giacomo Balla called for short-lived "hap-hap-hap-happy clothes" (Fig. 18) in brilliant colors, with asymmetrical lines;[132] and the following year, with the help of his daughter Luce, he began making unconventional clothes. There were echoes of women's fashion in the Futurists' constant clamor for speed and change—including demands for buildings and clothes with short life-spans—and in the self-conscious artifice and masquerade of their rhetoric and performances. But such parallels were not spoken. Instead, a model of male nudity—and male superiority—lurks more forcefully than ever behind all their words and actions. Although the Futurists changed their position on feminism (from outright rejection to halfhearted support for women's suffrage), they equated women with decoration, luxury, and sentimentality throughout their writings; for Marinetti in 1913, women's dress is analogous with historic bric-a-brac.[133]

Constructivism stands out as a major exception in this milieu. However masculine the emphasis on production and the bold engineering imagery, the concern for the decorative arts in Constructivism represents a break from earlier notions of *Gesamtkunstwerk*, in which women were merely an aesthetic extension of the environment. Designers such as Liubov Popova and Varvara Stepanova saw dress reform as part of a larger socialist revolution, changing domestic patterns and traditional sex roles; the radical

LE VÊTEMENT MASCULIN FUTURISTE
Manifeste

L'humanité a toujours porté le deuil, ou l'armure pesante, ou la chape hiératique, ou le manteau traînant. Le corps de l'homme a toujours été attristé par le noir, ou emprisonné de ceintures ou écrasé par des draperies.

Durant le Moyen-Âge et la Renaissance l'habillement a presque toujours eu des couleurs et des formes statiques, pesantes, drapées ou bouffantes, solennelles, graves, sacerdotales, incommodes et encombrantes. C'étaient des expressions de mélancolie, d'esclavage ou de terreur. C'était la négation de la vie musculaire, qui étouffait dans un passéisme anti-hygiénique d'étoffes trop lourdes et de demi-teintes ennuyeuses efféminées ou décadentes.

C'est pourquoi aujourd'hui comme autrefois les rues pleines de foule, les théâtres, et les salons ont une tonalité et un rythme désolants, funéraires et déprimants.

Nous voulons donc abolir :

1. — Les vêtements de deuil que les croque-morts eux-mêmes devraient refuser.

2. — Toutes les couleurs fanées, jolies, neutres, fantaisie, foncées.

3. — Toutes les étoffes à raies, quadrillées et à petits pois.

4. — Les soi-disants bon goût et harmonie de teintes et de formes qui ramollissent les nerfs et ralentissent le pas.

5. — La symétrie dans la coupe, la ligne statique qui fatigue, déprime, contriste, enchaîne les muscles, l'uniformité des revers et toutes les bizarreries ornementales.

Costume gris
Dessins noirs
Modifiants rouge bleu
Gilet vert (Jour)

FIG. 18 *Giacomo Balla, "Le Vêtement masculin futuriste: manifeste," Milan, 20 May 1914. Balla originally showed his designs in shades of yellow and blue, evoking a gay, carnivalesque atmosphere. Marinetti changed Balla's colors to "white-red-green" to create living flags that would serve as incitements to war. From Sergio Poggianella, ed.,* Giacomo Balla *(Modena: Edizioni Galleria Fonte d'Abisso, 1982), 413.*

reorganization of the "outward forms of daily life" was a requisite step.[134] They sought to design men's and women's dress on the basis of the activity of a particular profession or sport, and if this recalls Loos, they understood much better than their Viennese predecessor that this meant the dismissal of conventions and notions of stasis. The resultant designs were functional, but also colorful and playfully decorative, dramatically undermining traditional class and gender distinctions. And in contrast to most Modern Movement propagandists, they created more than avant-garde exercises for an artistic elite. Both women worked at the First Textile Printing Factory, where they became actively involved with industrial production.

REDUCTIO AD ABSURDUM

Between the wars, associations of dress and modernity extended, of course, far beyond architecture circles, as did the analogies and metaphors relating dress, nudity, and modern architecture. They were prominent in English psychologist and dress reformer J. C. Flugel's highly influential study *The Psychology of Clothes*, published in 1930. Even earlier, they played a seminal role in a small, idiosyncratic book (which Flugel cited), *Narcissus: An Anatomy of Clothes*, written by Anglo-Irish critic Gerald Heard and published in 1924.[135] In 1926 the De Stijl architect Cor van Eesteren recommended Heard's book as important reading to Knud Lonberg-Holm, a young Danish architect who had recently emigrated to the United States.[136] More important than the book's potential influence, however, is the contrast that it offers to the Modern Movement's celebration of English men's clothing as a paragon of modernity.

Heard reiterated the by-now familiar Semperian argument—that styles of architecture and dress are organically connected. But he declared that male dress is not dictated simply by functionalism and that men's "staged indifference" toward fashion (a word that he, like many writers after World War I, used interchangeably with dress and clothes) is not a sign of civilization but, rather, "nervous camouflage." In other words, those men who seem to care the least about their clothes are precisely those who give their tailors the most trouble (certainly a trait that Baudelaire, Loos, and Le Corbusier must have shared). In Heard's view, men's dress was moribund. However superior the quality of contemporary tailoring might be, it resulted in a creative impasse, since the striving for perfection brings death. "The bowler hat," he wrote, "has lasted a hundred years—an outrage unparalleled—and is yet and will be till the Deluge a prime favorite of gentlemen." Like Oscar Wilde, Heard rejected the division between functionalism and ornament in men's clothes and condemned those qualities in men's fashion that Wagner, Loos, and Le Corbusier had so appreciated: its anonymity and its resistance to change—its denial of the very attributes of fashion. However, he did not advocate the artifice and masquerade of women's fashion as a solution. In the last chapter of *Narcissus*, entitled "The Future's Fashions," he proposed two alternatives for the future of clothing and architecture, which he regarded as integrally linked. The first, reminiscent of the Futurists, is "a lighter, stronger architecture, [reciprocally] imposing cleaner, closer, more convenient clothing. Color will come back onto building surfaces, and men's dress will begin to flush in reflection." The second is that "architecture may take the place of clothing, and some other art, more austere, less intimate [such as engineering] may take the place of architecture."[137] In essence, Heard's prescription was brighter, more functional clothing, or else nudity. History, he claimed, had already indicated progress in this second direction. Today we wear far less clothing than medieval gentlemen did; "the three purposes of clothing [modesty, protection, and display] seem outworn, and our last garment is in danger of falling to the ground." New architectural inventions, such as central heating, made this an inviting possibility. Heard's nudity, like modern architects', was functional; but its *raison d'être* was not truth, or timeless nature. Heard believed that as architecture has affected clothes, so clothes have modified anatomy. "The razor, the corset, and the boot are only clumsy initial efforts to reduce our barbarian bodies to something smooth and delicate, which we have never been." He then mentioned, in words anticipating Thomas Pynchon's novel *V*, "manipulative surgery, facial operations, grafting," and "endocrine dosages." Functionalism has brought "a constant aim at reduction of mass." "Our bodies may actually be on the way to disappear[ing]."[138] This image, almost a parody of minimalism and efficiency, both dismantles one of the myths of modern architecture—that the body is a bearer of truth—and anticipates what has almost become a truism in current post-structuralist rhetoric—that the body is a construction.

Paradoxically, as Heard's vision of fashion moved from clothes to nudity, his vision of architecture encompassed a new version of the Semperian dressing thesis. The architect's role must henceforth be more like the tailor's and less like the builder's. The "lesser men of the profession" must dress the body that the engineer gives them, taking their themes from the present, namely engineering and machines. The aesthetic model—"the smartest male fashions"—was to be found not on Savile Rowe, but on Great Portland Street, where the "perfectly turned out" young mechanics were reflections of their gleaming limousines. This implied extending the democratization of men's dress another step. Just as the Great Renunciation in men's dress in the nineteenth century reduced overt class distinctions between the aristocracy and the middle classes, Heard's proposal, if followed, would reduce those between the lower and middle classes. He cited women's dress only as a model for temporal change: "We may live to change our buildings as quickly as a woman her clothes."[139]

Without conscious acknowledgment—but how typical—Heard concentrated almost exclusively on masculine dress; for instance, he claimed that the impact of World War I on fashion, which had initiated such dramatic changes in women's dress, was paralysis.[140] It is tempting to speculate to what extent this bias may have led him to his extreme of nudity as a fashion solution, and to his morbid obsession with doctored bodies as opposed to doctored clothes. Perhaps to a well-bred British man of the 1920s, however bohemian, the pleasure suggested by colors without function was more threatening than a nudity—historicist or not—based on function.

WOMEN'S SARTORIAL SUPERIORITY

FIG. 19 *Charlotte Perriand with Alfred Roth in her studio, Paris, 1927. Perriand is wearing her famous ball-bearing necklace. Photograph courtesy of Alfred Roth.*

Although a male-oriented view of modernity predominated in architecture throughout the 1920s, by the end of the decade there were a few chinks in the armor, even among the bastions of the Modern Movement. This is conveyed by a passage in Le Corbusier's *Précisions*, published in 1930, six years after his *Esprit Nouveau* articles on the decorative arts; and even before then, his personal contacts with women appear to have undergone a change. In the fall of 1927, after some resistance, Le Corbusier hired a woman for the first time as an active collaborator: Charlotte Perriand (Fig. 19), a talented young furniture designer, with an original personal style, who wore a necklace of ball-bearings and had cropped hair. In 1929, on his return voyage from South America he apparently had a serious shipboard flirtation with Josephine Baker, Loos's former client and the current Parisian inspiration of *la vogue nègre*.[141] And in his three trips to the Soviet Union from 1928 to 1930, he encountered for the first time a group of talented women working in architecture and design, many of whom had dispensed with traditional dress.[142] Probably more important, however, than these biographical events was that a revolution had occurred in women's fashion. In 1923 skirts were still long (Fig. 20), but by 1925 they had risen to the knee (Fig. 21), and several of the great firms of *la belle époque*—Doucet, Douillet, and Drescoll—had closed their doors; even Paul Poiret, who had done so much to transform prewar fashion, found himself out of touch with the latest currents. A new generation of dress designers emerged: Madeleine Vionnet, Jeanne

Women's suits, L'Art et la mode, *12 January 1924. From JoAnne Olian, ed.,* **FIG. 20**
Authentic French Fashions of the Twenties *(New York: Dover Publications,*
1990), 69.

Dresses, L'Art et la mode, *12 December 1925. Many assume that World War I* **FIG. 21**
brought short skirts to France, but although ankles became commonplace and
some designers showed dresses at mid-calf lengths, it was not until 1925 that
skirts began to appear regularly at lengths just below the knee. This trend contin-
ued until 1927. From Olian, Authentic French Fashions of the Twenties, *91.*

Lavin, and the legendary Coco Chanel (Fig. 22); two years later
they were joined by another great innovator of the interwar period
and Chanel's only real rival—Elsa Schiaparelli. Women now controlled fashion.[143] Here is the passage in *Précisions*:

> Woman has got there before us. She has brought about the
> reform of her dress. She found herself in this dilemma to
> follow fashion and by doing so gave up what modern tech-
> nology modern life had to offer. To give up sport and, more
> materially, the chance of employment which has given her a
> productive role in modern life and enabled her to earn her liv-
> ing....To carry out the daily construction of her dressing and
> grooming: hairdo, boots, buttoning her dress, she would have
> had to give up sleeping.

FIG. 22 *One of Chanel's little black dresses that inspired Paul Poiret to utter his famous retort, "What has Chanel invented? Poverty de Luxe." It was published in Paris* Vogue, *January 1927. From Edmonde Charles-Roux,* Chanel and her World *(London and Paris: Hachette Vendome Press, 1981), 157.*

So woman cut off her hair and her skirts and her sleeves. She goes around bare-headed, bare-armed with her legs free, and she can dress in five minutes. Moreover she is beautiful; she enchants us with the grace of her figure....

The courage, the enterprise, the inventive spirit with which woman has revolutionized her dress are a miracle of modern times. Thank you!

What about us men? A dismal state of affairs! In our clothes, we look like generals of the Grand Army and we wear starched collars! We are uncomfortable.[144]

Women had gained a new freedom, but not by equaling men. Even though Le Corbusier's remarks, like Baudelaire's, tended to objectify women in their aestheticizing gaze, is it too much to wonder if Le Corbusier's own architecture, which changed so dramatically in the early 1930s—in its more colorful, tactile, and sensuous forms—was not touched by these new options of what it meant to be modern?

Finally, it would seem that the pervasive model of architecture as timeless truth—removed from the artifice, play, *and* femininity of fashion—had been undermined.

AFTERWORD: ARCHITECTURE AS WOMEN'S FASHION?

Le Corbusier's assessment of women's dress in *Précisions* is remarkably close to Flugel's in *The Psychology of Clothes*, published the same year.[145] Although Flugel delineated certain advantages of the male dress in the nineteenth century—the elimination of competition, reduction in the time expended for dressing, improvements in taste for those without aesthetic judgment, the stabilization of the clothing economy—he believed that any superiority that men's clothing could once rightly claim had abruptly vanished. He then enumerated all the ways in which women's clothing allows greater satisfaction than that of men: in its variety of colors, innovative materials, lighter weight, individual liberty in selection, seasonal adaptation, adjustment to temperature, freedom of movement, exposure of parts of the body, convenience in dressing and in traveling, and overall hygienic superiority. Flugel considered this a historical stage of considerable cultural and ethical significance, as it implied "an increasing harmonization of erotic and cultural ideals with the actual realities of the human body."[146]

Flugel characterized his overall philosophy as securing "the maximum of satisfaction in accordance with the 'reality' principle"; short of nudity, this meant a synthesis of the best attributes of fashion and traditional dress:

> Costume must be freed, alike from the ruinous competition and commercialism of fashion, and from the unadaptable conservatism of 'fixed' dress. Reasonable consideration of ends and means, together with an appeal to the highest standards of contemporary aesthetic taste, must replace a frantic search for novelty at any cost, or a blind adherence to tradition.[147]

Flugel thus sought to counter fashion's ever-increasing ties to the market and its frenetic pace of change, intensified by the dramatic increase in industrialization and the wide-ranging dissemination of styles following World War I. But despite these economic trends, women's fashion had in many ways already answered his plea for aesthetic quality and functionalism, variety and continuity, femininity and masculinity, as Flugel himself had clearly

FIG. 23 *Parallels between fashion and style. From Adolf Behne,* Eine Stunde Architektur *(Stuttgart: Akademischer Verlag Dr. Fritz Wedekind, 1928), 28.*

acknowledged. By the late 1920s women's fashion also combined the advantages of female and male dress: the simplicity and utility of the man's suit—frequently surpassing it in terms of comfort, ease of movement, and maintenance—and the traditionally feminine pleasures of eroticism, fantasy, and self-fabrication. In the hands of Chanel, women's clothes were both classic and novel, practical and fanciful. Sexual difference remained, but in a more playful, even ironic vein. Chanel wore layers of costume jewelry and, on other occasions, men's suits; *la garçonne* defiantly applied garish lipstick and rouge in public. Codes of rigid sexual differentiation, as well as class divisions, had given way to greater individual choice.

Architecture underwent similar changes during the next decade. Just as the reductive vocabulary of the Modern Movement in the 1920s followed the men's suit in dispensing with many overt signs of social stratification, architecture's new emphasis on texture, color, and local conditions in the 1930s paralleled women's fashion in offering greater variety without traditional references to wealth, class, or gender. In Le Corbusier's own architecture, the highly diverse small houses of the 1930s—Errazuris, Mandrot, Mathes, Maison de Weekend—contrast sharply with the more aesthetically homogeneous villas of the 1920s. The universalism of the Modern Movement had given way to more modest, contextually specific visions of modernity, acknowledging a wider range of "differences."

Yet, to assume that architecture followed the same patterns as fashion is to accept too uncritically the zeitgeist rhetoric that characterized the association of architecture with fashion from the start, and that was promulgated so relentlessly by polemicists of the Modern Movement. Although there were real and vivid connections between the two fields, architecture and fashion did not always march in step. In fact, some of the appeal of the fashion analogies in modern architecture stemmed from this very gap, with men's fashion from 1890 to 1925 serving as a progressive model for architecture one or two decades later.

By the late 1920s, however, this relation had begun to falter: not only had architecture begun to embrace women's fashion as a paragon of modernism, but it became unclear whether fashion was leading architecture or vice versa. Already in 1924, Gerald Heard had argued for engineering as a model for men's clothes and nudity; in 1928, Varvara Stepanova made a similar plea, claiming that men's fashion needed to catch up with women's in following the lead of new discoveries of industrial architecture and engineering;[148] and in 1930, Flugel reiterated that idea.[149] But this model of women's fashion as functionalist instigator was short-lived. Almost immediately after Le Corbusier's statement appeared in *Précisions*, women's fashion took a seemingly backward slide— hemlines dropped and waists came in—while men's fashions remained unchanged. Nonetheless, in *Quand les cathedrales etaient blanches* (1937) Le Corbusier continued to pay homage to women's dress and deplored the funereal sobriety of men's clothes. Masculine dress, he complained, was the proof that the "machine age revolution has not reached maturity." More than functionalism, feeling and fantasy were now his battle cries.[150] Here, his continued interest in women's dress was inextricably linked to his reassessment of the values of the Modern Movement itself. Though far from an endorsement of Baudelaire's aesthetic of appearances, this reassessment included eroticism, theatricality, and even, at times, ornament as integral components of architecture's "nature." In other words, the domain of functionalism itself had been expanded.

However, the ideological meanings of this embrace of women's fashion remain a vexing question. As feminist theorists such as Elizabeth Wilson, Kaja Silverman, and Jane Gaines have shown, traditional theories of fashion as oppressive to women in the Loosian sense ignore the possibilities of creativity, self-expression, pleasure, and even the protective mask that fashion has offered women.[151] Yet for all the enduring transformations in women's dress during the 1920s, fashion continues to constrain women physically, psychologically, and economically. It is a capricious and often irrational product, alternating between styles of exagger-

Le Corbusier, "Clothes [costumes] for the women of today," a drawing submitted **FIG. 24**
by Le Corbusier to Harper's Bazaar *for publication, February 1952. The publisher*
declined to print the sketch. From Formes et Vie 2 (1951), 11.

ated artifice and what poses as naturalism. Each approach contains
elements of potential oppression and liberation, of masculine
objectification and female desire. In modern architecture, issues of
gender, which are so often linked to fashion, are similarly ever-
changing and ambiguous. Although the 1930s brought a new
appreciation of tactility and tradition, these qualities coexisted
with earlier models of male strength and nudity—sometimes at different scales or in different contexts. These last attributes resurged
with a renewed vigor in postwar America, most visibly with the
corporate skyscrapers of the 1950s. But even there, seemingly
masculine overtones coincided with strains of organicism, mannered historicism, and exuberant expressionism, carrying other,
often complex gender connotations.

After World War II, only a few architects publicly expressed an interest in clothes. In 1952, Le Corbusier sketched for *Harper's Bazaar* some women's dress designs (Fig. 24) which he labeled "costumes"—colorful, functional designs that avoided the cinched waist of the "New Look."[152] Carlo Mollino offered women another extreme with his witty pornographic dresses and underwear that revealed bare buttocks, in one instance branded CM.[153] More generally, however, the analogy of architecture to clothing had faded in architectural rhetoric. Its disappearance was possibly symptomatic of a new refusal to cope with the artifice of modernism itself, just when the underlying belief structures of modern architecture had been deeply shaken by World War II and the political and economic crises of the preceding decade. Though not articulated, it could also be that fashion analogies themselves came to be viewed as superficial and effeminate, with the pejorative connotations of fashion—so pervasive in modernist rhetoric—wholly retained. Or, more optimistically, it could be that the relevance of fashion analogies diminished as women's fashions challenged the male suit as a paragon of modernism, revealing its functional limitations and artifice. As the 1960s made blatantly evident, sexual categories in fashion had themselves lost their meaning.

Today fashion may again offer a model for architecture, though one quite different from that which prevailed during the first part of the century. The fluid boundaries in contemporary women's fashion underscore the continued rigidity in architecture discourse, an avant-garde moralism that is all too evident in the peculiarly puerile debates—deconstructivism versus postmodernism, abstraction versus figuration, technology versus decoration, and modernity versus history—that continue to plague the profession. Just as the lines between dress reform and fashion, function and fantasy, have blurred, so too have oppositions between surface and substance lost their meaning. Both the exterior and interior are part of architecture. Surface is as much substance as any other dimension of architecture. In her essay "All the Rage," Elizabeth Wilson states:

Deconstructionist fashion as portrayed in the Sunday "Styles of the Times" section of The New York Times, *25 July 1993, 1.* **FIG. 25**

> Traditionally western Christian culture has created a division between appearances and an inner and spiritual truth. Appearances, the immediate, sensual impact of life, are denigrated; only the superficial is real. Yet the light and shade of change which plays across the surface of life *is* reality. Fashion in our culture is elaborate, fetishized, neurotic, because it goes against these dominant values, against the grain of the cultural norm, representing the return of the repressed and the profound importance of the superficial.[154]

As the history of fashion and modern architecture reveals, appearances *are* profoundly important to both modernity and gender.

It is not accidental that the term "deconstructionist" entered the vocabulary of fashion (Fig. 25) shortly after the Museum of Modern Art's Deconstructivist Architecture show in 1988.[155] While this recent trend in architecture lacks the irony and humor of the parallel movement in women's and men's fashion, it has underscored the ambiguities between construction and ornament. In much contemporary work, construction and ornament are synonymous, creating style not in Otto Wagner's sense but in a manner more akin to Baudelaire's views on women's fashion. This congruence may have the potential for opening up new, progressive options for architecture *and* gender. Yet, lest we forget the revulsion that Baudelaire felt for women's nature, other questions arise. Is this new, aggressive display of construction and technique, with its celebration of collisions, cuts, and crashes—however decorative—yet another male body? Does ornament, whether the exaggerated caricature of historicist postmodernism or the structurally acrobatic scenography of deconstructivism, risk becoming (like so much of contemporary culture) the exclusive province of men? Does the exultation of indeterminacy, in its refusal of any universal social or ethical values and in its rejection of notions of political agency, threaten to become an end in itself, leaving gender definitions essentially untouched? Or is it possible that, as women continue to enter the profession, they will remove the imprint of male control that has long dominated the surface and body of architecture?

I want to express my debt and immense gratitude to Leila Kinney, who is respon-sible for sparking the development of the themes in this paper, and whose com-ments have helped me clarify my argument, although she may disagree with por-tions of it. Many of the issues raised in this essay first emerged in our prepara-tions for a workshop that we organized for the Feminist Art History conference at Barnard College in October 1990. For a sophisticated and insightful exploration of the relationships among women, fashion, and modernity in late-nineteenth-century painting, see Leila Kinney, "Boulevard Culture and Modern Life Painting," (Ph.D. dissertation, Yale University [forthcoming]). This essay has been long in gestation, and my debts are many. Barry Bergdoll, Rosemarie Haag Bletter, Stephen Robert Frankel, John Goodman, Harry Mallgrave, Robin Middleton, Joan Ockman, Kenneth Silver, Marc Treib, and the editors of this publication have all read earlier versions of this essay, and I am grateful to them for their numerous comments and suggestions. An earlier version of this paper was delivered at a Mellon seminar at Princeton University's School of Architecture in November 1990, which was sponsored by the architecture doctoral students there.

NOTES

1   Ozenfant is alluding to the objective that he and Charles-Edouard Jeanneret (Le Corbusier) had in mind in founding Purism. Amédée Ozenfant, *Foundations of Modern Art*, trans. John Rodker (New York: Dover, 1952), 326.

2   Harry Francis Mallgrave, Introduction to Otto Wagner, *Modern Architecture* (Santa Monica, Calif.: The Getty Center for the History of Art and the Humanities, 1988), 45. Wagner alludes to Muthesius's rejection of *Stilarchitektur* in the preface of his fourth edition of *Moderne Architektur* (ibid., 142). I am grateful to Harry Mallgrave for his assistance with this issue, and for giving me a copy of Stanford Anderson's translation of Muthesius's text. See Otto Wagner, *Style-Architecture and Building-Art, Modern Architecture*, trans. Stanford Anderson (Santa Monica, Calif.: The Getty Center and Chicago: University of Chicago Press, 1994).

3   Walter Gropius, "Program for the Establishment of a Company for the Provision of Housing on Aesthetically Consistent Principles," in Tim and Charlotte Benton, eds., *Form and Function: A Source Book for the History of*

Architecture and Design 1890–1939 (London: Crosby Lockwood Staples and The Open University Press, 1975), 190. It should also be noted, however, that Gropius's position shifted in the period immediately following the war, when he was most influenced by Expressionism and folklore. In a talk delivered in 1919, he applauded the color of folk costume. See Walter Gropius, "'Sparsamer Hausrat' und falsche Dürftigkeit," *Das hohe Ufer*, 1:7 (July 1919), 180, as quoted by Iain Boyd Whyte, *Bruno Taut and the Architecture of Activism* (Cambridge: Cambridge University Press, 1982), 166.

4   These questions first arose in preparations for a workshop that Leila Kinney and I jointly organized for the Feminist Art History conference at Barnard College in October 1990, and are as much a product of Kinney's thinking as my own. See the Introduction to this volume.

5   A variety of sources have been consulted with regard to the etymology of the terms "fashion," "mode," "clothes," "costume," and "dress." In particular, see: *The Compact Edition of the Oxford English Dictionary* (Oxford: Oxford University Press, 1971); Edward Pinkerton, *Word for Word* (Detroit: Verbatim, 1982); Dr. Samuel Johnson, *The New Royal and Universal English Dictionary* (London: A. Millard, 1763); *Grand Dictionnaire Encyclopédie Larousse* (Paris: Larousse, 1982); *Dictionnaire de l'Académie française*, 8th ed. (Paris: Hachette, 1932); *Dizionario etimologio italiano* (Florence: G. Barberra, 1954); *Dizionario etimologio della lingua italiane* (Bologna: Zarichella, 1984); Wolfgang Pfeiffer, ed., *Etymologisches Wörterbuch des Deutschen* (Berlin: Akademie Verlag, 1989); *Vollständiges Wörterbuch der Deutsch Sprache* (Vienna: Theodor Heinsius, 1840).

6   Although we usually associate the meaning of "costume" with theater and festivities, its use in English before World War II (and in French still today) was more general, referring to the proper clothes of a region, epoch, or certain condition. While the etymology of "costume" can be traced back to the Latin word *consuetudin-*, *consuetudo* (custom), its modern history dates back to the seventeenth-century Italian word *costume*, referring to the appropriate dress of characters in a painting. "Dress" initially carried suggestions of "arrangement" or "embellishment" and still does, to some extent (to dress a turkey, to dress for a ball) but in much usage is indistinguishable from clothing and costume. In German the word *Tracht* is used to refer to regional or peasant dress. In the beginning of the seventeenth century, when *Mode* first appeared as a distinct noun in German, *Tracht* had very much the same meaning as *Mode*, referring simply to the clothes one wore. (However, while aristocratic clothes might have been referred to as a kind of *Tracht*, it is unlikely that peasant clothes would have been described in terms of a *Mode*). See Daniel Leonhard Purdy, "Reading

to Consume: Fashionable Receptions of Literature in Germany, 1774–1816," dissertation, Cornell University, 1992 (Ann Arbor: University Microfilms, 1992), 6. I am also grateful to Daniel Purdy for the insights and information he provided concerning fashion in several conversations that we had.

7   According to Gottfried Semper, an even earlier example comparing clothes and architecture can be found in a surviving fragment of a book on the Temple of Ephesus by the Ephesian Democritus. He linked the highly ornamented, colored clothing of the Ephesians with the rich decorations of the Temple of Ephesus. Athenaeus, *Deipnosophists* 12: 525, as cited by Gottfried Semper, "Style: The Textile Art," in *The Four Elements of Architecture and Other Writings*, trans. Harry Francis Mallgrave and Wolfgang Herrmann (Cambridge: Cambridge University Press, 1989), 240–41.

8   Vitruvius, *The Ten Books on Architecture*, trans. Morris Hicky Morgan (New York: Dover, 1960), 103–04. Vitruvius's interpretation is probably more a reflection of Hellenist values in first-century Rome than of those which inspired the orders' initial use. Nevertheless, as John Onians points out, the Dorians, who were aggressive warriors, tended to worship male deities, while the more peaceful, wealth-accumulating Ionians tended to worship female deities, often linked to fertility. By the late fifth century, the Dorians were widely regarded as strong and manly and the Ionians as weak and effeminate; this prejudice undoubtedly only reinforced the tendency to see their architectures as embodying the two sexes. John Onians, *The Bearers of Meaning: The Classical Orders in Antiquity, the Middle Ages, and the Renaissance* (Princeton: Princeton University Press, 1988), 35.

9   Sebastiano Serlio, *Tutte l'opere* (Venice: de Franceschi, 1619; rpt. 1964), bk. 4, ch. 1, as trans. by Onians, *Bearers*, 273. Serlio's adaptation of Vitruvius's rule of decor to the saints was already indicated in Luca Pacioli's *De devina proportione* (Venice, 1509). See Onians, *Bearers*, 221.

10   Charles Blanc, *Grammaire des arts du dessin, architecture, peinture, jardins...*(Paris: Raynouard, 1882 [1867]); and Charles Blanc, *L'Art du parure et dans le vêtement* (Paris: Raynouard, 1875); trans. as *Art in Ornament and Dress* (London: Chapman and Hall, 1877), 150, 161. These gender connotations of the orders even reappear in the writings of structural rationalist Auguste Choisy, for whom the Doric represents a reformist style, countering the effeminate decoration of the Mycenaeans: "They needed a more masculine tone, a stronger form of expression: they placed their ideal in an architecture that scorned the easy seductions of ornament. An architecture...more abstract and simpler." Auguste Choisy, *Histoire de l'architecture* (Paris, 1899; rpt., Geneva and Paris: Slatkine, 1987), 266.

11   Paul Valéry, *Eupalinos or the Architect*, trans. from the original 1921 French edition by William McCausland Stewart (London: Oxford University Press, Humphrey Millford, 1932), 21–22. I have altered the translation slightly, as I do in several other instances of published translations in this text.

12   Christopher Wren, letter from France, 1665, in *Parentalia: or, Memoirs of the Family of the Wrens...*(London, 1750; rpt. London: Gregg Press, 1965), 69. In contrast, during the first half of the eighteenth century the rococo, which was in part a product of the female patronage and power in France that so frightened Wren, was often praised, in language heavily laden with feminine overtones, for its grace, delicacy, charm, and artifice. Furniture of this *style moderne*, created for women's intimacy and pleasure, gained anthropomorphic female names: *la causeuse* (the chatterer); *la bergère* (the shepherdess); *la chif-fonnière* (the rag woman); *la duchesse brisée* (the broken duchess); *la chaise à la reine* (the chair in the queen's style); and especially, *la toilette*. But this passion for the feminization of style was short-lived. By the mid-eighteenth century critics such as Charles-Nicolas Cochin and the Comte de Caylus vehemently attacked the rococo style for being *de mode*, capricious, bizarre, seductive, extravagant, and disorderly—for wantonly flouting the "truth" thought to be inherent in *la bonne architecture*. With the advent of neoclassical architecture, the pendulum swung back again, bringing a return to austerity and eternal virtues: in 1787 Luc-Vincent Thiéry praised Ledoux's toll houses "for their simple and masculine character which seems to us to correspond with the purpose for which they are destined." Nor was the rhetoric of the "manly" discarded with the Gothic revival. As Kenneth Clark has revealed, in the battle about styles surrounding the 1836 Houses of Parliament competition both the Gothic and the neoclassical were heralded for their masculine attributes. The "chaste plainness" of classical architecture was undeniably manly; so was the gloom and force of the Gothic. The feminine as a more positive attribute did not reemerge until the last half of the nineteenth century with the rococo revival and art nouveau, although very shortly thereafter the latter was criticized for its "elusiveness" and "moral anarchy." Just as the vocabulary that was used to praise art nouveau was similar to that used for rococo ("grace," "finesse," "elegance," "refinement," "aristocratic delicacy"), criticism of art nouveau echoed the language used in mid-eighteenth-century dismissals of the rococo style. For connotations surrounding both rococo and art nouveau design, see Debora L. Silverman, *Art Nouveau in Fin-de-Siècle France: Politics, Psychology, and Style* (Berkeley: University of California Press, 1989), chps. 1, 4, and 11, especially pp. 27–28. This ground-breaking study was fundamental to my thinking about the "gendering" of style. Similarly, Silverman's *Selling Culture: Bloomingdale's, Diana Vreeland, and the New Aristocracy of Taste in Reagan's America* (New York, Pantheon, 1986), which discusses the links among

Bloomingdale's, the Metropolitan Museum of Art, and the Reagan era, sparked my interest in the cultural and political meanings of fashion. For further information concerning the critical reactions to rococo, see Wolfgang Herrmann, *Laugier and Eighteenth-Century French Theory* (London: Zwemmer, 1962), 221–34; and Dorothea Nyberg, "Meissonnier: An Eighteenth-Century Maverick," *Oeuvre de Juste Aurèle Meissonnier* (New York: Benjamin Blom, 1969), 14–19. Other sources for this quick survey of gender and style are L. V. Thiéry, *Guide des amateurs et des étrangers voyageurs à Paris* (Paris: Hardouin and Gattey, 1787), as quoted by Alan Braham, in *The Architecture of the French Enlightenment* (London: Thames and Hudson), 194; both *The Works of James Barry* (London: T. Cadell and W. Davies, 1809), 1:23; and *The Oxford Dictionary*, s.v. "manly," as cited by Kenneth Clark, *The Gothic Revival: An Essay in the History of Taste* (New York: Icon, Harper and Row, 1962 [1928]), 116; G. Bans, "Les Gares du Méropolitain de Paris," *L'Art décoratif* 3 (25 October, 1900), 38–40; and V. Champier, "Le Castel Béranger et M. Hector Guimard," *Revue des Arts Décortatifs* 19 (January 1899), 1–10, as quoted by Franco Borsi and Ezio Godoli, in *Paris 1900: Architecture and Design* (New York: Rizzoli, 1976), 130 and 82.

13   Charles Baudelaire, "The Painter of Modern Life," in *The Painter of Modern Life and Other Essays*, trans. Jonathan Mayne (London: Phaidon, 1964), 31, 32.

14   Ibid., 12.

15   Ibid., 35.

16   In this sense, women play a role similar to that of the dandy. Michel Foucault's provocative essay "What is Enlightenment?" raises the theme in Baudelaire's writings of modern man as self-invention. What is curious, however, is Foucault's total neglect of the major role that women play in Baudelaire's account. He is not unique among critics of Baudelaire. Although much has been made of Baudelaire's male dandy, the poet's extensive discussion of women's fashion and makeup is only occasionally cited. In art historical commentary, the work of Valerie Steele and, to a greater extent, that of Leila Kinney begins to address this imbalance. See Michel Foucault, "What Is Enlightenment?" in Paul Rabinow, ed., *Foucault Reader* (New York: Pantheon Books, 1984), 32–50; Valerie Steele, *Paris Fashion: A Cultural History* (New York and Oxford: Oxford University Press, 1988), 88; Kinney, "Fashion and Figuration in Modern Life Painting," this volume, and Kinney, "Boulevard Culture and Modern Life Painting." Another theme that Baudelaire's essay suggests but does not mention is the relationship between his notions of artifice

and homosexual self-representation. Although speculations on the relation between personality, appearance, and sexual orientation were still not commonplace in the mid-nineteenth century, in other writings Baudelaire does discuss lesbians in terms of these themes.

17   Elizabeth Ann Coleman, *The Opulent Era: Fashions of Worth, Doucet, and Pingat* (Brooklyn: The Brooklyn Museum, and London: Thames and Hudson, 1989), 12; Sima Godfrey, "Baudelaire, Gautier, and 'une toilette savamment composée,'" in Barbara T. Cooper and Mary Donaldson-Evans, eds., *Modernity and Revolution in Late Nineteenth-Century France* (Newark: University of Delaware Press; London and Toronto: Associated University Presses, 1992), 74–87. France, of course, could boast of many couture houses before the House of Worth, but what set this establishment apart was the scale of its business, its international scope, and the fact that clients came to Worth instead of him going to their residences.

18   See Alison Gernsheim, *Fashion and Reality* (London: Faber and Faber, 1963), 47–48; Max von Boehn, *Die Mode: Menshen und Moden im neunzehnten Jahrhundert*, vol. 3, 1848–78 (Munich, n.d. [1919]), as cited by Gernsheim, 48.

19   While crinolines undoubtedly inhibited women's movements (though less so than the weighty layers of cloth wore by women in preceding decades), they were frequently viewed by contemporary male critics as signs of women's power. In 1878 F. T. Vischer, a well-known commentator on fashion, described crinolines as "impertinent" because they made women look larger than men. Friedrich Theodor Vischer, *Mode und Zynismus* (Stuttgart: K. Wittwer, 1879), as quoted by Valerie Steele, *Fashion and Eroticism: Ideals of Feminine Beauty from the Victorian Era to the Jazz Age* (New York and Oxford: Oxford University Press, 1985), 131.

20   It would seem that Baudelaire could admire women only to the extent that they created an artificial persona. In "The Painter of Modern Life," for instance, he wrote: "She is a kind of idol, stupid perhaps, but dazzling and bewitching....She is not I must admit, an animal whose component parts, correctly assembled, provide a perfect example of harmony." The essay suggests an unfortunate objectification and essentialist view of women, which is most apparent in Baudelaire's assertion, "I need hardly tell you that I could easily support my assertions with reference to many objects other than women." His two examples? Modern ships and thoroughbred race horses. Baudelaire, "The Painter," 32, 14–15.

21   Charles Baudelaire, "Mon coeur mis à nu," *Oeuvres complètes*, ed. Claude Pichois, 2 vols. (Paris: Gallimard, 1975) 1: 677.

22   In *The Nude: A Study in Ideal Form* (Garden City: Doubleday, 1956), Kenneth Clark distinguishes between "nude," which is idealized and noble, and "naked," which is bare nature, frequently distorted and defenseless. For the most part I have tried to follow this distinction, but in modern architecture the meanings begin to blur, since nudity as an ideal is frequently associated with the brute realities of matter. A further complication emerges in discussing French texts, since there is only one word, *nu*, to refer to both meanings. One might argue a similar trajectory from the clothed to the nude for one dominant trend of modern painting, which gradually eliminates not only clothes but the body—indeed all figuration. See also Leila Kinney's remarks in "Fashion and Figuration in Modern Life Painting," in this book.

23   Baudelaire, "The Painter," 3.

24   See, for instance, Semper's section, "The Textile Art," in *Der Stil*, where he noted: "Art had begun to separate itself from handicraft. Before this separation our grandmothers were indeed not members of the academy of fine arts or album collectors or an audience for aesthetic lecturers, but they knew what to do when it came to designing an embroidery. There's the rub!" Gottfried Semper, *Style in the Technical and Tectonic Arts or Practical Aesthetics*, originally published as *Der Stil* (1860), in *The Four Elements of Architecture and Other Writings*, trans. Harry Francis Mallgrave and Wolfgang Herrmann (Cambridge: Cambridge University Press, 1989), 234.

25   For a concise and excellent summary of Semper's thought in English, see Rosemarie Haag Bletter, "Gottfried Semper," *Macmillan Encyclopedia of Architecture*, ed. Adolf K. Placzek (New York: The Free Press, Macmillan, 1982) 4: 25–33. See also Rosemarie Haag Bletter, "On Martin Fröhlich's Gottfried Semper," *Oppositions* 4 (October 1974), 146–53; Wolfgang Herrmann, *Gottfried Semper: In Search of Architecture* (Cambridge, Mass.: MIT Press, 1984); and Harry Francis Mallgrave, Introduction to Gottfried Semper, *Four Elements*, 1–44.

26   As Wolfgang Herrmann explains, Semper's initial plan for *Der Stil* was to begin with pottery, which Semper associated with the hearth and regarded as the most important formal symbol. But as a result of a quarrel, his publisher did not return his manuscript on ceramics, and consequently, Semper began work on textiles, which he now treated as the most important technical art. In a later essay he cites both the hearth and the enclosure as the two primordial elements and links both with family industry. See Herrmann, *Semper*, 116.

27   Gottfried Semper, *Style in the Technical and Tectonic Arts*, 241.

28   Ibid., 255.

29   Ibid., 257.

30   It is interesting to compare Semper here to Heinrich Hübsch and the position that he outlined in an essay entitled "The Differing Views of Architectural Style in Relation to the Present Time," published in 1847. Hübsch made a distinction between decorated buildings for festive occasions (such as theatrical sets) and monumental buildings that "last too long for any such playful improvisation," and he claimed that "of necessity, such an architectural carnival can produce only buildings that are not thoroughly thought out, are false in conception, or are carelessly planned." Whereas Semper believed that decoration historically preceded construction, Hübsch and, later, most modernists, thought that it was, or should be, the reverse. Hübsch associated the carnival of styles of nineteenth-century architecture with fashion, and more enduring architectural values with established custom ("consuetudo est altera natura"). He articulated, with a clarity rare in later architectural discourse, the difference between "fashion" (rapid stylistic change) and "dress" (relative stasis), unequivocally choosing the latter in the name of naturalness and a more enduring modernity. "With regard to naturalness we are thus divided ...into two factions....With the modern faction...outer appearance and custom change faster than inner life; and since the outer person is no longer shaped by his inner self, all expression is affected and only half-true. Yet there is, thank goodness, a second, old-fashioned faction, whose outer appearance and custom have not markedly changed over many generations and whose expression is still true and natural." Although Hübsch did not use the word "fashion" [Mode] in this passage to characterize the first position, he did so in the preceding two paragraphs, specifically equating the "frenetic pace of change" of personal fashion to the current emphemerality, superficiality, and narcissism of architectural styles. One of the questions that might be explored further is if Wagner, Loos, and Le Corbusier's subsequent appreciation of the man's suit wasn't just such a choice of dress—and of truth and naturalness—even though they rejected any use of historicist imagery, which both Hübsch and Semper, though for differing reasons, still permitted. See Heinrich Hübsch, "The Differing Views of Architectural Style in Relation to the Present Time," in Wolfgang Herrmann, trans., In What Style Should We Build: The German Debate on Architectural Style (Santa Monica, Calif.: The Getty Center for the History of Art and the Humanities, 1992), 170–71, 173.

31   Throughout his career Semper was equivocal about the extent to which traditional forms can be used in present-day architecture. In Science, Industry, and Art (1852) he seemed to express the belief that industry and modern social

conditions would result in a new and better architecture; but by 1869 he concluded his lecture "On Architecture Styles" by stating that "nowhere has a new idea of universal historical importance...become evident....Until that time comes...we must reconcile ourselves to make do as best as we can with the old." Herrmann, *Semper*, 284.

32   Ibid., 257.

33   Gottfried Semper, "Structural Elements of Assyrian-Chaldean Architecture" (1850), in Herrmann, *Semper*, 209–10 and 143–44.

34   This connection between nature, construction, and adornment was even more clearly stated by Semper in "The Attributes of Formal Beauty" (1856–59). Here Semper gave his famous definition of tectonics: "Tectonics is an art that takes nature as a model—not nature's concrete phenomena but the uniformity and the rules by which she exists and creates. Because of these qualities, nature seems to us who exist in her to be the quintessence of perfection and reason." He then went on to assert, "Tectonics is a truly cosmic art; the Greek word *koÓµos*...signifies cosmic order and adornment alike. To be in harmony with the law of nature makes the adornment of an art object; where man adorns, all he does more or less consciously is to make the law of nature evident in the object he adorns." Herrmann, *Semper*, 219.

35   See, for instance, Gottfried Semper, "A Critical Analysis and Prognosis of Present-Day Artistic Production" (1856/59), in Herrmann, *Semper*, 251–53, 258; Semper, "On Architecture Styles," in *Four Elements*, 266–68.

36   Hübsch, "The Differing Views," 172. In other respects Semper's and Hübsch's attitudes differ significantly. As Harry Mallgrave pointed out to me, Semper despised Hübsch's religious sentiments.

37   Semper, "A Critical Analysis," 258; idem, "On Architecture Styles," 267. The original German passage appeared in Gottfried Semper, *Kleine Schriften*, eds. Manfred and Hans Semper (Berlin: Spemann, 1884), 399. As early as 1852, Semper referred to the French as "fashionable and fickle" [modesüchtig und wandelbar] although he did consider their design superior to that of other Western European nations at the 1851 World's Fair. See Gottfried Semper, *Wissenschaft, Industrie und Kunst, und andere Schriften uber Architektur, Kunsthandwerk und Kunstunterricht* (Mainz: Kupferberg, 1966), 51, trans. as "Science, Industry, and Art," in Semper, *Four Elements*, 149.

38   Semper, "On Architecture Styles," 266; idem, "A Critical Analysis," 253.

39   Blanc, *Art in Ornament and Dress*, 85. Blanc cited M. Challemel-Lacour's translations, appearing in the *Revue des cours littéraires* (1865), as his source.

40   In *Le Théâtre*, Garnier wrote: "La lumière qui étincellera, les toilettes qui resplendiront, les figures qui seront animées et souriantes, les rencontres qui se produiront, les saluts qui s'échangeront, tout aura un air de fête et de plaisir, et sans se rendre compte de la part qui doit revenir à l'architecture dans cet effet magique, tout le monde en jouira et tout le monde rendra ainsi, par son impression heureuse, hommage à ce grand art, si puissant dans ses manifestations, si élevé dans ses résultats." Jean-Louis-Charles Garnier, *Le Théâtre* (Paris: Hachette, 1871; rpt., Paris: Actes Sud, 1990), 101. I am grateful to Robin Middleton for alerting me to this quote, which also appears in Robin Middleton and David Watkin, *Neoclassical and Nineteenth Century Architecture* (New York: Harry N. Abrams, 1977), 244–45. Richard Etlin also encouraged me to examine Charles Garnier's writings.

41   Charles Garnier, *À travers les Arts* (Paris: Hachette, 1869), 159–60; in François Loyer, *Paris Nineteenth Century: Architecture and Urbanism*, trans. Charles Lynn Clark (New York: Abbeville Press, 1988), 361.

42   As quoted in Gerald Heard, *Narcissus: An Anatomy of Clothes* (New York: E. P. Dutton, 1924), 3–4. I have combed through many of Morris's essays and have not found this exact quotation, but it is certainly in accord with his basic precepts.

43   Morris declared that "no dress can be beautiful that is stiff, drapery is essential." He substituted aniline dyes for vegetable dyes, which produce the softer, more subdued colors also advocated by Ruskin. Jane Morris's unusual dress is evident in the numerous paintings and photographs of her by Morris, Burne-Jones, and Rosetti. For an early design by Morris (c. 1857) prior to their marriage, see Charles Spencer, ed., *The Aesthetic Movement 1869–1890* (London: Academy Editions and New York: St. Martin's Press, 1973), 51. Despite the plethora of literature on Morris, very little is written on this aspect of his prolific production.

44   One development in the Aesthetic movement was the establishment in 1884 of a costume department at Liberty's in London. It was supervised by the architect E. W. Godwin, who had already made a study of historic costume, was Hon. Secretary of the Costume Society, and had lectured on "Dress and Its Relation to Health and Climate" at Albert Hall. See Barbara Morris, *Liberty Design 1874–1914* (London: Pyramid Books, 1989), 43–55. Another designer

engaged in dress design and its reform was Walter Crane. He wrote a paper entitled "The Progress of Taste in Dress" for The Healthy and Artistic Dress Union, which was published in their journal, *Aglaia*, and which Crane later included in his book of essays, *Ideals in Art* (London: George Bell, 1905; rpt. New York: Garland, 1979). In this paper, Crane decried "the giddy, aimless masquerade of fashion," which he associated with the exigencies of the factory and the market. He concluded that modern architecture and modern dress are in much the same position—that is, without an organic style—and recommended that we must "revive certain types, and endeavour as best we can to adapt them to modern requirements." For literature on the Glasgow School clothing design, see Jude Burkhauser, ed., *"Glasgow Girls": Women in Art and Design 1880–1920* (Edinburgh: Canongate, 1990); Anthea Callen, *The Angel in the Studio: Women in the Arts and Crafts Movement 1870–1914* (New York: Pantheon, 1979); and Linda Coleing, "Ann Macbeth and the Glasgow School," in Juliet Ash and Elizabeth Wilson, eds., *Chic Thrills: A Fashion Reader* (Berkeley: University of California Press, 1993), 213–24.

45   Wagner, *Modern Architecture*, 76. The Getty translation is of the third, 1902, edition, but passages added to or deleted from the first (1896) as well as other editions (1898, 1914) are clearly indicated.

46   Some of these writings include Vischer, *Mode und Zynismus*; Julius Lessing, *Der Modeteufel* (Berlin: von Leonhard Simion, 1884); Friedrich von Kleinwächter, *Zur Psychologie der Mode* (Berlin: Carl Habel, 1885). Francesco Dal Co, who is one of the few architecture historians to touch upon issues of fashion, mentions two of these sources in *Figures of Architecture and Thought: German Architecture Culture 1880–1920* (New York: Rizzoli, 1990), 80.

47   For references to Semper, see Wagner, *Modern Architecture*, 62, 89, 91, 93. In the first two editions of the book Wagner referred to one of Semper's Vienna projects as an "immortal design," and he also credited Semper as the author of his much cited slogan "ARTIS SOLA DOMINA NECESSITAS" (necessity alone is the ruler of art), which dates back to Semper's more materialist period in the 1830s. Wagner's early biographer Joseph August Lux wrote, "After Schinkel and Semper comes Wagner"—a lineage that is still very much present in contemporary histories of modern architecture. Joseph August Lux, *Otto Wagner: eine Monographie* (Munich: Delphin Verlag, 1914), 8, as quoted by Mallgrave in his introduction to Wagner's *Modern Architecture*, 4.

48   Wagner, *Modern Architecture*, 93. I have slightly modified the translation.

49   Ibid., 131 n89.

50   Ibid., 77.

51   From a contemporary perspective, most of Semper's writings are amaz-ingly non-sexist in tone, although his criticisms of late Greek architecture and contemporary Parisian fashions suggest a preference for simplicity and continu-ity that in both traditional and modern architecture theory might be viewed as reflecting a masculine bias.

52   Wagner, *Modern Architecture*, 77.

53   Ibid., 146. Like Charles Garnier, Wagner believed that "the appearance and occupation of the inhabitant should harmonize with the appearance of the room," but his aesthetic intention was the opposite of that of the Opéra designer. Wagner stated: "The room that we inhabit should be as simple as our clothing."

54   Ibid., 121. Wagner's 1902 addition to *Moderne Architektur* appears to be a response to the flurry of recent efforts of artists and architects to engage in dress design. In the fourth edition (1914), there is one other cryptic reference to women's dress: "Equally ridiculous is to make villas meant for town dwellers look like farmhouses, and to let them be inhabited by drawing room peasants and urban women wearing dirndls." Ibid., 135.

55   Obviously the functionalism of dress is not strictly one of comfort and efficiency, but includes symbolic functions of a more enduring nature. One of the frequently noted differences between fashion and dress is that the novelty of fashion is divorced from any notion of function—that changes in style are merely for the sake of change.

56   Wagner, "Inaugural Address to the Academy of Fine Arts" (1894), in *Modern Architecture*, 159.

57   Viscountess Florence Wallace Pomeroy Harberton, *Reasons for Reform in Dress: A Lecture Given at the Monthly Conversations of the London Literary and Artistic Society on May 30, 1883* (London: Hutchings and Crowsley, 1883), as quoted in Gernsheim, *Fashion and Reality*, 72.

58   For a brief account of Wright's dress designs, see David Hanks, *The Decorative Designs of Frank Lloyd Wright* (New York: E. P. Dutton, 1979), 24–26. Aside from this, almost nothing has been written about Wright's dress designs. However, the Frank Lloyd Wright Home and Studio Foundation in Oak Park has photographs of dresses that Wright seems to have designed for Catherine Wright, Mrs. Darwin Martin, and Mrs. Avery Coonley.

59   Paul Schultze-Naumburg wrote an important book in the German campaign for clothing reform, *Die Kultur des weiblichen Körpers als Grundlage der Frauenkleidung* [The Culture of the Female Body as a Foundation for Women's Clothing] (Jena: E. Diederichs, 1901). This study reveals a pairing of reformist and conservative ideals. He argued that corseting impaired health and child-bearing capacities, and that a return to the study of the naked body was essential to clothing reform. In his projected "natural" culture, women would function primarily in their traditional maternal role. See also Stephen Kern, *Anatomy and Destiny: A Cultural History of the Human Body* (Indianapolis and New York: Bobbs-Merrill, 1975), 14–15.

60   This is even the case for "street clothes," which were photographed (perhaps for convenience) in interior settings. See, for instance, the photograph of Maria van de Velde in her article "Sonderausstellung Moderner Damenkostüme," *Dekorative Kunst* 4:1 (October 1900), 46. In his novel *Das graue Tuch und zehn Prozent Weiss* [The Gray Cloth and Ten Percent White: A Ladies' Novel] (Munich: Müller, 1914), the Berlin Bohemian and Expressionist muse Paul Scheerbart parodied architects' obsession with women's dress. The novel's architect, Herr Edgar Krug, who is renowned for colored-glass structures, insists that his wife wear clothing that is ninety percent gray with ten percent white to set off his designs. Here, the architect sees clothing as a formal counterpoint to the physical environment, rather than as an integral part of the *Gesamtkunstwerk*, with architecture now triumphing over, instead of coordinating with, the female occupant. I am indebted to John Stuart for giving me his translation of this amusing novel, which, I hope, will be published in the near future.

61   August Endell, *Die Schönheit der grössen Stadt* (Stuttgart: Strecker und Schröder, 1908). While Endell's appreciation of existing women's fashion was qualified, his appreciation of the transitory and excessive qualities of women's fashion (and urbanity) was unusual among architects of his generation. One passage (69–70) is worth quoting at length:

> The pedant who considers fashion idiotic on account of its transitoriness commits a sin against life. Fashion is in fact a symbol of life itself, which showers its gifts fickly, wastefully, without calculating timidly whether the effort stands in a sensible relationship to that which is achieved. Nature strews thousands of seed everywhere. Perhaps one will sprout. It is precisely this extravagance of thought, this eternal beginning, this colorful richness that makes fashion so pleasurable. Doctors rightly condemn the corseting of bodies, and anyone

who has appreciated nude beauty will agree. Their objections will do no good until communal water and fresh air bathing reveal the beauty of nakedness and make it once again desirable. Until then, the reformers will have to make different pleas to taste and sensibility in order to confront the usual fashion seriously. That fashion is far above them in sense of color, in elegance, in loveliness and inherent clarity [*Selbstverstaendlichkeit*]. The only achievement of the past few years, a greater awareness of color, is happily applied here. And rather than to denigrate missteps in a curmudgeonly way, one should recognize how much more lovely fabrics have become, how much finer their colorations, how much more developed the capacity is today to combine colors, to give hierarchy to them, and to accentuate the few important points. Perhaps the lace and embroidery, in fact all the detail, leave something to be desired. The whole is nonetheless lovely enough, more successful in any case than many of the highly praised modern rooms, which are seen as great achievements, but which are significant only in terms of color. Their formal poverty, if not roughness, is naturally more obvious and embarrassing than a toilette, whose charm is increased by the wearer's movements, which blur detail and allow it to be forgotten.

I am grateful to Lynette Widder for translating this passage for me.

62   For information on Krefeld, see "Sonderausstellung Moderner Damenkostüme," *Dekorative Kunst* 3:7–12 (April–September 1900), 414; Maria van de Velde, "Sonderausstellung Moderner Damenkostüme," 41, 44–47; Henry van de Velde, "Das neue Kunst = Prinzip in der modernen Frauen = Kleidung," *Deutsche Kunst und Dekoration* 9 (October 1901–March 1902), 363–86; Margarete Bruns-Minden, "Der Stil der modernen Kleidung," *Deutsche Kunst und Dekoration* 8 (April 1901–September 1901), 374–88; Max von Boehn, *Bekleidungkunst und Mode* (Munich: Delphin, 1918), 99–128. Aside from a brief reference, in Othmar Birkner's article, "The New Life-Style," in Lucius Burckhardt, ed., *The Werkbund: History and Ideology* (New York: Barron's, 1980), 52–53, I have found no recent literature giving a historical account of this show, which was greeted by its contributors as a major event.

63   Although Loos objected to some of Wagner's chair designs and his advocacy of total design, he clearly exempted the Master from the animosity that he felt toward the Secessionists. In his essay "Interiors in the Rotunda" (1898), Loos wrote, "I draw the line at the genius of Otto Wagner. For Otto Wagner has

one quality that I have found in only a small number of English and American architects: he is able to slip out of his architect's skin and into the skin of any craftsman he chooses." See Adolf Loos, *Spoken into the Void: Collected Essays 1897–1900*, trans. Jane O. Newman and John H. Smith (Cambridge, Mass.: MIT Press, 1982), 27. Loos's famous essay "Potemkin City," which was published in *Ver Sacrum* in July 1898, may also well have been inspired by Wagner's own reference to Potemkin villages in *Moderne Architektur*. See Wagner, *Modern Architecture*, 108.

64 In his essay of 1929, "Josef Veillich," Loos mentioned that when the Wiener Werkstätte was founded, he told the group: "You cannot be denied a certain talent, but it lies in an entirely different area than you suspect. You have the imagination of a ladies-taylor. You should design dresses." Later in the essay, Loos noted that his assessment of the Secessionists was confirmed when the Wiener Werkstätte opened a ladies' fashion department, the one enterprise of the group that he thought could be pursued on a "sound commercial basis." In this prediction he also proved to be correct. The fashion and the textile divisions were the mainstay of the Werkstätte during its declining years. See Adolf Loos, "Josef Veillich," *9H* 6 (1983), 86; and Jane Kallir, *Viennese Design and the Wiener Werkstätte* (New York: George Braziller, 1986), 95.

65 Adolf Loos, "Glass and Clay" (1898), in *Spoken*, 35. Loos's reading erases all of Semper's symbolic dimensions. From 1890 to 1893 Loos studied at the Dresden Polytechnic, where the precepts of Semper's teaching were still very much alive; in addition, he had spent time in Chicago, where Semper had a strong following among American architects.

66 Adolf Loos, "The Principle of Cladding" (1898), in *Spoken*, 66–69. I prefer Harry F. Mallgrave and Wolfgang Herrmann's translation of *Bekleidung* as "dressing" rather than "cladding." See Semper, *The Four Elements*, 240.

67 Adolf Loos, "Men's Fashion" (1898), in *Spoken*, 11.

68 Herman Muthesius, *The English House*, trans. Janet Seligman (New York: Rizzoli, 1987), 149. In his 1908 essay "Cultural Degeneration," Loos expressed his admiration of Muthesius's "fine series of instructive books on English domestic life." Muthesius commented more extensively on fashion in his magnum opus of 1902, *Stilarchitektur und Baukunst*. Here, he followed Loos in praising the general simplification of men's dress and in citing as a positive development the Englishman's tailor-made costume. Muthesius was also skeptical of "reform clothing," which he said "affects us emotionally like a caricature." One of the most intriguing observations that he made was that modern men's dress stems not only from functional concerns for cleanliness, but also

from symbolic concerns to show "that everything is neat and in the best of order." Hermann Muthesius, *Style-Architecture and Building-Art*.

69   Ibid., 11–13. The references in Loos's writings suggest that he was well-informed about contemporary fashion literature. In "Men's Fashion" he also referred—unfavorably—to F. T. Vischer, the well-known German aesthetic philosopher and author of *Mode und Zynismus*. Although Loos's objections are not completely comprehensible to a present-day reader, Vischer's nationalism and his psychological readings of dress seem to have been the focus of Loos's objections.

70   Dress was clearly a battleground for Hoffmann and Loos. As late as 1930, they were issuing bitter complaints about each other. In a letter to the editor of *Querschnitt* (Vienna), Hoffmann claimed that Loos slandered him with the statement that Hoffmann wore pre-tied ties and that Loos's description of the Secessionist checkered frock coat with a velvet collar was "fabrication." See *Spoken*, 75; also, Adolf Loos, "Cultural Degeneracy" (1908), in *The Architecture of Adolf Loos* (London: Arts Council Exhibition, 1985), 98–99. Paradoxically, the clothes of the two men look remarkably alike in photos—at least after 1900—and legend has it that by 1902 they were using the same tailor.

71   As Loos told it, the architect hired by the Rich Man scolded his poor client for wearing his slippers in the living room, where their embroidery clashed with the room's carefully calibrated decor. Adolf Loos, "The Poor Little Rich Man," 1900, in *Spoken*, 124–27.

72   As Loos wrote in another article for *Neue Freie Presse*: "Fashion advances slowly, more slowly than one usually assumes. Objects that are really modern stay so for a long time. But if one hears of an article of clothing that has already become old-fashioned by the following season—that has become, in other words, unpleasantly obvious—then one can assume that it was never modern, but was trying falsely to pass itself off as modern." Adolf Loos, "Men's Hats" (1898), in *Spoken*, 53.

73   Adolf Loos, "Architecture" (1910), in *The Architecture of Adolf Loos*, 107. Loos made no reference to American mass-produced goods in his essay "Men's Fashion," but in "Culture" (1908), the American worker, "the man in overalls," became his foil to the Secessionist aesthete. Overalls were another form of perfected clothing, which evolved over time, and one suspects that it was their functionalism, simplicity, and anonymity rather than their mass-production per se that Loos valued. The links between mass production and these attributes, which were to become so central to Le Corbusier and Ozenfant, were

erature. There are numerous affinities between Carlyle's and Loos's ideas of clothes and architecture, not the least of which is their marvelously sarcastic tone. Carlyle detested the late Regency dandy, and in his chapter "The Dandical Body" offered the following unrivaled definition: "A Dandy is a Clothes-wearing Man, a Man whose trade, office, and existence consists in the wearing of Clothes." Carlyle also equated architecture with dress, understanding both as "construction," and had Professor Diogenes Teufelsdröckh [Devil's Excrement] declare, "In all his Modes and habilatory endeavors an Architectural Ideal will be found lurking." As has been frequently noted, Ruskin was deeply influenced by Carlyle, and Ruskin's use of the word "Monstrification" with regard to decoration undoubtedly came from the Scottish writer. Edward Timms compares Loos's and Ruskin's attitudes toward adornment in "Facade and Function: The Alliance Between Karl Kraus and Adolf Loos," *9H* 6 (1983), 11. Loos's close friend Karl Krauss published an anonymous homage to Ruskin in *Die Fackel* (February 1900). According to Eduard Sekler, the only work of Ruskin's that appears in what remains of Loos's library is *Sesame and Lilies*, but Loos's essays contain scattered references to Ruskin, suggesting a general familiarity with his work. See Eduard F. Sekler, "Hoffmann, Loos and Britain: Selective Perceptions," *9H* 6 (1983), 2.

86   The similarities in the positions of Loos and Spencer are discussed in Lubbock, "Adolf Loos and the English Dandy," 47–48. There are no works by Spencer in the surviving portion of Loos's library, but he was probably the most widely read social evolutionist in the late nineteenth century.

87   Loos, *Spoken*, 100–02.

88   Ibid., 102–03.

89   Ibid., 103. For the reference to "protofeminist," see Miriam Gusevich, "Decoration and Decorum: Adolf Loos's Critique of Kitsch," *New German Critique* 43 (Winter 1988), 111.

90   A few published photographs of Lina Loos show her wearing loose reform-style gowns, but most show her in rather lavish attire. Assessments of Loos's personal life by his contemporaries are considerably different from those of most feminists today. Richard Neutra equated Loos's humanity with his happy relationships with women, including former spouses. See Richard Neutra, "Ricordo di Loos," *Casabella* 233 (1959), as quoted in Benedetto Gravagnuolo, *Adolf Loos: Theory and Works* (New York: Rizzoli, 1982), 28. In her memoirs Elsie Loos was extremely generous about Loos's relationships to women, but she also revealed aspects of Loos that many women today would abhor. Not only was he convicted in 1927 of a liaison with someone underage in

a notorious court case (he was not punished), but he maintained and valued a large collection of photographs of child pornography, taken by his client of Villa Karma, Theodor Beer. As a result of a report made by his own wife, Beer was arrested and imprisoned, and he eventually committed suicide. Elsie Loos recorded Loos as saying, "They [the photographs] will remain here as a memorial to a wonderful man who was sacrificed to the stupidity and evil of his fellow men." And despite Loos's critique of the dictatorial tendencies of the Secessionist designers, it is obvious that he was extremely rigid in maintaining aesthetic control in his own household. Elsie Loos recalled knitting a luxurious red silk cushion as her first Christmas present to Loos in 1917, which he rejected for not fitting with the decor of his apartment. Nor was she allowed to help decorate the Christmas tree. His control even extended to the aesthetics of food, such as calling her "stupid as the proletarian kids" for salting her tomatoes. Americans, he asserted, "eat their tomatoes without salt." See Elsie Altmann-Loos, *Mein Leben mit Adolf Loos* (Munich: Amalthea Verlag, 1984), esp. 46–48, 82, 84, 86, 95–96, 132, 178, 202, 210–19, 284–300. I am grateful to John Stuart and Rüdiger Krisch for helping me with translations of this book.

91   Loos's attitude toward women's fashion appeared to change somewhat after World War I. He no longer felt as compulsive about imposing male standards on women's dress and seemed to exclude women's fashion from issues of modernity and timelessness. In a 1924 essay "Ornament and Education" he wrote, "Whenever I ornamentally misuse a use-object, I reduce its durability, because anything subject to the rule of fashion passes away more quickly. Only the whims and ambition of women can vindicate this murder of material—for ornament in the service of women lives on eternally." In a passage in another essay, "Short Hair: Answers to a Poll" (1919), he almost seemed to be compensating for his earlier role in dictating his first wife Lina's dress when he wrote: "But the man who wants to dictate fashion to women admits by doing so that he considers the woman as his sexual serf. He ought rather to worry about his own clothing. And the women will get along fine with theirs." See Loos, "In Spite Of," 177–78, 208.

92   Simmel, "Fashion," 310.

93   Joan Riviere, "Womanliness as a Masquerade," *The International Journal of Psychoanalysis* 10 (1929); rpt. in Victor Burgin, James Donald, and Cora Kaplan, eds., *Formations of Fantasy* (London and New York: Methuen, 1986), 35–44.

94   Adolf Loos, "Heimat Kunst" (1914), *Trotzdem*, trans. "In Spite Of," 121.

95   Adolf Loos, "Architecture" (1910), in Tim and Charlotte Benton, eds., *Form and Function*, (London: The Open University, 1975), 44–45.

96   In his essay "Lou's Buttons," written in the 1970s, Massimo Cacciari juxtaposes the masculine visibility of Loos's exteriors with the feminine quality of "inhabitability" that permeates his interiors. See Massimo Cacciari, *Architecture and Nihilism: On the Philosophy of Modern Architecture*, trans. Stephen Sartarelli (New Haven: Yale University Press, 1993), 183. Beatriz Colomina has extended this observation of Cacciari's in a series of essays, which open new grounds for feminist analyses of architecture. In her essay "Intimacy and Spectacle: The Architecture Production of the Modern Subject," in *AA Files* 20 (Autumn 1990), Colomina refers to the split between inside and outside in Loos's Architecture as "gender loaded" and the interior as "the scene of sexuality and of reproduction," although she qualifies this "dogmatic division" by discussing the threshold or boundary spaces between inside and outside in his architecture. She further argues that the interior becomes a place for women's control—that Loos's alcove spaces for women (*Zimmer der Dame*) serve as a kind of theater box, in which the woman of the house can inspect and supervise activity. However, in some instances, it is not clear if the spaces operate in the manner that she suggests. In the Müller house, the built-in seating faces the opposite direction of the *Halle* or major living area; contemporary photographs also show a pulled curtain reinforcing the separation between the two spaces. In the Moller house, where seating in the alcove may well provide views to the sitting room five steps below, the alcove is labeled as the entry to the *Herrenzimmer* in the photographs published in Burkhardt Rukschcio and Roland Schachel, *Adolf Loos: Leben und Werk* (Salzburg: Residenz Verlag, 1982), 603. The label in Loos's published plans is simply *Sitzerker* (seating alcove). The alcove was adjacent to the library, which was generally still a man's space in the 1920s.

97   As Joan Ockman pointed out in a seminar at Columbia University, in November 1993, Loos's residential facades may have looked less masculine than his interiors to an observer in the first part of the century. The abstract language of the exterior surfaces stood outside gender conventions, in contrast to the forms of the interiors, which relied on more familiar imagery. Paradoxically, the very minimal quality of Loos's residential facades must have made them highly conspicuous in pre-World War I Vienna.

98   "The Austrian housewife tries to bind her husband to the family with her good cooking, while her American and English counterparts do so with a cozy (*gemütlich*) home." Adolf Loos, "Die Frau und das Haus," in *Die Potemkin'sche Stadt: Verschollene Schriften 1897–1933*, ed. Adolf Opel (Vienna: Georg

Prachner, 1983), as quoted by Christiane Crasemann Collins in her review of Adolf Loos's *Spoken into the Void*, in Society of Architectural Historians Journal 43:1 (March 1984), 88.

99   *Die Kunst* 1 (1903), 12.

100   Although similar prints appear in some of Loos's other, less gender-defined spaces, especially in his later houses, the gender connotations of the woman's alcove are visible in Ludwig Munz and Gustav Künstler's description of the space as "out of the ordinary and precious," in contrast to the master's room, which is "somewhat heavily restful." They also add that the rooms could not be readily exchanged. Ludwig Münz and Gustav Künstler, *Adolf Loos: Pioneer of Modern Architecture*, trans. Harold Meek (New York: Praeger, 1966), 159.

101   Gravagnuolo, *Adolf Loos: Theory and Works*, 191; Münz and Künstler, *Adolf Loos: Pioneer*, 195. See also Colomina, "Intimacy and Spectacle," *AA Files*, 14.

102   Loos did design one house of alternating bands of green and white for a male client, the Spanner Country House of 1922. This time, however, the stripes ran vertically.

103   I am grateful to Thomas S. Hines, who met with me in February 1991 and discussed his ideas concerning Baker's rejection of Loos's design. See his article "Historic Architecture: Adolf Loos in Paris," *Architectural Digest*, April 1991, 112. Baker did not discuss Loos's design in her autobiography *Les Mémoires de Josephine Baker* (Paris: Editions Corréa, 1949). In 1929 she and her husband Giusseppi Abatino [Pepito] bought a turn-of-the-century mansion at Le Vésinet, where she lived until 1947. The gap between her taste and Loos's is perhaps most evident in the Temple of Love that she created in the gardens that surrounded the house. This structure consisted of a semicircle of Corinthian columns with statues of Diana, Venus, and Circe; in the center was a large pool, with gold fish and water lilies, where she often bathed.

104   Loos, "Architecture," in *The Architecture of Adolf Loos*, 104 (I have revised this translation). In his essay "Furniture for Sitting" (1898), Loos wrote: "The beautiful man? He is the most perfect man, the man whose bodily structure and intellectual capacities offer the best assurance for healthy offspring and for the maintenance and sustenance of a family. The beautiful woman? She is the perfect woman. It is her responsibility to kindle a man's love for her, to nurse her children, and to give them a good upbringing." He then went on to provide a long list of her physical attributes with no mention of "intellectual

capacities." One realizes here the ambiguity of Loos's sarcasm in "Ladies' Fashion." While he may not have liked the function of woman's clothes, he still very much believed that woman's primary role was "to kindle a man's love for her"—that nature, rather than fashion, was woman's destiny. *Spoken*, 29.

105   Le Corbusier, "L'Art décoratif d'aujourd'hui," *L'Esprit Nouveau*, 24 (1924), in *The Decorative Art of Today*, trans. James I. Dunnett (Cambridge, Mass.: MIT Press, 1987), 85.

106   Ibid., 7–8. In the French edition the caption falls entirely under the photo. Le Corbusier, *L'Art décoratif d'aujourd'hui* (Paris: Crès, 1925; rpt. Vincent, Fréal, 1959), 8. Here, as in several other passages, I have slightly altered the translation.

107   Le Corbusier, *The Decorative Art*, 87. Le Corbusier's examples include Saderne men's shoes, Hermès sports bags and cigar boxes, and Comoy's pipe.

108   The smaller box ad for Jove, which appeared in the first issue of *L'Esprit Nouveau*, was replaced by issue 11/12 with a full-page advertisement that featured a sketch by Marie Laurencin. (This advertisement appeared again in issues 13 to 16.) Jove was founded by the fashion designer Germaine Bongard, who had earlier designed children's clothes. Bongard's clientele included women from intellectual and artistic circles, among them Mme. Henri Matisse, Mme. Marcelle Meyer, and Mme. Juan Gris, whose husband gave Bongard a painting in exchange for a dress. In a conversation with Francesco Passanti, Pierre-André Emery, who worked for Le Corbusier on the Pavilion of L'Esprit Nouveau, described the shop as one for *cocottes* [prostitutes or tarts], but this choice of words may be more indicative of Emery's attitudes than of the women themselves. Many of Bongard's clients were young (the daughters of artistic figures) and, most likely, not completely conventional in their lifestyle. I am also grateful to Susan Ball, Francesco Passanti, and Kenneth Silver, who all helped me find information about Germaine Bongard; Ball interviewed Bongard in 1977. See also *Musée de la Mode et du Costume, Paul Poiret et Nicole Groult: Maîtres de la Mode Art Déco*, exhibition catalogue, Palais Galliera, Paris, 5 July–12 October, 1986, 31.

109   Jenny Sacerdote founded her own couturier house in 1908, and moved it to the Champs-Elysées in 1915. The firm was probably most famous in the 1920s for its "little gray suit," which became a kind of uniform for chic Parisian women in the 1920s. Robert Mallet-Stevens designed the decor of Jenny's fashion rooms, and it is possible that he is the connection between *L'Esprit Nouveau* and Mme. Jenny. Mallet-Stevens (whose work as a teacher Le Corbusier praised in *L'Esprit Nouveau*) had strong connections to haute couture. In 1914 he

designed the interiors to Mme. Paquin's villa "Les Roses Rouges" at Deauville, and in 1924 he designed a project for Jacques Doucet and a house that was built for Paul Poiret. See Musée Richard-Anacréon, *Femmes créatrice des années vingt* (Paris: Editions Arts et Culture, 1988), 52, 74; see also Ara, *Un Artisan de la haute couture—Ara* (Libourne: Mira, 1988).

110 Amédée Ozenfant, *Memoires 1886–1962* (Paris: Seghers, 1968), 93–94. By the 1920s the distinctions between "costume" "dress" and "fashion" had become blurred. In the paragraph of *Mémoires* that follows the passage quoted above, Ozenfant himself used *mode* neutrally, or even positively, to refer to historical dress, where Purist lessons are to be found; the assumption seems to be that clothing was always fashion. Fashion was not a passing fancy for Ozenfant, who in 1927 he opened his own *maison de couture*, Amédée. See Susan Ball, *Ozenfant and Purism: The Evolution of a Style* (Ann Arbor: UMI Research Press, 1981), 31.

111 Despite the plethora of literature on Le Corbusier, almost nothing is known about his wife. The personal papers of Le Corbusier are not available to scholars at the Fondation Le Corbusier. Yvonne Gallis (née Jeanne Victorine Gallis) is frequently referred to as a former model, and some sources (including her friends Mme. Ducret and Henri Bruaux) specifically say a fashion model, but no evidence is cited. Her identification papers state "née à Monaco, sans profession." Evelyne Trehin, letter to author, 9 December, 1993. William Curtis refers to her as a couturier in his biography, *Le Corbusier: Ideas and Forms* (New York: Rizzoli, 1986), 108.

112 Le Corbusier, *The Decorative Art*, 85.

113 Ibid., 55. This passage alludes to Émile Zola's novel, *Au Bonheur des dames* (1883).

114 Ibid., 87, 90.

115 Ibid., 90.

116 Ibid., 85.

117 Ibid., 134.

118 Le Corbusier, like Loos, was opposed to the Secessionist notion of *Gesamkunstwerk*, in which the architect designed everything. But he strongly believed that the architect should "order" everything.

119   Amédée Ozenfant and Charles-Edouard Jeanneret, "Le Purisme," *L'Esprit Nouveau*, 4 (January 1921), 386, in Robert L. Herbert, ed., *Modern Artists on Art: Ten Unabridged Essays* (Englewood Cliffs, N.J.: Prentice Hall, 1964), 73.

120   Ibid., 66, 71, 63, 64. Revealing their debt to Loos, Ozenfant and Le Corbusier cited Papuan tattoos and peasant embroidered shirts as nostalgic remnants of another epoch.

121   *The Decorative Art*, 96.

122   Le Corbusier wrote: "Then the fashion [*mode*] for *expressing the construction*, the sign of a new construction. Then the ecstasy before *nature*, showing a desire to rediscover (by however circuitous a path!) the laws of the *organic*. Then the craze for the *simple*." Ibid., 99.

123   Ibid., 23.

124   Ibid., 165–66. In an essay of 1919, Loos also cited Diogenes and the story of his cup. See "Answers to Questions from Readers" (1919), in "In Spite Of," 147, 123.

125   Ibid., 188.

126   Le Corbusier, *Towards a New Architecture*, trans. Frederick Etchells (London: John Rodker, 1931; rpt. New York: Praeger, 1960), 18.

127   *The Decorative Art*, 192.

128   Walter Gropius, "Principles of Bauhaus Production," 1926, in Conrads, *Programs and Manifestoes*, 95; Hugo Häring, "Formulations toward a Reorientation in the Applied Arts," 1927, in Conrads, *Programs and Manifestoes*, 105; George Howe, "Monuments, Memorials, and Modern Design—an Exchange of Letters," *Magazine of Art* 37: 6 (October 1944) 202–07, as quoted in Christine C. and George R. Collins, "Monumentality: A Critical Matter in Modern Architecture," *Monumentality and the City, Harvard Architecture Review* 4 (Spring 1984), 24. Gropius and Hannes Meyer both applauded fashion over costume, as they associated the latter with regionalism and nationalism. Meyer, very much along the lines of Loos, applauded changes in women's fashion, by then much more evident, as "the external masculinization of woman" which "shows that inwardly the two sexes have equal rights." Hannes Meyer, "The New World" (1926) in *Hannes Meyer: Bauen, Projekte und Schriften*, ed. Claude Schnaidt (Teufen: Niggli, 1965), 91.

129   Theo van Doesburg and Cor van Eesteren, "Towards Collective Building" (1923), in Conrads, *Programs and Manifestoes*, 67.

130   Bruno Taut, *Modern Architecture* (London: The Studio, 1929), esp. 2–3, 168–69, and 205. In fairness to Taut, it must also be noted that other writings suggest a more complex attitude toward fashion than this reference suggests. Although Taut generally praised men's fashion in England, by 1927 he came to the conclusion that its slow process of change kept many men enslaved to certain antiquated traditions, such as wearing vests. See Bruno Taut, *Bauen: Der neue Wohnbau* (Leipzig and Berlin: Klinkhardt and Biermann, 1927), 14.

131   Marcel Breuer, "Where Do We Stand?" (1934), in Benton and Benton, *Form and Function*, 180. Besides examples such as these which allude to fashion or clothes, there are frequent comments by modern architects that suggest a masculine bias. One blatant example was published in the first issue of the Swiss magazine *ABC*, in 1924. The editors rejected American culture as too "feminine," due to its emphasis on outward decorative appeal, and asserted that real art, "the highest form of male activity" was exemplified in the bold, stripped-down forms of Soviet architecture.

132   Giacomo Balla, "Futurist Manifesto on Men's Clothing" (1913), in Umbro Apollonio, ed., *The Futurist Manifestos*, trans. Robert Brain et al. (New York: Viking, 1973), 132. The editor gives the date of this first draft as 29 December 1913. A French version was issued in Milan, in May 1914. One source of Balla's designs was undoubtedly Sonia and Robert Delaunay's "simultaneous clothes," worn at the Ball Bullier in Paris, in March 1913. See Sergio Poggianella, ed., *Giacomo Balla* (Modena: Edizioni Galleria Fonte d'Abisso, 1982), 57. In 1914 Balla wrote a second manifesto on clothing "Il Vestito antineutrale," rpt. in Giorgio De Marchis, *Giacomo Balla: L'Aura Futurista* (Turin: Giulio Einaudi, 1977), 102–05.

133   F. T. Marinetti, "Destruction of Syntax-Imagination without Strings-Words in Freedom," in Poggianella, *Giacomo Balla*, 97, 104.

134   For information on Soviet clothing design, see Tatiana Strizhenova, *Soviet Costumes and Textiles, 1917–1945* (Paris: Flammarion, 1991); Alexander Lavrentiev, *Varvara Stepanova* (Cambridge, Mass.: MIT Press, 1988); and M. N. Yablonskaya, *Women Artists of Russia's New Age* (New York: Rizzoli, 1990).

135   Gerald [Henry Fitz Gerald] Heard (1889–1971) had a varied career as novelist, philosopher, teacher, and pacifist. Of Irish descent, he was born in England but lived briefly after World War I in Ireland where he was involved in a movement to start agricultural cooperatives, a venture that ended abruptly

when his office was blown up by Irish freedom fighters. Among his many books are *The Ascent of Humanity* (1929), *The Social Substance of Religion* (1931), *Man the Master* (1941), *A Preface to Prayer* (1944), *The Black Fox* (1950), and, as H. F. Heard, two notable mysteries: *A Taste for Honey* (1941) and *Reply Paid* (1942). In England he became best known as a popular science commentator for the British Broadcasting Corporation in the 1930s. In 1937 he emigrated to the United States and lived in California, where he led a group participating in monastic community life. He was an active pacifist and a friend of Christopher Isherwood and Aldous Huxley. Heard figured in Huxley's novel *After Many a Summer Dies the Swan* as the mystic William Propter. He may also have been the model of Bruno Rontini in Huxley's *Time Must Have a Stop*. Flugel referred to *Narcissus* in *Psychology*, 150–51.

136   I am indebted to Marc Dessauce, who is currently writing a doctoral dissertation on Knud Lonberg-Holm at Columbia University, for telling me about van Eesteren's letter of 1926, in the Knud Lonberg-Holm Archives in New York, and for recommending that I examine Heard's book.

137   Heard, *Narcissus*, 135. Heard said that these options may be experimented with concurrently in the same or different societies, but that in all probability they will occur sequentially. He dismissed the notion of "national styles" as political propaganda and saw the world as increasingly unified.

138   Ibid., 147–48.

139   Ibid., 136–37, 146.

140   Here, it is interesting to speculate what role Heard's own sexuality may have had in coloring his perspective. He was never married, and several people who remember his public persona say that they always assumed he was gay. His appreciation of male adornment and his refusal to see that as antithetical to function can be linked to a lineage of male dress reform, starting with Oscar Wilde and continuing into the 1930s with Flugel and the Men's Dress Reform Party.

141   Josephine Baker, famous for her nearly nude attire, made her mark on Parisian fashion, encouraging the taste for suntan and shaved armpits. Chanel's 1926 collection was worn by models whose hairstyles resembled Baker's. See Edmonde Charles-Roux, *Chanel and Her World* (London and Paris: Vendome Press, 1981), 152.

142   There is little record of Le Corbusier's encounters with women in the Soviet Union, although several photographs show him in groups with women. Olga Kameneva, president of Voks and Trotsky's sister, welcomed him to the

offices of Voks in 1928. See Jean-Louis Cohen, *Le Corbusier and the Mystique of the USSR* (Princeton: Princeton University Press, 1992), 41–43, 54, 117.

143 This ascendancy of women was not without some resistance on the part of the old fashion establishment, which frequently saw Chanel's sport clothes and little black dress as nihilistic and anti-fashion. After seeing two Chanel designs published in the Paris *Vogue* of January 1927, Paul Poiret commented: "Formerly women were architectural, like the prows of ships, and very beautiful. Now they resemble little undernourished telegraph clerks." See Charles-Roux, *Chanel and Her World*, 157. In *The Psychology of Clothes* (148–64) Flugel argues that *haute couture* never really accepted the short skirt, citing an interview in *La Liberté* (12 December 1929) in which Jean Patou claimed it was "born from the brain of some 'Boetian.'" Although there had been prominent women dress designers before Coco Chanel—most notably Jeanne Paquin—Chanel's dominance in Parisian fashion in the 1920s was widely accepted by her contemporaries. In his classic study, *The Glass of Fashion* (London: Weidenfeld and Nicolson, 1954), 192, Cecil Beaton noted: "Sandwiched between two world wars, between Poiret's harem and Dior's New Look, two women dominated the world of *haute couture*—Schiaparelli and Chanel."

144 Le Corbusier, *Précisions* (Paris: Crès, 1930), trans. in Benton and Benton, *Form and Function*, 233–34. Le Corbusier's appreciation of women's contemporary dress as opposed to men's contemporary clothing recalls Bruno Taut's commentary in 1927, in which he pointed out the absurdity of men wearing "silly" vests, line coats and "laughable decorative' ties, associating such blind conformity to outmoded traditions with the risks of standardization in architecture. Taut wrote:

> We see with gentle horror how rationalization of industrially produced houses, by now an old demand, has led to mere cliché, and we are afraid in many respects that there is the establishment of types and rationalization before one knows what [should be rationalized]....Old laws and rules are not only perpetuated like a sickness but false forms continue as well, if they are turned too quickly into norms. An example of this is men's dress, which turned into a binding norm in England and has retained its mistakes already for over a hundred years, unchanged in its essence, regardless whether pants are worn sometimes tight or sometimes loose. Women's dress, on the other hand,, reveals a different aspect. Its changes are rapid and capricious, but they are fluid and have achieved today a fairly good simple form."

He then noted the similarities between contemporary women's clothes and ancient Egyptian and Greek dress, and stated that, while no definite conclusion should be deduced concerning modern architecture, "a curious relationship between the search for absolute precision in contemporary architecture and in that of the Egyptians and Greeks exists." Taut seems to have been implying that the temporality of women's fashion had resulted in a set of forms that were timeless in their precision and functionalism. Taut, *Bauen*, 13–14. I am indebted to Rosemarie Bletter for pointing out this passage and translating it for me.

145   John Carl Flugel (1884–1955) was one of a group of British psychologists who studied at Oxford under William McDougall, the American pioneer in physiological and social psychology. Although McDougall's work deeply influenced Flugel's research, which initially involved such practical issues as intelligence testing and measurement of mental fatigue, Flugel's own writings were especially important for their synthesis of contemporary British psychology and early psychoanalytic theory. He was the first professional psychologist in Britain to make a serious examination of Freud's work, and he did much to popularize Freud's doctrines in England, by recasting them in a somewhat more commonsensical vein. He taught at the University of London, had an active psychoanalytic practice, and presented a series of British Broadcasting Corporation radio programs. Aside from his most popular book, *The Psychology of Clothes*, his works include *The Psychoanalytic Study of the Family* (1921), *A Hundred Years of Psychology* (1933), *Men and their Motives* (1934), and *Man, Morals, and Society* (1945). He was also an active member of the Men's Dress Reform Party. See Cyril Burt, "Prof. J. C. Flugel," *Nature*, 17 September 1955, 533–34; and "J. C. Flugel, M.A., D.Sc.," *British Medical Journal*, 27 August 1955, 569–70.

146   Flugel, *Psychology*, 225–26.

147   Ibid., 218.

148   Varvara Stepanova, "From Costume to Designs and Fabric," *Vechernyaya Moskva* [Evening Moscow], 28 November 1928, in Yablonskaya, *Women Artists of Russia's New Age*, 156.

149   Reversing the earlier proclamations of Wagner and Loos, Flugel declared: "It seems obviously inappropriate, for instance, that clerks working in the spacious, light, and airy buildings of the 'new' architecture should be dressed in the same styles as their grandfathers who were housed in offices of the more intimate and secretive type favored in that period." Flugel, *Psychology*, 228.

150   Le Corbusier, *Quand les cathèdrales étaient blanches* (Paris: Plon, 1937), 161–62, published in English as *When the Cathedrals Were White*, trans. Francis E. Hyslop (New York: Reynal and Hitchcock, 1947), 108. Le Corbusier wrote:

> It is a curious end-result of civilization that men who used to wear ostrich plumes on their heads, rose, white, and royal blue, a vesture of brocades or shimmering silk, should no longer know how to do anything but thrust their hands into the pockets of black trousers. Ten years ago Maurice de Waleffe felt this decadence; but his crusade broke its nose on silk stockings and shoes with incongruous buckles. The question has to be reconsidered and the transformation of masculine costume is necessary. It is as difficult as changing the ethics and the institutional state of a society. Costume is the expression of a civilization. Costume reveals the most fundamental feelings; through it we show our dignity, our distinction, our frivolity, or our basic ambitions. Though standardized, masculine dress does not escape individual decision. But it is no longer suitable. From what persists, we have proof that the machine age revolution has not reached maturity.

It should be noted that Le Corbusier used the word *costume* instead of *mode*.

151   See especially Elizabeth Wilson's seminal study *Adorned in Dreams: Fashion and Modernity* (Berkeley: University of California Press, 1985); Kaja Silverman, "Fragments of a Fashionable Discourse," in Tania Modleski, ed., *Studies in Entertainment: Critical Approaches to Mass Culture* (Bloomington: Indiana University Press, 1986), 139–52.; and Jane Gaines and Charlotte Herzog, ed., *Fabrications: Costume and the Female Body* (New York and London: Routledge, 1990).

152   In a letter to *Harper's Bazaar* dated 25 February 1952, Fondation Le Corbusier, Le Corbusier described these designs as "contemporary" without sacrificing "feminine charms." He claimed that he patented the design, and hoped that he could earn a "maximum of dollars" from it. The magazine, however, declined to publish Le Corbusier's "invention" and text. Lily van Ameringen, letter to Le Corbusier, 18 March 1952, Fondation Le Corbusier. Le Corbusier did publish his designs and a description of his intentions in an article, "Le Costume de la femme d'aujourd'hui," *Formes et Vie* 2 (1951), 11. In his first paragraph he explicitly separated himself from the ephemerality of fashion: "This [is] a costume for a modern woman and no fashion creation, it has therefore a character more durable than ephemeral; this differentiation is

not absolute but simply designates two perfectly admissible stages in dress-making." Le Corbusier's text appears with a series of brief statements and sketches concerning the relation between architecture and fashion, including contributions by Fernand Léger and Pierre Balmain. L. Bruder introduced the issue with the article "Evolution in Dress in Keeping with Architecture," which links architectural styles with clothes. Like Le Corbusier after 1930, Bruder sees women's dress as the model of modern design: "Buildings became cubic, women rectangular....Architecture frees itself from 'pastrywork' as the woman from her corset. " Le Corbusier's letter of 25 February and his text in *Formes et Vie* are reprinted in *Le Corbusier: le passé à réaction poétique*, exhibition catalogue, Hôtel de Sully (Paris: Caisse nationale des Monuments historiques et des Sites, Ministère de la Culture et de la Communication, 1987), 211–13. Le Corbusier had made English translations of these texts, which are available at the Fondation Le Corbusier.

153   See Giovanni Brino, Carlo Mollino: *Architettura come Autobiografia* (Milan: Idea Books, 1985), 31–45.

154   Elizabeth Wilson, "All the Rage," in Gaines and Herzog, *Fabrications*, 38.

155   A recent article in the "Styles" section of the Sunday *New York Times* attributes the use of the term "deconstruction" in fashion to Bill Cunningham in *Details* magazine. See Amy M. Spindler, "Coming Apart," *New York Times*, 25 July 1993, "Styles," 1. Again, fashion seems to have almost immediate international currency. I first discovered the term "deconstruction" in reference to fashion in a Kenzo announcement that my husband, Robert Heintges, found in Kuala Lumpur in 1990. However, I have seen no signs of "deconstructionist" dress among professional architects, who continue to follow relatively conservative models of fashion.

"In" Ar

OBSERVING THE

VAL K. WARKE

Since fashions are ubiquitous and inevitable, it is not productive to assert that the concept of fashion is bad per se. One would be safer in saying that there are good fashions and that there are bad fashions; the fashion for jogging was arguably better, for example, than the fashion for opium-eating.[1]

The association of fashionability with weakness of personal will or of intellect is largely an invention of certain intellectuals belonging to a culture where it is fashionable to dismiss fashion.[2] Wherever there is a choice susceptible to influence and a group of peers (or imagined peers as dreamt by a wanna-be) who will be aware of the selection, fashion will advance its propositions.

tecture

Still, one finds that Frank Lloyd Wright's aphoristic chant—

I'll live
As I'll die
As I am!
No slave of fashion or sham[3]

ISMS OF FASHION

—continues to reverberate through architectural schools and offices, particularly in America. Why would architecture be construed as being immune to the vicissitudes of fashion? First, because architectural production has for so long been occluded by the phantom of the *zeitgeist*, most architects continue to be lulled by Wright's insistent mantra.[4] And second, because the cost and scale of architectural works themselves have traditionally caused architecture to be seen as being exempt from any fashion system.

And yet, just as fashion requires a consumer system, consumer systems require fashions. The capacity for an object-type (a piece of costume jewelry, a pair of shoes, a car, an office building) to undergo formal change as a result of a fashion shift is related directly to the size of the object, its cost, the time lag between its

FIG. 1 *"Mondrian" Dress, Fall/Winter Collection, 1965–66. From* Yves Saint Laurent, *exhibition catalog, The Metropolitan Museum (New York: The Metropolitan Museum of Art and Clarke & Potter, Inc., 1983).*

initial design and the final act of its consumption, the total amount of production occurring within a specific market, and the time interval between the production of the object and the dispersal of its carefully delimited representations throughout the market. The purchase of a fashion artifact (not necessarily the object itself, but often one of a series of representations of an object, e.g., a Björk compact disc, a Morphosis retrospective) operates as an endorsement, the nature of which is the acceptance of the producer's concept of the purchaser as one of a specific class.[5]

As a result, while these factors might slow the movement of a full-scale architectural construction through the fashion network, the merchandizing of contemporary architectural drawings and illustrated texts by architects who have produced only a limited number of constructions has had a diarrhetic effect on architecture's movements through the market.

FASHION'S DISCURSIVE REFASHIONING

Before considering these movements as they operate within architecture's various systems, it will be helpful to uncover the methods whereby fashion's machinery refashions ostensibly virginal works of art and architecture; for architecture and art have often been absorbed by other fashions in addition to being controlled by the mechanisms of the fashion system. Looking at the more overt associations established between the garment industry's fashion component and the realms of art and architecture will be helpful in isolating components central to the structure of fashion itself and in evaluating fashion's operation upon another enterprise: architecture.

The periodic compulsion by the garment fashion industry to appropriate superficial formal aspects of various art icons for the service of designing and manufacturing garments has resulted in a number of uneasy liaisons between the products displayed in the museum and those displayed in the clothing store. Fashion always desires a facile *association* with novelty and adventurousness, the *implication*—without the related liabilities—of the *risqué*. Fashion, concerned with the magnitude of its market, will resist referring to the genuinely novel (and therefore unrecognized) as well as to the religiously or politically laden (and therefore potentially ill-received in the popular marketplace). Thus, when fashion turns to art, it seldom turns to the most provocative; it turns to the most readily identifiable, culturally accepted icons that a society can furnish. Even when exoticism is the intended fashion statement, fashion will turn to internally generated cultural stereotypes of an outside culture—to the Other only insofar as it has been pre-measured against the Self.

Garment fashion often finds these associational sources in museums of modern art—culturally approved institutions of canonical modernism where even the renegade is neatly categorized and conventionalized. Works in the museum that might possess some of these latent characteristics of being provocative are either avoided or voided (i.e., purged of their connotations). Yves Saint Laurent's "Mondrian" collection (1965–66) and his "Picasso" collection (1979–80) were successful because of the already accepted iconographic qualities of their referents. By the latter third of the twentieth century, only in certain *retardataire* circles, where "high fashion" would never consider looking for a market anyway, would Mondrian or Picasso still be considered controversial.[6]

When the fashion component of the garment industry turns to architecture, its reproduction of artifacts is necessarily less mimetic and more conceptually oriented.[7] Occasionally, though, a specific building may inspire—or be said to inspire—a localized fashion in clothing. For example, Linnea Lannon of the KNT news service wrote in 1987:

> The best thing about Paris is not the fall 1987 fashion shows...the best thing I've seen so far in Paris this season is the Musée d'Orsay....What one comes away with from the Musée d'Orsay is not necessarily a Monet image. It is the image of color and texture and the combination of old and new materials that is so striking.
> So how does the Musée d'Orsay translate to clothes?
> First, in the coolness implicit in the materials and color.

> Colors are very subdued, very Italian. Black, which has been
> dubbed the color of the '80s, is destined to be replaced in our
> wardrobes, and the palette Aulenti has chosen for the museum
> quite likely is what is to come in clothes. The grays and tau-
> pes are almost exactly the shades Giorgio Armani used in the
> winter collection he showed recently in Milan.
>
> Then there is the mix of the spare and the ornate in the Musée
> d'Orsay. Ultimately, clothes that are too spare are judged bor-
> ing by many women; clothes that are too detailed end up look-
> ing fussy. I haven't heard it said, but I can just imagine some
> fabric designer or stylist looking at the museum and thinking,
> "That's the way women want to look."[8]

To Lannon, whose milieu is writing on garments, a museum is
appreciated for its "clothing": for its colors and for its exotic flair.
In the traditionally self-conscious and nationalistic Parisian design
circle, concerned about its waning supremacy in the fashion world
(especially since Chelsea and the 1960s), the fact that Aulenti is
an Italian architect immediately renders the building an Italian
import. Like a Romeo Gigli, an Alfa Romeo, or a Centre Pompidou,
its contextual abrasiveness is made acceptable by being accredited
to its otherness.

In a less literal association between architecture and fashion,
Susan Sidlauskas, then curator of the Committee on the Visual
Arts at M.I.T., wrote in the exhibition catalog accompanying the
1982 "Intimate Architecture: Contemporary Clothing Design"
show at the Hayden Gallery:

> This exhibition...concerns designers who, with varying
> degrees of austerity, are committed to boldly stretching the
> formal possibilities of their craft while maintaining a respect
> for the realities of the human frame. The expressive tools that
> are a traditional part of the designer's trade coexist with a pre-
> occupation for solving spatial and structural problems more
> commonly expressed in architecture. These artists view and
> design clothes to contain and define space. Their skills are
> those of builders rather than decorators. The garment is con-
> ceived and assembled as a three-dimensional entity, not as a
> facade for frontal display. As in the paradigms of certain
> utopian architectural visions, such as those of the Russian

Constructivists and the Bauhaus, the structural decisions (cut, seams, darts, pleats) compose the decoration. Blueprints and graphs often are used to plot out and transfer designs to fabric. The grid, that emblem of industrial design and a recurrent ordering device in avant-garde art of the last twenty years, surfaces as pattern.[9]

In a review of the exhibition (albeit one that depends on a rather nascent form of gendered discourse) that originally appeared in *The New Yorker*, Kennedy Fraser addressed the use of "architecture" as a formative concept in the realm of garment fashion, writing:

> I have referred to the new mood of fashion as modernist, but fashion, in spite of its new sense of worth as a branch of design, would still not quite have the temerity to use such a grandiose term. What it took to calling itself instead was either linear or architectural. As feminine fashion began to be self-conscious and to search for a language capable of expressing more serious thoughts than where to buy what, it looked with awe and envy to its big brother architecture. Here was a domain that simply swirled with theories, that had a tradition of debate leading back to Socrates and Plato, and that was confident enough to mantle itself in big words like "modern," and even "post-modern." Little fashion pressed its nose to the windowpane and saw architects moving freely in a bright and privileged world—long established, powerful, public, and masculine (to the point of being, especially with skyscrapers, notoriously phallic). And then, in recent times, architecture has been generating publicity and excitement, which spilled over into fashion—as most excitement must, in one way or another. To fashion designers, architecture gave the appealing impression (probably illusory for the most part) that creative theories could influence the course of style, and that designers could be actively in control....Fashion drew near to architecture for all these reasons, and also because architecture provided the look that it was after....What fashion found was a certain impassive, hard-edged, sharply outlined quality, traditionally associated not with female forms clothed in fabric but with edifices clothed in steel, concrete, glass, stone, or marble. What fashion took up, in short, was precisely the kind of "modernism" from which post-modern architecture was vociferously in flight.[10]

Versions of some of the theoretical constructs of "architectural post-modernism," appreciated for their having already received publicity (i.e., made their way into the marketplace), reappeared in the editorials of popular fashion magazines. Interestingly, they were used in this context to combat post-modernism's perceived calcification of forms; architecture, which seemed so effective in leading the way, was taking garment fashion backwards (a direction it, naturally, did not wish to take). Argues Fraser:

> ...It is even tempting to see Philip Johnson's A. T. & T. Building, with its neo-Chippendale twiddly bits, as some kind of giant late flowering of the historicism that the fashion world knows as "thrift-shop chic," and which [fashion] seems to be trying to leave behind.[11]

And so, the fashion critics, more competent than architects or theorists at the manipulation of textual significations, successfully opposed the postmodernism of the 1980s with postmodernism's own rhetorical structures. For example, note the brilliant manipulation of critical language wielded by Peter Carlsen, senior editor of *Gentlemen's Quarterly*, when he faced the gloomy prospect in 1980 of an apparent classical revival:

> Although conventional wisdom maintains that the white-heat of invention is always followed by a cooling down, we don't buy that theory; something more serious, more potentially damaging is happening.
> ...[E]ven Giorgio Armani has stamped his seal of approval on the decade's new nondirection....[He] has signaled that wit and clarity are no longer valid, but that an inchoate, timeless look is.
> The trouble with timelessness, of course, is that it's also featureless....The truth is that fashion is simply "on hold" at the moment....What's certain, however, is that sooner or later, the interrupted current will begin to flow, a new direction will emerge, and we'll all be off and running again.[12]

Carlsen advocates a series of remedies: the "*non sequitur*" (e.g., the silk suit with the motorcycle jacket); the "transformed object" (the tie as a belt); and the fashion "mannerism" (a Hungarian peasant vest with an otherwise restrained ensemble).[13] The terminology and constructs of literary, art, and architectural criticism are used to resist the "damaging" tendencies of the regressive products of these same disciplines. Architectural discourse provides fashion with a wave of publicity that can be ridden and a verisimilous base that can form a beach-head (note, for instance, Sidlauskas's citation of an abbreviated Bauhaus functionalism in arguing the propriety of "Intimate Architecture"); however, the apparently conclusive manifestations of this latest new architecture are disappointing. In order to maintain verisimilitude, a selective outlook is necessary: fashion retains architecture's new lingo, but uses it in opposition to the new forms, preferring, instead, to evoke the easily apprehended forms of conventional modern architecture, if at all.

FASHION'S SUBSCRIBERS

Not only do relationships exist between the fashion industry as it is commonly understood (i.e., as an industry focused primarily on the production of garments) and art and architecture, but the structures that direct the fashion system (i.e., the product of a fashion theory) have a profound, though hushed and even denied, effect among the producers of architecture.

As E. H. Gombrich points out in "The Logic of Vanity Fair" (1965), many of the attributes accredited to the phenomenology of the *Zeitgeist* may be seen as normative phenomena in a study of the structure of fashions, style, and taste.[14] Expanding on Gombrich's considerations, one could conclude that in a study of the production of art works, the concept of the *Zeitgeist* might be replaced by Walter Benjamin's notion of the *Jetztzeit*, wherein the immediate present—*this* moment—is understood to exist as the apotheosis of a series of continuously shifting instants of revelation, where fragments from relevant pasts are incorporated into a plausible depiction of the present.[15]

Those who find their messianic revelations in their present, who find this *jetztzeit*, seem to find it in the operation of fashion. Oscar Wilde states that "the feeling of being in harmony with fashion gives a person a measure of security religion can never offer." Auden, in "Making, Knowing and Judging,"[16] finds fashion and its operant structure—snobbery—to be extremely helpful to the poet in making a decision in the midst of an infinity of choices. Picasso states that only by operating within the various fashions of his time—fashions for subjects and fashions for techniques—did he feel completely free to turn his attentions to the real subject of his work: the nature of art.

For the more sentient artists, fashion offers a set of quasi-rules, providing a formal system within which one is free to focus on the art of art. By bracketing an art's appurtenances, fashion can facilitate the investigation of its fundamental operations.

For less inquisitive practitioners, however, fashion provides a method, a measure, and a subscription to a ready-made messianic illusion. Seduced by a fashion's appliances, the uncritically fashionable artist may find prosperity in dandyism and the comfort of being associated with a pre-defined movement (the polemics of which she or he may or may not comprehend); but this *artiste*, while perhaps enjoying a profitable practice at first, will eventually be puzzled, then resistant, and finally devastated by the undertow generated by the next major fashion challenge.

There is, of course, a third type: the fashionably savvy practitioner who profitably associates with the right fashion at the right time, literally di-vesting one architecture for the next at the most propitious moment. Fashions are the currency—in both senses of the word—of most successful large architectural firms.

FASHION'S EPISTEMIC APPARATUS

The formulation of a fashion tends to follow a generally pre-dictable pattern. First, sources are identified, often from a multi-tude of choleric voices. Second, the sources are de-radicalized, their "roughness" is tempered; they are subtly transformed from being sources of antagonism to being objects of desire: the eroti-cism of animus. Third, a primary icon or set of icons is selected; these become emblematic of the fashion and must be qualified to represent a homogenized, tangible version of the fashion, capable of being "sold." The fourth phase, once a fashion has taken hold, is marked by the repetitive atrophy of its forms' associated con-tents, with the eventual loss of virtually all original significations; during this phase, most fashions descend through the various con-sumer classes, beginning with the class wherein it had been intro-duced at the end of the third phase. The final phase of a fashion is its death, when it becomes *poncif*, literally a "pounced drawing" and figuratively a "commonplace piece of work." At this point it may either be overthrown by another fashion challenge or con-sumed as part of a generic style.

A fashion is always understood to represent that which is beautiful, even if it is a beauty founded upon some form of cultivated ugli-ness. Especially for fashions, verisimilitude—not truth—is beauty. A verisimilous base forms the foundation of a fashion's opposition to a style as well as to other competing fashions: the fundamental gambit of a fashion is its ability to unmask its opponents' verisimil-itudes. A fashion will always confront an existing, firmly entrenched fashion or an ascendant style by appearing as either a seducer or an antagonist. As seducer, a fashion may urge the adherents of the established fashion or style to reevaluate their allegiances by suggesting a plausible, though previously forbidden, variation on the apparently stable style's primary tenets. The fashion as antagonist will confront a popularly held fashion or style by underscoring the fallacies of the target's basic advertised pre-sumptions and propositions (that is, of its soft-bellied verisimili-tude). Since verisimilitude is not verity, it is always sensitive to opposition from similar constructs, particularly when those constructs insist upon their own opposing truth. Abetting the drive for new fashions is the fact that it is in the nature of the always-desired Progress to demonstrate that one now knows more (and better) than one once knew—a daily reaffirmation of the *Jetztzeit*. While a theory of "style" is too complex to be discussed herein, one might consider a style to be the *post facto* identification of a cluster of formally similar fashions. Any given moment my be occupied by a variety of fashions, each operating within a different stratum of a culture or society, and each lasting only the length of a season or publishing cycle. The life of a style is usually described as an "age" or an "era." Whereas fashions tend to be "written," (i.e., delineated, described, and disseminated) by publicists and critics, styles tend to be "written" by historians and anthropologists. In many ways, a style operates as a metafashion.[17]

During their challenging phase, fashions are contentious by nature; styles, defensive. Whereas styles depend upon the policing effects of taste, fashions depend upon the subversive effects of antipathy or distaste. Taste operates as the arbiter of a style; antipathy as the motivator of a fashion.[18] Just as a style is comprised of a constellation of "similar" fashions, fashions often find their origins by collecting a variety of relatively current and "similar" avant-gardes, occasionally mixing them with shards of deposed fashions from a not-too-distant past and historically recorded avant-gardes that are sufficiently distanced, in time or location, so as to be largely nostalgic (again, plundering the museum).

An avant-garde almost always welcomes the attention it receives from those promising to make its polemic (or, at least, its presence) known to a larger audience. The struggling avant-garde is generally not concerned with the context of its publicity, so thankful is it for exposure. Because a fashion must operate within the marketplace, it is necessary for the marketers of a fashion to *de-radicalize* the various avant-gardes as they are consumed. Avant-gardes are inevitably positioned in antipathy to established middle- and upper-class canons. A fashion, even when apparently opposed to those canons, must continue to operate within the rules of a culture. Therefore, a fashion will render harmless, perhaps even adorable, an avant-garde's attempted negation of an established cultural operation, carefully permitting the *sensation* of being radical to persist. This is an essential ingredient of a fashion, considering fashion's insistence upon its own novelty and urgency and its need to be conspicuous within the marketplace. Fashion must combine sharp elbows with sharper doggerel.

An avant-garde's entanglement with a fashion concludes with the achievement of a general acceptance that the avant-garde simultaneously desires and disdains. Even the most anarchic avant-garde falls victim to this process, eventually becoming subverted by fashion's compelling need to establish a process of standardization.

During the second phase of the fashion process, when the identified sources are presented for the first time to a public, there is a need for some distance: the forms have not yet been tempered, the public's resistance has not yet been tested. A meticulously staged ritual, bordering on the theatrical, is required. For clothing, the fashion show provides this milieu, and the artifacts that are insinuated into the public sphere in this way belong to a category of costuming known as *haute couture*. Literally "high needlework," *haute couture* poses as being representative of the future. Its insistence on its own inevitability as a cultural artifact is at once both charming and threatening.[19]

Haute couture is intrinsically anti-populist. It exists in the realm of parody and hyperbole.[20] Simulating an avant-garde, it functions as a battering ram on the consciousness of the public. By positing an extreme alterity, *haute couture* facilitates the eventual acceptance of a compromised, intermediate position teeming with the de-radicalized artifacts of the second phase of fashion development (which, in the fashion of attire, facilitates the final transferral from the singular, handcrafted garment to the mass-produced lines of ready-to-wear garments).

Haute couture speaks the language of the manifesto. It is shrill, bleak, irate, and ever-so-subtly disingenuous. *Haute couture's* hopeful manifestos utilize Swiftian ironies to promote the previously unthinkable and to facilitate the acceptance of the previously unconsumable. (The manifestos of twentieth-century architecture operated in a virtually identical manner: they functioned within conventional language, but with the discrete program of initiating a new language; they were intermediate objects asserting a directed intention.)[21]

One could, for example, easily trace the fashion network followed by modern architecture in its early days, leading to its show at the Museum of Modern Art in 1932 and ending in eventual style-dom.[22] The names accompanying the works tell an abbreviated story. First, there was "Modern Movement," with "movement" being a traditional sign of the presence of an avant-garde polemic. At this stage, modern architecture was a collection of dispersed movements; its singularity was a necessary goal of its marketers. Then it became "Modern Architecture," with an apparent solidification of its subject and of its intentions. With "Modern Style" there came a perception of the stability of the fashion. While not yet assimilated into a style, it developed the pretense of one, asserting the stability it desired. Finally, with "International Style," the Museum of Modern Art, through Henry-Russell Hitchcock and Philip Johnson, freed modern architecture from a specific, and therefore limiting, environment, increased its marketability, and formulated the basis of its verisimilitude: volume, liberated by reduced structural dimensions; balance instead of symmetry; regularity (especially when measured by the economic benefits of orderly structure and repetitive components: the beauty of mass-production); decoration only as a constitutive element of mechanized building fabrication; and so on.

The phenomenon continued with many of the same patterns. For the 1988 "Deconstructivist Architecture" show, held at the same venue as the 1932 show, Philip Johnson and Mark Wigley elegantly fabricated a formidable—and fashionable—challenge to the fatigued "Po-Mo." In their introductory essays in the catalog for the show, they resisted identifying "Deconstructivist Architecture" as an avant-garde (that is, as a "movement"), which would make the project too unstable, or as a style, which would clearly be too presumptuous. Instead, the curators chose to locate it within the realm of the "trend": slow but inevitable, a new direction, a marketable fashion. The catchy, neologistic title, "Deconstructivist Architecture," is a synthetic formulation, like "Ivory Snow," trading on the familiar and recently revived (i.e., Constructivism, some of the icons of which were trotted out in a sort of testimonial to the new stuff, decorating the antechambers the way Debussy's music might be used at a show where a collection evoking nineteenth-century romantic costumes is being premiered), avoiding the dowdiness of an "-ism" by using an adjectival form, and hybridizing the name of a popular analytic philosophy (Derridean deconstruction). The only other plausible title for the show, considering its content—"Postmodernism"—had already been taken by another fashion once eager for substantiation.

The exhibition presented a collection of diverse architectural projects by individuals whose stated polemics, when they existed, had little in common. What the designers shared was the desire to be made public. The museum could be counted upon to temper the roughness, asserting this architecture's Oedipal bad-boyism, while simultaneously and disingenuously proffering the work as a radicalization of a dead avant-garde. A museum of modern art—a shrine to the *Jetztzeit*, where a selected present is instantly legitimized (through juxtaposition with that which is considered historically important) and commodified (tickets and catalogs are sold, works are insured, guards are hired)—implicitly states "the present shown here *will* be as important as this past that we have collected."

Through most of the 1980s, architectural practice fell out of fashion with the fashion publishers. It is only recently that practice, always coyly soliciting the limelight, once again makes itself available so that the fashion industry can project its desires onto architecture's surfaces. This was largely due to the fact that the Deconstructivist Architecture show was a *tour de force* of architectural *haute couture*. However, in successfully infiltrating architecture schools and popular magazines throughout the world, any of the ideological content that may have been present in the individual originals has, through the process of combining and recombining the disparate icons, largely been allowed to atrophy in content and to hypertrophy in figure.

FASHION'S ANTI-DISCOURSE

If a fashion hopes to persist for any period of time (that is, if its vendors desire its longevity), it is necessary to put in place its own system of criticism and network of critics: one of the most powerful techniques a fashion has in its process of intimating itself with the public is its ability to introduce or invent new terminologies and to assign values to existing ones. By manipulating language, a fashion can eliminate its opposition: it can simply become impossible to discuss, due to its lack of conformity with a specialized critical language; or it can be denied positive assessment by a re-valuation of its own critical terminologies. For example, a number of modern architecture's avant-garde progenitors assigned a very positive value to "dynamic." This was opposed by the very negative "static." During the first stage of postmodernism in the 1970s, "static" and "dynamic" were replaced by "stable" (good) and "unstable" (bad) and the valuations were reversed. The recent trend reassesses "unstable" by means of its incarnation as "destabilized" (now good; as a word it is active and implies intentionality) and opposes it with "normative" (indicative of the *status quo*, a very negative term indeed).

As one of the premier "machines of fashion," to use Roland Barthes's phrase, the fashion magazine (and in architecture, this means magazines such as *Architecture, Architectural Record, Progressive Architecture* [P/A], *House and Garden* [HG], *Elle Decor,*

Metropolis, and so on) depends upon its ability to force a controlled focus on the reader. The function of a fashion journal is neither to initiate discourse nor to broaden perceptions; fashion journals operate from a position of authority dependent on a virtually monological form of utterance that functions to disengage the image from critical speculation and, therefore, from the dangers of uncontrolled discourse.[23] The text within the fashion journal is saturated with implicit valuations and contrived tautologies intended to underscore the apparent verity of the prescribed verisimilitude of the representations it has to offer.

For example, in *House & Garden's* coverage of Frank Gehry's Winton Guest House (built as an addition to Philip Johnson's Davis House of 1952), plans and photographs are centered on a text (written by Martin Filler, a frequent contributor to architecture magazines) that asserts:

> Although Gehry's seemingly loose ensembles have the air of random occurrences, they are in fact carefully plotted, first through models and then in drawings, accounting for their strong compositional logic.[24]

In this sentence, Filler fabricates an undereducated reader who uses superficial cognizant responses to judge a work and for whom Gehry's volumes *seem* to be loose and random. He then declares that Gehry's works "are in fact carefully plotted" and that this (the "fact" of being plotted) is the reason for their "strong compositional logic." Within the body of the text, Filler states that "the sequence of interior spaces seem[s] more spontaneous than it is."[25] Filler's text counters what is apparent, at least to the eyes of the average reader, with unbuttressed statements of "fact." The format of fashion magazines—abridged texts appended to abridged presentations—ensures this shorthand, and a concurrent and requisite trust of the author ensues.

In the fashion journal, the images themselves are selected more often for their seductive qualities as images (illustrating the eroticism of the architecture's animus) than for their ability to operate as relatively neutral representations. The architecture depicted in the architectural fashion journal is the publicly adept architecture, the architecture purged of its potentially antagonistic polemics. It has the cute pugnaciousness of a pouting youngster rather than the potentially offensive contentiousness of a bully.

The magazine's verbal structures, especially in the form of captions, will further erode the content of the building's physical ones. For instance, it is not unusual to see a caption that avers:

> An appropriately respectful "thickened wall," the North Range modules form a sense of enclosure for the space...but keep well clear of the library....Care was exercised in preserving existing trees on the property.[26]

Words like "appropriately respectful," "well clear," and "care" indicate that the illustrated building complies with an unstated but generally accepted code of manners, if not of morality. The quotation marks around "thickened wall" simultaneously flag this phrase as belonging to an external linguistic system (designer jargon) while implicitly disclaiming the exteriority of the more prevalent ethical phrases.[27]

Within fashion's house, no building should stand out as more important than any other. A building that is of the first phase of an ideological development should not appear to be unnecessarily superior to those where the ideological content has atrophied. A magazine must guarantee the continued supply of its goods by equalizing their apparent quality.[28]

FASHION'S END

The death of a fashion is inevitable. While asserting its conspicuousness and distinctiveness, a fashion simultaneously desires its integration and acceptance within a culture. A fashion dies when it becomes completely accepted and stereotyped. In order to reconcile these opposite urges, fashion requires a type of carnivalized ritual.[29] When an individual's relation to the discotheque, special sporting event, fashion show, or music video station begins to be participatory, that is, when the individual begins actually to *become* rather than merely to *observe* the physiognomy and manners of a fashion's proposed models, then the individual is succumbing to the allure of a carnivalized present. Once they have passed beyond the early, theatrical stages of their public debuts (where involvement is limited to spectating), fashions never put their audiences at a distance. Like carnivals, they abandon the theater for the market square, engaging their participants directly: *they will always speak in the first person plural.*

> Carnival is, so to speak, functional and not substantive. It absolutizes nothing, but rather proclaims the jolly relativity of everything. [30]

The disseminative operation of fashion within a culture represents one of carnival's generic strains.

It is virtually impossible to avoid being implicated in some fashion or another: no school exists completely unaffiliated with any fashion network, at either a local or global level; no journal subsists completely unconcerned about its market; no museum survives without the charity of its donors and visitors. In soliciting the fondness of a public, almost every institution requires the facile contemporariness fashion is always willing to provide. [31] Fashion frees an institution from stifling changelessness while promising the benefits of a continued expansion of its membership and, ultimately, financial development.

While the producer of a latter-generation fashion icon may believe that she or he is producing a legible social statement (legible with regard to the conditions, aspirations, or sympathies of a culture or sub-culture), the most legible statement is the producer's *interpretation* of that culture, or, more accurately, of her or his version of *fashion's intentions* for that culture. This is the principal dialogism of the fashion object.

Should an architect feel the compunction to be "fashion-free," that architect must either be unfashionable (a posture that requires some knowledge of prevalent fashions) or be completely independent of those systems that survive through the marketing of fashion. One could receive a vocational education; ignore all work published in journals; and, should one's work meet with critical acclaim, assiduously resist all overtures made by clients as the result of the publication or exhibition of one's work by anyone else. In other words, one would have to reconfigure the nature of architectural practice.

Fashion poses a doubled view of a culture: a view of how those in power want to present that culture;[32] and a view of how, at least within a range of choices, a culture wishes to depict itself. While fashion's options are emptied of their original polemical structures, the fashion process renovates these options into more socially prolific phenomena, capable of permeating every stratum of a society without regard to economic or ideological diversities.

The development of a critical cognizance of the operation of fashion within a culture, and within architecture in particular, is an essential stage in the development of a critical cognizance of the embedded cultural connotations of the artifacts we are given to see. The disavowal of fashion as a determinant of formal dissemination can only lead to histories that buttress the mysticism of the *Zeitgeist*, critical commentaries that dismiss a work on the basis of its superficial physique while ignoring its conceptual underpinnings, theories that measure a form's dispersal throughout a culture and mistakenly assume that its content has been transferred intact, and designs and design methodologies that perpetuate the belief that a description of a culture's self-prescribed desires can be interpreted as a map of its needs and hopes.

NOTES

1   However, better poems and essays were produced under the influence of the latter than the former.

2   It is tempting to speculate further that the distaste many critics and theorists in "serious" subjects (such as architecture) have had when confronting fashion is associated with the traditional conception of fashion as an intrinsically feminine phenomenon. Just as "fashion" itself is a feminine noun in all of the major gendered Western languages, so has its subsidiary language and discourse been predominantly feminine in nature and focus. The feminization of fashion by masculine-dominant cultures has perhaps caused it to be continuously relegated to the realm of less consequential subjects, its importance particularly denied by the various historical and theoretical establishments. Interestingly, "style," which enjoys a more favorable reputation among historians and theorists, is virtually always a masculine noun.

3   Frank Lloyd Wright, "Work Song" (Oak Park: Oak Park Workshop, 1896).

4   One example is the case of Craig Webb, a fallen Princetonian, who left college disgruntled with what he believed was Michael Graves's domination of the school, to return to the "table-saw part" of his persona in order to become involved with community design workshops. While he states that "Architecture is not fashion," he is quoted as saying this in one of a series of articles entitled "Careers: 'Men at Work: Tales from the Front Line'" in *Details*, May 1991, 53. The paradox here, of course, is that it is fashion that provides Webb with a platform from which he can make this anti-fashion statement. *Details* is not unaware of this irony; they print this quotation in bold, red, 36-point letters. It is clear that Webb was considered for inclusion in this issue—sandwiched between a comedian and a U.S. Representative—because he is a project architect at the fashionable firm of Frank O. Gehry & Associates.

5   The exception, of course, is that case of a purchase made in the interest of ritualistically redirecting the social status of a culture or subculture by appropriating its most identifiable simulacrum and grafting it into a clearly disparate context: heavy metal rockers dressed in the uniforms of elite prep schools; or nun-garbed transvestites, like the Sisters of Perpetual Indulgence.

6   The 1991 revival of the "Mondrian" collection was, interestingly, concomitant with the revival of the sixties. This dress is now more familiar to the general public than its precedent. It has developed a connotative value as an

artifact of the 1960s, blocking any potential reference to De Stijl and to the first third of the century. Such is the magnitude of fashion's revisionist authority.

7   Interestingly, a number of well-known *couturiers* received architectural educations, including Pierre Cardin, Gianfranco Ferré, and Ronaldus Shamask.

8   Linnea Lannon, *The Allentown Morning Call*, 29 March 1987.

9   Susan Sidlauskas, *Intimate Architecture: Contemporary Clothing Design*, exhibition catalog (n.p.: 1982), unpaginated.

10   Kennedy Fraser, *The Fashionable Mind* (Boston: Godine, 1985), 290–91.

11   Ibid., 290–91.

12   Peter Carlsen, "Personal Effects: Combatting Fashion Conformity with Individuality," *Gentlemen's Quarterly* 50:3 (April 1980), 74, 79. Note that the urgent, alarmist rhetoric of this editorial, particularly in the final paragraph, is very similar to that of the architectural manifesto (see, for example, Le Corbusier's *Vers une architecture*). Indeed, even a superficial stylistic analysis of Carlsen's text reveals its inherent contradictions and tensions. We are to assume, for instance, in the juxtaposition of "although" and "conventional" that the latter is being derided and that a more appropriate, *un*conventional wisdom is being proffered.
Similarly, "heat" has been accumulating positive connotations since the late nineteenth century: to be "hot" is to be lively and vital (e.g., Hemingway's "hot town"); to be a "sure thing"; to be sexually appealing; and to be very much in demand. Thus, the implication is that a period of cooling down is less vital, less certain, less appealing, less in demand: a fatal condition in the fashion world.
The first-person plural pronoun—one of fashion's most powerful proselytizers—is used by Carlsen in all of its glorious ambiguity: is this "we" the editorial board or the "we" who have purchased *GQ*? There is a literalness to "we don't buy," because our acceptance of a fashion theory is directly transcribed into our purchases. The more accurate future tense of "we *won't* buy" is not used because Carlsen is speaking of what he hopes is a secure immediacy.
Likewise, by shifting "conventional wisdom" to "theory," Carlsen demotes wisdom to uncertainty. Notice the equation of seriousness with damage, and the use of the passive "is happening," indicating an unnamed external force. Evidently, "nondirections" are more distressing when they occur at the beginning of a decade. Fashion always uses a ten-year version of millenialistic anxiety to its own benefit. Then, too, there is the implication of timelessness as being without wit, and the subtle juxtaposition of "clarity" with "inchoate"

(meaning "incipient") that coerces the innocent, yet relatively uncommon word to be read as "incoherent" by the casual reader. The "truth" that is spoken in the fashion journal is always a spectral verisimilitude.

Finally, to be "on hold" is to be victimized by a system of communication technology; it is the tangible communication of a lack of communication. As a result, "current" also resonates with ambiguities; an interrupted current is not only of the power blackout sort, but also evokes the image of a dam in the river (one of the basic metaphors for time and inevitable progression) and of this current time (i.e., the present) and all that is "with it." Thus, the equation of "timelessness" with that which is "featureless" indicates that the formal reductivism accompanying most genres of (neo)rational (neo)classicism is intrinsically a futile effort to dam time.

13   Carlsen, "Personal Effects," 76, 79.

14   E. H. Gombrich, "The Logic of Vanity Fair: Alternatives to Historicism in the Study of Fashions, Style and Taste" (1965), in *Ideals and Idols* (Oxford: Phaidon, 1979), 60–92.

15   Walter Benjamin, "Theses on the Philosophy of History," 14, reprinted in *Walter Benjamin, Illuminations*, trans. Harry Zohn, ed. Hannah Arendt (New York: Schocken Books, 1968), 261.

16   W.H. Auden, "Making Knowing and Judging," in W.H. Auden, *The Dyer's Hand* (New York: Vintage Books, 1968), 40.

17   I thank Seonaidh Davenport for suggesting the notion of style as metafashion.

18   It should be possible to write alternative histories, especially of architecture, that do not present architectural progress as a chain of positive events, but rather as a sequence of negative reactions: histories of antipathy.

19   For example, Karl Lagerfeld's 1991 Fall *haute couture* show in Paris (for Chanel) was entitled "City Ballerina." Asked why, Lagerfeld responded, "She dances through the grave life of the city in a weightless way, sophisticated to death." Quoted in Michael Gross, "Why the Caged Bird Sings," *New York* 24:31 (12 August 1991), 19.

20   The models used during shows of *haute couture* are often called "high fashion" models. Like their garments, they are generally quirky in appearance, having exaggerated features. High fashion models don't usually smile; their physiognomies range from the aloof to the apocalyptic. They transfer what

might normally be considered unacceptable into the realm of the unapproachable, and therefore desirable.

21   On the function of the fashion text, see Roland Barthes, *Système de la Mode* (Paris: Seuil, 1967), trans. by Matthew Ward and Richard Howard as *The Fashion System* (New York: Hill & Wang, 1983).

22   Each commodity has its own sites of fashionalization. Architecture, for example, becomes fashionalized at the moment that it engages its popular distribution systems: museums, galleries, glossy magazines, and schools.

23   On captions, see Barthes, *The Fashion System*, 13.

24   Martin Filler, "The House as Art," *House & Garden* 159:10 (October 1987), 158–59.

25   Ibid., 244.

26   Jim Murphy, "Scholarly Wall," *Progressive Architecture*, February 1991, 70–73. The subject of the article is Barton Phelps & Associates' North Range addition to Robert Farquhar's Clark Library (1926) at UCLA.

27   That "sense of enclosure," a more jargonistic phrase, is not set off by quotation marks reinforces the argument that the function of the citation is to divert attention from the more abundant and latently value-laden phrases at work in the text.

28   The practice of redrawing architects' drawings for publication is largely intended to develop a graphic consistency throughout the magazine while homogenizing the apparent level of representational development in the projects presented; in this way, authorial voice is drowned by the choric voice of the editorial board.

29   It is necessary to point out that, following Mikhail Bakhtin, I use "carnival" to refer to an internalized aspect of society's operation, one not limited to those past and present societies that once practiced or still do practice carnival in its most literal, traditional form.

30   Mikhail Bakhtin, *Problems of Dostoevsky's Poetics*, ed. and trans. Caryl Emerson (Minneapolis: University of Minnesota Press, 1984), 125.

31   The exceptions, of course, include those institutions that have no need for marketing themselves, where membership guarantees social status and all the benefits commensurate with such a position. The private club is the most

conspicuous of these institutions, where anti-progressive social and political practices are an intrinsic component of its "charm" and where the membership roll provides a microcosmic version of the membership's proposed ideal society or counter-society.

32   The French government's ownership of Yves Saint Laurent's fashion house makes this liason between fashion and power—both financial and political—starkly apparent.

MARK WIGLEY

> I met a whole swarm of architects who were seeking for the
> New, and sometimes found it.
>
> —Paul Poiret. *En habillant l'epoque*, 1930

How to talk about fashion and architecture today? It seems like an easy question. Too easy perhaps. After all, the symptoms of some kind of complicity between fashion and architecture can be found everywhere. In addition to the traditional sense of architectural styles as fashions, there are the obvious symptoms like architects appearing in advertisements for clothing designers and stores, the featuring of architects and buildings in fashion magazines, fashion supplements in architectural magazines, fashion designers branching out into architectural design, architects branching out into designing clothes and other fashionable objects, the signature architecture of fashion stores, the emergence of fashion magazines specializing in promoting architecture, and so on. But perhaps the question harbors some surprises within its very obviousness, not to mention its less obvious symptoms: the strategic role of architecture in fashion images, the architecture of the fashion show itself, the actual "look" of architects, the architectonics of clothing, the ongoing transformations in the language used by architects and critics, the oblique but critical role of architect designed objects and spaces in establishing identity in the mass media, and so on. Indeed, a whole terrain of effects presents itself, if not imposes itself, and demands some kind of sustained reading.

ite Out

ING THE MODERN

FIG. 1

Advertisement for Mercedez Benz model 8/38, using Weissenhof Siedlung house by Le Corbusier and Pierre Jeanneret (1927). From Franz Schultze, "La época de Weimar: Vivienda y vanguardia," Monografías de Arquitectura y Vivienda 6 *(1986), 38.*

The phenomenon is often referred to. Even the 1988 annual conference of the less-than-progressive American Institute of Architects featured a panel of starlets addressing the ever "thinner" line between fashion and Architecture in a suitably disapproving fashion.[1] But its symptoms have rarely been carefully examined in any detail. Rather, they are simplistically and repeatedly identified as unquestionable evidence of the commodification of architectural discourse that is by now routinely associated with "postmodernism." In the most developed of such arguments, architectural discourse is not understood as postmodern simply because of the concern some of its participants might have with eclectic practices of decoration. Rather, it is the way the discourse itself operates as a form of superstructural decoration in contemporary society— despite architecture's ostensibly structural relationship to the dominant economic forces, given the amount of resources it inevitably mobilizes. This decorative role is portrayed as a loss of political agency, or, more precisely, the loss of a critical political agency in favor of a relentlessly conservative maintenance of given power relations. The conservatism of the discipline is not identified with the static nature of its forms, its conservation of an aesthetic or technological tradition, but rather with its fluidity, its capacity to circulate and recirculate heterogeneous forms in response to the eccentric rhythms of a fickle market. Architecture's complicity with the most transient aspects of commodity culture is seen to parallel and support its apparently tangential cultural role—one whose very tangentiality masks a fundamental complicity, a passivity that actively preserves suspect socioeconomic structures. Its fashion-conscious concern for "the look" that can be sold to an empowered client assumes political force, sustaining both the overt and covert mechanisms of that empowerment.

It is in these terms that the discipline of architecture is seen to participate in the general phenomenon of postmodernism, understood as a collapse of the millennial discourses organized around the unified subject, originality, authorship, identity, and so on. Each of these threatened values is identified with a sense of interior.

The phenomenon is no more than a crisis of interiority in which a whole series of supposedly stable interior values are displaced onto seemingly ephemeral exterior surfaces. Indeed, it is often explicitly described as a fetishistic obsession with surface at the expense of (what was once understood as) a concern for material and economic structure. It should go without saying that this generic description becomes all too literally applied when architecture is described as postmodern inasmuch as it is dedicated to the production and reproduction of fashionable surfaces. But it is important to note that this generic account is not simply applied to architecture. On the contrary, architecture is its paradigm. Since 1984, almost all the influential writers on the question of the postmodern, whether for, against, or sideways, have addressed architecture in order to elaborate their position, arguing that not only is it the field in which the term first gained currency but also that it articulates the phenomenon more clearly than any other. Architecture has become the vehicle of both the celebration and condemnation of the so-called postmodern condition.

Indeed, it can be argued that the construction of the very category "postmodern" turns on a certain account of architecture, or, more precisely, a certain account of "modern" architecture. Contemporary trends in diverse fields, trends which threaten the very identity of those fields, are contrasted with the rejection of decorative surface by modern architects in favor of fundamental social structure. Images of white buildings by Le Corbusier are surprisingly often used to exemplify this social project. The rejection of nineteenth-century eclectic styles in favor of the clean-edged smooth white surface is used as a model for the contemporary critic's own rejection of postmodernism. In a quirky, but common, form of transference, the apparent rejection of particular forms by a particular historical avant-garde is tacitly extended into a model for the contemporary rejection of the means by which forms are reproduced, circulated, and consumed in the, by now, electronic marketplace. The white surface is deployed, as it were, against surface. It apparently neutralizes the seductions of surface exploited by postmodernism and thereby makes available the structural issues that the fashionable play with external effects is designed to cover.

These images of white walls are usually installed without discussion, as if they have a unique ability to exemplify the complex arguments they punctuate. Their pale, almost ghostly surface haunts the discourse like a spectral guarantee of some unspoken order. The polemical struggle over the contemporary economy of fashion is somehow underwritten by these less than innocent images. And when that discourse, as it were, returns to architecture, their already complicated role is, at the very least, further convoluted. Or, more precisely, some of the convolutions that already structure architectural discourse become evident. The strategic status of these images is transformed. Some of their already strange effects become even stranger, while others are normalized in institutionally crucial ways. Likewise, the argument about the general phenomenon of fashion that the images supposedly secure is displaced and other arguments emerge that, in turn, open up new readings of architecture.

To even begin to address the complex role that fashion plays in the contemporary commodification of architecture, we must return to the sense of modern architecture that is seen to precede it. In particular, we must return to the white wall and scratch its surface to see, as they say, exactly what it is made of.

THE FASHION POLICE

Modern architecture was indeed explicitly launched against fashion, and its white surfaces played a key role in that attack. Its very modernity was repeatedly identified with the rejection of architecture's nineteenth century immersion in the world of fashion. As the movement's most influential manifesto—*Vers une architecture*, published by Le Corbusier in 1925—puts it, the "styles" of nineteenth century architecture are but "the old clothes of a past age,"[2] clothes that "are to architecture what a feather is on a woman's head; it is sometimes pretty, though not always, and never anything more."[3] For Le Corbusier, it is not just that this feminine clothing is a superfluous accessory added to the body of architecture, a decorative mask irresponsibly changed according to the dictates of the latest fashion. Even the organization of the building's structure that such fashions mask has been subjected to the seasonal mentality of fashion, since "architects work in 'styles' or discuss questions of structure in and out of season."[4] But with the relentless emergence of new technologies that both mark and instigate modernity, the old clothes no longer even fit the body: "construction has undergone innovations so great that the old 'styles,' which still obsess us, can no longer clothe it; the materials employed evade the attentions of the decorative artist."[5] It would seem that modern architecture literally begins with the removal of the florid fashionable clothing of the nineteenth century. The first act of modernization strips architecture and the second disciplines the structure that has been exposed. Both are explicitly understood as acts against the suspect forces of fashion. Modern architecture disciplines itself against fashion from the beginning.

Each of Le Corbusier's polemics is framed by such a rejection of fashion. His original manifesto for Purism, written with Amédée Ozenfant in 1920, concludes by saying: "One could make an art of allusions, an art of fashion, based upon surprise and the conventions of the initiated. Purism strives for an art free of conventions which will utilize plastic constants and address itself above all to the universal properties of the senses and the mind."[6] The seminal "Five Points of a New Architecture," written with Pierre Jeanneret in 1927 to describe the thinking behind their houses for the Weissenhof Siedlung, begins by asserting: "Theory requires precise formulation. We are totally uninterested in aesthetic fantasies or attempts at fashionable gimmicks. We are dealing here with architectural facts which point to an absolutely new kind of building."[7] Likewise, Le Corbusier's account of the overall trajectory of his work in the 1929 introduction to the first volume of the *Oeuvre*

Complète symptomatically begins by opposing fashion:

> As I believe profoundly in our age, I continue to analyse the
> elements which are determining its character, and do not con-
> fine myself to trying to make its exterior manifestations com-
> prehensible. What I seek to fathom is its deeper, its construc-
> tive sense. Is not this the essence, the very purpose of archi-
> tecture? Differences of style, the trivialities [*frivolités*] of pass-
> ing fashion, which are only illusions or masquerades, do not
> concern me.[8]

The text then literally applies this generic image of fashion—as
the exterior mask of an age that contradicts or dissimulates its
inner structure—to buildings. The inner truth of modern construction is opposed to the exterior lie of the decorative masquerade that
conceals it. The mask worn by a building veils its construction
both by literally covering it and by misrepresenting it. But it is not
simply the disorderly surfaces of ornament that pose a serious
threat. Rather, it is their concealment of an internal disorder. Le
Corbusier goes on to cite his mentor Auguste Perret's claim that
ornament "always hides some fault of construction." Indeed, it is
not that the superficial ornament is necessarily disorderly. On the
contrary, it is precisely by representing a nonexistent order that the
ornament can most threaten order. As such representations are
rapidly changed according to the whims of fashion and independently of the structures they appear to articulate, this threat is
greatly intensified.

Fashion is therefore the greatest danger of ornament, the extreme
case of the ever present risk of "mere" decoration against which
architecture must be constantly disciplined. Le Corbusier predictably describes his own work as proceeding while "the architects of all countries were still busy *decorating*" but adds in paren-
theses: "whether with or without the direct application of ornament."[9] The crime of the architect-as-decorator is not simply decorating architecture by adding gratuitous ornament to it, but rendering architecture itself decorative by making it subservient to the
fickle sensibility of fashion rather than to fixed standards like

those offered by the new means of industrialized production. The risk of decoration is nothing more than a certain mobility of representation, an instability of the surface that effaces the ancient sense of order that the latest technologies unconsciously revive. The modern is advertised as the return of the transcultural and trans-historical truth that Le Corbusier repeatedly associates with the architecture of ancient Greece.

Regardless of its particular relationship to ornament, the change to a "modern" architecture has to be disassociated from a change of fashion in every detail. It must be presented as a change of an entirely different order—a difficult claim to make and one that must constantly be reasserted because it is so vulnerable to the counter-charge that nothing could be more fashionable, more *a la mode*, than "the modern." Furthermore, once architecture has changed, there cannot be very much additional mobility. Each subsequent change, no matter how minor, has to be differentiated from fashion by being tied to the logic of a fundamental break necessitated by new materials and the technologies by which they are assembled. Construction and function must be seen to immobilize and thereby subordinate all the surfaces of architecture.

Indeed, the building must somehow exhibit this subordination. Or, more precisely, its surfaces must exhibit their subordination to something hidden within them that is of a higher order. The inevitably time-bound surface must somehow exhibit timeless values. In the very name of modernity, time must be brought to a standstill. In the end, it is this exhibition of the subordinated surface, rather than an exhibition of the new means of production, that renders architecture modern. In a strange way, architecture can become modern before it fully engages with the forces of modernization. Its surfaces are not simply cleansed of ornament, the structure stripped of clothing, the layers of representation scraped off to expose the abstract forms of modern life, and so on. Rather, the surfaces are trained to represent the very process of cleansing, stripping, and scraping. The resistance to fashion is not so much achieved as constantly staged. Modern architecture is a kind of performance, both in terms of the specific details of buildings and the discourse that frames them. The white surface obviously plays a key role in this performance by announcing that the building is naked.

FIG. 2 *Sigfried Giedion (seated) with Walter Gropius, at CIAM meeting. From Siegfried Gideon,* A Decade of Contemporary Architecture *(New York: G. Wittenborn, 1954), 21.*

Much of the discourse around modern architecture can therefore be understood as an ongoing pre-emptive defence against the charge that it is itself a fashion. Fashion is portrayed as an insidious phenomenon that will inevitably return to contaminate the pure logic of architecture unless it is consciously held in check. To resist it requires a special vigilance. Most of the discourse of modern architecture is written by self-appointed watchdogs though which it constantly monitors itself, publicly censoring certain architects, building types, compositions, materials, and details as "decorative." The surfaces of both buildings and the texts that describe them are religiously scrutinized for signs of such "degeneration," "deviance," "contamination" and so on; each such term being explicitly mobilized in reference to suspect stereotypes of race, class, gender, and sexual orientation. But it is the word "fashion" that usually marks the ultimate moment of excommunication. To be branded as "merely" fashionable is to be ostracized.

This watchdog mentality is exemplified in the writings of Sigfried Giedion, the leading promoter of the movement and the very active secretary of C.I.A.M, its at once promotional and defensive—if not disciplinary—body. He describes modern architecture as the effect of an ethical refusal of the seductions of fashionable clothing in *Space, Time and Architecture: The Growth of a New Tradition*, a heavy book that was published in 1941 and immediately became the standard textbook on modern architecture for generations of architects—it was regularly updated until a revised and enlarged version of the fifth edition came out 1969, a year after his death. Like Le Corbusier, Giedion identifies the styles of nineteenth-century architecture as fashion conscious clothing, describing them as "the Harlequin dress of architecture." In so doing, he picks up the expression used by nineteenth-century critics to condemn stylistic eclecticism but argues that it refers to "a disease which is still malignant in our day," before adding, "nevertheless, beneath all the masquerade, tendencies of lasting importance lay hidden and were slowly gathering strength."[10] Underneath the dissimulating and distracting layers of fashion that cover architecture, new technologies of construction were supposedly developing. The removal of fashion is again literally identified with the removal of ornamental clothing. Without fashion, there is "no disguise of structure." Relieved of the burden of carrying a mask, structure is able to develop freely and a new architecture emerges that embodies truths of material construction and functional utility independent of the vagaries of fashion.

This argument had already been put in place by Giedion's *Bauen en Frankreich. Eisen, Eisenbeton* of 1928, which, in turn, was based on a series of articles he had published in the Berlin art journal *Der Cicerone* over the two previous years. Again, nineteenth-century architecture is seen to wear a "historical mask," which veils the emerging forms of construction that are fundamentally changing a building's mode of operation: "the new system was shrouded in the old formal decorations."[11] The endless search for "style" is dismissed as but "wrinkles on the surface," "academic encrustations," the "haut-goût" of "architectural appendages" that "suffocate the building spirit." The book attempts to "peel off an outer layer from the century" in order to expose the modernity trapped underneath this suffocating mask. It does so by looking at the various transformations of buildings that occurred before architects got a chance to wrap them up in fashionable clothes and at those parts of buildings that architects did not bother to clothe because they thought no one was looking, at the adventurous developments hidden, as Giedion puts it, "behind the scenes" of architecture. To go around and behind the architects, he examines everyday, anonymous and temporary constructions that had been put in the hands of engineers. The architects are then measured against the engineers. Their role is simply to transfer the new engineering realities to the sphere of "living space" by subordinating all surface play to the rigors of structural work, smoothing out the prematurely wrinkled skin of the building's young body, then putting that attractive body to work on new tasks.

The book is highly selective of the architects, buildings, and details with which it makes its case; praising those who, like Henri Labrouste, "saw the construction as the intimate side of architecture—the outside of buildings being mere wrapping (envelope) or skin"[12] and slighting those like the "elegant" "formalist" Rob Mallet-Stevens,[13] who apparently concern themselves only with the skin and thereby assist architecture's regression into the decorative folly of fashion. The book everywhere discriminates between progressive and regressive developments, monitoring architectural discourse like some kind of surveillance device looking for small flaws, traces of decorative play that act as tell-tale signs of a recurrence of fashion. *Space, Time and Architecture* resumes this surveillance operation, but on a much larger scale, broadening the field of inquiry and adding more and more territory with each successive edition, while remaining just as selective, if not more so. Those modernists who were previously identified with fashion, like Mallet-Stevens, are no longer even mentioned, a gesture that, as Richard Becherer has argued, was faithfully repeated by subsequent historians.[14] As the years pass, the book maintains its alert stance against any possible contamination of the cause by fashion.

It is crucial to note that this sense of fashion—operative, if not an organizing force, in so much of the discourse around modern architecture—is explicitly associated with a psychology. *Bauen en Frankreich* identifies the new reality hidden behind the dissimulating layers of ornament mobilized by fashion's obsessive logic of compulsory change with the "unconscious" of architecture: "In the 19th century, the construction only played a subconscious role. On the outside the old-fashioned pathos reigned ostentatiously. Underneath, hidden behind the facade, the foundations of all our present being took shape."[15] The story of modern architecture is the story of how this unconscious constructive reality came to the surface and "leaked out." This quasi-therapeutic narrative is continued in *Space, Time and Architecture*, which again describes modern construction technologies as "the unconscious," and elaborates the point by associating the role of the historian with that of the psychoanalyst who patiently reads the surfaces, looking at the marginal traces of everyday life for the small and easily overlooked gaps, slips and displacements that mark the relentless operation of a repressed system.[16] The book attempts to trace the way these unconscious tendencies gave rise to a new architecture by eventually forcing their way to the surface.[17]

It is only in the less obvious, usually overlooked, domain of anonymous industrial buildings, or the backs and hidden details of public buildings, that these developments occur. They necessarily occur out of sight, away from the eyes that would find them shocking and demand that they be covered with clothes. As Giedion puts it, "the moment the nineteenth century feels itself unobserved and is no longer conscious of any need for making a show, then it is truly bold."[18] Unrestricted by ill-fitting clothes designed only to please a nervous external eye, construction is finally able to emerge and transform itself. As the new forms of construction gain confidence, they are able to gradually move from the back stage to the foreground, such that "the undisguised shapes...that mark the rear and unobserved portions of railroad stations and factories begin to make themselves felt in the front walls of buildings,"[19] particularly in temporary constructions like Paxton's Crystal Palace, which, symptomatically, "aroused feelings that seemed to belong only to the world of dreams."[20] The dream-world of architecture starts to become visible. Eventually, architects are able to

world in permanent buildings in
th Peter Behrens's engagement
l slowly develops until finally,
ll of Walter Gropius's 1925/6
os itself around the corner, the
ecome the consciousness of the
hitecture arrives as such when
understood "not as unconscious
ing but as the conscious realiza-
ot that the unconscious of archi-
or even absorbed into the archi-
tect's consciousness. Rather, it has been relocated, accommodated
and disciplined.

This discipline is required because, for Giedion, the suspect desire
to adorn architecture with fashionable clothing is not produced by
a love of clothing but by an anxiety about what that clothing will
cover. The historicist clothes are not simply old garments that are
no longer necessary or fit the new body of architecture badly.
Rather, they have only recently been put on to deny that there is a
new body. *Bauen en Frankreich* specifically identifies the use of
historical clothes as a mask that is worn to cover new anxieties
about industrialization:

> The 19th century disguised its new creations with a historical
> mask, indifferently in all fields. This is just as true for archi-
> tecture as it is for industry or society. New building methods
> were invented, but they created a climate of fear which suffo-
> cated them with an uncertainty, relegating them to behind the
> scenes of stone.[22]

The apparently gratuitous changes of fashion are actually a form of
nervous resistance to the real changes going on. Hidden by the
apparently playful surfaces of eclectic decoration is the serious
fear of mechanization. As a result, "all the century's buildings
were put up with a guilty conscience or with insecurity, so to
speak."[23] Ironically, inasmuch as fashion is a symptom of the
repression of modernity, it becomes, for Giedion, an inadvertent
symptom of modernity itself. The more frenetic the changes in

clothing, the more insecurity must have been produced by modern techniques, encouraging the historian to uncover their hidden operations. For the psycho-historian, the dissimulating movements of fashion end up pointing to the very reality they attempt to conceal.

This association between fashion and insecurity is elaborated in the article "Mode oder Zeiteinstellung" ("Fashion or the Condition of the Times") that Giedion published in a 1932 issue of *Information*, the anti-fascist magazine he edited. It warns against being again "suffocated," as in the nineteenth century, by "complexes about the past" that cover up the nightmares of the present: "Insecurity and the need to come out in favor of second-hand issues only reigns everywhere. Fashion reigns everywhere in place of seriously taking sides on the issues of the age."[24] People use fashion to "shield themselves on two sides." But this defensive layer of "surface appearance" is not simply made up of old styles laid over new structures. It is also made up of new styles laid over old structures. Objects are chosen that look modern: "That is, the external formula of new products that really stem from their own time are borrowed and applied to the old body or the old mentality, just as one glues on ornament."[25] Consequently, most contemporary objects are neither old nor new. They neither promote nor resist the modern age. Rather, they replace the "condition of the times" with a persistent code of "fashionable conduct" that affects all objects, including architecture and urban design. This "intrusion of second-hand fashion in all areas of design," both produces and is produced by a profound psychological insecurity in which "we are internally divided." More precisely, "self-certainty has dwindled" and "everyone feels it in their own person."[26] Giedion actually proposes that history is the only agent of recovery from this malaise because it can provide "an overview of our ego" that tracks the way in which modern developments have already, albeit slowly, "penetrated the general consciousness" despite fashion's concerted attempt to stall them.[27] History is literally prescribed as the appropriate therapy for the neurotic addiction to fashion. By systematically uncovering the fundamental condition of modern life that lies beneath the dissimulating layers of fashion, the historian can facilitate the emergence of the "new order" without anxiety. Writing history is a form of construction rather than a commentary on it. As Giedion concludes: "Today categorizing is more important than inventing."[28] New forms are produced by reclassifying old ones.

It is not surprising, then, that such a bond between fashion and the insecurity of the modern underwrites *Space, Time and Architecture*, Giedion's explicit attempt at such a therapeutic history. The text guards itself against the darker side of industrialization as much as it guards itself against fashion: "the destruction of man's inner quiet and security has remained the most conspicuous effect of the industrial revolution. The individual goes under before the march of production; he is devoured by it."[29] Indeed, for Giedion, the threat to humanity is made emblematic by the figure of the *automaton*, the mechanized human, the unfeeling robot. Industrialization is seen to have produced a fatal split between feeling and thought, a split that would, of course, become the major theme of his extraordinary 1948 *Mechanization Takes Command*. The stac-cato attacks on fashion that punctuated Giedion's early essays were gradually propped up by a detailed analysis of the conditions that are seen to have forced the adoption of fashion as a kind of psychological defence.

This analysis was continued in Giedion's Mellon lectures, delivered at the National Gallery of Art in 1957. He looked at the origins of the arts in order to find some prehistoric condition that

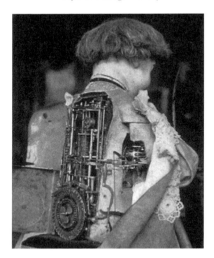

FIG. 3 *"Automaton: writing doll, made by Pierre Jaquet-Droz, Neuchatel, about 1770." From Sigfried Giedion,* Space, Time and Architecture *(Cambridge: Harvard University Press, 1941), 100.*

could be found within contemporary artistic practices, grounding their radical explosion of space and time in some fundamental condition of the human psyche. The lectures attempted to find a fixed structure that underpinned current changes and distinguished them from changes in fashion. For some years, the lectures were elaborated into manuscript form and then summarized in the inaugural Gropius lecture at Harvard in 1961 under the title "Constancy and Change in Architecture" before being published in two large volumes: *The Eternal Present: The Beginnings of Art*, which came out one year later, and *The Eternal Present: The Beginnings of Architecture*, which was published in 1964. The first volume begins by repeating the quasi-psychoanalytic claim that a history "of what has been suppressed and driven back into the unconscious," is needed to counter the "incessant demand for change for change's sake."[30] The relentless and psychologically damaging logic of fashion can only be blocked by "restoring" these buried conditions. Giedion argues that while the historical avant-garde produced radically new work, effecting an "optical revolution" that launched a "new tradition," its very newness involved the recovery of trans-historical constants, such that by the sixties "a painting of 1910 does not hurt the eye as something 'out of fashion,' something alien to the present day."[31] Furthermore, such work is understood as a weapon against fashion to be deployed in the everyday battle for psychological security. The same argument underwrites the second volume, which attempts to isolate modern architecture from fashion by grounding it in prehistory, producing a history of three "space conceptions" through the millennia in which the third one, still being produced, is seen to recover much of the first one that "develops instinctively, usually remaining in the unconscious."[32] No matter how high-tech it is, an architecture is only modern inasmuch as it reconnects anxious people to their pre-technological roots.

Giedion would go on to elaborate this history in his last book *Architecture and the Phenomenon of Transition*, whose final manuscript he delivered the day before his death in April 1968. His lifelong attempt to find a solid ground from which the restless movements of fashion could be distinguished from the necessary evolution of a new order had mobilized massive historiographic resources and produced a succession of monumental volumes that monitored a millennial field with a series of simple but globalizing arguments.[33] The surveillance operation that began on the pages of *Der Cicerone* had covered an ever-increasing territory with a methodical sweep—whose encyclopedic quality was already established with Giedion's barrage of articles for *Cahiers d'Art* between 1928 and 1934, which systematically surveyed the production of modern architecture in each country of the world—before being literalized when he was asked to do the architectural entries for *Encyclopedia Britannica* in 1957.

But, as this sheer weight of material might indicate, Giedion had long been on the defence. It is not by chance that he was reaching back as far as the Egyptians for security at the very moment that he was adding a new introduction to the final edition of *Space, Time and Architecture* that portrays contemporary architecture as having to purge itself of fashion in the same way as it had at the turn of the century. Modern architecture is seen to have regressed into a form of stylistic eclecticism resembling that of the nineteenth century which it had worked so hard to displace. He condemns the new "fashions" of the architecture of the sixties that, after the International Style "fashion" had "worn thin," exhibit a "tendency to degrade the wall with new decorative elements."[34] The purity of modern architecture has not merely given way to the immoral excesses of the sixties that disfigure the smooth white wall. Rather, modern architecture has itself been appropriated as a fashionable style of "*en vogue*" superficialities. Insisting that modern architecture is "not a sudden, quickly devalued, fashion,"[35] Giedion defends the original polemic of his own textbook from appropriation as a set of fashion tips.

In so doing, he echoes his original defense of the first polemic on the subject—Otto Wagner's 1896 manifesto *Modern Architecture*— which, like *Space, Time, and Architecture*, was, as Giedion put it, "soon translated into many languages" and "became the textbook of the new movement." Just as he had defended that manifesto against the critics who claimed when it was first published that Wagner was "a sensation-monger, a train-bearer of fashion,"[36] Giedion resists the possibility that his own attempt to detach fashion from architecture is nothing more than the preparation for a new fashion. In fact, he had already defended modern architecture against the threat of dismissal as a new fashion in a newspaper article of 1927 entitled "Ist das neue Bauen eine Mode?" ("The New Building, is it a Fashion?")[37] The argument about fashion written into all of his work is, from the beginning, at once an attack and a defence.

The double-sided quality of Giedion's engagement with the question of fashion is exemplary of the whole discourse. The very same identification of fashion with a generalized psychopathology of insecurity in the face of modernity can be found throughout the promotion of modern architecture. And it is not that this generic argument is simply applied to the ready-made forms of that architecture, or even used to supervise their construction. Rather, modern architecture is constituted as such by that very argument. The argument produces what it appears to merely describe. Giedion, for example, does not pretend that his writing simply offers a commentary on an existing tendency, acknowledging, with his very first lines, that he actively constructs that tendency as such because the historian inevitably rearranges the past in the light of present conceptions and "the backward look transforms its object."[38] In an extraordinary gesture, the reader of *Space, Time and Architecture* is first taken through a lengthy chapter on the active role of history in both everyday life and the production of architecture. But perhaps only the acknowledgement that this is the case is unique. The larger discourse, and the events that it addresses, including the specific details of architectural designs, are likewise structured by particular arguments about fashion. In fact, the fashion argument has a unique privilege, a special hold on the protagonists, a vice-like grip on the discourse which appears to employ it only occasionally, if not tacitly.

If modern architecture haunts contemporary debates then it is itself haunted by the specter of fashion. Fashion provides the basic frame of the discourse, its limit condition. While the phenomenon is rarely, if ever, analyzed as such, and the term itself is only occasionally invoked to reestablish the limits, the space of modern architecture is defined by its exclusion of fashion. Furthermore, fashion is everywhere inscribed within the very system it delimits. Throughout Le Corbusier's canonic writings, for example, the rhetoric of "eternal truth," "spirit," "work," "order," "vigorous," "erect," "virginal," "rational," "standard," "essential," "honest," "life," "deep," "internal," and so on, is routinely opposed to that of "disorder," "chaos," "congestion," "intoxication," "play," "dishonesty," "illusion," "weakness," "sentimental," "trivial," "lies," "prostitution," "caprice," "arbitrary," "dishonesty," "death," "cosmetic," "seduction," "superficial," "veneer," "fake," "substitute," "superficiality," and so on. Each in the latter set of terms, which are always used to mark that which his work attempts to resist, is, in the end, and at symptomatic moments (whose specificity needs to be carefully analyzed in detail), identified with fashionable clothing styles. Fashion is always the key.

Still, these isolated identifications offer but a preliminary map of the complex network of associations between clothing and architecture that underpin Le Corbusier's texts, organizing them—even if often against their apparent grain. The line of argument about fashion only occasionally becomes evident because it is twisted, folded over on itself in an eccentric geometry, a series of knots that, in their very convolution, tie together the discourse on modern architecture. It is not the overt argument about fashion that structures the texts but the complications of that argument, complications that rarely become visible as such. These complications, which not only bind Le Corbusier's texts together but also bind them to other texts in architecture and in other disciplines, profoundly disrupt traditional accounts of the so-called Modern Movement. It is only by actively neglecting them that those accounts have been able to sustain certain suspect institutional structures. And it is only by reopening the question of fashion that these structures can begin to be interrogated.

CLOSET OPERATIVES

Clearly, the enigmatic argument about fashion that underwrites modern architecture needs to be patiently tracked through its conceptual variations and historical specificity in much more detail to comprehend its considerable strategic effects. But how exactly should this be done? Fashion is never simply an object that can be scrutinized by a detached theory. The phenomenon, if that is what it is, can never be detached from the way it is read. Just as Le Corbusier passes seamlessly from describing himself as a kind of archeologist of his own time who recovers the inner logic of the age by going beyond the outer layers of fashion, to describing his work as being likewise stripped of fashionable ornament, Giedion's account of the modern architect is exactly the same as the account of the historian that precedes it. Supposedly, both the architect and the historian strip their objects of fashion. The opening chapter of *Space, Time, and Architecture* clarifies the therapeutic mission of history that had been prescribed in "Mode oder Zeiteinstellung?" by describing the task of the historian as clearing away the layers of fashion to discover the elemental truth they conceal and building a structure devoid of misleading superficial detail. The historian must distinguish between the "transitory facts" and "constituent facts" that are usually "intermingled" in each site of investigation. Transitory facts are those with the seductive "dash and glitter" of fashions whose surface disorder must not be confused with the inner order of constituent facts, which, "when they are suppressed, inevitably reappear":

> [the historian] can tell more or less short-lived novelties from genuinely new trends...At first appearance they may have all the éclat and brilliance of a firework display, but they have no greater durability. Sometimes they are interlaced with every refinement of fashion...These we shall call transitory facts.

> Transitory facts in their dash and glitter often succeed
> in taking over the center of the stage. This was the case
> with the experiments in historical styles that went on—
> with infinite changes in direction—throughout the whole
> nineteenth century.[39]

Here, as everywhere else, Giedion does not so much talk about fashion as invoke it. What is fashionable is, by definition—a definition that does not have to be offered—bad. The successive generations of historians of modern architecture have presupposed the same condemnation of fashion, sharing it with the historical figures they describe. More precisely, they share it with the historical figures that they have constructed. It is in this way that they are, in the end, "operative" in Manfredo Tafuri's sense. In the very moment of asserting their neutrality under the guise of scholarly detachment, they insist on a particular ideological formation by projecting present values onto the past in order to project them into the future.[40] Even Tafuri, for whom Giedion is the very model of the operative critic, is "operative" by virtue of the way he positions fashion as an unproblematically pejorative term. Indeed, it can be argued that the very concept of "operative criticism" is itself operative inasmuch as the strategic abuse of history it refers to is aligned with fashion.

When Tafuri's influential *Theories and Histories of Architecture* introduced the category of operative criticism in 1968 precisely to counter it, a footnote identifies its most degenerate forms as those organized by fashion: "One cannot sufficiently condemn the naive or snobbish attempt to read historical phenomena by 'present' yardsticks of those, who, for the sake of feeling 'alive' and up-to-date, reduce critical transvaluation to exhibitionism and fashion."[41] This opposition between history and fashion, which he symptomatically shares with the openly operative Giedion,[42] is exhibited in the opening lines, which identify the book's task as that of mapping the specific "obstacles" facing "historians who refuse the role of fashionable commentator, and who try to historicize their criticism."[43] These obstacles, in turn, are identified in the book's introduction with the unavoidable contradictions at work in the very idea of a history of the modern, given the ostensibly anti-historical stance of modern architects. When noting that contemporary architectural tendencies actually maintain this stance "behind the mask" of the new myths used to distance themselves from the avant-garde, Tafuri preserves the traditional opposition between a history that is critical in that it "digs deeper" and one "swallowed up by the daily mythologies," understood as fashionable masks:

> The present moment, so totally bent on avoiding, through *new myths*, the commitment of understanding the present, cannot help turning even the researches that, with renewed vigor and rigor, try to plan a systematic and objective reading of the world, of things, of history and of human conventions into *fashion and myth*.[44]

Tafuri actively resists the possibility, embedded within his own text, that what actually bonds contemporary practices to those of the avant-garde might not be what lies behind the fashionable mask but the fashionable mask itself. This resistance is tested when the text later addresses the affinity between what seems to be a fashionably historicist use of "architectural images" by the Neo-Liberty school in Italy and the anti-historical stance of the modern movement it appears to emphatically reject. But the affinity is quickly described as being "underneath an immediately fashionable phenomenon"[45] rather than at the same level. The "garish" "farce" of Neo-Liberty that the text symptomatically identifies with Art Nouveau, the Baroque, and Fellini; and whose "equivocal quality" parallels the bourgeoisie's "own evasive costume," is seen to occur "on the fringe" of the modern project rather than contradicting or opposing it.[46] But it is seen to participate in that project because it only "flirts" with history and fails in its attempted "fetishism" of the architectural object, while leaving unquestioned the avant-garde's own fetishistic flirtations. Furthermore, what Neo-Liberty merely appears to reject is not the avant-garde itself but the consequence of its transformation into a fashionable form of eclecticism with the so-called International Style. In this way, modern architecture is doubly immunized against prosecution on the charge of fashion.[47]

Likewise, the book attempts to negotiate the specific terms of the same immunity for the historian, looking for the ways in which research can avoid becoming "another transient fashion under the flag of evasion,"[48] even if that involves a sustained silence.[49] The historical avant-garde acts here, as it does for so many contemporary writers, as the model of Tafuri's own practice. Consequently, it is exempted from certain interrogations that might threaten that practice, even in the middle of such a comprehensive and nuanced reading. Despite the book's constant call for a vigilantly self-critical stance like that supposedly assumed by the avant-garde, its analysis is, from the beginning, vulnerable to its own arguments about operative criticism. It is surprisingly reluctant to acknowledge the institutional practices it leaves intact, if not tacitly defends, most of which have survived the subsequent transformations in Tafuri's work. Despite the invaluable insights of his at times explicitly Nietszchean accounts of the ruses of history, his equally sophisticated accounts of the complex economies of the mask operating in different historical sites are never quite extended to his own practices as a historian, or even to those of his practices that he later emphatically rejects.[50] Nietzsche's own refusal of a distinction between fashion and history is never mobilized. On the contrary. Ten years after he distances himself from the final edition of *Theories and History of Architecture*, Tafuri is still able to criticize the work of postmodern architects because "history has been reduced to fashion" and, like Giedion, he associates this with "anxiety" and "the sense of insecurity."[51] The term "fashion" retains its old disciplinary role in his argument, as it does throughout the economy of architectural theory that he is analyzing.

Indeed, later generations of "critical" writers have preserved this role for the term, deploying it at key points in their analysis without ever subjecting it to that analysis. The critical writer is understood to be, by definition, detached from fashion. Alternative modes of scholarship that are skeptical of the possibility of such a detached position are themselves often dismissed as "fashionable," "chic," "modish," and so on by proponents of well established modes of research who presuppose that fashion is inherently bad and have difficulty recognizing their own adherence to one mode amongst others, let alone acknowledging the structural role of fashion in those sections of the archives that they privilege. As a disciplinary concept, fashion itself necessarily remains untheorized. To address the question of fashion here, as anywhere else, will necessarily be to address the role of theory. To address "Architecture: In Fashion" will necessarily be to re-address the role of theory in the constitution of architecture.

But can one suggest here that any inquiry into fashion must reform or deflect the modes of inquiry, if not tease the limits of a discipline that constitutes itself by ostensibly rejecting fashion, whether that discipline be that of architecture or scholarly argument in general, without having that very suggestion either uncritically embraced by certain well defined groups of readers or uncritically censored by other groups as too fashionable? Probably not. And wouldn't a rigorous interrogation of fashion, whatever that might mean, be rigorous only insofar as it confused the distinctions between such groups? Probably.

Anyway, it goes without saying that no discourse can simply isolate itself from fashion. At the very least, one is bound to ask here whether the question of fashion is now a fashionable question. To what extent does the very posing of the question commit us to a particular fashion regardless of our ostensible position on the subject? Either way, a more detailed (and fashion is, of course, always a question of details) account of fashion and its multiple and often conflicting relationships with architecture is needed. In the end, it is a question of the precise way that fashion is usually "intermingled," as Giedion says of the "dash and glitter" of transitory facts, with what seems to be its other. To scratch the white surface here will therefore be to look for the ways in which it is constructed out of the very operations of fashion whose exclusion it supposedly

confirms. To show, that is, that the white surface glitters—dazzling
its audience in a way that fosters a series of bizarre, but extremely
influential, collective hallucinations.

MODERN ARCHITECTURE AS CLOTHING

After all, the stripping of fashionable clothes, advertised by both
the original promoters of modern architecture and its contemporary
dealers, is not simply a stripping of all clothing. While everyone
seems to be everywhere concerned with the beauty and purity of
the naked body, modern architecture itself is not naked. From the
beginning, it is painted white. And this white layer that proclaims
that the architecture it covers is naked clearly has an extraordinarily ambiguous role. Supposedly, it is inserted into the space once
occupied by clothing, without being clothing as such. But, symptomatically, the nature of that insertion is not addressed by the historiography. The white surface is almost completely ignored by the
very historians whose attack on fashion it is meant to exemplify.
The scholars are blind to it, or they are blinded by it.

In fact, it is typically only books aimed at a general readership,
rather than a specialized architectural audience, that address the
white surface, let alone criticize it. Lionel Brett's 1947 contribution on houses to the book series entitled *The Things We See*,
which aims "to encourage us to look at the objects of everyday life
with fresh and critical eyes," for example, has a section called
"Clothing" that accompanies an image of some generically modern
apartment houses with the following text:

> The skeleton thus poised upon the ground must next be
> clothed, and the purpose of this clothing, like any other, is
> partly protective, partly decorative...But by the twentieth cen-
> tury the traditional ways of dressing-up a building had become
> stale; every possible way had been disinterred and rein-
> terred...Ornament was banished...Houses, like their occu-
> pants, flaunted their anatomy, and while some had beautiful

bodies that (while they remained young) delighted the passer-by, others had not. Any kind of clothing for the bare concrete seemed dishonest. Pure white was *de rigueur*, partly because of its exciting novelty, partly because it emphasized the smoothly mechanical texture, and pointed the contrast between it and surrounding nature.[52]

But Brett immediately calls this white surface into question, showing an image of a pristine modern house upon its completion alongside one whose white paint is peeling off after a few years. The white wall is seen to have "presented a surface which could neither be cleaned nor happily left to weather. The modern house arrived in a blaze of glory and after a brief summer of astonishing beauty faded like a flower in the frost."[53] It is precisely this fragility that mainstream architectural discourse attempts to avoid. Not simply to protect the white surfaces from further abrasion, but in order to protect certain institutional assumptions. The delicate layer of paint holds together a social and conceptual structure that is not exposed when it cracks or flakes. After all, no matter how thin the coat of paint is, it is still a coat. It is not simply inserted in the space vacated by clothing. It is itself a very particular form of clothing. And by sustaining a logic of clothing, modern architecture participates in the very economy from which it so loudly announces its detachment. At the very least, the sustained attack on fashion has to be carefully distinguished here from an attack on clothing.

Indeed, as I have suggested elsewhere, the "Law of Ripolin" with which Le Corbusier rationalizes his choice of the smooth white surface is actually a modification of Adolf Loos's "Law of Dressing" that is, in turn, a modification of Gottfried Semper's mid-nineteenth century "Principle of Dressing," a principle that makes architecture not merely analogous to clothing but an art of clothing from its beginnings, or, more precisely, the very origin of clothing itself.[54] In these terms, modern architecture is nothing more than a particular form of clothing. To understand the precise relationship between this clothing and the psychic and material economies of fashion, it is necessary to trace the elusive role of Semper's identification of architecture and dress right up into the formulation of high modern architecture in the 1920s, following closely its seemingly relentless trajectory through the discourse as it affects, and even organizes, diverse and well-known formulations—many of which might appear, at first, to contradict it.

Firstly, we must take account of the direct influence of Semper's argument. Take, for example, Louis Sullivan and Adolf Loos, the two so-called father figures of modern architecture who are repeatedly and simplistically identified with the two dominant advertising slogans of the movement: "form follows function" and "ornament is a crime." In each case, Semper's arguments are evident in both the architect's writings and designs. Not only does Loos explicitly formulate his "Law of Dressing" as a slight modification of Semper's "Principle of Dressing" but he repeatedly identifies architecture with clothing design throughout his many essays, defending this association in the decisive "Architecture" essay of 1910 by paraphrasing Semper's basic premise:

> Many will have had doubts over my last remarks, doubts which are directed against the comparison which I have drawn between tailoring and architecture. After all, architecture is an art. Granted, it is for the time being. But have you never noticed the strange correspondence between the exterior dress of people and the exterior of buildings? Is the tasselled robe not appropriate to the Gothic Style and the wig to the Baroque?[55]

Likewise, Sullivan participated in the circle that studied, translated, and published Semper's theory in Chicago.[56] Its effects on his writing—in its specific privileging of ornament—and his work—in its fabric-like weaving of ornamental surfaces—is obvious,[57] as it is in the work of his apprentices Frank Lloyd Wright and Walter Burley Griffin (when working in partnership with Wright's assistant Marion Mahony). It even becomes a kind of manifesto in Sullivan's use of "tapestry brick" arranged to give the building a finely textured surface like that, as he puts it, of an

Louis Sullivan. Carlson Pirie Scott Department Store (1899–1904), as original- **FIG.4a-d**
ly published in Architectural Record, *16: 1 (July 1904), 58.*
Detail of CPS fenestration. Illustration from Sigfried Giedion, Space, Time and
Architecture, *312., with the caption, "Outstanding for strength and purity of
expression even in the work of Louis Sullivan."*
Detail of CPS fenestration, from Juan Pablo Bonta, Architecture and its
Interpretation *(New York: Rizzoli, 1979), 97.*
*Detail of the ornamental patterns along the reveal of an upper story window,
from Joseph Siry,* Carlson Pirie Scott: Louis Sullivan and the Chicago
Department Store *(Chicago: the University of Chicago Press, 1988), 231.*

"oriental rug," and Wright and Griffin/Mahony's simultaneous development of "textile" construction systems. In each case, the decorative surface is literally woven into a structural frame for the building or, rather, the structure itself is woven into a decorative pattern. After all, Semper's argument does not simply privilege ornament. It equally involves the clarification of the structural frame.

Indeed, it can be argued that it is precisely the influence of Semper that leads to Loos and Sullivan's stereotypically modern call for a stripping of ornament. Loos visited Sullivan during the time that he was studying Semper, initiating a lifelong correspondence of mutual admiration, and later, as is often pointed out, based his infamous "Ornament and Crime" essay (1908) on Sullivan's well known "Ornament in Architecture" essay (1892), which proposes a moratorium on ornament in favor of "nude" buildings.[58]

As "fathers," Loos and Sullivan are, of course, treated ambiguously by the historiographers of modern architecture. Giedion is clearly nervous about both of them. This nervousness is arguably produced by their debt to Semper, which commits them at once to ornament and to its reduction, making them both exemplars of the modern project and historical figures who must be held apart from that project lest their ambiguity contaminate and irreducibly complicate the formulation of a marketable canon. While this early isolation has been successively renegotiated as each figure—and the image of modern architecture with which they are both held in ambiguous tension—is repeatedly reconstructed, the nervousness remains. While images of Loos's Villa Steiner and Sullivan's Carlson Pirie Scott building (Figs. 4a–d), for example, still populate most of the standard histories and cement certain key transitions in the respective arguments, the images almost always show the undecorated white orthogonal rear of the villa and privilege the orthogonal frame faced with white terra cotta tiles of the department store, rather than the curved front (let alone the more ornate interior) of the former or the heavily ornamented ground floors and entrance of the latter. Giedion goes as far as to insist that the curve of the entrance was imposed on Sullivan by his client and publishes a second image that zooms in to exclude all the ground-floor decoration and leave only the white surfaces above. The successive readings of each figure have depended on holding these tendencies apart, maintaining, as it were, the thin line between simple, abstract, white surfaces and complex, sensuous, colored decoration, a line that seems to be actually marked across the face of Sullivan's building.[59] But this task has proved increasingly difficult. In the end, the line is not so straight. If Giedion had zoomed in even further, his canonic image would have revealed that the white frame actually participates in an extraordinarily dense ornamental scheme. Indeed, the icons carry a specific threat to the canon they supposedly represent: the threat raised by Semper's argument that the clean white abstract frame cannot in the end be separated from the very decorative play it appears to have decisively neutralized.

After all, Sullivan's call for the removal of ornament is not a call for the eradication of ornament. On the contrary, it is an attempt to rationalize the building precisely to better clothe it with ornamentation that is more appropriate and more carefully produced, such that "our strong, athletic and simple forms will carry with natural ease the raiment of which we dream, and that our buildings thus clad in a garment of poetic imagery, half hid as it were in choice products of loom and mine, will appeal with redoubled power."[60] Sullivan goes on to say that, despite the "fashion" to consider ornament as something that can be either added or removed from a building, ornament can never simply be separated from the structure it clothes, regardless of how decorative or plain the building is, or of the merely contingent fact that it might be applied later in the process of construction. The woven ornamental surface, which he elsewhere calls "the fabric of a dream, a fabric of enduring reality," produces the spirit of the building rather than receiving it from the structure. Likewise, in 1924, Loos writes "Ornament und Erziehung" ("Ornament and Education"), a follow-up to

"Ornament and Crime," to correct those who took it to advocate the banning of ornament.[61] Both of them closely follow Semper's own call for a tactical reduction of ornament that would in the end liberate it from the structure it is meant to cover and subordinate, allowing one to "devote oneself lovingly to the innocent needlepoint of decoration,"[62] a convoluted but decisive argument that at once organizes and deeply threatens the discourse of modern architecture.

The, by now institutionalized, nervousness in the face of this threat points to the more oblique, and perhaps ultimately more decisive, undercurrent of Semper's "Principle of Dressing" in architectural discourse, as it passes through the complex filter of one of Loos's contemporaries, the Viennese art historian Alois Riegl, who at once promotes and counters Semper's thinking. Riegl had an extremely strong influence on the so-called "pioneers" of modern architecture. His 1893 treatise *Stilfragen* ("The Problem of Style: Foundations for a History of Ornament") presents itself as an attempt to counter the "materialist interpretation of the origin of the art" promoted in the 1860s by writers who wrongly associated it with Semper. Arguing that Semper never privileged material technique and function over art,[63] the text attempts to restore the privilege of ornament over structure, acknowledging that it is merely echoing Semper's basic "proposition" when asserting: "It is the urge to decorate that is one of the most elementary of human drives, more elementary in fact than the need to protect the body,"[64] and footnoting the passages of Semper's *Der Stil* that argue that buildings were produced and elaborated before any clothes—the very passages upon which Semper based his central argument that architecture is itself nothing more than a form of clothing. Riegl does not counter this claim. On the contrary, it is precisely Semper's "theory of dressing as the origin of all monumental architecture" that persuades him that Semper was not simply a materialist as his followers had interpreted. Nevertheless, Riegl's relationship with that argument is ambivalent. In fact, he identifies the basic project of his book as playing down the importance of textiles and clothing by countering Semper's use of the production of clothing as a general theory of all art. Textiles and clothing are now to be understood as but a subset of the general category of "surface decoration."[65]

But while textiles and clothing do literally appear as mere subsections of the text, it is crucial to note that Riegl (who began his career as the keeper of the textile collection at the Museum of Art and Industry in Vienna and whose first two books were on textiles) is actually employing Semper's argument in the very act of criticizing it. It is Semper, after all, who argues that the basic role of clothing is not physical protection but surface decoration. For him, all decoration is clothing. Through a kind of transference, or, rather, countertransference, Riegl ends up taking over Semper's argument—and the whole logic of the internal elaboration of ornamental motifs that follows from it—in the guise of dismissing it. In reducing the importance of textiles, he clearly reduces the importance of the specific technology of decoration that Semper privileges as the origin of all decoration, but he does not reduce the importance of clothing as such. The "law of *kunstwollen*" he formulates is not simply substituted for that of dressing. Rather, the conceptualization of dressing is suppressed only to resurface throughout his writing in a displaced form.

It is precisely through this kind of displacement that Semper's thinking, without being acknowledged as such, infiltrates much of the discourse around modern architecture—even organizing many of those texts that explicitly claim to counter his views. In its displaced form, the clothing argument is very elusive but all the more decisive in its effects. Ironically, it can be argued that Riegl became influential in architectural discourse precisely because his view, unlike Semper's, subordinates architecture and thereby sustains a tradition fundamental to that discourse. While Riegl accepts the idea that clothing is the origin of architecture, he rejects the idea that it is the origin of all the arts. Architecture, as an art of clothing, is a merely a subsection of art rather than, as Semper maintains, its mother. But—and this is the twist crucial to the institutional politics of the discipline—this subsection is then given unique exemplary power.[66] It is architecture that is seen to exemplify the condition of art. When Riegl repeats the argument about Semper in his *Late Roman Art Industry* of 1901, he goes on to assert that the laws of *kunstwollen* are best revealed in architecture.[67] Following the strange dynamics, at once conceptual and institutional, that have always organized the architectural discipline, the clothing that is architecture becomes the paradigm of a general theory in which it is actually subordinated.

Not surprisingly, Riegl's ambivalence about Semper made its way into architectural discourse. In fact, the ambivalence assumed a specific strategic effect, a disciplinary function without which "Modern Architecture" could not be constituted as such. Despite the fact that he saw himself as waging a largely unsuccessful campaign against the materialist position, Riegl was extraordinarily influential on architectural discourse. This influence is particularly evident in the various institutions from which modern architecture is seen to emerge, like the Vienna Secession, the German Werkbund, the Bauhaus, and so on. His arguments are explicitly cited by figures as diverse as Otto Wagner, Henry van de Velde, Hermann Muthesius, Walter Gropius, Peter Behrens, Richard Neutra, and Ludwig Hilbesheimer, to name but a few. Typically, they deploy Riegl's rejection of materialism against the kind of extreme functionalism or structural rationalism that the canonic accounts of modern architecture promote as the very core of the movement, even though those accounts are supposedly based on their work. In fact, it is precisely their resistance to the cartoon accounts of the modern pushed by the successive generations of propagandists that allows clothing argument to be smuggled into the basic thinking of modern architecture. And it is only by systematically playing down this resistance, in order to avoid certain enigmas of functionalism, that the strategic role of the argument has been overlooked. After all, the unique capacity of architecture to exemplify the transcendence of material by art to which Riegl refers is, in the end, its Semperian capacity to mask that materiality, to clothe the body of the building with art, since architecture is, from the beginning, nothing more than an art of clothing, or, rather, the very art of clothing itself.

The rejection of "materialism" is most explicitly spelled out by Peter Behrens, who is routinely identified as the first architect to successfully apply the signature of the artist to previously anonymous industrial structures. In his 1910 lecture "Art and Technology," he argues for a "battle" against the emerging credo of function, materiality and technology, crediting it, and the associated call for the excessive reduction of decoration, to the influence of Semper's theories, citing Riegl's critique in order to claim the architect's superiority over the engineer.[68] In this complicated maneuvre, the basics of Semper's argument are again transferred into Riegl's name and its misreadings are transferred to Semper's name.[69] By being, like Riegl, ambivalent about whether the fault lies with Semper or his disciples, Behrens is able to maintain a commitment to both technology and art's capacity to transcend the materiality of that technology. Riegl's argument is particularly attractive since it establishes a place for the architect in an industrialized world that threatens to make such a figure redundant.

And this position is not simply passed over with the formation of high modernism. On the contrary, it defines it. Gropius faithfully repeats the argument in his famous 1913 essay "The Development of Modern Industrial Architecture," which singles out Behrens's factory design.[70] Then Giedion, who seems to privilege the engineer and the new modes of construction more than anyone else, applies the same argument to Gropius himself. When he identifies Gropius's Bauhaus building as the paradigmatic work of the newly conscious modern architect, it is not due to the dominance of function in it but to its domination of function. In this moment of enlightened self-consciousness, in which architecture finally becomes as modern as the society it is designed for, the realm of construction governed by the unconscious engineer is transcended by the sense of art unique to the architect: "In this building Gropius goes far beyond anything that might be regarded as an

achievement in construction alone."[71] The decorative surfaces frenetically manipulated by fashion up to that point have not simply
been abandoned in favor of the self-evident rigors of structure.
Rather, the structural unconscious is mastered by the architect,
disciplined by art. Function is no longer the source of art but
something that must be tamed by it.

Giedion eventually credits Riegl with this argument. In 1962, his
The Eternal Present: The Beginnings of Art identifies Semper as the
source of the "materialist" argument summed up in the expression
"form follows function," in which art history was "trapped" until
Riegl identified its "crippling influence."[72] Two years later, this
claim is elaborated further when *The Eternal Present: The
Beginnings of Architecture*, which organizes itself around Riegl's
analysis of space, argues that "few conceptions have been so fruit-
ful for research in art history as his conception of the *kunstwollen*.
This was the battering-ram used against the materialist aesthetic of
Gottfried Semper, which had held the stage for sixty years."[73]
Giedion's analysis is everywhere indebted to Riegl. In fact, he
repeatedly argues that all he is doing is updating Riegl's accurate
history of two space conceptions by adding a third one that only
started to emerge after Riegl's analysis was published. Throughout
his writings, he echoes Riegl by insisting that architecture is the
spiritual transcendence of material conditions.

Clearly, much of Le Corbusier's writing is devoted to establishing
the same position (although its sources in German discourse—let
alone art history—are, of course concealed). The rhetoric of function and structure is invariably covered by an argument about art.
The opening pages of *Towards an Architecture*, for example,
rehearse exactly the same argument about the engineer and the
architect in the face of the architect's apparent redundancy in the
modern world, concluding, in typically propagandist style:

> Finally, it will be a delight to talk of ARCHITECTURE after
> so many grain-stores, workshops, machines and sky-scrapers.
> ARCHITECTURE is a thing of art, a phenomenon of the emo-
> tions lying outside questions of construction and beyond them.
> The purpose of construction is TO MAKE THINGS HOLD
> TOGETHER; of architecture TO MOVE US.[74]

In these famous pages, the fundamental difference between the engineer and the architect has to do with the "look." It is by satisfying the eye that the materiality of buildings can be transcended. While the engineer's calculations of the internal logic of structure necessarily involve a certain "taste," the architect must consider the external appearance of the forms and "reward the desire of the eyes." The machine is a model for architecture only insofar as it has already transformed the "outward appearance" of the world, a transformation that has been ignored by clients, who only ask for historical styles because they have "eyes which do not see." This concern with the look of transcended industrialization follows from Behrens's lecture, which is not so surprising given that Le Corbusier was working in Behren's office during the same year that the lecture was delivered. And, as Behrens's argument is ultimately based on Semper's account of the bond between clothing and architecture, the clothing argument has not simply disappeared. It is precisely the ultimate privileging of the external "look" over the internal structure that renders the role of the modern architect one of choosing the correct clothing for the newly industrialized body of architecture.

ADDRESSING ARCHITECTURE

The literal question of clothing does not fade away in favor of a disciplined, or, rather, disciplinary, "look." On the contrary, Behrens (like his wife Lilli) was actually designing dresses at the turn of the century. In so doing, he rigorously practiced the collapse of the traditional distinction between the high and low, fine and applied, arts, which Semper had repeatedly called for after his 1850 contact with the design circles in London, whose intense debate about the status of ornament initiated the thinking behind the Arts and Crafts movement. This thinking, which would eventually be associated with William Morris before being gradually exported to Germany, had, as Harry Mallgrave argues, an enormous and immediate impact on Semper's position. It encouraged him to privilege

FIG. 5 *Peter Behrens, house dress, 1901. From Leonie Wilckens,* Peter Behrens und Nürnberg

the "Principle of Dressing" that he had only formulated the year before, completely reversing the traditional prioritizing of fine over applied art and placing new emphasis on "style" by giving "ornament" the central role in art.[75] Likewise, Morris repeatedly argued that clothing articulates social relations, and designed fabrics and dresses accordingly. Indeed, his own work started when he joined the group of "Pre-Raphaelite" artists who were able to launch a new movement by painting women wearing particular dresses in particular interiors. Semper's and Morris's respective privileging of textiles was to have a major impact on subsequent discourse. As Giedion notes in *Mechanization takes Command,* Semper remained the key figure for the Arts and Crafts movement up until 1910. This, of course, is the year that Behrens explicitly voiced Riegl's criticism of Semper's theory but tacitly maintained that very theory, moving it, as it were, underground, but in no way weakening its influence. And not by chance is it the year that Giedion's texts repeatedly choose to mark the end of the rule of fashion.[76] In both the general commitment to applied art and the specific privilege in the arts of clothing, the Arts and Crafts movement was Semperian from the beginning. Having started as a painter and forming his own Arts and Crafts organization in 1898, Behrens's dress designs were an almost inevitable consequence of his commitment to a movement indebted to Semper's "Principle of Dressing."

Maria Sèthe and Henry van de Velde in the first floor studio of their house at **FIG. 6**
Blomenwerf, ca. 1898. Dress made in a William Morris fabric to a design by
Henry van de Velde. From Francoise Dierkens-Aubry, Art Nouveau in Belgium
(Paris: Duculot, 1981), 190.

This integration of architectural design with clothing design is even clearer in the work of another architect who was influenced by Riegl, Henry van de Velde, who faithfully imported the philosophy of Morris (publishing a book on him in 1898) and launched Art Nouveau in Belgium along with Victa Horta before distributing it in both France and Germany. Like Frank Lloyd Wright, he faithfully sustained Morris's polemic by first designing many dresses for his wife (Maria Sèthe) to match his innovative design for their own house, and then designing dresses to go with the houses he did for the clients that the house attracted. Following the Arts and Crafts tradition, which, like its gurus Morris and Semper, gives ornament a structural rather than subordinate role, van de Velde elevated ornament into the major creative force of design, arguing that it is the "heart's blood" of art and that the territory it needs to enrich includes all everyday objects, including buildings, furniture, clothing, jewelry, books, utensils, wallpaper, textiles, light fittings, and so on. The revision of dress design is understood as a necessary part of a revision of the entire environment to produce the infamous *Gesamtkunstwerk* ("total work of art"). As Karl Ernst Osthaus—whose wife wore gowns and jewelry designed by van de Velde to match the house they commissioned from him—said in 1906, a year before the house was completed: "woe to the lady who would enter such a room in a dress that was not artistically suitable."[77] But such dresses did not simply complete an ornamental scheme. Rather, the privileging of ornament is linked, from the beginning, to a certain sensibility about clothes. Clothing is not understood as an accessory to an architectural space but as its very condition.

Is this concern with clothing a concern with fashion? Van de Velde's critics certainly thought so. His opponent in the famous fight at the 1914 meeting of the German Werkbund in Cologne was Hermann Muthesius, the architect who (following the lead of Robert Dohme's *Das English Haus* of 1888) had introduced the Arts and Crafts philosophy to Germany in a long series of essays and books; who had long been an outspoken critic of fashion. In 1902, for example, his "Die Moderne Umbildung Unserer Äesthetischen Anschauungen" ("The Modern Reorganization of our Aesthetic Points of View") had condemned the relentless cycles of fashion, offering his own psychological explanation for its degenerate influence and arguing that "fashion is not limited to clothing; there are also fashions in art" which produce rapidly changing styles.[78] Repeatedly declaring Art Nouveau (and its German variation, Jugendstil) to be just such a fashionable style that had already "mummified" architecture with an excess of ornamentation, Muthesius called for a massive reduction in the amount of ornament. His promotion of the need to "discover the functional form without decoration, without ornament, without any trace of the activity of old decorative aesthetics,"[79] was based on the claim that excesses of ornamentation are always produced by fashion. Art Nouveau is seen to continue the subjection of architecture to fashion. For Muthesius,

as his "Weg und Ziel" (Means and Goal) of 1905 argues, this subjection began with the "regurgitation" of old styles in the nineteenth century. The "basic principle" of the "demand for variety
led by fashion" is to compromise utilitarian form by drowning it in
ornament.[80] The removal of this regressive layer makes available
the new art of the machine. Muthesius's "Kunst und Machine" (Art
and Machine) essay of 1902 had already extended Morris's thinking by overturning his refusal of the machine, insisting that to not
show how something is produced today is merely to produce a
degenerate form of "dressing" (*Verkleidung*).[81] To accept the new
condition of the object is to refuse to clothe it in a fashionably old-
fashioned dress, a point that was emphatically restated in
Muthesius's address on "Architektur und Publikum" (Architecture
and the Public) delivered to the 1907 International Congress of
Architects in London:

> If we were not so caught up in the prejudices of our time to the
> point of being unable to judge, the striving to dress modern
> tasks in historical forms would appear just as ridiculous as if a
> person possessed different masquerade costumes and under-
> took to appear today as a gothic knight tomorrow as a french
> courtesan the next day as an ancient greek. Because these
> strivings for style are nothing other than artworks of dressing
> which come out of a certain characterlessness and groundless-
> ness of architecture.[82]

Even the attempt to reject historical dress in favor of a modern
style is to dress, and thereby suffocate, the object. For Muthesius,
the very search for a modern look is not modern. Modernity is not a
look. The modern is an unconscious effect of new conditions rather
than something produced by artists. Indeed, to seek it is necessarily to lose it, as he argues in a 1903 article on English country
houses:

> Herein lies the unconsciously modern. To want to be "mod-
> ern" on principle is unobjective and is therefore very unmod-
> ern. One is modern when one is as objective as possible and
> thinks of nothing other than the demands at hand. To look for
> the modern in external details is the erroneous way of the
> nineteenth century, to look at artistic things from the wrong
> side.[83]

Inasmuch as Art Nouveau actively seeks a modern look, it is seen to be, like the historical eclecticism it rejected, a degenerate form of dress. More precisely, its decorative excesses are seen to be nothing more than those of fashion—excesses whose model is to be found in women's dresses. In contrast to such architectural fashions, Muthesius insists on the need to standardize architectural practice by settling on certain generic type-forms. Indeed, it can be argued that while the ostensible theme of the 1914 debate in Cologne was the freedom of the individual artist versus the establishment of such shared standards, the tacit argument is about disciplining design against fashion. At a key point early in his speech, Muthesius touches the question of fashion. His central argument is that the obsessive application of the word "art" to all domains (including, symptomatically, the idea of "Art in Men's Suits," along with art in the house, the street, the shop-window, and so on) has lead to a proliferation of excessive ornament that destroys the aesthetic order produced by anonymous craftspeople. And it is preceded by the claim that purely commercial interests are already seeing the Werkbund's designs as "the new fashion" to be exploited.[84]

Without addressing, let alone defending, fashion, van de Velde responded in favor of the individual artist over the anonymous worker and was supported by the other older members of the Werkbund, and even the young turks like Walter Gropius and Bruno Taut. The rights of the individual artist were repeatedly aligned with a sense that modernity involved ongoing aesthetic change, changes of mode guided by the artist controlling everything in the environment. The signature designer was successfully defended against the anonymous, collective production of standards. But the debate is usually understood as a watershed in the formation of modern architecture because the proposed agenda that Muthesius reluctantly withdrew, with its extreme reduction of ornament and attempted standardization, ended up becoming the ostensible agenda of modern architecture. Consequently, historians tacitly, but routinely, identify Muthesius with the final rejection of fashion that supposedly allowed modern architecture to emerge. In fact, it is remarkable the extent to which they reproduce, but rarely cite, Muthesius's opinions. In a sense, Muthesius is responsible for an entire historiographical tradition within which he only appears at one key point, if at all. Precisely because the whole project to discipline fashion turns around him, it overlooks him.

The rejection of fashion is, of course, even more explicit in the writings of another of van de Velde's critics, Adolf Loos. Like Muthesius, Loos rejects the very idea of architecture as a high art sealed by a signature. While accepting and elaborating Semper's argument that architecture is a form of clothing, he condemns fashion in favor of the anonymous evolution of standards. Writing extensively about fashion, in successive articles about hats, shoes, underclothes, fabrics, men's and women's clothing, uniforms, and so on, his opinion is seemingly clear-cut and extreme:

> Ladies' fashion! You disgraceful chapter in the history of civilization! You tell of mankind's secret desires. Whenever we peruse your pages, our souls shudder at the frightful aberrations and scandalous depravities. We hear the whimpering of abused children, the shrieks of maltreated wives, the dreadful outcry of tortured men, and the howls of those who have died at the stake. Whips crack, and the air takes on the burnt smell of scorched human flesh.[85]

Women's fashion is identified with ornamentation, which in turn is identified with sensuality, in particular man's "sickly sensuality," which the ornaments are intended to attract. For Loos, ornament is the mark of servitude. The woman uses ornament to make the man a slave to his own pathological sexuality precisely because she is herself a slave. After all, when ornament is identified with crime in the notorious essay, the crime is explicitly sexual, or, rather, is sexuality itself. The critique of the immoral seductions of fashionable clothing is extended into a critique of the immoral seductions of the clothing of buildings. Such dissimulating layers of clothing are repeatedly opposed whether they are draped over the inside or the outside of buildings. On the outside, Loos condemns the use of architectural styles, fashionable facades that are literally "nailed on" to the structure, as mere "costume" (in the sense of dead clothing, imitation clothes). Likewise, on the inside, he condemns the fashion-conscious search for a "stylish home" assisted by the new figure of the "decorator" who single-handedly, like the fashion designer, establishes a particular style for the inhabitant. This figure displaces the traditional selection of furnishing and clothes produced by different craftspeople whose anonymous work fits together because they are independently harmonious with their own time.[86] Inside and out, modernity is effaced by the very fashions that claim to express it.

While attacking the Arts and Crafts movements for attempting to impose their individual signatures on the whole environment, Loos repeatedly singles out van de Velde, as in his famous line: "there will come a time when the furnishings of a prison cell designed by Professor Van de Velde will be considered a harshening of the punishment."[87] He constantly teases the designer, even parodying the designing of clothes to match architectural interiors by suggesting that one would have to change clothes when changing rooms.[88] But the problem is not simply the actual designing of such clothes by an architect. Loos sees all of van de Velde's architectural work as the design of women's dresses. When the infamous "Ornament and Crime" essay attacks van de Velde as a "modern producer of ornament" pathologically "disowning his own products after only three years," it counters this subordination of design to fashion with the principle that "the form of an object should be bearable for as long as the object lasts physically" and illustrates the point in terms of dress: "A suit will be changed more frequently than a valuable fur coat. A lady's evening dress, intended for one night only, will be changed more rapidly than a writing desk. Woe betide the writing desk that has to be changed as frequently as an evening dress, just because the style has become unbearable."[89] The problem with van de Velde is not simply that he designs dresses but that he confuses the specific demands of architecture with those of dresses.

Loos likewise attacks Josef Hoffmann, Josef Maria Olbrich and the other Viennese secessionists. Again, he criticizes their use of internal and external masquerade in architecture but does so by literally criticizing the clothes they wore as being a form of masquerade, accusing them of using imitation ties, an accusation taken so seriously that Hoffmann angrily denies it in print. It's not just that the error in their own clothes supposedly reflects the error of their whole project. The project literally involves the redesign of clothing. Hoffmann, like van de Velde, was designing dresses and even teaching fashion design within his class at the School of Arts and Crafts (an institution that, as Kenneth Frampton notes, had originally been founded to carry out Semper's educational program[90]). While it was a special architecture class, it embraced the entire design, or, rather, designable, environment; architecture and dress being seen to have the "same preconditions of creation" as his assistant of the time put it.[91]

Furthermore, in 1903 Hoffmann founded the Wiener Werkstätte with the painter Kolomon Moser. This was modeled on the English workshop tradition initiated by Morris that Hoffmann had seen on a tour guided by Muthesius the year before. The new workshop, which was devoted to all the applied arts and had its first exhibition the next year in a Berlin "Shop for Art and Craft" run by van de Velde, was extremely influential in design circles throughout Europe, especially those of fashion design. Given that it assumed responsibility for the total environment (furniture, table settings,

Josef Hoffmann, Summer dress. **FIG. 7**
Published in Mode *(Vienna),*
1911. From Wolfgang G. Fischer,
Gustav Klimt and Emilie Flöge:
An Artist and his Muse *(London:*
Lund Humphries, 1922), 87.

flower arrangements, garden layouts, wallpapers, utensils, book design, and so on, in addition to buildings), dress was necessarily a major concern. Moser, like Hoffmann, designed dresses in the same spirit as the decorations he painted for so many of Hoffmann's interiors. While it did not have a fashion department with its own tailor's workshop until 1911, the Werkstätte was designing dresses from the beginning and having them constructed at the Schwestern Flöge, a fashion salon run by the three Flöge sisters that catered to the progressive upper middle classes, itself designed by Hoffmann in 1904. When the Werkstätte's own fashion department opened, its director, Eduard Wimmer, set about "the creation of a modern 'Viennese fashion' appropriate for women living in Wiener Werkstätte designed dwellings."[92] But the Werkstätte dresses were to have a major impact on not only Viennese fashion circles but also those of Germany and even Paris.

In 1910, the Werkstätte had opened its own fashion salon selling fabrics, dresses, hats, shoes, leather goods, bags and accessories.[93] By 1924, it was employing 150 people and was growing into a chain of stores that eventually had branches in Karlsbad, Zurich, New York and Berlin before the Werkstätte itself collapsed in 1931. Unlike the Schwestern Flöge, which had from the beginning participated in both the emerging ready-to-wear trade (through Emilie Flöge's biannual appropriations of Paris fashions) and the one-off art dresses designed by her and the Secessionist circle (some by Hoffmann but most by Wimmer and the notorious Gustav Klimt), the Werkstätte specialized in the latter exclusive and expensive market.[94] In the face of the increasing mass production of fashions, its obsessive concern for handicraft was unable to hold a market. Nevertheless, it was the last department of the Werkstätte to close and its designs had greatly influenced the very ready-to-wear trade that made it redundant.

The relationship between the workshop and the evolving international fashion world was complex. From the beginning, all the Werkstätte dresses were widely published in Paris and the original salon had been regularly visited by Paul Poiret, the leading French fashion designer who was Hoffmann's friend at the time and whose neo-empire line had clearly influenced the original Werkstätte designs. Poiret, who pioneered most of the modern apparatus of fashion publicity (like trained models), held a major fashion show in Vienna in 1911 and was, in turn, influenced by the dress designs he saw at the Werkstätte, organized a show of them in his Paris salon, and had a huge quantity of their fabrics and accessories sent back to Paris for use in his own collections.

Furthermore, while describing Hoffmann's control of both the house and the dresses worn within it as a form of "slavery" that subordinates the inhabitant's personal taste,[95] Poiret was sufficiently affected by Hoffmann's interiors that he commissioned a house from him in 1912. While the scheme was abandoned, it is no coincidence that the eventual architect for the house, Mallet-Stevens—who was greatly influenced by Hoffmann, designed fashion stores for shoes, clothing and jewelry, and whose architecture was used in films as sets framing clothes designed by Poiret—is singled out by Giedion as the paradigm of the ever present danger that modern architecture might become nothing more than surface fashion design and then effaced from the historical canon. In fact, Poiret had even been inspired by all this to branch out into the field of interior design himself, opening a workshop based on the Wiener Werkstätte called Atelier Martin that, as Isabelle Anscombe puts it, "established the tradition in France of not only bringing fashion closer to the fine arts, but also allowing fashion to flow outwards into the decorative environment."[96] To do this, Poiret hired and trained a group of designers that produced very Hoffmann-like objects, fabrics, interiors, and buildings.

Such a blurring, if not effacement, of the line between architecture and fashion had been going on at the Werkstätte since at least 1903. Wimmer had been trained as an architect with Hoffmann at the *Kunstgewerbescule* (School of Industrial Arts) before becoming the director of the fashion department. Indeed, he was repeatedly described in the press as the workshop's "architect of fashion." This blurring continued after Hoffmann's architectural office was separated off in 1912 (as a result of a legal suit over the division of fees). In the Primavesi country house of the following year, for example, the guests (frequently including Hoffmann and Klimt), whether male or female, had to wear specially designed silk gowns made of Werkstätte fabric that matched the dense abstract patterns that dressed most surfaces of the building itself.[97] Klimt, who promoted his art dresses as an anti-bourgeois "symbol of independence and informality, as the epitome of fashionable freedom and one's unique individual style,"[98] had long advocated and designed such unisex gowns, and often wore them. A crucial part of this sense of freedom was the effacing of the distinction between fashionable dress and architecture. What was, for Loos, the new prison-house of fashion was, for the Secessionists, the long awaited release.

DRESSING DOWN THE FEMININE

With the Secessionists' inclusion of the domestic domain—traditionally associated with women—within the space of high art; the production of designs for women; the opening of an institutional space for women designers (after 1913 the majority of Werkstätte designers were women); the blurring of traditional markings of gender; and their overall concern with the stereotypically feminine domain of ornamentation, it is not surprising that Loos, like Karl Kraus, attacks the Werkstätte as "feminine" in its contaminating use of fashion:

> Whenever I abuse the object of daily use by ornamenting it, I shorten its life-span, because since it is then subject to fashion, it dies sooner. Only the whim and ambition of women can be responsible for this murder of material—and ornamentation at the service of woman will live forever.[99]

In 1927, Loos went even further in a public lecture entitled "The Viennese Woe: Wiener Werkstätte," whose goal was, according to a newspaper report, to "finish the dying Wiener Werkstätte with the claw-stroke of his speech." It attacked the "feministic eclectic rubbish arts and crafts of the Wiener Werkstätte" in such vitriolic terms that it lead to a reply from Hoffmann, much debate in the newspapers, and a libel suit.[100] Both the workshop and its products were vilified as feminine:

> To bring us first-rate work no architects are needed, no arts and crafts students and no painting, embroidering, potting, precious-material-wasting daughters of senior civil servants, or other *Frauleins*, who regard handicrafts as something whereby one may earn pin-money or while away one's spare time until one can walk up the aisle.[101]

Emilie Flöge and Gustav Klimt (ca. 1905). From Traude Hansen, Wiener Werkstätte Mode, Stoffe, Schmuck, Accessories *(Vienna: Christian Branstätter, 1984), 9.*

FIG. 8

Loos's attack exploits the millennial tradition in which ornament is identified as a feminine principle which needs to be disciplined, literally domesticated, restrained if not actually contained within the interior by a masculine structure. Despite his personal vendetta against Hoffmann, his argument is not so much idiosyncratic as it is institutional. Indeed, it faithfully echoes Germain Boffrand's mid-eighteenth century attack on Rococo in the *Livre d'Architecture*:

> Fashion, at various times (and especially in Italy) has taken pleasure in torturing all the parts of a building, and has often tried to destroy all the principles of architecture, whose noble simplicity should always be preserved...Ornamentation has (in the work of Guarini and Borromini) passed from the interior decoration of houses, and from the carved woodwork for which delicate work is suitable, to exteriors, and to works in masonry, which require to be worked in a more vigorous and more masculine way.[102]

Likewise, the Secessionists are seen to have released ornament from the interior and allowed it to contaminate the very structure that is supposed to control it. The Arts and Crafts principle that decoration should become the structure is seen as a direct threat to masculine authority. This perception that Hoffmann and his circle had feminized architecture by concentrating on a "surface style" was not a passing sentiment in the literature framing modern architecture.[103] Loos's reaction is far from isolated. Rather, it acts as a structuring claim in the discourse around modern architecture that must apparently be repeated in order to be effective, even within Loos's own writing. When his 1908 essay "Cultural Degeneration" dismisses the aims of the newly established Deutscher Werkbund as laid out by Muthesius, for example, he argues that it is necessary to re-launch his earlier successful attack on both the clothes worn by the Secessionists and their attempt to "infect" the world of tailoring.[104] Likewise, the Wiener Werkstätte is often invoked by other writers as the model for the way fashion mobilizes the greatest dangers implicit in all ornament, the danger against which modern architecture must vigilantly guard by disciplining not only buildings but the people that produce them, those that live in them and even, if not especially, those that write about them.

Even Giedion uses a 1950 essay on Neutra to credit Loos with turning to England and America to find "a cure for the effeminate Viennese taste."[105] In fact, Giedion, who has little time, and even less space, for Loos, condemns the Wiener Werkstätte in the first of his periodic surveillance sweeps against fashion in architecture. His 1926 "Zur situation deutscher architektur" (The State of German Architecture), which launched the series that became *Bauen en Frankreich*, attacks what he sees as the revived precedence of decoration over architecture, criticizing the Wiener Werkstätte in particular for its "playful and irrelevant quality," which he calls "the curves of a nervous feminism (*nervösen Feminismus*)."[106] This association of fashion with the dangers of femininity occurs again when the essay later identifies the Arts and Crafts movement in general with an "over-cultivated feeling for the surface charm of materials linked up with *soigné* and somewhat effeminate (*verweichlichten*) feeling for plushy furnishings."[107] In contrast, he insists again that modern architecture is "inartistic, unfashionable." In France, it is supposedly easier for Le Corbusier to "fight...against the adjustment of taste, which is all the more dangerous," because the decorative arts were never so dominant there. But still, it is only by assuming an extreme functionalism that resists "external assimilation" by the style-mongers that "a movement stays almost safe from fashionable dilution (*modischen Verwässerungen*)."[108] The essay concludes by objecting to "this 'taste' which so easily lets architectural matters slip into dangerously fashionable realms (*Modezone*). Now is the time to attempt once again to break away from superficial attraction and to re-establish architecture as functional art."[109] It is not enough for architecture to be "almost safe." "Almost safe" is apparently unsafe. Fashion is lethal in even the smallest of doses.

In fact, Giedion implies that even the most extreme commitment to function cannot inoculate architecture against fashion. Inasmuch as it is an art, albeit a "functional art," it cannot leave the surface behind and so remains open to the very appropriations it tries to resist. While the very shape of modern architecture is actually produced by its ongoing attempt to resist the fashion market, it remains, for Giedion, all too attractive to that market. The threat of fashion, which is to say the feminine threat of "superficial attraction," is permanent, as must be the masculine resistance to it. After all, the threat is, as it was for Loos, that of sexuality.

Throughout Giedion's texts, the psychological complex in which fashion necessarily participates is tacitly linked to questions of sexuality. The "schizophrenic" division between feeling and thought produced by the mechanization of everyday life and covered over, if not repressed, by fashionable decoration, is a form of sexual degeneration, as is the decorative cover itself. Ornaments are understood as sexual lures. *Space, Time and Architecture* identifies the licentiousness of fashionable ornament when it literally speaks of the "erotic facade" which must be stripped off buildings and abandoned to produce the "impersonal, precise and objective spirit" of modern architecture.[110]

But this spirit, which is exemplified by the engineering triumph of the huge spans in the 1889 Galarie des Machines, is not desexualized because the structures are naked, or even clothed in a modestly plain dress. The sexuality is displaced rather than effaced. Alongside images of the Galarie's apparently naked steel frame, Giedion publishes a "popular" nude from the same year, arguing, in the caption, that "with its facile histrionics and its full share of erotic facade, it met all the demands of its day."[111] Symptomatically, the stripping off of this erotic facade is identified with the way a Degas painting of a clothed ballerina apparently locates "the nascent prostitute in the young dancer." Giedion sees the labor of the modern architect, and his own as a historian, as being, like Degas, that of taking sexuality away from the surface, relocating it in some interior rather than abandoning it. Like the psychoanalyst, they locate a cauldron of sexuality behind apparently innocent surfaces. If the modernists' "stripping" off of decorative clothes is a moral act, the morality is sexual. The disciplining of fashion is, in the end, an attempt to discipline, as distinct from reject, sexuality.

This puritan logic becomes even more evident in the introduction added by Giedion in 1962 to the final edition, which calls for the disciplining of the contemporary architects who have apparently transformed modern architecture itself into a "fashion" by decorating it. The sacrilegious "tendency to degrade the wall with new decorative elements" that has "infected" the architects is symptomatically condemned because it "flirts with the past" and produces "playboy fashions" in a "romantic orgy."[112] The crime of decoration is always sexual and the historian-therapist must constantly guard against flirtations with the surface that succumb to the inherently feminine ruses of fashion. Indeed, in the very name of resisting sexuality, the historian must, as the text variously says, "penetrate," "drive boreholes into," "enter into," "probe into," the surface.

These are not passing metaphors. Sex is not even a metaphor here (if it ever is). The opposition between the Degas and the popular nude is a trace of the extensive research that Giedion was carrying out in 1936 into what he called "the ruling taste," which was interrupted when Gropius invited him to come to Harvard to give the Charles Eliot Norton Lectures that would be published as *Space, Time and Architecture*. In 1955, he published some of this early research, analyzing the "erotic mode" of popular paintings of the mid-nineteenth century by the Dutch artist Ary Scheffer, whose "sentimentally veiled lasciviousness" apparently "paralyzes the capacity for judgement."[113] Already, his 1944 call for a "new monumentality" had chosen the seemingly copulating figures in 1930s sculptures by Gustav Adolf Vigeland as the "acme" of the "pseudo-monumentality" that is blocking the emergence of an appropriate urban architecture that would bring to the surface the unconscious feelings buried by such popular fashions.[114] Even his 1962 book, *The Beginnings of Art*, begins by arguing that most art originates in symbols of procreation but that these figures ("with their heavy breasts, protuberant belly, and exaggerated buttocks") should not be interpreted, as they would be by a nineteenth-century mentality, "merely as lust," "eroticism," and "pre-historic pin-up girls."[115] Giedion identifies the innocence of certain apparently sexual images in the same way that he had earlier identified the sexuality of certain apparently innocent images. Furthermore, he argues that images of seduction and seductive images actually inhibit sexuality. His 1954 book on Gropius, for example, argues that the seductive images of the "ruling" taste, which "have become part of the dream world of the masses and their representatives," are used "impotently" to oppose "truly creative art, whose roots reach back into the ancient ages."[116] The ancient potency of modern art, with which the impotence of overtly sexual images is to be cured, is always sexual. It comes as no surprise, then, that the later books argue that modern art's recovery of these ancient origins provides a weapon against the all too seductive surface: "spatial penetration." In an old, if not the oldest, story, seduction is to be countered with (phallic) control.

Giedion's sentiment, his argument, and even his methodology, is not unique. One by one, the historians of modern architecture, with their very different agendas, attempt to leave fashion behind by associating it within sexuality's (feminine) threat to (masculine) order and guarding against its return. They operate surgically on the available evidence, and change the terms of what constitutes evidence, within certain definite but undefined limits. The most obvious symptom of this operation is that all the figures being addressed here—Behrens, van de Velde, Horta, Hoffmann, Loos, Sullivan, and so on—are routinely divided into those elements of their designs or writing consistent with a canonic, almost cartoon-like, image of modern architecture, and those that are not. Each is tacitly or explicitly split into two clear-cut and gendered sets of qualities and their work is portrayed as the struggle between the two, any blurring of the distinction being associated with the feminine qualities that must be overcome to produce a modern architecture. The much-advertised clarity of modern architecture is no more than the drawing of a line that genders, and the effacement of any blurring, twisting or convolution of that line. It is not by chance that Giedion begins his final attempt to ground modern architecture in a trans-historical order by insisting that the prehistoric bisexual figures of procreation be disassociated from desire. The regulating lines of modern architecture turn out to be those that regulate desire. The modern erects itself as such by refusing the collapsing or weaving of these all too straight lines into a sensuous surface.

In this way, a pre-history is constructed and invested with a sense of momentum. Modern architecture is portrayed as the inevitable product of irreversible psychic forces long at work. The prehistory from which it emerges is both explicitly and tacitly identified with fashion. No matter how blurred, multiple, and unevenly developed (if not invisible) the line between the canon and its prehistory, fashion is clearly left behind. In the end, the line cordoning off fashion may be the only one drawn with any regularity and confidence—no matter how tacitly. Indeed, it is precisely the tacit nature of the argument, the sense that it almost goes without saying, needing only the smallest punctuation to mark its presence, that confirms the extent to which it is seen to be beyond question. The generic sense that modern architecture is preceded by fashion is so strong precisely because it is seen to require only the lightest prop.

Much is made, for example, of the fact that Le Corbusier sought and received a job with Hoffmann, accepted it but asked for a short delay to make a trip from which he never returned. His Arts and Crafts background is carefully split off from his "pioneering" work, treated as a necessary but insufficient and ultimately inadequate space whose critique provides the crucial step forward. In this way, the paradigmatic sites of an explicit parallel between dress design, fashion, and architecture are seen as but stepping stones to a new form of practice within which both the commitment to fashion and the dresses are literally left behind, rejected and forgotten. The designing of dresses is thrown back into the pre-history of modern architecture and, even there, any mention of it is hard to find. Behrens's many dress designs are almost never referred to in supposedly comprehensive monographs on his work.[117] Even van de Velde's and Hoffmann's dress designs are almost completely effaced from architectural scholarship,[118] including that which condemns the designers for embracing fashion. Not only is the activity of dress designing (to say nothing of the specific properties of the designs) suppressed; it is deemed somehow too embarrassing to even pick up in order to discard. With the notable exception of Beatriz Colomina's persuasive analysis of Loos's arguments about fashion,[119] even the decisive question of clothing is withdrawn. It is as if to touch the question is somehow to already be contaminated by the danger of fashion it carries. A simplistic account of the "modern" attack on ornament is all that survives from the extremely complex and contradictory attempt to discipline clothing at the turn of the century in which architects played such and important role.

But clearly things are not so simple. It's not just that the historians, unlike Loos, do not analyze fashion or its relationship to architecture. It is precisely this absence that structures the discourse.

When the line between modern architecture and fashion does become explicit and the rejection of fashion by that architecture is addressed, it is always in isolated moments (even with such anti-fashion zealots as Giedion) and almost always to clarify some point about the status of function. In fact, what usually happens is that the tacit argument about fashion is encouraged to slide into and over the argument about function. All we learn is that function is what fashion is not. Function ends up appearing more certain without having been opened up any further. On the contrary, some uncertainty about it has been covered up. In this sense, a map of the confident rejections of fashion in the historiography of modern architecture would actually be a map of its insecurity: a map of cracks in the apparently smooth surfaces of the cartoon image it constructs, cracks which harbor the very uncontrollable forces whose presence is being denied. The explicit rejections of fashion might actually be the most precise map of its enigmatic operations, operations that structure the discourse, but only appear within it at idiosyncratic moments.

UNSECURING THE LINE

Modern architecture cannot be separated from dress design. On the one hand, the architects working as dress designers are completely modern in terms of the stereotypical image of modern architecture as the systematic reduction of ornament and dedication to function. On the other hand, the anti-ornamentalists are completely dedicated to clothing. And these gestures cannot simply be separated. The aspects that mark certain figures as precursors to the modern cannot be separated from those the modern means to leave behind. The line between fashion and modernity, if there is such a thing, does not pass between modernity and dresses.

Both sides of the stereotypical opposition between fashion and modern architecture frustrate the terms that are usually used to hold them apart. While Hoffmann, for example, instituted a fashion department at the Weiner Werkstätte, his 1898 essay "Das individuelle Kleid," which first announced his committment to dress design, defended individual clothing styles that express individual character against the uniform styles that have been imposed by the "tyranny of fashion."[120] Standardization is understood as an effect of fashion rather than a form of resistance to it. When Hoffmann later appears to consolidate his commitment to fashion by writing to a newspaper and proposing a "fashion bureau" for Vienna, he again sounds like all the outspoken critics of fashion in arguing for modern clothing styles that are consistent with the automobile and in opposing any form of masquerade.[121] Likewise, van de Velde rejects stylistic eclecticism as masquerade, as if "one had to end up by completely wearing out the tattered clothes of one's older brother."[122] After all, his primary influence was Morris, for whom the poverty of historicism, as Pevsner points out, was "masquerading in other people's clothes."[123] Indeed, when van de Velde opposes Muthesius's ideal of universal standards at the Cologne meeting of the Werkbund, he does so precisely because, in his view, any "universally valid form" would be but a "mask."[124] His whole project is governed by an obsessive rationalism directed against the dissimulations of clothing, as can be seen when his *Memoires* describe the logic with which he designed the dresses to match the interiors of his house as a pervasive rationalism understood as a moral code which excludes all "fantasy."[125] The house is not intended as a fashion statement. On the contrary. Giving ornament the privileged role does not mean the total subordination of construction and function. Rather, it involves blurring the difference between them. Van de Velde's argument is precisely that which is typically used to mark modern architecture's rejection of fashion: "its construction and exterior form must adapt themselves completely to the aim for which they were created...no ornament which does not insert itself organically can be considered as valid. Anything which lies outside this constructive vision is, in applied art, senseless, irrational and sterile."[126] His concern with ornament is a concern with the particular qualities of line, understood as that which fuses construction and ornament. The line of ornament has to be disciplined, restrained in a way that liberates the "line of construction" that "refuses to conceal its activity behind an unjustified excess of ornamentation."[127] From the beginning, van de Velde employs smooth surfaces with simple decoration, favors mass production and finally, like Hoffmann, has no hesitation in placing his rationality in a historical trajectory with canonic modern architecture.[128] He explicitly opposes fashion, insisting that his own work was never a "vogue" and bitterly opposing the transformation of Art Nouveau itself into one.[129]

In his 1929 lecture "Le nouveau: pourquoi toujours du nouveau?" ("The New: Why Always the New?") van de Velde opposes the "newness" of his architecture to the "novelty" of fashion. He argues that the individualist variations of the early Art Nouveau work were seized upon by manufacturers who appropriated only its most superficial elements and transformed them into a fashion with the eager backing of the magazines for the "new art" that emerged precisely in order to promote such trends. No matter how rigorously the artist strips away the degenerate layers of old fashions, it is always possible that "a 'false newness' under some clever disguise may come into vogue" through the "specter of ornamentation" that haunts all forms of production and "has not changed its methods of seduction since men first began to barter."[130] To resist such a seduction of artworks into a fashion, "we had to disabuse those who saw us only as 'purveyors of the new' of the idea that after *this* new style, we should bring them another"[131] by demanding an unchanging, essential order. The newness of contemporary architecture had to be seen as the product of logic rather than the dictates of fashion. Van de Velde's repeated call for rational principles that uncover "essential forms" by insisting on "the fatal determination of shape by function" is therefore explicitly directed against fashion. He symptomatically concludes that the constant "menace" of ornamentation can only be resisted by a rigid "submission to discipline" which transforms the early individualist experiments into a single unified style, a *"style of the machine,"* no less, that is protected from the ravages of fashion. Furthermore, the lecture's model for an architecture that "elevates itself above fashion," by "abstaining from ornament," is the "pursuit of pure forms and the pure line" in women's clothing. While Van de Velde is so repeatedly condemned for transforming architecture into fashion by treating it like dress design, he turns to dresses to resist fashion.

Likewise, the Secessionists oppose the transformation of their work into a fashion, objecting to their own influence as "a loud fashion" precisely because that fashion is not faithful to the fundamental principle of construction that organizes both their buildings and dress designs.[132] Indeed, they see their commitment to dress design as responsible for their principle of construction rather than a means to disregard it. Hoffmann's eloquent essay, "Simple Furniture," for *Das Interieur* in 1901, argues that modern dress should be the model for an environment that would "give a fitting shape to our modern feeling and thinking" and asks: "How does it happen that people who make an effort to be dressed according to the latest pattern, act at home as if they were living in the 15th or 16th century?"[133] The text immediately goes on to condemn stylistic dress as pathological masquerade.[134] And if each such style is "a borrowed lying mask," it is not just an ill-fitting and untimely set of clothes for the building. It is also a kind of fashionable but uncomfortable clothing for the designer. As Hoffmann says of other designers: "most of them are intent on squeezing themselves into some trend."[135] Against this hopeless quest for the latest fashionable style, he promotes structural and functional "honesty," arguing, "I think we must above all consider the respective function and the material,"[136] a sentiment he repeatedly identifies with his teacher Otto Wagner. Indeed, as Le Corbusier will do much later, the essay criticizes museums for neglecting the modern, asking, "have you ever seen a beautiful machine in a museum of arts and crafts?" and arguing that it is necessary for such institutions to "search out the traces of the 'Modern' in this and other infallible things."[137] This sensibility cannot so easily be separated from that which will reject it as mere fashion.

FIG. 9   *Josef Hoffmann, steel construction house, Vienna (1928) as illustrated in Bruno Taut,* Modern Architecture *(London: The Studio Limited, 1929), 145.*

Furthermore, as Jane Kallir points out, despite the apparent obsession with handicraft, the workshops of the Wiener Werkstätte were not only highly mechanized, even making a number of significant innovations in the modern workplace; many of their designs were licensed to outside manufacturers and mass-produced in large numbers.[138] And Hoffmann ends up designing the extraordinary, but largely and symptomatically overlooked, prefabricated steel house in 1928 (which Bruno Taut immediately publishes in *Modern Architecture* a year later, alongside one of his own house designs and Gropius's prefabricated house for the Weissenhof Siedlung of 1927). Its obvious modernity (in terms of the canonic cartoon) cannot be as easily detached from his earlier work as might be imagined. Again, like van de Velde, Hoffmann does not simply fit the stereotype constructed for him. The line between fashion and modern architecture is, at the very least, insecure.

Even Mallet-Stevens, Giedion's paradigm of the architect-as-fashion-designer, repeatedly opposes the excesses of decoration and writes a piece called "Modern Versus Modish" that refuses to privilege fashion over function. On the contrary, it condemns the continued presence of old fashions that block the emergence of a modern—because functional—form appropriate for the "man of today." He uses the example of all the anachronistic features of contemporary clothing,[139] but also argues against any superficially "modern" styling:

> Aerodynamics in the automobile is not always essential, it is often merely a fashion. It is no longer the result of calculations, it is a "shape" like a hat. The history of dress is a long one of nonsense, of unreasoned extravagance...If certain now useless fashions still survive, new ones arrive to impose themselves without reason.[140]

This complication of the line between fashion and modern architecture is not simply an example of the way that no historical event conforms to its description upon closer examination. Rather, these particular events are fundamentally enigmatic in their engagement with fashion. At the very least, it becomes clear that a figure's relationship to fashion can have almost nothing to do with what that figure says about fashion. Just because people design dresses does not mean that they will argue in favor of fashion. Likewise, those who attack fashion may actually be engaged with it. Both sides of the stereotype are irreducibly complicated. In the same way that the agenda of the dress designers is stereotypically modern in its attempt to discipline ornament, those who are ostensibly anti-ornamentalist are obsessed with clothes, a fixation that can never simply be separated from the very lure of fashion they claim to be staunchly resisting. Not only do their respective photographic portraits reveal a studious attention to the construction of a stylish ensemble; their respective polemics seem to find the question of clothing irresistible.

This is, of course, most evident in Loos, who appears to be the most outspoken opponent of fashion. Following Semper closely, he sees clothing not just as an analogy for architecture but as its very model, both as a general philosophical principle, as articulated in his "Law of Dressing," and as a literal exemplar (contemporary clothing styles). In the "Architecture" essay of 1910, he argues that nineteenth-century fetishists of ornament, who covered buildings with eclectic styles in an always-frustrated attempt to find a modern style, did not realize that the tailor and other craftsmen had already quietly and anonymously produced the style of the twentieth century—a style that would probably have been blocked had the brand-name architects deigned to enter the world of clothing design:

> In their arrogance, the warped people by-passed the reform of our clothes. For they were all serious men who considered it beyond their dignity to bother about such things. Thus our clothes were left alone to reflect the true style of our period. Only the invention of ornament was becoming to the serious, dignified man...what was true in the case of clothes was not the case for architecture. If architecture had only been left alone by those warped people, and if the clothes were reformed in terms of old theatrical junk or in the Secessionist manner—there certainly were attempts in this direction—then the situation would have been the other way around.[141]

This anonymous transformation of clothing is exemplified in the gradual evolution of the man's suit in England. Loos emphatically privileges the relative standardization of men's clothes over the variation of women's. Male attire is supposedly detached from the many dangers of sensuality that are carried by the ornament that defines women's fashion. He does acknowledge a certain mobility in male fashion as "the masses" appropriate the clothing styles with which the aristocracy attempts to differentiate itself, but draws a distinction between this regular, almost logical, movement from the uncontrollable sexual forces driving women's fashions:

> On the one hand, then, change in men's fashion is effected in such a way that the masses go rushing headlong in their desire to be elegant; in this way the originally elegant style is debased in value, and those who are genuinely elegant—or better, those who are considered by the multitude to be elegant—must cast about for a new style in order to distinguish themselves. On the other hand, the vicissitudes of women's fashion are dictated only by changes in sensuality. And sensuality changes constantly.[142]

For Loos, men's clothing is led by the people of highest standing while women's is led by those of the lowest standing, or more precisely, those who confuse the system of standings. The greatest enemy is the *parvenu*, the pretender who acts the part by assuming the costume of another class. If men's fashions are led by the gentleman, women's fashions are led by the coquette who employs her sexuality to bypass class distinctions. The sensuality of women's clothing upsets all forms of rationality, rendering insecure all distinctions, especially those of class, which are, for Loos, all too rational. In opposing the rationality of male dress to the sensuality of female dress, he is able to identify fashion at once with the dangers of women and with their subordination. As Elizabeth Wilson notes:

> In the nineteenth century fashion had come to be associated almost entirely with women's clothing, while men's clothes have since been perceived (inaccurately) as unchanging. Fashion as a mania for change could therefore the more easily be interpreted either as evidence of women's inherent frivolity and flightiness; or—the other side of the coin—as evidence of women's subjection and oppression.[143]

Loos identifies the designs of Hoffmann and the others with women's clothing, telling them just after the formation of the Wiener Werkstätte to give up architecture: "One cannot deny you a certain talent, but the area it covers is quite different from that which you imagine. You have the imagination of dressmakers (*damenschneiders*); so make dresses (*damenkleider*)!"[144] The designers are condemned for feminizing architecture by treating it as women's clothing, subordinating it to the suspect dictates of art. In contrast, his own designs, which deliberately refuse the label of art, are identified with men's clothing. He extracts from his articles on underclothes, hats, shoes, monocles, socks, uniforms, and so on, the coherence of a gentlemen's wardrobe turning around the restrained business suit that had evolved in England.[145] This suit is privileged because of its functional comfort, which results from the way the style of everyday street clothes gradually absorbed the innovations in sports clothes required to handle their specific functional demands.

But, as Beatriz Colomina has argued, the comfort of the modern suit, like that of modern architecture, is not merely physical. The function of modern clothes for the man is also—if not primarily—

psychological. More precisely, the look of function provides a newly required psychological advantage. Inasmuch as men's clothing is standardized, it is able to act as a mask behind which the individual is shielded from the increasingly threatening and seemingly uncontrollable forces of modern life (forces that were themselves understood as feminine). In the article "Men's Fashion," Loos determines that the ideal of modern dress is "being dressed in *such a way that one stands out the least*...to be conspicuous is bad manners."[146] As Colomina observes, this effacement of the individual relates to fundamental transformations in metropolitan life. Having tracked Loos's crucial identification of architecture with clothing, she notes that his architectural clothing corresponds with Georg Simmel's account of fashion as a mask:

> Loos writes about the exterior of the house in the same terms that he writes about fashion...[He] seems to establish a radical difference between interior and exterior, which reflects the split between the intimate and the social life of the metropolitan being: outside, the realm of exchange, money, and masks; inside, the realm of the inalienable, the nonexchangeable, and the unspeakable. Moreover, this split between inside and outside, between senses and sight, is gender-loaded. The exterior of the house, Loos writes, should resemble a dinner jacket, a male mask; as the unified self, protected by a seamless facade, the exterior is masculine. The interior is the scene of sexuality and reproduction, all the things that would divide the subject in the outside world. However, this dogmatic division in Loos's writings between inside and outside is undermined by his architecture.[147]

The mask is a means of mental survival. The man cannot afford to wear his sensuality or any other part of his private life on the surface like a fashionable woman does. Masculinity is no more than the ability to keep a secret; and all secrets are, in the end, sexual. The disciplinary logic of standardization is, of course, psychological.

In promoting the standardized mask, Loos circulated the same intelligence reports as his fellow anglophile, and "cultural spy," Muthesius, whose introduction to *The English House* of 1904–05 associates the simplicity and comfort of English houses with the simplicity of English clothes: "The Englishman...even avoids attracting attention to his house by means of striking design or architectonic extravagance, just as he would be loth to appear personally eccentric by wearing a fantastic suit. In particular, the architectonic ostentation, the creation of 'architecture' and 'style' to which we in Germany are still so prone, is no longer to be found in England."[148] Both architects explicitly interpret standardization in terms of clothes.

Given Le Corbusier's profound, but largely unacknowledged, debt to Loos, which Colomina uncovers, it is not surprising that when *Towards an Architecture* makes a Muthesian argument about standardization, it turns on the same distinction between men's and women's fashions. The illustration for the emphatic claim that "Architecture is governed by standards" carries the caption: "It is a simpler matter to form a judgement on the clothes of a well-dressed man than on those of a well-dressed woman, since masculine costume is standardized,"[149] and is preceded by the Loosian claim that "decoration is of a sensorial and elementary order, as is color, and is suited to simple races, peasants and savages...The peasant loves ornament and decorates his walls. The civilized man wears a well-cut suit and is the owner of easel pictures and books."[150] The well-cut suit again acts as the model for a modern architecture, an architecture of its own time. Le Corbusier's sporadic attacks on fashion are matched by equally sporadic appeals to men's fashion, understood not as fashion but as standardization.

The gendering line the protagonists and their promoters wish to draw between fashion and modern architecture is clearly an extremely complicated and fragile one. Its contours need to be traced much more carefully in order to identify the structural role of these complications, some of which are generic to fashion, while others arise in fashion's specific engagement with architecture.

The generic complication of fashion is that it is not possible to promote ephemeral fashions without making certain claims about truths beyond those fashions. Even the specific identification of a temporary style requires claims about systems of representation, effects of materiality, line, surface, structure and so on. These claims are not stable reference points against which "the look" is made to appear, such that precise changes of "look" become visible over time; they are properties of "the look" itself. Far beyond the ironic necessity that the fashion industry has to construct itself as one of the most stable institutions in order to register the variations that it promotes, there are elements embedded within any fashion that are seen to exceed the precise time and mood that the fashion supposedly marks. Likewise, it is not possible to withdraw oneself from fashion without deploying certain arguments governed by fashion. Opponents of fashion inevitably fall victim to the very mobility of external surfaces that they condemn. As the conditions of fashion change, the specific arguments against it must necessarily change. Fashion is not so much a specific set of institutional practices as it is a specific set of paradoxes.

Important here is the structural role that this ultimate impossibility of drawing a clear-cut line between fashion and anti-fashion plays in architectural discourse and, more particularly, the role it plays in the discourse of modern architecture. Inasmuch as that discourse turns on certain claims about fashion, these complications assume an unacknowledged (perhaps unacknowledged because so extraordinary) force. In order to interrogate the strategic effect of these irreducible paradoxes of fashion in modern architecture, it is necessary to patiently scan the broad field of its discourse to accumulate enough of their dispersed traces that their idiosyncratic but insistent rhythm can begin to emerge.

ARRESTING THE FASHION POLICE

The effects of the paradoxes of fashion can be seen in all the protagonists of the modern movement. Take Walter Gropius, the architect that Giedion, in his relentless crusade against fashion, singles out as the paradigm of the modern architect, as does Nikolaus Pevsner in the rival history published five years earlier under the title *Pioneers of the Modern Movement From William Morris to Walter Gropius* (1936). When Pevsner concludes with a celebration of Gropius, he goes out of his way on the very last page to insist (as he will do in *Industrial Art in England* a year later[151]) that modern architecture is "a genuine style, not a passing fashion."[152] Gropius is promoted as the model of the rejection of fashion. And indeed he does constantly attack fashion, siding with van de Velde against Muthesius in 1914 and campaigning persistently (if unsuccessfully) for several years to oust him from the Werkbund leadership, but eventually appropriating most of his arguments (claiming much later that the fight was really about Muthesius's "unpleasant" personality rather than about his ideas[153]). Gropius ends up as a leading exponent of the view that modern architecture is first and foremost the attempt to produce standard objects through "the elimination of the personal content of their designers."[154] Supposedly, by guarding against "arbitrary and aloof individualism," it is possible to produce standard types which exert a "settling and civilizing influence on men's minds" in the face of modernity, rather than perpetuating the neurotic cover-up achieved by putting on protective layers of fashion. It is on the basis of this quasi-utopian rejection of the economic and psychological imbalances of fashion that Gropius literally spends most of his career attempting to perfect a standardized system for the mass-production of housing units. But his supposedly generic resistance to fashion is equally explicit in the projects for which he was constructed as one of the "masters" of modern architecture: his hanging the first curtain wall on the Fagfuswerke building, his founding of the Bauhaus school, and his design of its new building when it later moved to Dessau.

The campaign against fashion is aligned with the strategic use of white. While the sheer curtain wall of Gropius and Meyer's Faguswerke was framed in exposed brick, the famous staircase that it exposed was white. And by the time Gropius completes the Bauhaus building at Dessau, even the brick construction has been plastered over and painted white. The curtain wall is now suspended between, and opens onto, smooth white surfaces. It at once frames and is framed by whiteness. If Giedion describes this building as modern architecture finally becoming conscious of itself, then that liberating moment is the one in which architects actively choose to use white, the point at which white is exhibited as such: when architects exhibit the exhibition value of white. To say the least, Gropius's architecture cannot be thought of outside its use of white. All the various technologies that he deployed were reconfigured with a white layer; whether it be the cinderblock walls of the Dessau housing units, the thin asbestos panels of the cement house for the Weissenhoff Siedlung, or the brick and boards of his own house in Lincoln, Massachusetts. More than a role model for the creative use of such technologies, Gropius stands for the tacit link between a politicized discourse against fashion and certain properties of white surfaces. Since this link is never addressed as such, its enigmas only become evident by patiently tracking the way in which his discourse is always underpinned by a specific argument about surface that is itself established by a generic narrative about clothing.

It must be recalled that the Bauhaus originally occupied the building that van de Velde designed for the Weimer Academy of Arts and Crafts he had founded in 1907, and which Gropius's new school literally replaced, along with the parallel Academy of Fine Arts, directed at the time by Fritz Mackensen. Given that van de Velde's school, like the Wiener Werkstätte, focused on the decorative arts, it is not surprising that Gropius described its curriculum as too superficial; or that he viewed this superficiality in explicitly gendered terms. The first letter from Mackensen soliciting Gropius's involvement (but veiling van de Velde's own recommendation that Gropius should take the position) argues of van de Velde's curriculum: "In time it turned out that architecture, the important element, was neglected, and what remained received a somewhat feminine character."[155] The second letter argues that the school made "only trivial things...almost nothing that fits in the framework of architecture. The students were for the most part ladies."[156] While the Bauhaus has often been described as the culmination of Semper's thinking in its polemical refusal of a distinction between fine and applied art, and despite its unacknowledged indebtedness to the training methodologies developed at both the Wiener Werkstätte and van de Velde's school, it is significant that not just dress design but clothing in general is eliminated from the program.

Only textile design remained, introduced as an autonomous workshop in order to meet the requirement of the Weimar Constitution that women students be admitted without restriction. Despite this official policy of equality, one publicly endorsed by Gropius when he took the position, all the women students were unofficially forced to take the textile workshop initially run by the painter Johannes Itten (although its looms, symptomatically, belonged to the crafts teacher, Helene Börner, who had previously taught weaving and embroidery in van de Velde's school) and were excluded from the other workshops, including the prestigious architecture department when it was finally introduced in 1926. In this way, the traditional split between high and low art supposedly undermined by the institution was actually maintained in traditionally gendered terms. After only a year of the school's operation, when women were already in the majority, Gropius—who wrote detailed articles on the way modern architecture actively facilitated the breakdown of the "patriarchal family" and the corresponding emancipation of women,[157] yet who would deny them access to his own workshops—even attempted to have the official policy changed by limiting the overall admission of women and legislating that they be confined to the textile workshop.[158]

Of the enormous production of fabrics by the workshop, many of which entered mass production under license with a Berlin textile company, most was intended for interior decoration. While some of the later designs for curtains were also purchased by clothing manufacturers, the only clothing designs in the comprehensive inventory of student work that the Bauhaus had bought, up until the 1925 move to Dessau, were some caps and children's clothes.[159] Outside of Schlemmer's famous theater designs (proposed, significantly, as "trial balloons" for a new architecture, in which the actor appeared "not as the vehicle of individual expression, but standardized through costume and mask"[160]), one of the few traces of clothing design was that of the teachers' own clothes. According to one of their students, van Doesburg "favored a stiff black hat and fashionably-cut suits...sporting a monocle, black shirt and white tie (both to the amazement of the local residents),"[161] while Itten designed special Bauhaus work clothes, "a monkish outfit" made at the school with "funnel-like trousers, wide at the top and narrow at the bottom, and a high-necked jacket fastened by a belt of the same material,"[162] which only he and his most devoted students wore and that was emphatically rejected by Gropius as gratuitous "fancy dress." Symptomatically, Itten was eventually forced out and replaced by László Moholy-Nagy who, as Pevsner points out, is symbolically photographed at the school in overalls, the American workman's uniform that Loos had predicted will eventually take over from the suit in the world of everyday dress.[163] It is not by chance that Herbert Bayer goes out of his way to praise Gropius for dressing like a regular person in restrained clothes in order to sustain his polemical call for standards:

> gropius wore black trousers, white shirt, slim black bow tie,
> and a short natural-colored leather jacket
> which squeaked with each movement.
> his short mustache, trim figure, and swift movements
> gave him the air of a soldier
> (which in fact he had been until recently).
> gropius' manner of dress was in contrast
> to the generally fantastic individualistic appearances
> around the Bauhaus.

it was a statement of his opinion
that the new artist need not oppose his society
by wearing dress that, to begin with,
would set him apart from the world he lives in,
that the step toward common understanding
would be acceptance of such standards
as would not infringe on a free spirit.[164]

The modern architect, like the modern city dweller and the modern building that Loos describes, is not meant to stand out. While the first modern buildings may stand out from the dominant architecture left over from a previous time, the end point of the modern project is standardization: if not a uniform per se, a certain uniformity. The look of the architect has to participate in the economy of modern architecture.

Gropius's comprehensive detachment from fashion, and women's clothes in particular, is again linked to a rejection of "masquerade" in architectural design. When his "The Development of Modern Industrial Architecture" of 1913 praises Behrens's factory designs, it is because they abandon the traditional use of a "sentimental mask" that covers the "naked form of utilitarian building," "distorting the true character of the building by allowing it to masquerade in borrowed garments from an earlier period...a period got up in fancy-dress."[165] But it is not a question of simply opposing the naked mechanized body to the fashionable clothes that disguise it. Like Behrens, Gropius follows Riegl in arguing against extreme functionalism understood as "materialism." Functionalism, like ornamentalism, is seen as the product of "superficial minds." While it is necessary to achieve what his *The New Architecture of the Bauhaus* calls the "liberation of architecture from a welter of ornament,"[166] this liberation is seen as only one side of the modern project. The other is to employ art to counteract the horror of the mechanization of the material world, the tyranny of the machine, whose "misuse" is creating what he elsewhere calls a "soul-flattening mass mind."[167] This horror of the "new world order"—of the machine—is symbolized, as it would later be for his promoter Giedion, by the "sub-human, robot-like automaton."[168]

Mechanization is seen as a means of liberation and not an end in itself. On the contrary, it is a nightmare if undisciplined by art, which must engage with the very structures of modern life, modifying new buildings even while lightly clothing them. It is the clothing that must engage with, rather than dissimulate, the newly mechanized body. As Gropius would argue in his "Eight Steps to a Solid Architecture" of 1954, the insecurity produced by a new organization of building cannot be disguised by a "new look" generated by the architectural fashion industry:

> The stark and frightening realities of our world will not be softened by dressing them up with the 'new look' and it will be equally futile to try to humanize our mechanized civilization by adding sentimental fripperies to our homes...architecture will reveal the emotional qualities of the designer in the very bones of the buildings, not in the trimmings only.[169]

For Gropius, a modern style would be just as evasive as the old styles, and ultimately just as much of a trap, sustaining the very nightmare it attempted to disguise. As he puts it: "it is just as easy to create a modern straightjacket as a tudor one."[170] The problems of the age cannot be solved by new clothes, no matter how modern they look. Gropius, like all his peers, is everywhere against fashion. His generic attack on style is an attack on "personal whims or fashionable styles,"[171] the "newest local fashions which disappear as fast as they appear."[172] This had already been made clear in his "Ornament and Modern Architecture" of 1938, which paraphrases Muthesius in arguing that "true ornament" is the product of the collective unconscious over a period of time rather than individual desires that can only produce "transitory fashions," which, like all fashions, are "doomed to failure."[173] Opposing any form of "masquerade," the text emphatically concludes that: "Instead of wearing again and again the self-deceiving garment of former periods...let's face the future. *Forward* to tradition. The Ornament is dead! Long live the Ornament!"[174]

It must be emphasized again that this promotion of standards against fashion is not against clothing per se. On the contrary, clothing acts as the very model of standards. In a 1924 article called "Housing and Industry" that promotes the industrialization of building, Gropius had argued that architecture should follow the modern standardization of clothes:

> Is it a reflection of man's way of life that each individual's dwelling should differ entirely from that of every other individual? Is it not a sign of intellectual impoverishment and fallacious thinking to furnish a dwelling in rococo or Renaissance style while identical modern clothes are worn in all parts of the world?...*The majority of citizens of a specific country have similar dwelling and living requirements; it is therefore hard to understand why the dwellings we build should not show a similar unification as, say, our clothes, shoes or automobiles.* The danger of undesirable suppression of legitimate individual requirements should be no greater here than in the case of fashions.[175]

When discussing standard types two years later in an essay on "Principles of Bauhaus Production," Gropius returns to the exemplary quality of "modern" clothes: "Modern man, who no longer dresses in historical garments but wears modern clothes, also needs a modern home appropriate to him and his time, equipped with all the modern devices of daily use."[176] It is not by chance that Gropius paid so much attention to the place of clothes in the modern house, using a 1930 Bauhaus book to publish cinematic sequences of coats, hats, shoes and shirts being stored away (symptomatically, the man's clothes are dealt with by a maid and the woman's are dealt with by herself).[177] The question of the house is first of all a question of clothing. Even when addressing Behrens in the 1913 essay, it was a question of dress. Behrens's architecture is modern because it "convey[s] the impression of coherent architecture which has at last discovered the right dress for the life style of the times and firmly rejects the romantic residue of past styles as cowardly and unreal."[178] And, as Gropius says of the enlightened industrial client: "a handsome outfit reflects on its wearer and the new design will encourage positive conclusions as to the character of the firm as a whole."[179] To dress oneself up in the right architecture is to modernize oneself. Likewise, a handsome surface reflects well on the building it

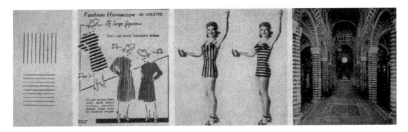

FIG. 10 *Illustration of psychological effects of visual patterns, from Walter Gropius, "Design Topics,"* Magazine of Art, *December 1947, 300.*

clothes. While a "new look" cannot, in the end, cover over the problems of mechanization, the solving of those problems is best exemplified by the correct choice of clothes.

In fact, the look is all-important. Gropius ends up arguing that the experience of architecture is fundamentally optical. Equating the human eye with a camera, he argues that architecture is not a question of material or structural reality but of the effect of the particular surfaces it presents to the observer. At one point, his "Is There a Science of Design?" of 1947 goes as far as comparing the effect on the psychological perception of a building produced by the addition of particular patterns to the effect of the same patterns on a woman's swimsuit. In adding these patterns of parallel lines to the original photos, he elaborates a "fashion tip" that he found in a newspaper. The optical effect of such lines is apparently "an important fact to know for architecture and fashion design."[180] In going on to describe a number of such optical effects, Gropius offers his own set of fashion tips, suggesting that the "surfaces" of architecture can be deployed in a way that produces the much needed "stimulation." These tips are presented as the "common denominator" of design, the basic "language" with which the designer can "organize the psychological effects of his creation at will." Modern architecture is understood as a kind of ongoing research into this language of sartorial effects.

While such theories of perception are used to determine the correct choice of clothes for architecture, this choice is not meant to restrict the choices of its occupants. On the contrary, Gropius uses his 1924 article on industrialized housing to argue that standardized clothes act as a model of individual variations within the collective social body: "Adequate freedom remains for the individual or national character to express itself, exactly as in the case of our clothing, and yet all of it will bear the stamp of our era."[181] A year later, when he publishes the work of the Bauhaus workshops (which, of course, does not include clothes), he renegotiates the long-debated relationship between standard types and individual expression by appealing to the standardization of clothes in the face of fashion:

> A violation of the individual by the production of types is to be feared as little as a full uniformization of clothing by the dictates of fashion. Despite the typical homogeneity of the separate parts, the individual reserves a free play of personal variation.[182]

It is not surprising that two years later Gropius's "How Can We Build Cheaper, More Attractive Houses?" literally argues that the standard parts of an industrialized architecture should be be purchased "off-the-peg," like shoes, and that their "recurrence in differently shaped buildings will have an orderly and soothing effect as does the uniformity of our clothes."[183] And by the time of *The New Architecture and the Bauhaus* (1935), these isolated claims had been gathered together and reformulated as a concise argument:

> The repetition of standardized parts, and the use of identical materials in different buildings, will have the same sort of coordinating and sobering effect on the aspect of our towns as uniformity of type in modern attire has in social life. But that will in no sense restrict the architect's freedom of design. For although every house and block of flats will bear the unmistakable imprint of our age, there will always remain, as in the clothes we wear, sufficient scope for the individual to find expression for his own personality.[184]

Indeed, Gropius's 1910 "Program for the Establishment of a Company for the Provision of Housing on Aesthetically Consistent

Principles" had already credited this "civilizing" transnational uniformity of clothing types to fashion itself: "National costumes tend to disappear and fashion is becoming a common factor in all civilized countries. In the same way there is bound to be a common factor in all civilized countries."[185] But having dislodged regional characteristics, fashion itself must be disciplined, brought into line—a line it cannot twist. Since standardizing clothes in this way is not to impose a uniform, Gropius uses a late address of 1953, to literally criticize the West Point military uniforms shown in a photograph for their "deliberate rigid conformity; de-individualization of the wearer" in contrast to the variations evident within a photograph of the traditional dress of Japan and India that is captioned: "Unity of basic cut, but individual variation of patterns and accessories."[186] Standardized architecture, the architecture that resists fashion, is a basic wardrobe of garments that go together in different combinations. Gropius's industrialized housing projects were always conceived as kits of standard parts that could be purchased and assembled in different combinations, mix-and-match architecture that, with the judicious addition of patterns and accessories, supposedly enables endless variations without participating in the degenerate economy of fashion. And, of course, each part, each garment, was coated in white to signal its resistance to that economy.

But this rejection of fashion in favor of standardized clothes, like all such attacks, threatens to turn against the person who makes it. From the beginning, Gropius preemptively defends himself against this threat by denying that the Bauhaus itself is concerned with producing a house style, a new fashion, a "vogue" of "bauhaus garb."[187] The constant threat is that the removal of ornament might itself be perceived as a fashionable move. Indeed, he must immediately defend himself against repeated claims that the role of the school was precisely to produce an easily marketed fashion line. *The New Architecture and the Bauhaus* notes that: "we had also to hold our own in another direction: against detractors who sought to identify every building and object in which ornament seemed to be discarded as examples of an imaginary 'Bauhaus Style'; and imitators who prostituted our fundamental precepts into modish trivialities."[188] The book attempts to defend the whole project of modern architecture from such accusations and appropriations:

> Although the outward forms of the New Architecture differ fundamentally in an organic sense from those of the old, they are not the personal whims of a handful of architects avid for innovation at all cost, but simply the inevitable logical product of the intellectual, social and technical conditions of our age...But the development of the New Architecture encountered serious obstacles at a very early stage of its development...Worst of all, 'modern' architecture became fashionable; with the result that formalistic imitation and snobbery distorted the fundamental truth and simplicity on which this renaissance was based. That is why the movement must be purged from within if its original aims are to be saved from the straight-jacket of materialism and false slogans inspired by plagiarism or misconception.[189]

Window interior of Walter Gropius's Faguswerke, Alfeld, Germany (1911–1914). From Casabella 311 (1966), 62. **FIG. 11**

From the beginning, the protagonists of modern architecture attempted to discipline not only the material building but also their colleagues. In a sense, Giedion attempted to carry out the "purge" Gropius called for, relentlessly negotiating between the danger of the straight-jacket on the one hand and that of fashionable clothes on the other, the encyclopedic scale of his work veiling the specific exclusions and censorships necessary to disassociate modern architecture from fashion. In the end, he fails to save his favorite architect. Gropius's defence eventually collapses; by the mid-sixties he is routinely condemned as a fashion-monger. Even his first curtain wall, hung at the Fagus factory in 1911, around which Giedion and Pevsner's extraordinarily influential narratives are organized, such that the building, as Banham puts it, "is frequently taken to be the first building of the Modern Movement properly so-called,"[190] is dismissed. It ends up being identified as but a decorative front added to give a modern "look" to a traditional structure whose internal layout and details (except for a very Hoffmannesque lobby) had in fact already been designed by another architect. The client literally commissioned Gropius to "see what you can do with the facade," providing the *künstlerische* ("artistic") design for the project "in order to give the whole plant a *geschmacksvoll* (tasteful, even "fashionable") appearance."[191] The famous floating glass wall that supposedly unmasks architectural space turns out to be but a fashionable mask of transparency disguising what it apparently reveals. And this masquerade is treated as exemplary of Gropius's life work rather than its necessarily limited beginnings, let alone as a clue to the operations of all modern architecture. He ends up being vilified in surprisingly dismissive terms by influential writers of the following generation, like Colin Rowe, and their followers. While marketing their own form of analysis (itself extremely vulnerable to the very same critique), they argue that he is an inadequate architect who produced a marketable style for easy consumption, even crediting his emphasis on a "camouflage of retinal excitement" that supposedly reinforces a logic of the "false front" with the emergence of postmodernism.[192] The anti-fashion argument has turned on its most dedicated promoter and devoured him.

Why is it that the other "masters," his fellow apprentices in Behrens's office, Le Corbusier and Mies van de Rohe, and all their colleagues, are not brought before the inquisition—even though so many of them seem more vulnerable to the charge? Indeed, Gropius's collapse into fashion is often opposed to Le Corbusier's resistance to it.[193] He is, as it were, the master who must be sacrificed in order to maintain the good name of modern architecture, removing the taint of fashion without threatening the movement. But the convolutions of fashion are clearly not unique to Gropius. They can easily be found in all his contemporaries who, while never being dismissed, employ exactly the same arguments against fashion in favor of standardized clothing but, in so doing, likewise organize modern architecture around the necessity for a certain "look" inextricably linked to the world of fashion. Gropius is not even an especially good example of the fashion trap. Indeed, he may well have been singled out for excommunication precisely because of his lifelong commitment to industrialized housing (where the aesthetic choices are supposedly made by the client rather than the name designer) and his parallel commitment to collaboration. Both gestures blur the artist's signature and thereby threaten the very idea of mastery. In the end, Gropius effaces the ostensible gap between high signature design and the marketplace, a move that had already been formulated in the Bauhaus ideal of the "anonymous designer" and was maintained by his refusal to disguise the "commercial" basis of his late work. It is one of the intricacies of the fashion trap that those who are dismissed as fashionable are usually dismissed because something in their practice exposes the duplicity of the anti-fashion argument. Precisely by being more rigorous in certain dimensions of his opposition to fashion and thereby redefining certain institutional practices, Gropius is dismissed by those who wish to preserve those practices. After all, the attempt to discipline figures like Gropius is no more than an attempt to preserve the discipline.

DISCIPLINING THE SURFACE

In fact, Gropius's use of the standardization of modern clothing as the model for modern architecture, and the corresponding promotion of the calculated "look" of modernity, is written into the entire discourse around that architecture. Take his colleague in the

Deutscher Werkbund, Bruno Taut, for example. His *Modern Architecture* of 1929 opens with the generic contrast between the "old-fashionedness" of the contemporary house and the style of modern clothes, asking how it would look if the "be-wigged, long coated gentlemen and ladies in hoops" that belong to that architecture were to ride in the latest car.[194] Taut concludes that "tailors and dressmakers," like the engineers and constructors of modern technical equipment, "have merely accomplished what we architects now consider necessary to accomplish in our own profession."[195] This general claim resonates throughout the specific details of the text, as when it criticizes the use of architectural styles to mask the new reality of engineering construction, so prevalent that the architectural term "facade" has become the general term for "mask"[196] and a pervasive logic of fashion has taken over:

> As in the face of an incontrovertible law of nature, we must bow to the fact that in architecture there will always be some who, like wholesale outfitters and costumers, will have saleable models and "designs" in stock, people who are ever on the look out for the newest patterns and "dernier cri," which, accordingly, they are able to turn into cash.[197]

Against such fashion retailers with their ready-to-wear architectural fashions, Taut later defends the standardized business suit as a model for architecture, arguing that neither modern business leaders nor their buildings need old-fashioned "costume" or "fancy-dress" to signify their prestige. Just as the business leader "might miss the ease of his tailored suit" if he were "attired in the trappings" of old wealth, "so would the fulfillment of purpose suffer under the stress of an architectural 'costume.'"[198] Nevertheless, almost all state buildings are seen to employ such an "absurd masquerade"; the new League of Nations building exemplifies it by adopting a "masquerading attitude" that establishes a "disguise covering the clean-cut reality of the building's purpose."[199] Not surprisingly, Le Corbusier's rejected scheme is offered as the model of a well-tailored building. Later in the text, the social consequences of removing the clothing of architectural styles are drawn out by comparing the way the building has traditionally been forced to labor "under the disguise and shrouding of the purpose itself" to the way the "workman" has traditionally been forced to "wear a special costume, just as waiters to-day still wear their dress-suits" when working in the presence of the ruling class.[200] While opposed to the whims of fashion, modern architecture is, from the beginning, an art of tailoring.

Similar arguments can be found in the influential essays of Theo van Doesburg of the same time. His 1925 article "The Ambiguous Mentality: Factory and Home," for example, explicitly argues that the new goal throughout European architecture is a form of tailoring that privileges form over decoration: "The architecture of the past, which over-indulged in decorative ostentation, was stripped of its earrings, necklaces and lace frills. What counted most was 'tailoring.' Everything that did not belong to the essence of the architectural *form* was eliminated."[201] Significantly, it is German architects, like Behrens, Gropius, Otto Wagner and Adolf Loos, who have been "reared with excellent theories (for instance Semper's *Der Stil*)"[202] that are seen to have effected this move towards a more functional dress for architecture—as distinct from an architecture in which all dress has been removed. Likewise, van Doesburg's 1926 article "Defending the Spirit of Space," with its emphatic subtitle, "Against a Dogmatic Functionalism," argues: "As during the course of time the tailoring of our clothing, the shapes of transportation vehicles, our hairdos, handwriting etc. have changed, so has the 'tailoring' of architecture changed—and because of the same reasons."[203] The specific role of this tailoring is identified in another essay of the same year that addresses the industrialization of architecture along assembly line principles. Symptomatically, this is illustrated with a photo of a "Ladies' Fashion Boutique" designed in 1923, called "Femina," that was described as "facade-architecture with reminiscences of the Wiener Werkstätte."[204] Such individual fashions are opposed to

the sense of standardized tailoring that had been promoted by
Loos:

> It is always a sign of a kind of narrow-mindedness when a per-
> son dresses very individualistically, according to his or her
> own design and own tailoring. "The modern, intelligent person
> must present a mask to other people," says Loos. This mask is
> the general life form, originating from necessity and culture, a
> person's life habits, his clothing and physiognomy, all crystal-
> lized together in his dwelling. His dwelling is his mask.[205]

The removal of the decorative mask of fashion is clearly not the
removal of all masks. If for Loos, as Colomina argues, the exterior
of the house should discretely mask its interior in the same way
that the nervous individual is securely walled in by a business suit
or dinner jacket within the crowded metropolis, then ornament is to
be disciplined rather than removed. After all, the structure it covers is not so secure. On the contrary, it is the source of all insecurity, including that experienced by the discipline of architecture.
Like the building, the architect has to blend in with the crowd. As
Margaret Olin puts it when describing Loos's use of Semper:

> [While Loos] cleansed his surfaces of ornament to reveal
> underlying structures, the same goal led the nineteenth-
> century architect to cover surfaces with ornament, revealing
> structure through clarification and punctuation...The covertly
> symbolic nature of self-representation in modernism is more
> obvious in human self-representation as expressed in clothing.
> Modernist architects were in agreement that such representa-
> tion should be forthright, and done without ornament. Yet the
> modernist demonstrated his lack of ornament only by cladding
> himself in the symbols, such as the 'correct hat,' that demon-
> strate one's membership in society.[206]

The logic of the well-cut suit is that of the disciplined surface, the
set of clothes whose smooth surface maintains certain distinctions
(notably, masculine versus feminine, upper versus lower, and so
on), yet gives nothing away. Everywhere, the discourse of modern
architecture turns on the privileged status of the smooth surface.
For van Doesburg, for example, the search for well-tailored archi-

tecture corresponds to the search for forms with "an *inner purity and with an outer surface of equal merit*."[207] Despite his rejection of the dangerously fashionable manipulation of surface, the end point is always the surface. In a Semperian sense, structure has to be disciplined in order to make the right surface possible. The final goal is the surface, not the construction that supports it. Architecture is no more than an effect of surfaces, an effect that is facilitated by the structure that props the surfaces up, but one that is, in the end, independent of that structure. Van Doesburg's review of the 1927 Weissenhof Siedlung makes it clear that for him as for Gropius, even while he criticizes Le Corbusier's excessively painterly concern with "surprising visual effects," it is the look of the surfaces presented to its occupants, understood as the look of its clothing, that determines the effect of architecture:

> It is my utter conviction...that only the *ultimate surface* is decisive in architecture...the ultimate surface is in itself the result of the construction. The latter expresses itself in the ultimate surface. Bad construction leads to a bad surface...the finishing touch is in the finish of the surface...the development of the ultimate surface is essential...only the surface is of importance to people. Man does not live within the construction, within the architectural skeleton, but only touches architecture essentially through its ultimate surface (externally as the city scape, internally as the interior). The functional element becomes automatic, only the summarizing surface is of importance, for sensory perception as well as for psychological well-being. It has an impact on the morale of the inhabitant...Houses, are like people. Their features, posture, gait, clothing, in short: their surface, is a reflection of their thinking, their inner life.[208]

This physiognomic privileging of the surface, and the smooth surface in particular, understood as a form of clothing, is especially evident in Giedion's writing. It is even written into his historiographical method which involves interrogating the multiple surfaces of everyday cultural life. He always describes history in terms of surface: the forward to *The Beginnings of Art*, for example, refers to "our attitude towards the past, that measureless container of human experience, only fragments of which come up to the surface, most of it lying dominant in unfathomable depths," before going on to argue that "both above and below the surface of our present age there is a new demand for continuity."[209] Giedion inherited this approach from his teacher, Heinrich Wölfflin, whose "psychology of art" involves scrutinizing all the surfaces of society, especially its clothes. Indeed, Wölfflin (an earnest supporter of clothing reform[210]) literally equates the surfaces of architecture with those of clothes.[211] Likewise, Giedion's approach remains Semperian, despite its overt rejection of Semper, inasmuch as it focuses on smaller-scale anonymous forms of production.[212] The qualities he seeks in *Space, Time and Architecture*, while everywhere opposing fashion, are "flat unmodulated surfaces...naked wall...flat surface...no restlessness or turbulence." Until "the pure flat surface" of modern architecture, the wall had been "either chaotically dismembered or deception." Indeed, modern architecture is seen to modern only insofar as it transforms the status of the surface:

> Surface, which was formerly held to possess no intrinsic capacity for expression, and so at best could only find decorative utilization, has now become the basis of composition...surface acquired a significance it had never known before.[213]

This new status is explicitly opposed to the superficial qualities of fashion. The flat wall, the plane surface, is "not simply another transitory fashion but an inner affinity,"[214] a moral identification with inner human needs that, as he says later, "were just coming to the surface." Since these fundamental needs transcend history, the place to find them is in pre-history. Giedion's last books, the two on *The Eternal Present*, go to a lot of trouble to demonstrate that art originates with the "smooth, shadowless plane surface."[215] Modern art is thus seen as therapeutic inasmuch as it recovers this primordial surface in the face of all the decorative excesses that actively suppress it. What comes to the surface, then, is the smooth surface. All Giedion's talk about the need to penetrate the surface in order to avoid its seductions does not lead to its rejection. On the contrary, it is all about the preservation of a particular kind of surface, one that can discipline the ornamentation that might be embroidered upon it. All the scholarly rhetoric about the need for depth gives way to a formidable regime of the smooth surface.

In fact, Giedion's grand narrative about the three space conceptions that have orchestrated the millennia is nothing more than a history of the status of surface. It follows Riegl in beginning with the Egyptian and Greek conception in which the pre-historic play of "endlessly changing surfaces" is reassembled to create a "smooth unbroken plane," a sensuous surface without any sense of space.[216] This in turn gives way in the middle of the Roman period to a conscious search for space, understood as the depth of an interior. When modern art begins to produce the third conception, this is framed as a return to the first conception, if not its prehistoric origins, inasmuch as there is no longer a clear-cut distinction between inside and outside; rather, there is a collage of suspended and mobile surfaces in which, in its definitive form, "solid and void, inside and outside, flow continuously into one another."[217] Naturally, Giedion sees modern architecture, and Le Corbusier's work in particular, as exemplifying this "rediscovery of the surface plane."[218] Indeed, Giedion's loyalty swings from Gropius to Le Corbusier in order to preserve this analysis; the new introduction to the last edition of *Space, Time and Architecture* insists that "Le Corbusier was more closely connected than others to that Eternal Present which lives in the creative artifacts of all periods."[219]

Clearly Le Corbusier, like Giedion, presents the smooth wall as a moral code rather than a fashion statement. The emphatic privileging of the surface is equally explicit in his writing. When he insists that architecture should be stripped of its outmoded fashions, he maintains that its body is still "clothed" by a surface—a surface that, no matter how thin, still has the capacity to threaten the mass it covers. That it must, therefore, be disciplined, is apparent in the second (and almost always omitted) part of what is probably Le Corbusier's most often cited statement:

FIG. 12 *Le Corbusier and Pierre Jeanneret, Villa Savoye, Poissy (1928–1930). Page from* L'Architecture Vivante, *1931.*

> Architecture being the masterly, correct and magnificent play
> of masses brought together in light, the task of the architect is
> to vitalize the surfaces which clothe these masses, but in such
> a way that these surfaces do not become parasitical, eating up
> the mass and absorbing it to their own advantage.[220]

It is no surprise that Giedion is one of the few writers to cite this
passage in full, which he does at the conclusion of *The Beginnings*

of Architecture.[221] His claim that Le Corbusier leads the way in the modern "revitalization" of the surface comes directly from Le Corbusier's writings, which present a comprehensive theory of the disciplined surface. Much more of *Towards an Architecture*, for example, is devoted to the question of surface than the section literally entitled "Surface." With the removal of the dead clothes, the surface fabric must be "appropriated" again by the internal logic of the building, "revitalized from within," such that forms "display

Le Corbusier and Pierre **FIG. 13**
Jeanneret, Villa La Roche (1923),
published by Sigfried Giedion in
Der Cicerone *19, 1927, 188.*

their own surfaces."[222] This requires a new kind of surface, a new kind of cloth that is neither completely opaque or completely transparent to the forms it covers. The thick "old clothes" produced by the "surface decoration of facades and of drawing-rooms" are to be supplanted by the recovery of the architecture of the "great periods" when "facades were smooth" and "walls were as thin as they dare make them."[223] The surface is not simply recovered by utility. Rather, it assumes its own utility, its function becoming more important than that of the building it clothes. Rather than lining an architectural space that facilitates certain functions, the surface produces the effect of space in the first place. For Le Corbusier, the specific dilemma is how to rupture this surface for functional reasons while maintaining the strategic effects of space and mass it produces.

Furthermore, this exemplary surface that actively resists the immoralities of fashion, and around which the discourse of modern architecture organizes itself, is not simply smooth. It is white. The disciplined surface is exemplified by the white wall. In the face of the wild colors of the old clothes embraced by the "sensualists," Le Corbusier counters: "There is only one color, white; always powerful since it is positive."[224] This stark opposition between fashion and the white wall becomes even more clear in *The Decorative Art of Today*:

> What shimmering silks, what fancy, glittering marbles, what opulent bronzes and golds! What fashionable blacks, what striking vermilions, what silver lamés from Byzantium and the Orient!
> Enough.
> Such stuff founders in a narcotic haze. Let's have done with it.
> We will soon have had more than enough.
> It is time to crusade for whitewash and Diogenes.[225]

It must be remembered that Diogenes is a key figure for all the writers that Le Corbusier appropriates extensively: Behrens, Loos, Muthesius and Morris. Like the other "ornamentalist," Semper (and his disciples Sullivan and Loos), Morris uses Diogenes's polemical refusal of excess (including the distinction between clothes and house) as a model for the reduction of ornamentation in favor of essentials that allows ornament to then be liberated without degenerating into gratuitous style. Symptomatically, Morris approves of Diogenes's minimalist house at the beginning of an essay that ends by arguing that the way the "simplicity" of contemporary women's dress design has resisted the "extravagances of fashion" is the appropriate model for reform in the other arts.[226] Le Corbusier's reference to Diogenes is therefore charged in a very particular way. His text, as always, is organized around its sporadic jabs against fashion. It attacks the Sun King's "coiffure of ostrich feathers, in red, canary, and pale blue; ermine, silk, brocade, and lace"[227] as an "intoxication." Elsewhere, it lampoons a book entitled *Fashionable Architecture* and a journal subtitled *Literature, Art, Fashion*. The historical styles, which are described as random surface "modalities," "narcotic fetishes," are yet again linked to misplaced sexuality. But still, this "quasi-orgiastic decoration" must be replaced rather than simply removed. Even the idea of "expressing the construction" is dismissed, as it had been by Sullivan, as being no more than a "fashion."[228] The body is not to be exposed. It is not a question of wearing clothing which represents the structure it covers, but of wearing minimal clothing, a decent cover. The surfaces which clothe architecture must remain a discrete mask.

Again, it is crucial to understand that for Le Corbusier these surfaces produce space as such rather than appear "in" it. The house, for example, is defined by surfaces. It is nothing but a set of surfaces. As can be seen *The Radiant City* of 1933, Le Corbusier's understanding of housing is literally that of the "habitable surface,"[229] which is to say, the surface that caters to all the body's needs and thereby frees the mind. It is in this sense that he associates surface, cleanliness, order, morality, and tailoring: "To walk over a clean surface, to look at an orderly scene. Live *decently*. Only the tailor, the shoemaker and the laundryman help us to hold on to the right to remain the intellects of the universe."[230] Le Corbusier's architecture is indeed a tailored architecture. While the body of the building has been exercised, has become leaner and fitter, like those that promenade within it, the design of its outfit is a separate problem. A thin mask is required but a mask nonetheless—one that transforms the psychological effect of the structure it veils.

This layer becomes visible as such when Giedion publishes before and after images of Villa la Roche in a 1927 issue of *Der Cicerone* (and later in *Bauen en Frankreich*) that demonstrate the extent to which the machine age finish of white painted stucco is but a "look" that veils the basically handcrafted structure beneath, just as Badovici's publication of before and after images of Villa Savoye will do in a 1931 issue of *L'Architecture Vivante*. While Le Corbusier himself never publishes such revealing images (and Giedion leaves them out of *Space, Time and Architecture*), it is clear that he actually perfects the mask before perfecting the construction underneath, mastering the image of modern functionality before functionality itself. He ultimately gives up on the white exterior surface only because he lacks the technical control to avoid cracks—cracks that completely subvert the status of the surface by revealing that it is but a coat. The central issue is always the technology of the surface itself rather than the technology of what it covers.

ANYONE FOR TENNIS?

The white wall has to be understood in terms of the specific argument about clothing and architecture that Le Corbusier imported, stripped of its signature, and redistributed (along with so much of the German discourse). This argument ties the "Law of Ripolin" back to Semper's "Principle of Dressing" through the intermediary of Loos's "Law of Dressing." The initially surprising connection is far from arbitrary. Not only was Le Corbusier drawing on a German discourse multiply indebted to Semper's arguments, but his particular translation of that discourse required at least a minimal staging of those very arguments. It is not by chance that the very first essay that Le Corbusier, Ozenfant and Demmer published in the first issue of *L'Esprit Nouveau*, written by Victor Basch, turns on Semper's account of the industrial arts, or that the second part of the essay begins the second issue in which Adolf Loos's "Ornament and Crime" is republished. Semper is, as it were, put in place to prop up the new discourse and then the prop is quickly thrown away.

Likewise, when Giedion produces an extreme version of Le Corbusier's argument, by elaborating on the trans-historical integrity of the smooth surface, it is not simply to establish a clear-cut opposition between the dissimulating texture of ornament and Art, which is seen to begin with such a surface. Giedion overtly follows Riegl (who is covertly following Semper) in arguing that art does not simply begin with the plane surface but with everything that might go on upon that surface, including and especially ornamentation. The plane surface is, then, no more than the mechanism for establishing that whatever goes "on" is ornamentation. The smooth surface is that which makes ornament visible. It is the very possibility of ornament as such, and therefore the possibility for a history of ornament as a history of culture's impressions upon it. But it cannot simply be separated from the ornament it makes visible as such. Giedion ends up, immediately after dismissing "the materialist approach of Gottfried Semper and his followers,"[231] by approving of Riegl's close echo of Semper that "sees ornamentation as the purest and most lucid expression of artistic volition."[232] In its very smoothness, the primordial surface participates fully in the ornamental economy of surface effects that it supposedly disciplines. Likewise, its whiteness participates fully in the economy of clothing whose excesses it supposedly restrains.

At first glance, it is clear that if women's fashion is almost invariably constructed as the limit of the discourse of modern architecture, the mark of its supposedly personal and feminine outside, then the mark of the inside, of the standard, of impersonal masculine detachment, is the white wall. Consequently, when fashion does become explicit, it is likely that the white wall, whose effects are usually mobilized without being marked, becomes explicit, and vice versa. When Marcel Breuer's 1934 essay entitled "Where do We Stand?" opposes the dangers of the "purely transient vogue" to the integrity of "winning color, plasticity, and animation from a flat white wall," for example, it is not surprising that it follows an explicit attack on women's fashions:

> The 'new' in the Modern Movement must be considered simply a means to an end, not an end in itself as in women's fashions. What we aim at and believe to be possible is that the solutions embodied in the forms of the New Architecture should endure for 10, 20 or 100 years as circumstances may demand—a thing unthinkable in the world of fashion as long as modes are modes. It follows that, though we have no fear of what is new, novelty is not our aim. We seek what is definite and real, whether old or new.

> ...we have tired of everything in architecture which is a matter of fashion; we find all intentionally new forms wearisome, and all those based on personal predilections or tendencies equally pointless. To which can be added the simple consideration that we cannot hope to change our buildings or furniture as often as we change, for example, our ties.[233]

For Breuer, as for all his colleagues, the Modern movement is the architectural equivalent of the masculine resistance to fashion. The white wall is an item of clothing, authorized at once by modernity and the classical tradition, a recovery of the spartan puritan dress that befits the controlled nobility required in the face of mechanized life. It is a kind of athletic dress. After all, Loos had argued that the rationalization of men's clothing derives from its adoption of the transformations in sports dress. The white wall is the sports outfit of architecture, a thin coat over the newly pumped-up body of the building, an exercise outfit like those that can be found in so many images of modern architecture that show its occupants working out, as in Breuer's own 1930 interior "for a lady gymnastics teacher." And it is not by chance that the figure is that of a woman: Loos had gone as far as to claim that the adoption of sports dress by women would not just

FIG. 14 *"The new practical tennis costume." From Siegfried Giedion,* Befreites Wohnen *(Zurich: Orell Füssli Verlag, 1929), 83. Taken by Giedion from* Illustriettes Blatt *(Frankfurt) 5, 1929.*

FIG. 15 *Traffic policeman in Milan. From Sigfried Giedion, "Situation de l'architecture Contemporani en Italie,"* Cahiers d'Art, *1931, 446.*

symbolize but actually effect their emancipation in its resistance to the immoral economy of fashion.[234] The body that needs to be tamed, disciplined by the emerging and regular rhythms of anonymous production, was understood to be feminine. The horror of mechanization is precisely its potential to release the very femininity it is supposed to control—the possibility that it might itself, in disordering the surfaces of everyday life, be feminine.

Perhaps the paradigm of modern architecture, in its simultaneous engagement with and resistance to mechanization, is the white tennis outfit (Fig. 14) at the end of Giedion's 1929 *Befreites Wohnen* (opposite an image of Andrè Lucrat's white rooftop gymnasium) that is worn by a woman that smiles coyly at the reader across the net—rather than the white uniform of the traffic policeman that Giedion smuggles into a 1931 survey of Italian architecture as if it is a kind of self-portrait of the historian directing the flow of architectural movements (Fig. 15). Or perhaps it is the white dress that Mercedez Benz associates with the surfaces of Le Corbusier's Weissenhof Siedlung building to advertise its latest sports car (Fig. 1).[235] But that makes us ask why Giedion's tennis outfit is also exhibited by a fashion model? Why has the image been taken from the fashion pages of an illustrated magazine? And why does the frontispiece of the book display a quote from Henry Ford—the very figure of mass-production and standardization—that appears to embrace the rapid turnover of clothing styles: "The form of housing will be transformed with the same speed that changes occur in the style of clothes and even the domestic situation will undergo alterations. Until now it took a lot of time, but from now on progress will set a very fast pace."[236] The logic of standardization seems to stand here for the accelerated circulation of fashions rather than the reverse. Which raises the possibility that the white wall, supposedly marking the loss of fashion, may itself be nothing more than a fashion statement, ready to be changed in the next season. All the elaborate attempts to isolate the white wall from fashion, locating it within a millennial tradition passing from ancient Egypt through the Mediterranean vernacular, may, in the end, be insufficient to block the obvious thought that it is just a look. But not just any look: it is the look of a resistance to fashion, the anti-fashion look.

The unique complications of this architectural fashion that so loudly proclaims its detachment from fashion need to be patiently traced and its historical specificities need to be carefully established in order to understand modern architecture's precise strategic role. Only after such an analysis would the nuances of the contemporary commodification of architectural discourse start to become visible. Clearly, the twisted but dominant (dominant because twisted) pathology of the anti-fashion look does not go away when white architecture is no longer in vogue. "White" architecture is itself not so white anyway. Most of the canonic walls were off-white (which necessitates an interrogation of the strategic role of a surface just short or long of white) and some of the most famous were actually lightly colored and only appear white in photographs, while the rest played a key role in organizing a whole system of polychromy. It is the "idea" of the white surface that plays a key role in holding together a specific conceptual economy, giving architecture a certain cultural status by maintaining certain assumptions about surface in general, rather than engaging with particular surfaces. The white surface marks the disavowal of the structural role of surface. The existence of one surface that denies surface—whether it be in one part of a building, or one part of a theory, or one historical moment—sustains an economy in which surface is everywhere subordinated. But this subordination is itself only ever a surface effect. It is the self-subordination of a surface that is more controlling than controlled. Modern architecture is never more than a surface effect. This is no way to call into question its force. On the contrary, it derives its force from the surface, concentrating its energies on the outer layer made available to the viewer, who is understood in Gropius's terms as a camera passing through the building. One photograph, that of the white wall, is seen to exemplify the whole process. It is the exposure of the exposure. The exposure of the surface that exposes everything.

To look closely at this white surface is to begin to call into question a cultural regime with wide-ranging effects, of which the glaring limitations of the dominant architectural historiography is but one symptom. A key symptom nevertheless, because that regime can only operate as a disciplinary mechanism by appealing to a certain image of architecture. It is not by chance that would-be cultural critics both within and outside architectural discourse actually consolidate the very economy they claim to critique by employing this image. They appeal to, and protect, a generic image of modern architecture, the image of the subordi-

White shirts framed by Louis Sullivan's Carson Pirie Scott department store (1899–1904), as originally published in Architectural Record *16:1 (July 1904), 58.* **FIG. 16**

nated surface. To see that this subordination is itself but a surface effect is not just to rethink modern architecture. It is also to displace the terms of political critique. To say the least, it becomes difficult to detach the so-called postmodern fashion industry from the so-called modern avant-garde.

Of course, these phenomena are very different and should never be confused. But neither can they simply be separated, let alone opposed, on the grounds that one accepts fashion and the other rejects it. Indeed, fashion is one of the things that bind them together in ways that the apologists for both forms of practice would find disconcerting. If the historical avant-garde still serves as the model for theorists who oppose fashion, it must be remembered that it is also the model for the very theorists and practitioners that they condemn. A more nuanced understanding of the way architecture participates in the contemporary economies of fashion would result from investigating the specific engagements with fashion that underpin critical practices rather than attempting to isolate architecture from fashion or mourning the loss of some mythical isolation in the near or distant past.

Since the extraordinarily overdetermined surface of the white wall is one of the strongest threads that stitch together the current marketplace of architectural discourse and that of the historical avant-garde, in ways that produce discomfort for the promoters of both, such an investigation might well begin by returning to the white surface to scratch the seemingly interminable itch produced by such an anti-fashion fashion.

After all, when Giedion tries to hold the line between the white surfaces of Sullivan's department store and the ornamental scheme of its ground-floors, it is not by chance that the role of that ornamentation is literally to frame fashion displays in the store windows. Giedion, who always associates fashion with ornament, and collected fashion plates of the period, was clearly aware of this. His text had already noted that American department stores emerged from "ready-to-wear clothing concerns" and even reproduced one of their earliest advertisements.[237] To exclude the ground floors was no more than the attempt to hold the line between modern architecture and fashion. To note that the fashions displayed in the windows were actually to be found above the line in the third and fourth floors (with "dress accessories" and "fabrics" on the lower floors) and, likewise, that Sullivan's ornament cannot be contained to the ground floor—that it passes up through the building's very structure, such that the white surface emerges from it, rather than exposes and excludes it—is only to say that the line between architecture and fashion is endlessly convoluted. Not only can fashion never be cut off from modern architecture, modern architecture emerges from the very economy of fashion that it so loudly condemns. Indeed, its very rejection of fashion is a product of that economy. To return yet again to the white surface will be to explore the complications of this simple, if not obvious, thought.

This text is the first part of a two part essay. The second part is in Assemblage *22. I would like to thank Sarah Ogger for her assistance with the German translations.*

NOTES

1   "In the seminar entitled 'Star Architects and Designer Buildings'...all the panelists agreed that the line between architecture and fashion is becoming thinner." Lynn Nesmith, "Design Theme Seminars as Diverse as Today's Architecture," *AIA Journal*, July 1988, 22, 27.

2   Le Corbusier, *Towards a New Architecture*, trans. Frederick Etchells (London: John Rodker, 1931), 94.

3   Ibid., 25.

4   Ibid., 17.

5   Ibid., 286.

6   Le Corbusier and Amédée Ozenfant, "Purism," *L'Esprit nouveau* (Paris) 4, 1920, in Tim and Charlotte Benton, eds., *Architecture and Design: 1890-1939* (New York: Watson-Guptill, 1975), 91.

7   Le Corbusier and Pierre Jeanneret, "Five Points of a New Architecture," in Benton and Benton, *Architecture and Design*, 153–155.

8   Le Corbusier, *Oeuvres complètes: Volume 1, 1910–29* (Zurich: W. Boesiger, 1929), 11. Translation modified.

9   Ibid., 11.

10   Sigfried Giedion, *Space, Time and Architecture: The Growth of a New Tradition* (Cambridge, Mass.: Harvard University Press, 1941), 115.

11   Sigfried Giedion, *Bauen en Frankreich. Eisen, Eisenbeton* (Berlin: Klinkhardt and Biermann Verlag, 1928), 5.

12   Ibid., 14.

13   Ibid., 106.

14   Richard Becherer, "Monumentality and the Rue Mallet-Stevens," *Journal of the Society of Architectural Historians* 40:1 (March 1981), 44–55. A

recent example, which confirms Becherer's claim, employing Giedion's original term "elegant," can be found in Tafuri and Dal Co: "The elegant and refined works of Mallet-Stevens, beginning with the De Noailles villa of 1923 in Hyères, were yet another product of an intimate converse with the Cubist vanguard that nonetheless kept its eye on the latest modes and fashions." Manfredo Tafuri and Francesco Dal Co, *Modern Architecture* (New York: Rizzoli, 1986), 233.

15   Giedion, *Bauen en Frankreich*, 3.

16   "History can reveal to our period the forgotten elements of its being, just as our parents can recover for us those childhood and ancestral peculiarities which continue to determine our natures though they are not to be found in our memories. A connection with the past is a prerequisite for the appearance of a new and self-confident tradition." Giedion, *Space, Time and Architecture*, 30.

17   "We intend to see how our period has come to consciousness of itself in one field, architecture...For a hundred years architecture lay smothered in a dead, eclectic atmosphere in spite of its continual attempts at escape. All that while, construction played the part of architecture's subconscious, contained things which it prophesied and half-revealed long before they could become realities." Ibid., 23.

18   Ibid., 175.

19   Ibid.

20   Ibid., 184.

21   Ibid., 402.

22   Giedion, *Bauen en Frankreich*, 1.

23   Ibid, 15.

24   Sigfried Giedion, "Mode oder Zeiteinstellung," *Information* (Zurich) 1, June 1932, 9.

25   Ibid., 8.

26   Ibid., 10.

27   Ibid.

28   Ibid., 11.

29   Giedion, *Space, Time and Architecture*, 99.

30   "At the present time the problem of constancy is of special consequence, since the threads of the past and of tomorrow have been brought into
disorder by an incessant demand for change for change's sake. We have
become worshipers of the day-to-day. Life runs along like a television program:
one show following relentlessly upon another, barely glancing at problems with
never a notion of taking hold of them organically. This has led to an inner
uncertainty, to extreme shortcomings in all essential phases of life: to what
Heidegger calls "a forgetfulness of being." In this situation the question of what
has been suppressed and driven back into the unconscious and of what must be
restored if man is to regain his equipose becomes a prime requirement for any
integrated culture." Sigfried Giedion, *The Eternal Present: The Beginnings of
Art* (Princeton: Princeton University Press, 1962), 7.

31   Ibid., xx.

32   Sigfried Giedion, *The Eternal Present: The Beginnings of Architecture*
(Princeton: Princeton University Press, 1964), x.

33   "I was so fascinated by pre-history that I gave it a good many years of
my life, because in pre-history you see mankind struggling against huge odds,
making tools, and somehow finding (through the shamans or whatever it was)
direct contact with the unknown forces. And we are somehow today in a similar
position. We are also opposed by unknown forces which we have to conquer."
Sigfried Giedion, *Ekistics* 21:123 (February 1966), 82.

34   Sigfried Giedion, *Space, Time and Architecture* (Cambridge, Mass.:
Harvard University Press, 1962), liii.

35   Ibid., xliii.

36   Ibid., 239.

37   Sigfried Giedion, "Ist das neue Bauen eine Mode?" *Basler Nachrichten*
(Basel), 13 November 1927, 215–216. Giedion associates fashion with the cult
of the individual that he had emphatically condemned in "Gegen Das Ich
(1918)" [Against the Ego], one of his first articles, which calls for unification:
"This has been the malady of the century: the Ego! We stand where it falls
apart. We are at a point where desire wants to see form split into folds no longer
but wrapped in a grand curve; where form does not remain solitary in space,
aloof and separate from all others, but overwhelmed and swept away by the
curve, into the great chain...The more impious times have grown, and the more
lost in triviality, the more stress has been laid on this: show your Ego, develop
your singularity...what distinguishes you from others is valuable, not what
unites. We acknowledge this: what unites will turn into value!" Sigfried
Giedion, "Gegen Das Ich," *Das Junge Deutschland* (Berlin) 8/9 (1918),

242–243. Trans. Romana Schneider and Miriam Walther, in *Domus* 678 (December 1986), 20–24.

38   "The historian, the historian of architecture especially, must be in close contact with contemporary conceptions...History is not simply the repository of unchanging facts, but a process, a pattern of living and changing attitudes and interpretations. As such, it is deeply a part of our own natures. To turn backward to a past age is not just to inspect it, to find a pattern which will be the same for all comers. The backward look transforms its object; every spectator at every period—at every moment indeed—inevitably transforms the past according to his own nature...History cannot be touched without changing it...observation and what is observed form one complex situation—to observe something is to act upon and alter it." Giedion, *Space, Time and Architecture*, 5.

39   Ibid., 18.

40   "What is normally meant by *operative criticism* is an analysis of architecture (or of the arts in general) that, instead of an abstract survey, has as its objective the planning of a precise poetical tendency, anticipated in its structures and derived from historical analyses programmatically distorted and finalized...operative criticism plans past history by projecting it towards the future...this type of criticism, by anticipating the ways of action forces history: forces past history because, by investing it with a strong ideological charge, it rejects the failures and dispersions throughout history, and forces the future because it is not satisfied with the simple registering of what is happening, but hankers after solutions and problems not yet shown (at least, not explicitly so)." Manfredo Tafuri, *Theories and History of Architecture*, trans. Giorgio Verrecchia (New York: Harper and Row, 1976), 141. Operative criticism gives history an "instrumental value": "a typical feature of operative criticism: its almost constant presentation of itself as a prescriptive code." Ibid., 144.

41   Ibid., 169. While opposing history and fashion in this way, the book later acknowledges that fashion has its own history: "The proliferation of studies on the semantics and semiology of architecture is due not only to a snobbish keeping up with the current linguistic *vogue*: every snobbism, anyway, derives its reasons from historical events, and the snobbisms of architectural culture do not escape this rule." Ibid., 174.

42   It is symptomatic that Tafuri does not acknowledge that Giedion spells out in detail the operative role of history. Giedion is made into an example of a phenomenon he had in fact theorized in detail and then, characteristically, has the operative role of his history of certain Italian developments analyzed rather than his claims about historiography. In an almost comic turn, Giedion is, in the end, incriminated for being exactly what he announces that he is from the

beginning. The question that remains is not so much the role of operative criticism in the formation of modern architecture, but the role of its acknowledgment, and, it could be added, the role of its ostensible rejection today.

43   Tafuri, *Theories and History*, 11.

44   Ibid., 7.

45   "And it is certainly not difficult to see, underneath an immediately fashionable phenomenon, made evasive by those who appropriated it for snobbish reasons, a frustrated revolt against a modern tradition which often with sincere despair, one saw fail." Ibid., 50.

46   Ibid., 51.

47   When Tafuri condemns the "'fashionable' architect" Robert Venturi because his book "employs 'fashionable' analytical methods, turning them, without any mediation, into 'compositive' methods," for example, this practice is sharply distinguished from those of the historical avant-garde—particularly Le Corbusier, with whom Vincent Scully is seen to have mistakenly compared it. Ibid., 213.

48   A critical practice is understood to be one that removes fashionable masks without installing new ones. It must "unmask the current mythologies...without proposing new myths." Ibid., 201. For Tafuri, these masks are not simply ornamental covers which conceal some structural reality. Rather they actively resist that reality. He describes the way in which architectural discipline resists the danger of its own exposure posed by semiotics, for example, precisely by appropriating semiotics, instrumentalizing it and thereby transforming it into a fashion. The ongoing "comfort" of the discipline is maintained by the mechanisms of fashion: "After all, what is comfortable in the present confused and contorted cultural situation is the possibility of continuous exchange between game and evasion, essential needs and fashionable phenomena, research and rhetorical toying with worn out instruments, honest critical commitment and conscious skepticism *à la jongler*. We were saying that this is a desperate but comfortable situation." Ibid., 211.

49   "'Operative criticism' accepts the current myths, enters into them, tries to create new ones, judges architectural production by the yardsticks of the objectives it itself has proposed and advanced. A criticism that pays attention to the relations between the single work and the system to which it belongs tends to throw light on and to unmask the current mythologies, invites a pitiless coherence. Even the extreme coherence of those who decide to remain (but consciously and critically) in the most absolute silence.'" Ibid., 210.

50 For Tafuri's eloquent revision of the status of history, which proposes a extreme self-critique to deal with the consequences of accepting the constructive—i.e. operative—nature of history, see particularly "Introduction: The Historical 'Project'," trans. Pellegrino d'Acierno and Robert Connolly, in *The Sphere and the Labyrinth: Avant-Gardes and Architecture from Piranesi to the 1970's* (Cambridge, Mass.: MIT Press, 1987), 1–24. While stressing the need to "weave together" multiple methodologies, the text still detaches itself, and the idea of history it promotes, from the complex effects of surface masks that the subsequent essays will go on to analyze in detail (particularly in the section on avant-garde theater costumes). Despite his refusal of a distinction between historiographical method and content, Tafuri never acknowledges his own use of masquerade, pushing certain surfaces forward for at once aggressive and defensive reasons rather than, as he symptomatically puts it, "penetrating" them. On the contrary, he attempts to fragment and redistribute the apparently unified fabric of history in order to resist its own deployment of dissimulating masks: "To look for fullness, an absolute coherence in the interaction of the techniques of domination, is thus to put a mask on history; or better, it is to accept the mask with which the past presents itself." (Ibid., 7) And this understanding of a unified sense of history as but a mask is literally based on Simmel's account of the mask of conformity in his classic essay on fashion. (Ibid., 5) Once again, all of the sophistication of Tafuri's argument is marshalled against fashion. For comprehensive and invaluable analyses of the strategic role of the surface as mask, see: Manfredo Tafuri, "*Cives esse non licere*: The Rome of Nicholas V and Leon Battista Alberti: Elements Towards a Historical Tradition," trans. Stephen Sartarelli, *Harvard Architectural Review* 6 (1987), 60-75; and Manfredo Tafuri, "The Subject and the Mask: An Introduction to Terragni," *Lotus International* 20 (September 1978), 5–29.

51 Manfredo Tafuri, "There is no Criticism, only History," *Design Book Review* 9 (Spring 1986), 11. A few years later, in what can only be described as a fashionable art magazine, Tafuri again condemns fashion, dismissing talk of the crisis of modernism as "fashionable social chit-chat," and criticizing the once "fashionable" applications of structuralism and semiology to art before describing the "elaboration of what merely amounts to so many modes of European dress" by American architects in the 1970s as being like "that taste for the exotic that was so fashionable in eighteenth-century salons." Again, fashion is associated with anxiety and astonishingly simplistically opposed to the qualities of "science" with which Tafuri always associates "good" history: "It's clear that fashion performs the function of reducing anxiety caused by the new. In fact, if we weren't accustomed to being saturated by artistic phenomena, we'd have no capacity for aesthetic understanding, or at least there would not be our widescale acceptance of modernity as a fact of mass culture. But this

is a question of human behavior, and is not any basis for the existence of, say, fashion in scientific fields, since science is based on conditions that are independent of facts of daily human nature." Manfredo Tafuri, "Interview," *Flash Art International* 145 (March/April 1989), 68.

52   Lionel Brett, *The Things We See: Houses* (West Drayton: Penguin Books, 1947), 34-36.

53   Ibid., 37.

54   Mark Wigley, "Architecture after Philosophy: Le Corbusier and the Emperor's New Paint," *Journal of Philosophy and the Visual Arts* 2 (1990), 84–95.

55   Loos, "Architecture" (1910), Yehuda Safran and Wilfred Wang, eds., *The Architecture of Adolf Loos* (London: Arts Council, 1987), 107.

56   See Roula Geraniotis, "German Architectural Theory and Practice in Chicago: 1850–1900," *Winterthur Portfolio* 21:4 (1986), 243–306.

57   For an important anlysis of this weave, see Jennifer Bloomer, "D'Or," in Beatriz Colomina, ed., *Sexuality and Space* (New York: Princeton Architectural Press, 1992), 163–184.

58   "It would be greatly for our aesthetic good, if we should refrain entirely from the use of ornament for a period of years, in order that our thought might concentrate acutely upon the production of buildings well formed and comely in the nude." Louis Sullivan, "Ornament in Architecture" (1892), in *Louis Sullivan: The Public Papers* (Chicago: University of Chicago, 1988), 80.

59   For a thorough analysis of these successive readings, see chapter three of Juan Pablo Bonta, *Architecture and its Interpretation: A Study of Expressive Systems in Architecture* (London: Lund Humphries, 1979).

60   Ibid., 80.

61   Adolf Loos, "Ornament und Erziehung" (1924), in *Sämtliche Shriften* (Vienna: Verlag Herold, 1962), 391–398.

62   "May the material speak for itself and appear undraped, in that form and under those conditions that experience and science have tested and proven the most suitable. May brick appear as brick, wood as wood, iron as iron, each according to its own law of statics. This is the true simplicity based on which one can devote oneself lovingly to the innocent needlepoint of decoration." Gottfried Semper, *Vorläufige Bemerkungen über bemalte Architektur und Plastik bei den Alten* (Altona, 1834). Cited in Fritz Neumeyer, *The Artless Word: Mies van der Rohe on the Building Art* (Cambridge, Mass.: MIT Press, 1991), 365 n8.

63   "Whereas Semper did suggest that material and technique play a role in the genesis of art forms, the Semperians jumped to the conclusion that all art forms were always the direct product of materials and techniques. 'Technique' quickly emerged as a popular buzzword; in common usage, it soon became interchangeable with 'art' itself and eventually began to replace it...They were, of course, not acting in the spirit of Gottfried Semper, who would never have agreed to exchanging free and creative artistic impulse [*Kunstwollen*] for an essentially mechanical and materialist drive to imitate. Nevertheless their misinterpretation was taken to reflect the genuine thinking of the great artist and scholar." Alois Riegl, *Problems of Style: Foundations for a History of Ornament*, trans. Evelyn Kain (Princeton: Princeton University Press, 1992), 4. "Semper would surely have been the last person to discard thoughtlessly truly creative, artistic ideas in favor of the physical-materialist imitative impulse; it was his numerous followers who subsequently modified the theory into its crassly materialist form." Ibid., 18. "According to Semper...technology played its formative role at a more advanced stage of artistic development and not at the very inception of artistic activity. This is precisely my conviction." Ibid., 23.

64   "This is not the first time such a proposition has been made; Semper himself expressed it several times." Ibid., 31.

65   "It will become evident, namely, that the human desire to adorn the body is far more elementary than the desire to cover it with woven garments, and that the decorative motifs that satisfy the simple desire for adornment... surely existed before textiles were used for physical protection....Surface decoration becomes that larger unit within which woven ornament is but a subset, equivalent to any other category of surface decoration. In general then, one of the main objectives of this book is to reduce the importance of textile decoration to the level it deserves." Ibid., 5.

66   Elsewhere, I have discussed the complications of this disciplinary tradition in detail. See Mark Wigley, *The Architecture of Deconstruction: Derrida's Haunt* (Cambridge, Mass.: MIT Press, 1993).

67   "The clearest case is architecture, next the crafts, particularly when they do not incorporate figurative motives: often architecture and these crafts reveal the basic laws of Kunstwollen with an almost mathematical clarity." Alois Riegl, *Late Roman Art Industry*, trans. Rolf Winkes (Rome: Giorgio Bretschneider, 1985), 15.

68   According to Behrens,

It is true that the engineer is the hero of our age, and that it is to him that we owe our economic position and our international standing...But it cannot be claimed that the creations of the engineers are in themselves already elements of an artistic style.

A certain modern school of aesthetic thought has promoted this misconception by wishing to derive artistic form from utilitarian function and technology. This view of art stems from the theories of Gottfried Semper, who defined the concept of style by demanding that the work of art should be the product first of its function and second of its materials and the tools and procedures involved. This theory comes from the middle of the last century, and should, like many others from this period, be seen as one of the dogmas of Positivism (Riegl).

Admittedly, when one recalls the "artistic" goods produced by industry over the last decades, one can understand how Semper's view could have been seen as a new truth...The bad workmanship and cheap materials of these products were covered up by as rich a decoration as possible...I am convinced that this shortcoming cannot be overcome by instructing the manufacturers to keep only to the most functional form. On the contrary, it seems to me much more important to try to understand the essential nature of art.

Art originates as the intuition of powerful individuals and is the free fulfillment of a psychological need...Or, as the Viennese scholar Riegl has put it, "Semper's mechanistic view of the nature of the work of art should be replaced by a teleological view in which the work of art is seen as the result of a specific and intentional artistic volition that prevails in the battle against functional purpose, raw materials, and technology." These three last-named factors lose, thereby, the positive role ascribed to them by the so-called Semper theory, and take on instead an inhibiting, negative role: "...they constitute, as it were, the coefficient of friction within the overall product."

Peter Behrens, "Art and Technology" (1910), trans. Iain Boyd Whyte, in Tilmann Beddensieg, *Industriekultur: Peter Behrens and the AEG, 1907–1914* (Cambridge: MIT Press, 1984), 213.

69   Even the subsequent, and apparently anti-Semperian claim that "architecture is the creation of volumes, and its task is not to clad but essentially to enclose space" (Ibid., 217), is Semperian, following Semper's basic argument that cladding is the production of space rather than an addition to it.

70   Walter Gropius, "The Development of Modern Industrial Architecture (1913)," *Jahrbuch des Deutschen Werkbundes* (Jena), 1912, 28–30 and 34–36, trans. Benton and Benton, *Architecture and Design: 1890–1939* (New York: Watson-Guptill 1975), 53–54.

71   Giedion, *Space, Time and Architecture*, 402.

72   Giedion, *The Beginnings of Art*, 15. For the argument's elaboration, see ibid., 40-42.

73   Giedion, *The Beginnings of Architecture*, 499.

74   Le Corbusier, *Towards a New Architecture*, 19.

75   See Harry Francis Mallgrave, "The Idea of Style: Gottfried Semper in London," dissertation, University of Pennsylvania, 1983.

76   For Giedion, 1910 is a key date: "a decisive year, marking the break-through of the movement." Giedion, *The Beginnings of Art*, 40. It is the year of the "optical revolution," beyond which artworks are no longer "out of fashion." Ibid., xx. By identifying Semper with the period before 1910, Giedion systematically associates him with the pre-modern rule of fashion. It is significant that Semper plays almost no part in *Space, Time and Architecture*, which tries to detach Modern Architecture from the Arts and Crafts Movement.

77   Karl Ernst Osthaus. "Austellung wiener Künstler im Folkwang," in *Hagener Zeitung* (Hagen), December 1, 1906. Cited in Werner J. Schweiger, *Wiener Werkstätte: Design in Vienna 1903–1932* (New York: Abbeville Press, 1984), 90. Osthaus became van de Velde's first biographer in 1920. On the dresses designed for his house, see Klaus-Jürgen Sembach, *Henry van de Velde* (New York: Rizzoli, 1989), 126.

78   "It is known that fashion loves to fall from one extreme to another and one could perhaps explain the psychological causes for this change in that certain organs that are activated in admiring form become weary in time and then make another place for this activity by directing themselves towards other forms." Hermann Muthesius, "Die Moderne Umbildung Unserer Ästhetischen Anschauungen" (1902), in *Kulture und Kunst*, 2nd ed. (Jena: Berlegt Bei Eugen Diederichs, 1909), 39. The essay was originally published in *Deutsche Monatsschrift für das gesamte Leben der Gegenwart*, 1.

79   Ibid., 64.

80   "Incidently, however, a change was introduced: the demand for variety led by fashion steered toward imitation of other predominately later styles of baroque, of the French style of Ludwig, of the empire. Throughout all the

changes in style, the industrial arts held true basic principle of inciting the historical styles against utilitarian form...If the eternal regurgitation of past forms was already in its own right a dubious activity, then it finally became positively degrading after fashion had chased the artists from one style to another. This aroused an aversion against historical style itself." Hermann Muthesius, "Weg und Ziel," in *Kunstgewerbe und Architektur* (Jena: Berlegt Bei Eugen Diederichs, 1907), 5. The essay was originally published in *Deutsche Kunst* 8, 1905.

81   Hermann Muthesius, "Kunst und Maschine," *Dekorative Kunst* 5, 1902, 144.

82   Hermann Muthesius, "Architektur und Publikum," in *Transactions of the VII International Congress of Architects* (London: RIBA, 1906), 307.

83   Hermann Muthesius, "Landhäuser der Architekten J.W. Bedford und S.D. Kitson in Leeds," *Dekorative Kunst* 6, 1903, 82.

84   "Speculating business people think they have recognized a new specialty as being catchy, the Werkbund-specialty (german) as they call it. In many cases it is clear that here the driving element is a purely external spirit of commercialism and not an inner conviction, one that sees a new fashion in the Werkbund-specialty and wants to enjoys its advantages." Hermann Muthesius, "Die Werkbundarbeit der Zukunft Vortrag auf der Werkbund-Tagung Köln 1914," in *Zwischen Kunst und Industrie der Deutsche Werkbund* (Munich: Staatliches Museum für Angewandle Kunst, 1975), 85-96, 87.

85   Adolf Loos, "Ladies' Fashion (1902)," in Adolf Loos, *Spoken into the Void: Collected Essays 1897-1900*, trans. Jane O. Newman and John H. Smith (Cambridge, Mass.: MIT Press, 1982), 99.

86   "In those days one decorated his home the way one outfits himself today. We buy our shoes from the shoemaker, coat, pants and waistcoat from the tailor, collars and cuffs from the shirtmaker, hats from the hatter, and walking sticks from the turner. None of them knows any of the others, and yet everything matches quite nicely." Adolf Loos, "Interiors: A Prelude" [1898], in *Spoken*, 19.

87   Adolf Loos, "An Den Ulk (1910)," in his *Sämtliche Schriften*, 238.

88   Adolf Loos, "The Poor Little Rich Man (1900)," in *Spoken*, 125–127.

89   Loos, "Ornament and Crime" (1908), in Safran and Wang, *The Architecture of Adolf Loos*, 102.

90   Kenneth Frampton, *Modern Architecture: A Critical History* (London: Thames and Hudson, 1985), 81.

91   "...regardless whether it is a matter of architecture proper, of designing a piece of furniture, a metal utensil, a wallpaper, a dress: There are always the same conditions of creation from which the work comes." Leopold Kleiner, *Deutsche Kunst und Dekoration* 54, 1924, 161. Cited by Edward Sekler, *Josef Hoffmann: The Architectural Work* (Princeton: Princeton University Press, 1985), 240.

92   Cited in Werner J. Schweiger, *Wiener Werkstätte: Design in Vienna 1903–1932* (New York: Abbeville Press, 1984), 211.

93   Sekler notes: "At times he even used to appear personally in the salesroom of the textile department of the Wiener Werkstätte in order to suggest to customers, with the aid of improvised draping, which fabrics they ought to wear in what manner." Sekler, *Josef Hoffman: The Architectural Work*, 221.

94   "Against the background of this reality, 'aesthetic sermons' by ideologists of the Wiener Werkstätte claiming that they were well on the way to creating an art that was true to design and materials for the enlightened human race of the twentieth century must have brought a smile to the face to realistic social reformers, let alone dyed-in-the-wool Marxists." Wolfgang Gerd Fischer, *Gustav Klimt and Emilie Flöge: An Artist and His Muse* (Woodstock, N.Y.: The Overlook Press, 1992), 37.

95   Describing his visit to Hoffmann's Stoclet Palace, Poiret says "Hoffmann designed everything, including Madame's dresses and Monsieur's sticks and cravats. This substitution of the taste of the architect for the personality of the proprietors has always seemed to me a sort of slavery—a subjection that made me smile." Paul Poiret, *King of Fashion: The Autobiography of Paul Poiret*, trans. (of *En habillant L'epoque*) Stephen Haden Guest (Philadelphia: J. Lippincott Company, 1931), 159.

96   Isabelle Anscombe, *A Women's Touch: Women in Design from 1860 to the Present Day* (New York: Elizabeth Sifton Books, Viking, 1984), 115.

97   Sekler, *Josef Hoffman: The Architectural Work*, 129.

98   Cited in Traude Hausen, *Wiener Werkstätte Mode: Stoffe–Schmuck–Accessories* (München: Christian Branstätter, 1984), 14.

99   Loos, "Ornament und Erziehung (1924)," 395.

100   The newspaper reports that are the only surviving records of the lecture are cited in Sekler, *Josef Hoffmann: The Architectural Work*, 190.

101   Cited from newspaper reports, in Schweiger, *Wiener Werkstätte*, 118.

102   Germain Boffrand, *Livre d'Architecture*, 1745. Cited in Peter Collins,

Changing Ideals in Modern Architecture: 1750–1950 (Montreal: McGill University Press, 1967), 266.

103   "While they had to go back to simplified forms and clear-cut lines to find a new starting-point, they were animated most by the desire to create a sur-face style...No one...so charmingly feminized architecture; no one...so richly colored buildings without breaking up wall sense." Sheldon Cheney, *The New World Architecture* (London: Longmans Green and Co., 1930), 25. Partially cited in Sekler, *Josef Hoffmann: The Architectural Work*, 517 n65.

104   Adolf Loos, "Cultural Degeneration (1908)," in Safran and Wang, *The Architecture of Adolf Loos*, 99. "Ten years ago these artists went in search of new conquests and tried to bring the tailoring trade under their control, after they had already brought down the craft of joinery...They were dressed in frock coats of Scottish plaid and velvet lapels, a piece of cardboard stuck in their turned-down collars—trade-mark 'Ver Sacrum'— was covered with black silk and gave the illusion of a tie which had been wound around their necks three times. I managed to drive these gentlemen out of the tailors' and shoemakers' work-shops with a few forceful essays on the subject...The master tailor, who had shown himself to be so accommodating to these cultural and artistic endeavors, was abandoned, and gentlemen took a subscription with a Viennese bespoke tailor." Ibid., 98.

105   Siegfried Giedion, "R. J. Neutra: European and American," in Willy Boesiger, ed., *Richard Neutra: Buildings and Projects, Vol. 1 (1923–1950)* (Zurich: Verlag für Architektur, 1992), 8.

106   Sigfried Giedion. "Zur situation deutscher architektur (Die kunst-gewerbliche Infiltration)," *Der Cicerone* 18, 1926, 216–224. Trans. by Tim Benton as "The State of German Architecture," in Tim Benton, ed., *Documents: A Collection of Some Material on the Modern Movement* (Milton Keynes: The Open University, 1975), 12.

107   Ibid., 15.

108   Ibid., 13.

109   Ibid., 15.

110   Giedion, *Space, Time and Architecture*, 207.

111   Ibid., 209.

112   Giedion, *Space, Time and Architecture*, 5th ed., 1962, xxxii-liii.

113   Sigfried Giedion, "The Tragic Conflict (1936, 1955)," in *Architecture, You and Me* (Cambridge, Mass.: Harvard University Press, 1958), 25–39.

114 "There are forces inherent in man, which come to the surface when one evokes them. The average man, with a century of falsified emotional education behind him, may not be won over suddenly by the contemporary symbol in painting or sculpture. But his inherent, though unconscious, feeling may slowly be awakened by the original expression of a new community life. This can be done within a framework of urban centers and in great spectacles capable of fascinating the people." Siegfried Giedion, "The Need for a New Monumentality" (1944), in *Architecture, You and Me*, 25–39.

115 Giedion, *The Beginnings of Art*, 4.

116 Siegfried Giedion, *Walter Gropius: Work and Teamwork* (New York: Rheinhold Publishing, 1954), 36.

117 The notable exception is Leonie von Wilckens. Leonie von Wilckens, "Künstlerkleid und Reformmode—Textilkunst in Nürnberg," in Peter-Klaus Schuster, ed., *Peter Behrens und Nürnberg*, exhibition catalog, Germanisches Nationalmuseum Nuremberg (Munich: Prestel, 1980).

118 A significant exception is Kenneth Frampton's *Modern Architecture: A Critical History*, which illustrates one of van de Velde's clothing designs modelled by Maria Van de Velde and refers to Loos's parody of such designs. Even Osthaus, who wrote the first biography on van de Velde in 1920, doesn't describe the dress designs, though some of them were done to match his own house, which features prominently in his book. Francesco Dal Co illustrates one of these dresses, along with a design by Behrens and another by Wimmer, but does not discuss them in the text, even though it does address the general question of fashion in some detail. Francesco Dal Co, *Figures of Architecture and Thought: German Architecture Culture 1880–1920* (New York: Rizzoli, 1990). Sekler's comprehensive book on "The Architectural Work" of Hoffmann does address his dress designs briefly. Coffee table books on Art Nouveau and ornamentation that are not directed towards an architectural audience, however, do not hesitate to illustrate and discuss the dress designs. The line between dress design and architecture is almost always preserved, even in the face of a practice whose declared purpose is to efface that line.

119 See Beatriz Colomina, "On Adolf Loos and Josef Hoffmann: Architecture in the Age of Mechanical Reproduction." *9H* 6 (1983), 52–58; and Beatriz Colomina, "The Split Wall: Domestic Voyeurism," in Colomina, *Sexuality and Space*, 73–130. While this essay does not focus on the question of the mask as such, it does little more than explore some of the spaces opened up by Colomina's decisive reading of Loos's deployment of fashion as a mask, which is elaborated further in her *Privacy and Publicity: Modern Architecture as Mass Media* (Cambridge, Mass.: MIT Press, 1994). More recently, Mary

McCleod presented a careful reading of the question of fashion as part of the Graham Symposia at Princeton University (see her essay in this book).

120 Joseff Hoffmann, "Das individuelle Kleid," *Die Waage* 15:9 (1898) 251–252. Cited in Traude Hansen, *Wiener Werkstätte*, 13.

121 "We must be...modern, i.e., we must not refer back too much to old dead things. It is impossible to imagine the chauffeur of an auto in the Old Viennese costume of a coachman...We must advance to a unified form. England...instinctively knows only the city cut, and avoids every attempt at country folk costume which often leads to costume ball-like aberrations of taste...Respect for the frequent genius of the design of such folk costumes should force us not to masquerade frivolously in them." Josef Hoffmann, "Vorschläge zur Mode," *Neue Wiener Journal*, 17 July 1936. Cited in Sekler, *Josef Hoffmann: The Architectural Work*, 515 n11.

122 Henry van de Velde, *Die Renaissance im modernen Kunstgewerbe* (Berlin, 1901), 47, 48, 81f; *Die drei Sünden wider die Schönheit* (Zurich, 1918), 26ff. Cited in Frank-Lothar Kroll, "Ornamental Theory and Practice in the Jugendstil," 64.

123 Nikolaus Pevsner, *Pioneers of Modern Architecture: From William Morris to Walter Gropius* (Harmondsworth: Penguin Books, 1960), 18.

124 In his reply to Muthesius, van de Velde says that the artist resists anyone who "attempts to drive him into a universally valid form, in which he sees only a mask." Henry van de Velde, "Counter-Propositions," in Tim Benton, *Documents: A Collection of Some Material on the Modern Movement*, 6.

125 "Since it was inconceivable to me that beauty could ever be in part the product of reason and in part of its opposite, I refused to allow the presence of any object in my own home which was not as basically honest, genuinely straightforward and altogether above suspicion in design as the character of the friends we received there. An interior which displays downright shams, capricious whimsicalities or wild formal travesties clearly exerts just as immoral an influence as a man who deliberately bases his life on a tissue of false pretenses. Designs are moral as long as they do not transgress the dictates of reason; they become immoral so soon as they show signs of being subordered by the lure of fantasy." Henry van de Velde, "Extracts From his Memoirs: 1891-1901," *Architectural Review* 112:669 (September 1952) 143-155, 153.

126 Henry van de Velde, "Was Ich Will (1901)," in his *Zum neum stil* (Munich, 1955), 81. Cited in Christian Schädlich, "Van de Velde and the Construction of Rational Beauty," *Rassegna* 45, 1979, 41.

127   Henry van de Velde, "Die Linie (1910)" in *Zum neum stil*, 193. Cited in Schädlich, "Van de Velde and the Construction of Rational Beauty," 45.

128   "Just as evil is for ever seeking to corrupt virtue, so throughout the history of art some malignant cancer has ceaselessly striven to taint or deform man's purest ideals of beauty. The brief interlude of art nouveau, that ephemeral will o' the wisp which knew no law other than its own caprice, was succeeded, as I had foretold, by the hesitant beginnings of a new, disciplined and purposeful style, the style of our own age...[which] will synchronize with the realization of a rationalized aesthetic, whereby beauty of form can be immunized against recurrent infections from the noisome parasite fantasy." Van de Velde, "Extracts From his Memoirs: 1891–1901," 155.

129   In fact, van de Velde argues that the reason his work would not become a vogue was that its lack of familiar ornament always aroused the same kind of antagonism as that directed towards his own house: "One can only suppose this excited the suspicion that the virus of some dangerously subversive tendency must lurk beneath my wholesale elimination of conventional ornament." Ibid., 154. As Christian Schädlich puts it: "It is necessary to bear in mind that Van de Velde's architectural production was only marginally influenced by the current denominated as Jugendstil...he kept a distance...both because it was a widely diffused movement, often influenced by fashion and by the orientations of the market, and because of the formal excesses to which it was subject during the phase around 1900 with the affirmation of the new ornamental art." Schädlich, "Van de Velde and the Construction of Rational Beauty," 38.

130   Henry van de Velde, "Le nouveau: pourquoi toujours du nouveau?" (1929), in his *Pages de doctrine* (Brussels, 1942) Reprinted in Henry van de Velde, *Deblaiement d'Art* (Brussels: Editions des Archives d'Architecture Moderne, 1979), 91.

131   Ibid., 80.

132   Sekler, *Josef Hoffmann: The Architectural Work*, 37.

133   Josef Hoffmann, "Simple Furniture (1901)," trans. in Sekler, *Josef Hoffmann: The Architectural Work*, 483. Compare the passage in Hoffmann's 1924 essay, "The School of the Architect," which argues that when art scholars out of touch with contemporary design recommend the purchase of old buildings and furnishings: "a modern gathering in tailcoat and uniform with ladies in modern dresses had to have a disturbing effect in such a room." Josef Hoffmann, "The School of the Architect," trans. in Sekler, *Josef Hoffmann: The Architectural Work*, 494. This essay also contains the Behrens-like argument: "We know today that, without using decorative forms, we can arrive at a new

design that aims only for the causative. But we also know that the best calculated form of construction does not achieve a satisfying product, that in addition to a command of the technical requirements, one must have a culti-vated taste, a feeling for relationships and the rhythm of the visual, as well as that secret sensitivity which only artistically oriented people possess, in order to bring satisfying results." Ibid., 494. It is precisely this sense that enables Le Corbusier to identify with Hoffmann: "And among the ordinary productions, often devoted to narrowly circumscribed utilitarian tasks, the works of Hoffmann left a deep impression because he, like myself, starts from the conviction that architectural work must possess a spiritual content, provided of course that it completely fulfills the demands of appropriateness...what remains is the 'indispensable superfluous,' art (a word today kicked around like a football). *And in the history of contemporary architecture, on the way to a timely aesthetic, Professor Hoffmann holds one of the most brilliant places.*" Le Corbusier, "The Wiener Werkstätte" (1929), in *Die Wiener Werkstätte: 1903–1928*, trans. in Sekler, *Josef Hoffmann: The Architectural Work*, 496.

134   "Is that again the disgusting mania of the parvenu to seem more than he is, or is it a resigned retreat after deep disappointment...seized by the giddiness of the masquerade with its spurious, false knickknacks, with its lack of style despite all the styles of all times and countries." Josef Hoffmann, "Simple Furniture" (1901), 483.

135   Ibid., 484.

136   Ibid.

137   Ibid., 483.

138   Jane Kallir, *Viennese Design and the Wiener Werkstätte* (New York: George Brazilier, 1986), 32.

139   "Fashion dictates if the silhouettes of women's hats are pure fancy; the almost universal adoption of the soft hat for men is an aberration. This soft material, folded upwards to gather the rain and which loses its shape in the wind, is at the very least comic. Custom demands that man's suits have buttons at the cuff as a reminder of the rows of copper buttons sewn on the jackets of Zouave soldiers in order to prevent their blowing their noses on them! And what can be said about the two buttons nicely placed on the back of evening suits, which once served to raise the coat-tail in order to permit the wearer to rise a horse! Fashion." Rob Mallet-Stevens, "Modern Versus Modish," text dated February 1938, in *Rob Mallet-Stevens: Architecte* (Brussells: Editions des Archives d'Architecture Moderne, 1980), 377.

140   Ibid.

141   Loos, "Architecture" (1910), 107.

142   Loos, "Ladies Fashion" (1902), 100.

143   Elizabeth Wilson, "All the Rage," in Jane Gaines and Charlotte Herzog, *Fabrications: Costume and the Female Body* (New York: Routledge), 1990, 28-38, 29.

144   Loos cites himself in "Josef Veillich" (1929), *Sämtliche Schriften*, 437.

145   Adolf Loos,"Culture" (1908), in Safran and Wang, *The Architecture of Adolf Loos*, 97–99. He describes the influence of riding clothes on the evolution of "dress suit," and predicts the influence of workers clothes, arguing that the "man in overalls" from America "has conquered the world."

146   Adolf Loos, "Men's Fashion" (1898), in *Spoken*, 11.

147   Colomina, "The Split Wall: Domestic Voyeurism," 93. "For Loos, the interior is Pre-Oedipal space, space before the analytical distancing which language entails, space as we feel it, as clothing; that is, as clothing before the existence of readymade clothes, when one had to first choose the fabric...The spaces of Loos's interiors cover the occupants as clothes cover the body (each occasion has its appropriate 'fit')...But space in Loos's architecture is not just felt...The 'clothes' have become so removed from the body that they require structural support independent of it. They become a 'stage set.' The inhabitant is both 'covered' by the space and 'detached' from it." Ibid., 90.

148   Hermann Muthesius, *The English House*, trans. Janet Seligman (New York: Rizzoli, 1987), 10.

149   Le Corbusier, *Towards a New Architecture*, 145.

150   Ibid., 143.

151   "To abuse or ridicule any nostalgia for ornamentation can only deter people from studying the modern style and from trying to appreciate it...I need hardly add that I have tried not to mistake the modern for the beautiful, nor a fashion for that much profounder expression of a new period in the history of humanity which we call a style." Nikolaus Pevsner, *Industrial Art in England* (Cambridge: Cambridge University Press, 1957), 10. The book, which Pevsner prepared at the same time as his book on modern architecture, promotes the modern style (because ninety percent of British industrial art is "devoid of any aesthetic merit") but opposes the "modernistic fashion," understood as the "disease of modernism."

152   Pevsner, *Pioneers of the Modern Movement from Morris to Gropius*, 206.

153 "The reasons for the fight were more against the person of Muthesius than the content of his thesis. He was an unpleasant man who used tricky methods to get into the lead. His mind was also much too rigid and 'unartistic.' I was the youngest Board member in the *Werkbund* and acted as *enfant terrible* to bring Muthesius's methods into the open. But you are quite right; when one looks at the substance of that fight, one wonders about the strange distribution of participants on both sides." Walter Gropius, "Letter to the Editor," written in reply to an article by Pevsner, *Architectural Review* 134, July 1963, 6.

154 Walter Gropius, *The New Architecture and the Bauhaus*, trans. P. Morton Shand (London: Faber and Faber, 1935), 34.

155 Letter from Fritz Mackensen to Walter Gropius dated 2 October 1915, in Hans M. Wingler, *The Bauhaus: Weimer, Dessau, Berlin, Chicago* (Cambridge, Mass.: MIT Press, 1969), 22.

156 Letter from Fritz Mackensen to Walter Gropius dated 14 October 1915, in ibid., 22.

157 See, for example, Walter Gropius, "Sociological Premises for the Minimum Dwelling of Urban Industrial Populations" (1929), in his *Scope of Total Architecture* (New York: Collier Books, 1955), 91–102. See also Walter Gropius, "The Formal and Technical Problems of Modern Architecture and Planning (1934)," trans. P. Shand, *Journal of the Royal Institute of British Architects*, 19 May 1934, 694.

158 On women at the Bauhaus, see Magdalena Broste, *Bauhaus 1919–1933* (Berlin: Bauhaus-Archiv Museum für Gestaltung and Benedikt Taschen, 1990), 38–40. As Broste earlier points out, the number of women trained in the Prussian handicraft schools had increased from the moment that the government revised them all by adding workshops and appointing artists as teachers on Muthesius's advice. Ibid., 11. Note that this contrasts markedly with Isabelle Anscombe's optimistic version: Anscombe, *A Woman's Touch*, 131–144.

159 Broste, *Bauhaus 1919–1933*, 74.

160 Dirk Scheper, "Die Bauhausbühne," in *Experiment Bauhaus* (Berlin, Bauhaus Archiv 1988), 256. Cited in Broste, *Bauhaus 1919–1933*, 158.

161 Werner Graeff, "Bemerkungen eines Bauhäuslers," in Werner Graeff, *Ein Pionier der Zwanziger Jahre*, exhibition catalog, Skulpturenmuseum der Stadt Marl, 1979, 7. Cited in Broste, *Bauhaus 1919–1933*, 57.

162 Ibid., 31.

163 Nikolaus Pevsner, "Gropius and van de Velde," *Architectural Review*

133:793 (March 1963), 168. Loos praises overalls again in "Antworten auf Fragen aus dem Publikum (1919)," in *Sämtliche Schriften*, 365.

164   Herbert Bayer, "Homage to Gropius," in *Bauhaus and Bauhaus People* (New York: Van Nostrand Reinhold, 1993), 141. Compare to Hoffmann's dress: "Hoffmann always valued a good appearance, and the colors gray, black, and white were his preferred personal choice in dressing. As far as dressing for the evening was concerned, he was of the opinion that—in contrast to the many colors of women's fashions—man should wear only nonchromatic hues." Sekler, *Josef Hoffmann: The Architectural Work*, 235.

165   Walter Gropius, "The Development of Modern Industrial Architecture (1913)," in Benton and Benton, *Architecture and Design: 1890–1939*, 53. "Occasionally an architect was called in to add irrelevant decoration to the naked form of the utilitarian building. Points of conflict were concealed on the exterior, and because one was ashamed of it, the true character of the building was hidden behind a sentimental mask taken from an earlier age according to the whim of the owner...ornamental decoration is only a final touch." Walter Gropius, "Industrial Buildings" (1911), trans. Iain Boyd Whyte, in Beddensieg, *Industriekultur*, 247.

166   Gropius, *The New Architecture and the Bauhaus*, 23.

167   Gropius, *Scope of Total Architecture*, 12.

168   "Were mechanization an end in itself it would be an unmitigated calamity, robbing life of half its fullness and variety by stunting men and women into sub-human, robot-like automatons. (Here we touch the deeper causality of the dogged resistance of the old civilization of handicrafts to the new world-order of the machine.)" Gropius, *The New Architecture and the Bauhaus*, 33.

169   Walter Gropius, "Eight Steps Toward a Solid Architecture," *Architectural Forum*, February 1954, 182.

170   Ibid., 174.

171   Ibid.

172   Ibid., 178.

173   Walter Gropius, "Ornament and Modern Architecture," *American Architect and Architecture*, January 1938, 22.

174   Ibid.

175   Walter Gropius, "Housing Industry" (1924), *Bauhausbücher* 3, *Ein*

Versuchshaus des Bauhauses (Munich: Albert Langen Verlag, 1924).
Republished in Walter Gropius, *Scope of Total Architecture*, 128.

176   Walter Gropius, "Bauhaus Dessau: Principles of Bauhaus Production"
(1926), in Benton and Benton, *Architecture and Design: 1890–1939*, 148.

177   Walter Gropius, *Bauhausbücher 12, Bauhausbauten Dessau* (Fulda:
Parzellar and Co., 1930), 99–121.

178   Gropius, "The Development of Modern Industrial Architecture" (1913), 54.

179   Ibid.

180   Walter Gropius, "Is There a Science of Design?" in *Scope of Total
Architecture*, 35. The article originally appeared as "Design Topics" in
Magazine of Art (December 1947, 301), in which the line reads: "This is an
important fact to know for fashion design." Gropius removes the newspaper's
fashion tip, however, for the revised article's publication in the well-known collection of essays.

181   Gropius, "Housing Industry" (1924), 134.

182   Walter Gropius, *Bauhausbücher 7, Neue Arbeiten der Bauhauswerkstät-
ten* (Munich: 1925), 7.

183   "*The provision of housing for people is concerned with mass needs.* It would
no longer occur to 90 per cent of the population today to have their shoes specially made to measure. Instead, they buy *standard products* off-the-peg, which,
thanks to much improved production methods, satisfy the requirements of most
individuals. Similarly, in the future the individual will be able to order a house
from stocks which suits his needs...Standardization of parts places no restrictions
on the individual design. Their recurrence in differently shaped buildings will
have an orderly and soothing effect as does the uniformity of our clothes." Walter
Gropius, "How can we build cheaper, better, more attractive houses?" (1927), in
Benton and Benton, *Architecture and Design: 1890–1939*, 195.

184   Gropius, *The New Architecture and the Bauhaus*, 40.

185   Walter Gropius, "Program for the Establishment of a Company for the
Provision of Housing on Aesthetically Consistent Principles," manuscript trans-
lated in Dennis Sharp, ed., *The Rationalists: Theory and Design in the Modern
Movement* (London: The Architectural Press, 1978), 53.

186   Walter Gropius, "The Inner Compass," a lecture of May 1958 published
in Walter Gropius, *Apollo in the Democracy: The Cultural Obligations of the
Architect* (New York: McGraw Hill, 1968), 14.

187   Gropius, *Scope of a Total Architecture*, 11.

188   Gropius, *The New Architecture and the Bauhaus*, 91. An example of such an accusation is made by Ernst Kallai: "Bauhaus style: one word for everything. Wertheim sets up a new department for modern-style furniture and appliances, an arts-and-crafts salon with functionally trimmed high-fashioned trash...A fashion magazine in Vienna recommends that ladies' underwear no longer be decorated with little flowers, but with more contemporary Bauhaus-style geometrical designs. Such embarrassing and amusing misuses in the fashion hustle of our wonderful modern age cannot be prevented...exchanging the historical robe for a sort of pseudo-technological raciness...a taste-oriented arbitrariness decked out in new clothes." Ernst Kallai, "Ten Years of Bauhaus" (1930), in Benton and Benton, *Architecture and Design: 1890–1939*, 172.

189   Gropius, *The New Architecture and the Bauhaus*, 23. Note that Gropius had published this claim a year earlier. Gropius, "The Formal and Technical Problems of Modern Architecture and Planning," 679.

190   Reyner Banham, *Theory and Design in the First Machine Age* (Cambridge, Mass.: MIT Press, 1960), 79.

191   Letter from Carl Benscheidt to Walter Gropius, dated 20 March 1911. Cited in Reyner Banham, *A Concrete Atlantis: U. S. Industrial Building and European Modern Architecture* (Cambridge, Mass.: MIT Press, 1986), 187.

192   Klaus Herdeg, *The Decorated Diagram: Harvard Architecture and the Failure of the Bauhaus Legacy* (Cambridge, Mass.: MIT Press, 1983), 12. On the back of the book, Colin Rowe offers the following: "The persistence of the mystique of Walter Gropius is very hard to understand. For, as both architect and educator, Gropius was surely inept...it was supposed that Gropius was a supreme Moses-figure, preparing and illuminating *the way*; but, then, when *the way* turned out to be little more than relentless *kitsch* catastrophe, the mystique survived and it continues to plague architectural education to this day. For the confusions of so-called Post Modernism are not only a reaction to Gropius but also an explicit product of that abysmal failure to recognize the complex nature of architectural discourse, which Klaus Herdeg here alleges was the ultimate result of the Harvard 'establishment' sponsored by Gropius."

193   Herdeg's argument that the works of the Gropius school "devalue what were the once rigorous standards of architecture," (ibid., 2) for example, depends on being able to successfully contrast Le Corbusier's "ironic" use of the "false-front" to that of Gropius's school and of Main Street USA (the paradigm for postmodernists).

194   Argues Taut:

> The same person who transacts his shrewdly calculated busi-
> ness affairs in the most modern up-to-date office, actually
> inhabits a dwelling which is its very antithesis in its old-fash-
> ionedness, despite the installation of electric light, wireless,
> etc. The man who travels abroad in his car, with which he is
> familiar to the minutest detail, prefers to stay at an inn with
> tiny diamond-paned windows and, if possible, with a steep,
> thatched roof—an inn frequented once upon a time by be-
> wigged, long coated gentlemen and ladies in hoops. What
> would he say, were a crinolined lady with powdered locks to
> settle herself in the driver's seat of his car? What would he say
> were whole compartments in express trains be occupied by
> these ladies and gentlemen? According to his present views
> on architecture he should by rights say nothing, for he prefers
> crinolines and wigs in house and home."

Bruno Taut, *Modern Architecture* (London: The Studio Limited, 1929), 2.

195   Ibid., 3.

196   "For those who are only capable of visualizing the surface of architecture—the facade, so to speak—all remains facade. This term has become the
figurative expression for the veiling of makeshifts and doubtful moral characteristics, in respect of individuals, firms, and political parties. The expression
"facade" has already been adopted in Germany in the sense of disguise, a
mask, intended to conceal personality, as if to say, the wolf in sheep's clothing." Ibid., 8.

197   Ibid., 8.

198   Ibid., 140.

199   Ibid., 139.

200   Ibid., 169.

201   Theo van Doesburg, "The Ambiguous Mentality: Factory and Home"
(1925), in *Theo van Doesburg: On European Architecture*, trans. Charlotte I.
Loeb and Arthur L. Loeb (Berlin: Birkhäuser Verlag, 1990), 62.

202   Elsewhere, van Doesburg identifies Semper, along with Viollet-le-Duc,
as "the starting point of what is being completed in our time, or more correctly:
what is still in the process of being completed, an elementary architecture, *of
an inner purity and with an outer surface of equal merit*." Theo van Doesburg,

"Swiss ABC for a Logical Building Method (1927)," in *Theo van Doesburg: On European Architecture*, 157.

203   Theo van Doesburg, "Defending the Spirit of Space: Against a Dogmatic Functionalism," in *Theo van Doesburg: On European Architecture*, 88.

204   Theo van Doesburg, "Misunderstanding Cubist Principles in Czechoslovakia and Elsewhere" (1926), in *Theo van Doesburg: On European Architecture*, 113. "By applying cubist forms the Czech architects simply replaced Wiener-Werkstätte-Ornamentik, which had oppressed them for years, by cubist ornamentation." Ibid., 115.

205   Ibid., 113.

206   Margaret Olin, "Self-Representation: Resemblance and Convention in Two Nineteenth Century Theories of Architecture and the Decorative Arts," *Zeitschrift für kunstgeshte* 49:3 (1986) 397.

207   Doesburg, "Swiss ABC for a Logical Building Method" (1927), 157.

208   Theo van Doesburg, "Stuttgart-Weisenhof 1927: Die Wohnung" (1927), in *Theo van Doesburg: On European Architecture*, 167.

209   Giedion, *The Beginnings of Art*, xix-x.

210   I would like to thank Mark Jarzombek for pointing this out to me during a seminar at Princeton University.

211   Harry Francis Mallgrave, Introduction, *Otto Wagner, Modern Architecture*, (Santa Monica: Getty Center for the History of Art and the Humanities, 1988), 23.

212   "Modern artists have shown that mere fragments lifted from the life of a period can reveal its habits and feelings...the furniture of daily life, the unnoticed articles that result from mass production—spoons, bottles, glasses, all the things we look at hourly without seeing—have become part of our lives without our knowing it." Giedion, *Space, Time and Architecture*, 4. "The most important developments are the changes that have come about in daily life." Ibid., 8.

213   Ibid., 462.

214   Ibid., 315.

215   Giedion, *The Beginnings of Architecture*, 522.

216   "The dimension of depth...is suppressed, whenever possible, by ancient art...the visual arts to be responsible for representation of objects as individual material phenomenon not in space (here after meaning always deep space), but

on the plane...not the optical plane, imagined by our eye at a distance from the objects, but the tactile plane suggested by the sense of touch...From the optical point of view, this is the plane which the eye perceives when it comes so close to the surface of an object, that all the silhouettes and, in particular all shadows which otherwise could disclose an alteration in depth, disappear." Riegl, *Late Roman Art Industry*, 24.

217 Ibid., 525.

218 Giedion, *Space, Time and Architecture*, li.

219 Ibid., xxxix.

220 Le Corbusier, *Towards a New Architecture*, 37.

221 Giedion, *The Beginnings of Architecture*, 507.

222 Ibid., 48.

223 Ibid., 94.

224 Ibid., 161.

225 Le Corbusier, *The Decorative Art of Today*, 135.

226 William Morris, "The Lesser Arts of Life" (1877), in *Architecture, Industry and Wealth: Collected Papers by William Morris* (London: Longmans, Green and Co., 1902), 73. First published in *The Architect*, 8 December 1877.

227 Ibid., 6.

228 Ibid., 99.

229 Le Corbusier, *The Radiant City*, trans. Pamela Knight et al. (New York: The Orion Press, 1967), 107.

230 Ibid., 8.

231 Giedion, *The Eternal Present*, 41.

232 "Everything must take place upon the plane surface: space is excluded. This explains how Worringer, almost in the same way as Riegl, sees ornamentation as the purest and most lucid expression of artistic volition." Ibid., 42.

233 Marcel Breuer, "Where do We Stand?" (1934), in Sharp, *The Rationalists: Theory and Design in the Modern Movement*, 87.

234 "But only in the last fifty years have women acquired the right to develop themselves physically. It is an analogous process: as to the rider of the thirteenth

century, the concession will be made to the twentieth-century female bicyclist to wear pants and clothing that leaves her feet free. And with this, the first step is taken toward the social sanctioning of women's work...we are approaching a new and greater time. No longer by an appeal to sensuality, but rather by economic independence earned through work will the woman bring about her equal status with the man. The woman's value or lack of value will no longer fall or rise according to the fluctuation of sensuality." Loos, "Ladies' Fashion," 102.

235   I would like to thank Beatriz Colomina for directing my attention to this image.

236   Citation from 1929 interview with Henry Ford on frontispiece of Sigfried Giedion, *Befreites Wohnen* (Zurich: Orell Fübli, 1929). Cited by Stansilaus von Moos, "Giedion e il suo tempo," *Rassegna* 25, 1979, 7.

237   Giedion, *Space, Time and Architecture*, 236.

Fashion and I

IN

LEILA W. KINNEY

An emblematic monument to France's commercial and artistic cultures stood on the rue de Rivoli during the second half of the nineteenth century. There, two Louvres confronted one another. Completed in 1855, the block across from the Palais du Louvre featured a large hôtel and a group of arcade shops united under the sign of "The Louvre."[2] The firm grew rapidly into one of the most prominent Parisian department stores.[3] Three decades later, in 1882, when Paris was in the throes of a serious economic depression, a *Figaro* journalist, one Pierre Giffard, attacked the *arriviste* establishment. Using the two buildings as his figure for the cultural crisis, he complained that the venerable Louvre, the "palace of kings," repository of the fine arts, had been abandoned by a younger generation enthralled by the "*revolution du bon marché.*"[4] Giffard's argument that the store had usurped social leadership is alarmist, to be sure, yet it announces that the realms of art and commerce had become interlocking, competitive models of cultural formation in the second half of the nineteenth century.

guration

ERN LIFE PAINTING

A promotional pamphlet published at the end of the century by the upstart "Louvre" proclaims as much. Offered as a guidebook to the museum, the publication provides an inventory of the collection alongside an account of the store's merchandise. Black ink is used to itemize the works of art, which are tabulated by school, while descriptions of the commercial goods are printed in red ink on the facing pages. The irony, one presumes, was unintended. Still, a grandiose parallel is established:

FIG. 1   *Detail, Georges Seurat,* Un dimanche à la Grande Jatte *(A Sunday on La Grande Jatte) 1884–86, oil on canvas, 81 x 120 inches, The Art Institute of Chicago, Helen Birch Bartlett Memorial Collection, 1926.224.*

The singular thing is that this palace, which symbolizes the French monarchy, was not completed until the time that France achieved the height of industrial grandeur. Opposite this palace consecrated to kings and the arts, the ground was ready to receive commerce and democracy—the Hôtel du Louvre and the Magasins du Louvre, themselves also symbols of an equally grand thing, the flowering of the industrial power of France.[5]

One can easily imagine this typographically explicit specimen of the loss—or theft—of the 'real' Louvre's aura being destined for Walter Benjamin's treasure-trove of fragments. For this "double-entry" account of the two Louvres, in its peculiar form of stasis, preserves with mute efficiency an exchange of functions between art and fashion otherwise difficult to describe.

Well before Benjamin (1892–1940) took up the problem of the loss of an artwork's "aura," though, French critics had articulated changes in the artistic economy that were altering the conception, distribution, and reception of paintings. The art criticism of Émile Zola (1840–1902), for example, records the transformation of the Salon into a massive "market for pictorial production." Indeed, not only do Zola's exhibition reviews of the 1860s and 1870s rehearse the descriptive task of his 1883 novel about department stores, *Au Bonheur des Dames*—slipping in statistics on the number of exhibitors and glimpses of the prevailing fashions—but the very staccato rhythm of his prose seems to maneuver us through the press of the crowd, the riot of "merchandise," and the stifling, yet exhilarating atmosphere.[6] In 1880, Jules Claretie expresses reservations about the merchandising of art in a succinct turn of phrase: "*l'objet d'art* has replaced *l'oeuvre d'art*."[7] The shops of the art dealers, Claretie continues, display the names of fashionable painters in their windows just as the department stores promote the latest imports of Japanese ceramics and Oriental rugs on their posters. And so, he concludes, "the name of the *Palais de l'industrie*, where each year the *products of painting* are exhibited," superbly characterizes "the epoch of artistic manufacture in which we live."[8] If it is customary by now to see the museum and the department store as intersecting domains in which the "cultural logic of capitalism" can be discerned and its effects evaluated,[9] it is because Walter Benjamin retraced the circuitous route between these two Louvres. And it is the Paris of Charles Baudelaire (1821–1867), of course, that prompted such an itinerary.

It comes as something of a mild shock, then, to realize that Benjamin gives so little credit to the essay that joins fashion to the definition of modernity, even as he is in the midst of proposing a "metaphysics of fashion" for the *Passagen-Werk*. Of Baudelaire's "Le peintre de la vie moderne" he merely avers:

> In summary form, his doctrine reads as follows: "A constant, unchangeable element...and a relative, limited element cooperates to produce beauty....The latter element is supplied by the epoch, by fashion, by morality, and the passions. Without this second element...the first would be not be assimilable." One cannot say that this is a profound analysis.[10]

Even so, the temporal dimension that structures Baudelaire's argument must have seized Benjamin's imagination; for to judge from the notes and textual fragments that he left behind for his arcades project, an analysis of fashion appears all but poised to reveal the mechanics of modern memory and of myth. Where Baudelaire envisions the temporal dimension of fashion as a perpetual renewal of the present, Benjamin would come to see fashion as an eternal recurrence of the same and, more importantly, as an engine for the destruction of historical consciousness.[11]

Perhaps Benjamin's formulation of the issue would have supplanted the role that Baudelaire ascribed to fashion, which, for all of the familiarity of his essay on modernity, remains something of a puzzle, if not an embarrassment.[12] Its peculiarities—or its inadequacies, if one prefers—arise in part from Baudelaire's attempt to argue simultaneously against both academic historicism and the naturalism that he deems vulgar, the emphasis, in the first instance, being placed on the historical rhythm embodied in fashion and, in the second, on what we might call displaced idealism. The fashion plates that are the models for a new "rational and historical theory of beauty" are presented in the opening paragraphs of his essay as so many semi-fossilized presentation of past contemporaneity. They derive their authority from a process of historical sedimentation that extracts the eternal from the ephemeral and that legitimizes in a complementary manner the present as the basis for the future "ghostly piquancy" of the past.[13] Seeing in these plates the traces of a personal process of transformation that we have since come to know as "self-fashioning," Baudelaire writes:

> The idea of beauty that man creates for himself affects his whole attire, ruffles or stiffens his coat, gives curves or straight lines to his gestures and even, in process of time, subtly penetrates the very features of his face. Man comes in the end to look like his ideal image of himself. These engravings can be translated into beauty or ugliness: in ugliness they become caricatures; in beauty, antique statues.[14]

A residual classicism lingers in this conception of the body as an artifact, one that has been rescued from the moribund historicism of academic doctrine, but which retains all the same an "immortal appetite" for beauty. In fact, so pronounced is this striving for perfection on the part of those who are most debased within Baudelaire's hierarchy (and therefore in greatest need of embellishment) that near the end of his essay, a part of his praise of women and of make-up, Baudelaire remarks:

> Fashion must therefore be thought of as a symptom of the taste for the ideal that floats on the surface in the human brain, above all the coarse, earthy and disgusting things that life according to nature accumulates, as a sublime distortion of nature, or rather as a permanent and constantly renewed effort to reform nature.[15]

Baudelaire's stereotyped idealization of women, one still tied to the classical tradition even in this "*mondaine*" version, would seem to be an unlikely component of his rejection of theories of general beauty, unless we keep in mind his concomitant desire to negate current as well as established doctrines of imitation—in particular, the materialist realism of his erstwhile artistic ally Gustave Courbet (1819–1877).[16] No doubt part of the beauty of Baudelaire's piece resides in the contingency of the argument (not to mention the circumstances of its publication).[17]

The essay, then, is not exactly an "analysis" of modernism, and only a crude beginning for a theory. It is Michel Foucault who, piecing it together with his interrogation of Kant, makes of it a good deal more. The temporal and collective dynamism that Baudelaire recognizes in fashion seems all the more striking when it is reformulated by the later Foucault as a "permanent critique" of the present and of the self.[18] In less lofty terms, however, we can also locate the significance of Baudelaire's essay in several adjacent domains. First, I believe, it is the place in aesthetic discourse where fashion is isolated from a history of costume, clothing, or dress itself. Costume had an established, if ancillary, niche in the decorative and ornamental arts, to which aesthetics proper lent a considerable, albeit secondary, level of prestige. It is this tradition that encouraged an intersection with architectural theory; its anthropomorphic understanding of the Greek orders and the long-standing analogy of the body made discussions of clothing and of adornment literally and metaphorically useful.[19] Fashion, on the other hand, was consigned either to *moeurs* or to the materially influential but symbolically impoverished subgenre of commercial journalism spawned to promote consumption—periodicals addressed specifically to women. To grant fashion a place in artistic theory, even with all of the qualifications and correctives that Baudelaire attached, was a considerable shift. Once grafted onto the discussion of the values that governed appearance, fashion proceeded to overtake aesthetics in setting the terms of representation, although the shifting points of demarcation in the reversal of function that has occurred over the last century are still being determined. The passage from "style" to "lifestyle" is just one indication of the range of fashion's territorial acquisition and of the breadth of its consolidation of social power.

FIG. 2   *Georges Seurat,* Un dimanche à la Grande Jatte *(A Sunday on La Grande Jatte) 1884–86, oil on canvas, 81 x 120 inches, The Art Institute of Chicago, Helen Birch Bartlett Memorial Collection, 1926.224.*

Secondly, in releasing fashion from the notion of costume, Baudelaire's essay makes a significant conceptual departure. By thinking about fashion as a principle or a system, he reserves for clothing the function, increasingly unworkable in the late nineteenth century, of social denomination.[20] Certainly the old physiognomies are at play in Baudelaire's essay, particularly and predictably in the section on "Women: Honest Ones, and Others." The urban iconography that he formulated survived avant-garde reinventions and migrations from medium to medium for years to come. And yet, here begins the trajectory as well that will lead us away from the perception of clothing as an intelligible index of social identity. It is precisely the breakdown of this system and its reconstitution in terms of a "dialectic of novation and imitation" that made it a subject of such intense scrutiny in the nineteenth century and has made it a privileged object of study for French thinkers ever since.[21]

Finally, and for my purposes most appropriately, this is a phenomenon better seen in modern life painting than in Baudelaire's essay
(and one connected ultimately, it might be argued, to the crisis of
figuration in turn-of-the-century painting). The chronological "set"
of paintings that engage the notions of costume and fashion in
Baudelaire's art criticism begins with Gustave Courbet's *Un enterrement à Ornans* [Burial at Ornans] (1849–50).[22] But it culminates
in Georges Seurat's *Un dimanche à la Grande Jatte* [A Sunday on
La Grande Jatte] (1884-86) (Figs. 1 and 2). In the distance tra-
versed between these two paintings reside the issues that I wish to
address.

The importance of fashionable attire in *La Grande Jatte* has been
noted as conveying, in John House's view, the artificiality of the
"peacocks of Parisian society" in contrast to the more "natural"
leisure of the working classes in Seurat's *Une Baignade (Asnières)*
(1884).[23] Yet Seurat's vision of fashion registers more than the
Baudelairean opposition of the artificial and the natural. Its "technique of the body"[24] is perhaps the first to depart from the residual
principles of physiognomic encoding that had characterized figurative painting and portraiture for several centuries. Instead, it
visualizes fashion as a reflexive activity in which individuality is
composed and recomposed within a fluid but ultimately finite field
of possibilities. It is the painting's iconic privilege to freeze this
momentum. The haunting quality of movement abruptly and temporarily arrested isolates a form of appearance that can resolve
identity only momentarily, if at all, before being submerged once
again in the painting's insistent patterning and regularity. In *La
Grande Jatte*, identity is replaced as the fundamental index of
social representation by appearance, in the most fragile and contingent sense.

Paradoxically, the relentless focus on socioeconomic class in
recent discussions of La Grande Jatte has brought the painting's
departure from the typical protocols of legibility into clearer view.
This trend begins with Meyer Schapiro's reorientation of the critical discussion towards the painting's revision of Impressionist por-

trayals of leisure and continues with T. J. Clark's proposal that Seurat realizes in the work an effective means for portraying the makeshift bourgeois identity cultivated by the petit bourgeoisie.[25] The crucial passage in Clark's text (which, it must be said, is no more—and no less—than an epilogue to his study) asserts that "[*La Grande Jatte*] attempts to find form for the appearance of class in capitalist society, especially the look of the '*nouvelles couches sociales*'; that the forms it discovers are in some sense more truthful than most others produced at the time; and that it suggests ways in which class might still be painted."[26] By stressing the latter part of this statement, one might conclude, as does Linda Nochlin, that the painting represents an "anti-utopian allegory."[27] However, the more significant aspects of the painting's visibility are captured, I think, by the first of Clark's reflections, in the "attempt to find form for the appearance of class." For if Seurat's painting turns back even provisionally the borders of class, it is within the realm, we might say, where representation engages the dynamics of fashion.

Four factors are especially important for assessing fashion's relations to modern life painting: leisure, comportment, *confection* (ready-made clothing), and conformity.

LEISURE

New forms of leisure that accompanied industrialization have been the primary focus for the analysis of the subjects of modern life painting; however, evidence of a perceptual, or better, of a somatic awareness of industrialization also appears in artistic production at mid-century. Phenomena such as refinements of technique, specifications of place, time, or season, and fragmentary, repeated, and serial treatments of imagery are artistic variants of the division of labor, clock time, and piece work that transformed France's economy in the period. Thus, the title of Seurat's painting specifies both the place—the island of La Grande Jatte, and the day—Sunday; while the designation of the time—four o'clock in the afternoon—appears to have been the contribution of the critic Félix Fénéon.[28]

As has been noted by a number of scholars, this day marks a division in working-class as opposed to bourgeois patterns of labor and leisure.[29] The special role of Sunday in the organization of time serves to amplify this division.

The French Revolution provided the great rupture in the history of costume, and Sunday was the day on which its fault lines were most visible. "Clothing being one of the most energetic of all symbols," writes Honoré de Balzac (1799–1850) in his *Traité de la vie élégante*, "the Revolution also was expressed in terms of fashion, a debate between silk and broadcloth."[30] At first, enfranchised men were the sole beings who figured in the symbolic order; their adoption of black clothing registered the overturning of class distinctions ordained by sumptuary laws under the *ancien régime*.[31] "Thus, in our society," Balzac proclaims, "differences have disappeared: only nuances remain."[32] True, these differences still derive their authority from the social order, but they have become clandestine, residing in details, rather than in an overt hierarchy of appearance.[33] Balzac assiduously pursues these nuances, interrogating external appearances in order to yield the revealing signs of character and class, or, to maintain his economy of words, signs of the separation of the man of leisure from the man who works. It is this crucial separation that Sunday, the day of rest, suspends. Balzac is precise: Sunday is the great leveler, the day on which the true man of leisure's distinction from his opposite becomes inoperative. In fact, he argues elsewhere, since on this day everyone amuses themselves and takes the air, everyone has a white shirt and a clean suit, "*l'homme comme il faut*" could hardly do "*comme tout le monde*."[34] On this one day of rest for the rest of the world, the man of leisure stays home.

It is important to recall here that for the first fifty years of the nineteenth century, physiognomic thinking held sway over the discourse of fashion. Purporting to have mastered the truths and falsehoods of external appearances, physiognomists peeled back the "outer skin" of modern man, hoping to reveal a point of origin; more often than not their atavistic project simply uncovered a

FIG. 3 *J. J. [Jean-Ignace-Isodore Gérard] Grandville*, Types Modernes, 1835: Observations Critiques. *Caption: "Le dedans de l'homme expliqué par le dehors." Lithograph published by Neuhaus. Bibliothèque Nationale, Département des Estampes et de la Photographie B81629*

provincial rather than a Parisian birthright and an acquired rather than an assigned identity. Scanning the effects of "The Great Masculine Renunciation" before it was even so named,[35] they hoped to extract principles of wealth and rank from those that had supplanted them: sobriety, self-control, and mercantile ideals of labor. The uneasy acceptance of the new denizens of leisure is well known from the tradition of ridiculing the bourgeois *endimanché* in the *physiologies* and *feuilleton* literature that burgeoned under the July Monarchy. Balzac, Honoré Daumier (1808–1879), and Théophile Gautier (1811–1872), among others, contributed to this mock-epic of the bourgeois, while Henri Monnier (as Joseph Prudhomme) impersonated him most vividly. His frock coat, observes Gautier, "in a happy combination, is both too large and too tight and flaps like the shutters of an open window to reveal a rounded paunch."[36] The ungainly fit of "this outer skin of the modern hero," in Baudelaire's ironic phrase from "The Salon of 1846," is of course the single most potent aspect of the travesty of provincial bourgeois in Courbet's *Un enterrement à Ornans*.[37]

A nostalgia for the coded hierarchy of the eighteenth century clings to the texts that resituate fashion in the 1850s. Balzac calls the passers-by on the boulevards "the chorus of a classical tragedy," but the scene reminds him more of comedy.[38] Other frameworks of representation are likewise assayed. For Grandville, the animal kingdom and the inorganic *nouveauté* furnish obvious poles of comparison for a disoriented species. His lithographs in the series *Types Modernes* (1835) retain, however, many of the familiar physiognomic assumptions. "The interior of man explained by the exterior," announces the frontispiece, but with the ironic twist that only articles of clothing are on display—hats, umbrellas, boots, and bonnets, all scattered in disarray and each awaiting the physiologist's census (Fig. 3). The best-known manifestation of nostalgia for the eighteenth-century social order is the Baudelairean dandy, an *aristocrate-manqué* who, in order to resist the vulgarity of the nineteenth century, carries his self-restraint to the point of aggressive stoicism. A somewhat belated arrival from the English scene at the turn of the century, the figure of the dandy in "Le Peintre de la vie moderne" coexists uncomfortably with the man of the crowd—with whom, to play upon a point made by Benjamin, he has little in common.[39] This confusion subsides, however, when the inability to rank the clothed figure is resolved by arranging the evidence in a temporal sequence. In reviewing the history of fashions down to the present, Baudelaire postulates that one will readily uncover the transitions: "No gaps, hence no surprises."[40]

Reformers, on the other hand, welcomed the upheaval of appearance and were more certain of its benefits. "Visible equality," asserts Jules Michelet (1798–1874), will elevate the working class:

"Fashion and taste are an initiation into art for them. In addition, and still more important, better dress changes a man; he wants to be worthy of it, and he tries to align his moral behavior with it."[41] Nevertheless, a strict timetable does regulate this aesthetic bonus. Popular prints from the 1840s unceasingly proffer Sunday as the day to exchange identity. No one was surprised when those employed in the fashion and retail trades exhibited the keenest appreciation of this fact. The tailor's assistant in a Gavarni print, for example, admires a fashion plate and exclaims: "This, however, is what I will be like on Sunday." (Fig. 4) In the 1880s, the obligatory word-picture of *le dimanche* in the *tableaux de Paris* makes this same point. Writes Jules Vallès:

FIG. 4 *Guillaume-Sulpice Chevallier Gavarni, "Violà pourtant comme je serai dimanche!...", 1839, lithograph printed by Aubert et Cie., appeared in* le Figaro *(6 June 1839). Bibliothèque Nationale, Département des Estampes et de la Photographie B22251*

It is the valiant class of people of the atelier and shop that one's eyes should follow early on these beautiful Sundays. And, watching this population wake up and dress themselves for strolling in this great bivouac that we call Paris, which has extinguished their fire for twenty four hours, it must be said that the French Revolution was not in vain, and that the Brutuses who isolate themselves from this joyous crowd to lament the Republic on the desert of the Champ-de-Mars are wrong....These republicans dressed in new clothes for a *louis* and embalmed with a bouquet for a *sou* feel, throughout the length of their skin and dress, the thrill of aristocracy.[42]

The lower end of the social stratum now bears the freight of distinction eliminated at the top, as Vallès further explains: their "*petit luxe*" insults the second-hand clothing ("*friperie*") of the underemployed (Fig. 5), here designated a bourgeoisie *déclassée*.

Nicolas-Toussaint Charlet, "Voilà pourtant comme je serai Dimanche," 1822, **FIG. 5**
lithograph, printed by Villain, distributed by M. Hulin. Bibliothèque Nationale,
Département des Estampes et de la Photographie B80946

"Under the Second Empire, textile laborers learned arithmetic,"
observes the historian William Reddy, adding that they had no
choice but to adapt to a new system of bargaining over units of time
and calculations of labor, rather than over yarn or cloth.[43] The so-
called democratization of luxury that spread during this
period engendered a new form of social calculus. Inventories of the
household possessions of workers, artisans, and petit bourgeois
compiled in the 1870s show two clearly marked sets of clothing,
one for workdays, one for Sunday.[44] The wardrobes of women
became a crucial unit of measure. The bourgeoise or *femme du
monde* did not divide her psychological week in half so much as
her day by four or more changes of costume: one for her morning
toilette, another for her afternoon calls, and so on and so forth. Her
outfits for promenades and for riding in the late afternoon were of

FIG. 6 *Gustave Courbet,* Les Desmoiselles au bord de la Seine (été), *1856–57, oil on canvas, 68 x 78 inches, Musée du Petit Palais, Paris. Photo: Giraudon*

dark fabrics, their austerity a prelude to the ebullience of evening dress. Seurat's painting is very mindful of these temporal distinctions. Associating *La Grande Jatte* with portrayals of *le monde*, therefore, he unwittingly obliterates the precise point as he makes it. *Le déjeuner sur l'herbe* (1865–1866) by Claude Monet (1840–1926), for example, would seem to anticipate the structural and thematic elements of Seurat's work. Yet these figures—Monet's friends and companions playing roles—are *"en grande toilette."*[45] Thus, where Monet isolates individualist, even extravagant uses of the new luxury goods, Seurat, in contrast, creates a monotonous replication of sartorial custom. In selecting this one day out of seven, his calendar of appearances is that of the working class who aspires *to become* petit-bourgeois. What this choice implies, however, is easily missed. Seurat's painting measures time by two sets of clothing, but neither this nor some commodified notion of democracy adequately describes its peculiar "look."

COMPORTMENT

Fashion in this period was regulated by two energetic discourses, etiquette and "publicity," the latter being a deferential term of the period for advertising. Fashion columns described the goods and encouraged hyperbolic emulation, while etiquette manuals prescribed appropriate behavior and offered exaggerated promises of self-transformation.[46] Together they created the staggered sequence of conformity and change that characterizes fashion, balancing the dual function of appearance as both a barrier and a bridge to social mobility.

In his second trilogy of paintings opposing the country and the city—the pair *Les Demoiselles de village* (1851) and *Les Demoiselles au bord de la Seine* (1857) (Fig. 6), separated by the working women of *Les Cribleuses de blé* (1855)—Courbet attempts to represent this impossible dynamic in his portrayal of young women, or *demoiselles*.[47] Here, clothing generates a tyranny of classification that measures the distance between the workers in their coarse woolen clothing and the village *demoiselles endimanchés*. Yet the outdated clothing of the latter also suggests their isolation from the Parisian center of fashion as well as from the *grande monde* that dictates it.[48] In contrast, the young women lounging in abandon in *Les demoiselles au bord de la Seine* display the finery that had become available as the result of the expansion of *confection*. Whereas in the 1830s work clothes and uniforms were the major ready-made items for sale in the capital, during the Second Empire, outerwear (shawls and overcoats), underwear (corsets and crinolines), and accessories (gloves, fans and hats) were marketed in increasing quantities.[49] Contemporary reactions to Courbet's painting read like aberrant versions of the *chroniques de mode* that were used to promote these items and of the *manuels de bon ton* that were used to teach their proper use. The *demoiselle* in the foreground, writes the informed reviewer in *L'Illustration*, is sprawled out more than napping, in a wanton attitude in poor taste; her bare arms are flung out haphazardly, and her hands squeezed into yellow gloves that are too tight; she has made a pillow of one part of her *cachemire*, while the other half, slung around her body, fails to hide the shapeless form beneath a mass of flounces of gauze ending in a stiff, tight, bodice [actually a chemise over a corset], as well informed as the rest....This figure is a scandal![50]

It took the combined efforts of capitalism and of social regulation to create a demand for material improvement that at the same time held in abeyance the acquisition of the higher social status that the possession of these goods appeared to promise. The two groups of *demoiselles* reveal the contradiction inherent in this project. Irreducible to the simple opposition of vice and virtue that Castagnary makes of this pair of paintings, they nonetheless present us with a set of antitheses—a dynamic of distance and approach, of imitation and excess that the fashion system itself has been designed to enforce.[51] Indeed, where *nouveautés* seem to create the possibility of crossing the boundary between *paysanne* and *bourgeoise*, between *paysanne* and *parisienne*, they in fact cause these boundaries to surface, making explicit fashion's latent structure as a system of classification, even in this period of increasingly generalized luxury.

Comportment, as the etiquette manuals of the period never tire of proclaiming, is the outward, visible sign of internalized values— sobriety, propriety, and respectability, all that is fused together to make the upright posture into a figurative symbol. And just as importantly, they advise, one must never be seen to *labor* for one's appearance; it should be carried off with a natural ease, such that it never appears to have been acquired, but rather to have been assigned by right of one's origins or birth. The aristocratic standard that will ultimately frustrate the behavioral program that these manuals put forward thus contains and limits at every turn the anxious readers to whom they are addressed. The effectiveness of these social rules is nowhere more evident than in their capacity for reversibility; they can be invoked to explain the signification of

Edgar Degas, Portraits en frise, *inscribed* "Portraits en frise pour décoration   **FIG. 7**
dans un appartément," *1879, pastel, 19.5 x 25.4 inches. Collection of Dr.
Herman J. Abs, Cologne, Lemoisne 532*

fashion as well as to coax one's obedience to its dictates. Consider
the precepts of Charles Blanc, former Director of Fine Arts,
founder of the *Gazette des Beaux-Arts*, and professor of aesthetics at
the Collège de France:

> In the July Monarchy, the triumph of the middle classes modi-
> fied female costume. Waving bows and short curls were worn
> on the temples; the shoulders were enlarged by leg-of-mutton
> sleeves, and...the hoop and puffed skirts were revived. Thus
> attired, women seemed designed for a sedentary and domestic
> life, because nothing in their dress indicated movement, or
> appeared favorable to it. All was revised under the Second
> Empire: family ties were relaxed, and a growing luxury so cor-
> rupted manners that an honest woman could no longer be rec-
> ognized by her style of dress. The female costume was trans-
> formed....Everything that could prevent a woman remaining
> seated was developed, and everything that could impede her
> walk was discarded.[52]

FIG. 8   *Georges Seurat,* La Promeneuse
au Réverbère, *ca. 1882, conté
crayon, 12 x 9 inches, de Hauke
510. Private collection*

The Second Empire costume, Blanc continues, is designed to be seen in profile. And the profile is the image of the passer-by who hurries past, "cleaving the air," leaving the home, the family, and stability behind.[53]

The profile, therefore, is judged to be legible, indicative of the habitual *flâneurisme*, mobility, and silent interaction of social life in Paris. Among Seurat's older contemporaries, it is Edgar Degas (1834–1917) who brings to bear the greatest acuity in the observations of these movements. His studies of strolling women aim to catch the "grimace" of posture, to achieve a gestural physiognomy.[54] A series of studies for a frieze of strollers intended to decorate an apartment interior (Fig. 7), for instance, varies the pose and the orientation of the women depicted; the twisting torsos and bumpy protrusions of clothing serve to differentiate rather than to affiliate the individual figures.[55] Seurat, too, was preoccupied with isolated figures in motion who were unaware of their being observed—and yet subject to being identified and classified. Numerous drawings made well before his studies for *La Grande Jatte* indicate his systematic study of female strollers.[56] (Fig. 8) But Seurat, we notice, adheres more strictly than does Degas to the profile view, here calibrating the forward momentum through the tilted arcs of a bonnet, back, or bustle, there deflecting it by an angle turned sharp and square. In *La Grande Jatte*, he freezes this forward movement, rendering it mechanical, self-contained, strange. Choosing uniformity over irregularity, he closes open contours, making the profile geometric, upright. Degas's figures have a supple, relaxed posture; they impart nonchalance and ease. Seurat's become simplified molds. In this way, he regularizes the appearance of the figures and, at the same time, conveys a sense of their rigidity and their reserve, bodies disciplined by the constraints of comportment. Indeed, his entire canvas is organized by a strikingly regular beat, with an emphasis on the upright posture, standing and seated. Whether military, musical, or theoretical in inspiration, the attitude of his figures is one of cultivated rectitude.

CONFECTION

Informal tutelage of artists in the new codes of dress had begun in the art criticism of Gautier and Baudelaire, who scorned their recoil from contemporary clothing. Each discovered a virtue in the modern redistribution of adornment across a gendered divide, celebrating the material splendor of women's appearance as a welcome relief from the grey platitudes of male clothing. Women, Gautier explains, understand the "dissonance" required to distinguish the *toilette* from the body.[57] Save the soldier, Baudelaire mentions no picturesque examples of male attire in "Le Peintre de la vie moderne"; the essay does devote considerable attention, however, to the artfulness of women's make-up. Misleading tributes to her commemoration of aristocratic elegance aside, Baudelaire's assumptions about women's lower order of being underlie his injunction to mask it with artifice. In contrast, Blanc depersonalizes the problem, since it is his intention to concoct a pragmatic textbook for French design in the service of the newly christened "industrial" arts—which are, for the most part, luxury goods. Construing the toilette itself as a work of art, Blanc is at pains, though, to extend the principles of his *Grammaire des arts du dessin* to fashion: "the umbrella," for example, "plays the role of *chiaroscuro*."[58]

Seurat's artifice is of a radically different order than that found in cosmetics or fabricated finery. It has most in common with Blanc's ideally aligned correspondence of the fine and applied arts and his

FIG. 9   *"Changement de Domicile...Bonnardet" [Facade of the Bonnardet store], wood-cut advertisement, 1848, 7 x 9.4 inches, Bibliothèque Nationale, Département des Estampes et de la Photographie, R5217*

utilitarian approach to what may be called "the aesthetics of appearance."[59] No doubt, too, Seurat aimed for the condensation of effect set down in Sutter's aphorisms about vision, which he had read: "Parallel lines establish the moral relation between two or more persons, expressing an identity of view and a conformity of sentiments."[60] Or perhaps for something like the "descriptive blocks" that filled Mallarmé's fashion magazine *La Dernière Mode* (1874), which he had probably not encountered. No verbs; no body; at most a mannequin provided support for the attachment of words to clothing and to accessories. Phrases are parceled out in segments: hat, collar, bodice, sleeves, skirt, shoes, parasol; the slightest indications of use: *toilette de visite, de promenade, de sortie, de dîner....*[61] Remarks Roland Barthes of this tactic, "Empty, but not absurd."[62]

The everyday lives of Seurat and of the artists in his circle disclose the extent of their familiarity with France's leading industrial sector —textile production—and its commercial outlets in the fashion trades and in retailing. "Au Père de Famille," the name of the fancy goods (*nouveautés*) shop owned by Seurat's maternal uncle, Paul Haumonté-Faivre, brings the point home.[63] And in 1882, we should recall, Lucien Pissarro held a position at Niel frères and Company, "a house well known for its Roubaix fabrics"— the leading center of popularly priced woolens.[64] "I don't think it's necessary that my son park himself in a particular line of business," writes Pissarro to his friend Théodore Duret, the critic and collector, "but what he knows best is the commerce of fabrics for ready-to-wear clothing."[65] A year

Georges Seurat, **FIG. 10**
Le Strapontin
(Silhouette de Femme),
pen and ink, 6.5 x 4
inches, de Hauke 615.
Whereabouts unknown.

later, in encouraging his son to pursue drawing while in London, Pissarro is conscious of its usefulness—"*un métier en main*"—for both trade and art.[66] In fact, the municipal drawing school of Justine Lequien that Seurat attended before entering the École des Beaux-Arts followed a teaching program inspired by the Saint-Simonian Alexandre Dupuis, whose pedagogy was aimed, as recent work has shown, at developing manual skill and visual literacy in "the language of industry."[67]

Raideur (stiffness) is the word that critics use so repeatedly to describe Seurat's painting, attempting to characterize the comic and the ridiculous in his figures and their simul-taneous sobriety and seriousness. Octave Mirbeau, for example, labels the painting "an Egyptian fantasy"; he is hardly alone.[68] But the visual associations activated by the figures encased in their rigid armature are consistent as well with the uniformity of mass-produced manufactured goods (Fig. 9). The *révolution du bon marché* had flooded the

FIG. 11 *Cover,* L'Art dans le Costume, *October 1885. Bibliothèque Nationale 4°V2586*

market with "shoddy" goods (*la camelote*) in the 1880s. Especially denigrated were cheap wooden toys imported from Germany. Thus a "flabbergasted" and "bewildered" Henry Fèvre asks rhetorically, "Who are these stiff people, these wooden dolls, this pack of Nurembourg toys?" before he comes gradually to the realization that the painting presents "the stiffness of Parisians strolling, formal and enervated, where even recreation is a pose."[69] Likewise, the *Journal des Artistes* calls the figures "wooden '*bonshommes*'" and declares: "They are a band of petrified, immobile beings, mannequins who make the mistake of grabbing the public's attention, only to make them laugh."[70] Of course, it need hardly be mentioned that Seurat's emphasis on the ready-made extends to that most banal of products, the umbrella, one of the principal motifs of the painting.[71] And the bustle was there from the start. The earliest drawings that can be associated with the painting feature this attribute of a woman's "urban armor"; in one, the prefabricated skeleton is laid bare (Fig. 10).

Then, too, the wooden quality that preoccupies these critics is part of the semblance of ready-made clothing, which was said to imitate—without achieving—elegance. The most frequently cited characterization of Seurat's painting recognizes this fact: "And even the stiffness of the figures, the stamped-out, cookie-cutter quality of the forms give *La Grande Jatte* a modern tone, a reminder of our tight clothing, stuck to our bodies, our reserved gestures, and the British cant imitated everywhere."[72] Beginning in the late 1870s and early 1880s, the expansion of *confection* and the increasing adoption of ready-made clothing was promoted vigorously by department stores as a response to structural changes in an economy already hard pressed by devastating competition from foreign goods and further crippled by the depression of the 1880s.[73] Indeed, the variety of fashion plates that Seurat's compositional structure most resembles promotes *confection*.[74] Lacking the hand-tipped tones, cozy domestic vignettes, or tantalizing *tête-à-têtes* in prints sold *hors-texte* in ladies' magazines, these plates show multiple, vertically arranged silhouettes in a standardized form. Trade publications in fact considered the constant regeneration of novelty celebrated by fashion writers to be a nuisance, and various tactics were devised to limit its impact on the couturier's labor and raw materials. In the 1880s, consequently, there developed a kind of publication that specialized in offering semi-assembled costumes, which then could be modified to give the effect of their having been tailored for the individual client.[75] Shortcuts for those who had not studied drawing extensively were provided in other publications: diagrams based on

"*Costume en velours uni et vigogne frisée*" (*Croquois 13*), L'Art dans le Costume, **FIG. 12** October 1885, 13. Bibliothèque Nationale 4°V2586

"*Étude de dessin professionel: Appliqué à la couture*," L'Art dans le Costume, **FIG. 13** 15 October 1885, 44. Bibliothèque Nationale 4°V2586

proportional units, tracings, silhouettes devoid of modeling and musculature, step-by-step instructions, and "correspondence" courses in cutting and construction (Figs. 11, 12, 13).[76]

This procedure of making multiple variations on a single, organizing pattern is found in Seurat's meticulous preparations and adapted to the project as a whole. That is, he evokes his training in "mechanical" drawing and simultaneously adjusts his formal vocabulary to the visual habits that characterize the realm of labor latent in the fashionability portrayed in his painting. The *pointillisme* so often casually associated with tapestry, weaving, or embroidery—textiles, in short—works in this new equation of regularity and the ready-made. Undoubtedly, Seurat's ambition was a grand synthesis. For this painting also represents a first step towards a new pictorial language, one that would not merely solicit but, ideally, predetermine a viewer's response to painting by stimulating physiological reactions to the emotional qualities of line and color; his later works elaborate this system.[77] There is something oddly poignant about "Seurat's science," its exploration of the elusive boundary between improvised and coerced forms of expression.

But what is at stake in *La Grande Jatte* is a larger signifying system for the human form, as Joris-Karl Huysmans, for one, recognized:

> Strip his figures of the colored fleas that cover them, what is beneath is void; no soul, no thought, nothing. A non-being in a body whose contours only remain. Thus in his painting of the Grande Jatte, the human scaffolding becomes rigid and hard; everything becomes immobilized and clots up.[78]

What Huysmans regrets is not just the loss of three-dimensional form, but the loss of the depth of human presence; only the inanimate quality of the figures remains. A denial of access is enforced through the absence of human contact or exchange among the figures—and between those figures and the viewer; only the child, near dead center, gazes out; and hers is a diminutive and insufficient gesture of address, shadowed beneath a large bonnet.

Seurat's emphasis on the common manner of the figures can be accepted: up to a point. But why, complains Alfred Paulet, has he "systematically sacrificed the rest?"[79] The stiffness and even the awkwardness of the figures in *La Grande Jatte*, their mock-gravity and their deadpan theatricality, display both the means and the results of fashioning the self in contemporary society. The painting's apprehension of the impersonal regularity of modern appearance (in a phrase, Seurat's embrace of the ready-made) re-presents the contradictions inherent in the classifying system of fashion itself. If the painting cannot really focus socioeconomic class with any precision, it is because the operation of fashion interferes with clothing's ability to function as an index. Rather, fashion defines an unstable, though not unbounded, distribution of identity.

CONFORMITY

The painting's tendency to itemize its contents leads the viewer to want to strike off, as on a list, the repetitive pattern of parasols, hats, and collars. This impulse to inventory extends as well to the assembled figures; it seems unavoidable in written responses to the painting. The typological system of classification that had informed a century of verbal and visual descriptions of Parisian inhabitants, however, is residual in *La Grande Jatte*, as is indicated by the facility and carelessness with which critics tick off the various characters in the painting: young shop girls, a nurse and old grandmother, soldiers, a young mother and her child, another *ménage* with a maid holding the child, and so on. The typology is generalized, diffused, until one comes to two "overdetermined" points in the painting: the figures that fill the lower corners, left and right, stretching an emphatic plane across the foreground of the canvas's minutely differentiated surface. On these figures hinges the problem of identifying the social types in the painting. Fouquire calls the reclining man a "jockey stretched out, who has lost a leg on his latest jump."[80] Or is he a *canotier*, as Jules Christophe writes later, "smoking his pipe without distinction?"[81] To Christophe we also owe the description of the "hieratic and scandalous couple, a young *élégante* on the arm of a foppish companion, holding a monkey on a leash."[82] The *canotier* and the *demimondaine* couple are deliberately opposed, the one lounging in a costume of impossibly scrambled codes—clay pipe, jockey's hat, vest and shirt-sleeves—whereas the couple is self-consciously adorned, correcting to an extreme the lounging posture of the former. They are the one note of excess in an otherwise restrained scene, setting in motion from the right edge of the painting a declension of form that unfolds throughout the scene.

The fluidity of sartorial custom noted as early as 1854 by Gustave Flaubert (1821–1880) would seem to close the search for stable identities. His advice to Louise Colet about how to write a fashion magazine bears repeating:

> But since our purpose here is not to sermonize the bourgeois (who aren't even bourgeois anymore, for since the invention of the public bus the bourgeoisie is dead; they sit there in the bus alongside the "lower classes" and not only think like them and look like them but even dress like them: take the fashion for coarse cloth, the new styles in overcoats, the jerseys worn for boating, and the blue work shirts for field sports, etc.)—still, since there is no question of sermonizing them, this is what I would do: I would accept it all, and write straight from the democratic point of view: point out that nowadays everything is for everybody, and that the greatest possible confusion exists for the good of the greatest number.[83]

In this modern, submerged mode of classification, identity fades and reemerges in affiliations not quite clarified.

In the late nineteenth century, the peculiar oscillation between conformity and differentiation in the dynamic of fashion inspired social scientists such as Herbert Spencer in England, Gabriel Tarde in France, and Georg Simmel in Germany to recast the occasional assessments of a Balzac or of a Baudelaire in an analytic mold.[84] It is as if, through some kind of mutation, the doctrine of imitation abandoned by the fine arts finds a renewed purpose in defining social space. As the poetic gaze gives way to the scientific, a comparative anatomy of imitation or social obedience—and distinction or semiotic resistance—pervades the contemplation of fashion. "It is characteristic of the dude," writes Simmel, "that he carries the elements of a particular fashion to the extreme....Thus he represents something distinctly individual, which consists in the quantitative intensification of such elements as are qualitatively common property of the given set or class. The spirit of democracy causes persons to seek the dignity and sensation of command in this manner, it tends to a confusion and ambiguity between ruling the class and being ruled by it."[85] Seurat's couple intensifies the qualities of the group of figures beyond them and determines the rhythm of the whole. The poses of the other figures fragment, multiply, and simplify the contrasting postures in the foreground. From one figure to another, Seurat constructs a geometry that links the figures in a series of groupings; one group becomes an intermediary transition to the next, so that identities gradually merge and dissolve into a haze of flickering light. He depicts all that the democratization of luxury and the general uniformity of dress promises but fails to deliver. Collected in the mirage of an afternoon on the island of *La Grande Jatte* are a series of differentiated people and classes that, in the end, are caught in the reproduction of a uniformity that the formal structure of the painting enforces and suffuses within itself.

The only words attributed to Seurat about *La Grande Jatte* stress the composure and the condensation of effect: "The Pan-Athenaic Frieze of Phidias was a procession. I want to make the moderns file past like the figures on that frieze, in their essential form, to place them in compositions arranged harmoniously by virtue of the directions of the colors and lines, line and color arranged in accordance with one another."[86] A grandiose parallel, assuredly. Nevertheless, mythic conceptions of the modern stroller cannot accommodate the figures here depicted. The *contrappósto* of the ancients has stiffened, hardened into the mold of the modern pageantry of appearance. It is left to the viewer to resolve the contradiction between

FIG. 14 *Georges Seurat,* Les Poseuses, *1888, oil on canvas, 79 x 98.4 inches. The Barnes Foundation, Merion Station, Penn.*

ugliness and beauty, between caricature and the antique; and to resolve the conflict inherent in a commerce of luxury goods that offers escape from one's class only to renew one's conformity within it. Seurat leaves us with a tense calm, a balance between the ritual and the rigidity of modern life that had come to dominate the conditions of appearance in the 1880s.

When interest in fashion again changed intellectual hands in the mid-twentieth century, it was perceived as "much more a semiological than a semantic order."[87] Something of the quandary in which Seurat's painting leaves the viewer could be described by Roland Barthes's verdict on fashion:

> Fashion thus proposes this precious paradox of a *semantic system whose only goal is to disappoint the meaning it luxuriantly elaborates:* the system then abandons the meaning yet does so without giving up any of the spectacle of signification.[88]

Lest we mistake Seurat's "disappointment" of meaning for an abandonment of critique, we should recall that *Les Poseuses* (1886–1888) (Fig. 14) in effect reverses the mechanism of concealment at work in *La Grande Jatte*. If the earlier painting permits identification with the illusion of fashionability, the latter offers us a reminder of the constructed nature of both painting and self-presentation. It becomes an intricate counterpoint to and

Paul Signac, **FIG. 15**
Apprêteuse et
garnisseuse (modes),
rue du Caire
(Les Modistes), 1886,
oil on canvas,
39.5 x 32 inches.
E. G. Bührle
Foundation, Zurich.

reconfiguration of *La Grande Jatte*, recovering the body as the primary unit of expression and scattering clothing as mere raw material in the atelier, awaiting the painter's synthesis. "Pseudo-scientific" fantasies aside, the umbrellas, hats, shoes, and stockings are self-sufficiently arranged, displaying themselves as so many finished goods. Taken together, the two paintings seem to demonstrate that the "form" for the appearance of modernity is to be found not in the supra-natural artifice that Baudelaire envisions, but in the displacement of the natural from the body to its inorganic accoutrements.[89] Among these are the goods being "trimmed" and "finished" in the precisely titled painting by Paul Signac (1863–1937), exhibited along with *La Grande Jatte* at the final Impressionist exhibition in 1886: *Apprêteuse et garnisseuse (modes), rue du Caire,* known as "The Milliners" (Fig. 15). Here the artifice returns to the labor expended on its formation. As we are shown by Signac and reminded by Barthes, "the world of Fashion is work in reverse."[90]

The arena for discussion has in recent years shifted once more, as feminist critics ponder not only the constraints but the possibilities inherent in fashion's performative aspects. Surveying the field, Jane Gaines muses: "self:role as body:costume and gender:identity, each term in the pairing at odds with the other and in the relation of constant flux, with the advantage that, as we confuse the world, we are allowed to maintain our ambivalence for a little while longer."[91] Only one thing is certain: the work of appearance remains an open realm of possibility.

NOTES

1   In the summer of 1984, just after this paper was first delivered, a version of *The Grande Jatte* appeared in my mailbox; the figures were decked out in sportswear on the cover of a *Land's End* catalogue. It was one of those uncanny experiences that seemed to render further comment on the argument superfluous. I would like to thank all those who have brought me back to it. Debora Silverman's invitation to participate in a panel on "Culture and Consumption in the Early Third Republic" at the American Historical Association in 1983 first prompted my work on fashion and modern life painting. A brief version of the discussion of Seurat's painting was presented at a symposium entitled "*La Grande Jatte:* The New Scholarship" and organized by Richard Brettell in the Spring of 1987. I was inspired by Robert L. Herbert's lectures and writings on Seurat and am grateful for his generous recognition of my unpublished paper in *Georges Seurat, 1859–1891*, exhibition catalog (New York: Metropolitan Museum of Art, 1991), 177.

2   The completion in 1855 of the hôtel and arcade complex brought to a close the first phase of Georges Eugène (later Baron) Haussmann's program for municipal improvements. The literature on Haussmannization is extensive, but Jeanne Gaillard's thesis, *Paris, la ville, 1852–1870: L'Urbanisme parisien à l'heure d'Haussman* [sic]*; Des Provinciaux aux parisiens; la vocation ou les vocations parisiennes*, 2 vols. (Paris: Honoré Champion, 1977), provided the most direct stimulus to art historical thinking about the impact of urbanization on art of this period. The results are best seen in T. J. Clark, *The Painting of Modern Life: Paris in the Art of Manet and His Followers* (New York: Knopf, 1985); and Robert L. Herbert, *Impressionism: Art, Leisure, and Parisian Society* (New Haven-London: Yale University Press, 1988).

3   The complex was designed to have a traditional appearance using modern materials, as George d'Avenel's description suggests: "Aussi le *Louvre* ôffre-t-il cette particularité assez rare de marier dans sa structure les pans de bois des vieilles maisons aux planchers en fer des constructions modernes," in *Le Mécanisme de la vie moderne*, 4 vols. (Paris: Armand Colin, 1896), 1:25. The Louvre's goods, according to Émile Zola, were upscale: "Les confections sont en général riches et destinées principalement à la classe aisée de la société." From "Dossier préparatoire à la rédaction de Bonheur des Dames," mss., Bibliothèque Nationale, Paris, as quoted in Philippe Perrot, *Les Dessus et les dessous de la bourgeoisie: Une histoire du vêtement au XIXe siècle* (Paris: Fayard, 1981), 123.

The origins of "The Louvre" are somewhat obscure. Usually assigned to 1855, the year the hôtel was completed, the enterprise actually seems to have been founded earlier, perhaps as early as 1853, certainly before 1854. Chauchard (1821–1909), the founder, was the son of a restaurateur and had been employed at the Pauvre Diable until he persuaded Hériot, the "premier aux soies" at la Ville de Paris, to contribute 100,000 francs to the enterprise; eventually, the Pereire's *immobilière*, or development corporation, became a silent partner, providing the bulk of the capital (i.e., 1,100,000 francs). See George d'Avenel, "Le Mécanisme de la vie moderne: les grands magasins," *Revue des Deux Mondes*, 15 July 1894, 340–41; idem., *Le Mécanisme de la vie moderne*, 1:21–30; Gilles Bertrand, "Recherches sur l'origine des grands magasins parisiens, notes d'orientation," in *Fédération des sociétés historiques et archéologiques de Paris et de l'Île de France*, Mémoire 7 (1955), 308–21; Gaillard, *Paris, la Ville*, 532; Theodore Zeldin, *France 1848–1945: Ambition and Love* (Oxford: Oxford University Press, 1979), 109–10; Michael B. Miller, *The Bon Marché: Bourgeois Culture and the Department Store, 1869–1920* (Princeton: Princeton University Press, 1981), 27–28; and Perrot, *Les Dessus et les dessous de la bourgeoisie*, 111–13.

4   Pierre Giffard, *Paris sous le troisième république: Les grands bazars* (Paris: Victor Havard, 1882). The phrase "revolution du bon marché" was coined by Jacques Néré, *La Crise industrielle de 1882 et le Mouvement Boulangiste*, 2 vols., Thèse d'état, University of Paris 1959, 1:113. See also Philip Nord, *Paris Shopkeepers and the Politics of Resentment* (Princeton: Princeton University Press, 1986).

5   *Les chefs d'oeuvres du Musée du Louvre publiées par les Grands Magasins du Louvre* (avec un introduction de Sigismond Marot) (Paris: n.p., n.d.). BN Estampes: Aa.30. x.4o.

6   See Emile Zola, "Lettres de Paris: Exposition de Tableaux à Paris," *Le Messager de l'Europe* (June 1875), in *Mon Salon, Manet, écrits sur l'art*, trans. from the Russian by M. Morozov, ed. Antoinette Ehrard (Paris: Garnier-Flammarion, 1970), 214. Compare the opening pages of Zola's articles on the exhibitions of 1872, 1874, 1875, 1876, and 1881 with those on the Salons of the Second Empire (reprinted in *Mon Salon*).

7   Jules Claretie, *La Vie à Paris* (Paris: Victor Havard, 1881), 27.

8   Ibid.

9   I am using Fredric Jameson's phrase without necessarily subscribing to the argument that he advances in his "Postmodernism, or the Cultural Logic of Late Capitalism," *New Left Review* 146 (July–August 1984), 59–92, and in his *Postmodernism, or, the Cultural Logic of Late Capitalism* (Durham, N.C.: Duke University, 1991). There is no single work that encompasses the argument that I have in mind about the museum and the department store, but two examples of scholarly research inspired by the work of Walter Benjamin are helpful: Miller, *The Bon Marché*; and Rosalind Williams, *Dream Worlds: Mass Consumption in Late Nineteenth-Century France* (Berkeley: University of California Press, 1982). For the convergence of the tactics of exhibition, publicity, and display at Bloomingdale's and at The Metropolitan Museum of Art in the 1980s, see Debora Silverman, *Selling Culture: Bloomingdale's, Diana Vreeland, and the New Aristocracy of Taste in Reagan's America* (New York: Pantheon, 1986).

10   Walter Benjamin, "The Paris of the Second Empire in Baudelaire" (1938/1968), in *Charles Baudelaire: A Lyric Poet in the Era of High Capitalism*, trans. Harry Zohn (1976; rpt. ed. London: Verso, 1983), 82. The "metaphysics of fashion" is mentioned by Benjamin in a letter to Hofmannsthal, 17 March 1928, *Gesammelte Schriften*, vol. 5 of his *Das Passagen-Werk* (Frankfurt: Suhrkamp Verlag, 1982), 1084–85, as cited by Susan Buck-Morss in *The Dialectics of Seeing: Walter Benjamin and the Arcades Project* (Cambridge, Mass.-London: MIT Press, 1989), 97.

11   On the shift in Benjamin's attitude towards fashion and historical change, which I suspect coincides with a critique of Baudelaire's essay on modernity, see Buck-Morss, *The Dialectics of Seeing*, 98.

12   See, for example, Marshall Berman, *All That is Solid Melts into Air: The Experience of Modernity* (New York: Simon & Schuster, 1982), 136: "Those who love Baudelaire will think it a pity that, as long as he was writing advertising copy, he couldn't arrange to get paid for it."

13   Charles Baudelaire, "The Painter of Modern Life," in *Baudelaire: Selected Writings on Art & Artists*, trans. P. E. Charvet (Cambridge-New York: Cambridge University Press, 1972), 392.

14   Ibid., 391.

15   Ibid., 426.

16   The essay was probably begun in 1859, not too long after Baudelaire's break with Courbet, which is memorialized in the poet's "Puisque Réalisme Il Y A," a series of hostile notes for a critique of the latter's painting. T. J. Clark deduces that "To analyse Courbet's talent would mean explaining Nature and its horrors, and mocking the Realist's worship of sanctified vegetables." T. J. Clark, *Image of the People: Gustave Courbet and the Second French Republic 1848–1851* (Greenwich, Conn.: New York Graphic Society, 1973), 21. I suggest that the celebration of artifice in "The Painter of Modern Life" is a response to the "horror" of naturalism, as is its mysterious central figure; to feature the unnamed illustrator Constantin Guys is an arch rebuke to the characterization of "Courbet saving the world" in Baudelaire's notes.

17   The article was offered to at least nine other publishers before finally appearing in three installments in *Le Figaro* on 26 November, 29 November, and 3 December 1863. See Charles Baudelaire, *Oeuvres complètes*, 2 vols., ed. Claude Pichois (Paris: Gallimard, 1975) 2:1413–20.

18   See Michel Foucault, "What is Enlightenment?" (1981), first published in *The Foucault Reader*, trans. Catherine Porter, ed. Paul Rabinow (New York: Pantheon, 1984), 32–50.

19   On the relation of costume to architectural discourse from the Greeks through Semper, see Mary McLeod's essay in this volume. For a short history of the analogy of the body in architecture, see Anthony Vidler, "The Building in Pain: The Body and Architecture in Post-Modern Culture," *AA Files* 19 (Spring 1990), 3–10, published as "Architecture Dismembered," in Vidler's *The Architectural Uncanny: Essays in the Modern Unhomely* (Cambridge, Mass.-London: MIT Press, 1992), 69–82. The question of when fashion became a constituent as opposed to a metaphorical model for architecture remains unresolved, I think, except insofar as it has become the silent partner of 'avant-garde' production in the realms of both art and architecture.

20   Hegel, as Barthes points out, went so far as to say that the body is "devoid of signification" without clothing. See Roland Barthes, *Système de la*

Mode (Paris: Seuil, 1967), trans. by Matthew Ward and Richard Howard as *The Fashion System* (New York: Hill & Wang, 1983), 258.

21   This is Barthes's characterization of sociology's interest in fashion since Herbert Spencer. See *The Fashion System*, 277 n1; also 9 n13.

22   Oil on canvas, 123 x 260.5 inches. Musée d'Orsay, Paris.

23   John House, "Meaning in Seurat's Figure Paintings," *Art History* 3:3 (September 1980), 351. But see House's later disavowal of certain aspects of this article in his "Reading the Grande Jatte," *Museum Studies* [The Art Institute of Chicago] 14:2 (1989), 241 n45.

24   The term is borrowed from Marcel Mauss, "Body Techniques," (1934/1935), *Economy and Society* 2:1 (February 1973), 70–88. Reprinted in *Sociology and Psychology: Essays*, trans. Ben Brewster (London-Boston-Henley: Routledge, 1979), 95–119. Claude Lévi-Strauss's introduction to an earlier collection of Mauss's writings underscores the significance of this aspect of Mauss's work—"Introduction à l'oeuvre de Marcel Mauss," in *Sociologie et Anthropologie* (Paris: Presses Universitaires de France, 1950), ix–lii.

25   For a succinct summary of the critical path Schapiro's writing opened up, see Holly Clayson, "The Family and the Father: *The Grande Jatte* and its Absences," *Museum Studies* [The Art Institute of Chicago] 14:2 (1989), 155–57.

26   See Clark, *The Painting of Modern Life*, 261–67. In an essay that is frequently cited as a rebuttal to this argument, Martha Ward suggests that it is at odds with the confident or disinterested accounts of contemporary critics. See Ward's "The Eighth Exhibition 1886: Rhetoric of Independence and Innovation," in *The New Painting: Impressionism 1874–1886*, exhibition catalog, ed. Charles S. Moffett (San Francisco: The Fine Arts Museums of San Francisco, 1986), 421–42. Further attempts to clarify the character-types and hence the class identities of the figures have reached an impasse.

27   Linda Nochlin, "Seurat's *Grande Jatte:* An Anti-Utopian Allegory," in *Museum Studies* [The Art Institute of Chicago] 14:2 (1989), 133–53.

28   Writes Félix Fénéon:

> Le sujet: par un ciel caniculaire, à quatre heures, l'île, de filantes barques au flanc, mouvante d'une dominicale et fortuite population en joie de grand air, parmi des arbres; et ces quelque quarante personnages sont investis d'un dessin hiéra-

tique et sommaire, traités rigoureusement ou de dos ou de face
ou de profil, assis angle droit, allongés horizontalement,
dressés rigides: comme d'un Puvis modernisant.

"Les Impressionnistes en 1886," *La Vogue*, 13–20 June 1886, in his *Oeuvres
plus que complètes*, ed. Joan U. Halperin, 2 vols. (Geneva: Droz, 1970), 1:37.

29   See House, "Meaning in Seurat's Figure Paintings"; Clark, *The Painting
of Modern Life*; Richard Thomson, *Seurat* (Oxford: Phaidon, 1985), 121–23; and
Clayson, "The Family and the Father."

30   Honoré de Balzac, "Traité de la vie élégante," *La Caricature* (1830), in
Oeuvres complètes, ed. Marcel Bouteron and Henri Longnon, 40 vols. (Paris:
Louis Conard, 1910–38), 39:162.

31   Sumptuary laws were finally abolished on 29 October 1793, although
during much of the eighteenth century, they were rarely enforced. See Nicolas
de Lamare, *Traité de police*, 2 vols. (Paris: J. and P. Cot, 1705), 339–426;
A[uguste] Debay, *Hygiène Vestimentaire: Les Modes et les parures chez les
français depuis l'établissement de la monarchie jusqu'à nos jours* (Paris: E.
Dentu, 1857), 73–122; Henri Aragon, *Les lois somptuaires en France*
(Perpignan: Le Coq Catalan, 1921); and Perrot, *Les Dessus et les dessous de la
bourgeoisie*, 31–46.

32   Balzac, "Traité de la vie élégante," 39:161.

33   For a wide-ranging discussion of "decoding" as a model of thought, see
Carlo Ginzburg, "Morelli, Freud and Sherlock Holmes: Clues and Scientific
Method" (1979), *History Workshop* 9 (Spring 1980), 5–36, published as "Clues:
Roots of an Evidential Paradigm," in *Clues, Myths, and the Historical Method*,
trans. John Tedeschi and Anne C. Tedeschi (Baltimore: Johns Hopkins
University Press, 1986), 96–125.

34   Honoré de Balzac, "Le Dimanche," *La Caricature* (1831), in *Oeuvres
complètes*, 39:330.

35   Flügel uses this term to designate "the sudden reduction of male sartorial decorativeness which took place at the end of the eighteenth century." See J.
C. Flügel, *The Psychology of Clothes* (1928), The International Psycho-
Analytical Library 18, ed. John D. Sutherland (London: Hogarth, 1971),
110–21.

36   Théophile Gautier, "Monographie du bourgeois parisien," in *Le Peau de
tigre* (Paris: n.p., n.d.), 247.

37   Charles Baudelaire, "The Salon of 1846," in *Baudelaire: Selected Writings*, 105. Champfleury [J. F. F. Husson], *L'Ordre*, 21 September 1850, puts forward the connection of *The Burial at Ornans* to Baudelaire's oft-quoted passage on the frock-coat, explaining that the painter had perfectly understood the ideas in the *Salon* of 1846. See Yoshio Abe, "'Un Enterrement à Ornans' et *l'habit noir* baudelairien," *Etudes de la langue et littérature françaises* 1 (1962), 35; and Clark, *Image of the People*, 142, who writes: "Costume fascinates and alarms the reviewers; they know that the peasants, if they are peasants, are dressed to kill; they recognize the *habit noir*. Is it the peasant in his Sunday best or are the figures at the graveside 'les hommes faits causant d'affaires'?"

38   Honoré de Balzac, "Histoire et Physiologies des Boulevards de Paris," *Le Diable à Paris* (1844), in *Oeuvres complètes*, 40:611.

39   Benjamin, *Charles Baudelaire: A Lyric Poet*, 128: "The man of the crowd is no flâneur. In him, composure has given way to manic behavior."

40   Baudelaire, "The Painter of Modern Life," 392.

41   Jules Michelet, *The People*, trans. John P. McKay (Urbana: University of Illinois Press, 1973), 44–45.

42   Jules Vallès, "Le Dimanche," in Marie-Claire Bancquart, ed., *Le Tableau de Paris* (1882–83) (Paris: Français Réunis, 1971), 363:

> C'est la classe vaillante des gens d'atelier ou de magasin qu'il faut suivre de l'oeil, dès le matin de beaux dimanches. Et, quand on a regardé cette population se lever et s'orner pour la flânerie, dans ce grand bivac qu'on appelle Paris, qui a éteint ses feux de guerre pour ving-quatre heures, il faut dire que la Révolution française n'est pas un vain mot et que les Brutus ont tort, qui s'isolent de cette foule joyeuse pour aller désespérer de la République dans le désert du Champ-de-Mars....Elles ont tout le long de la peau ou de la robe un frisson d'aristocratie, ces républicaines qui s'habillent à neuf avec un louis et s'embaument avec un bouquet d'un sou!

43   William A. Reddy, *The Rise of Market Culture: The Textile Trade and French Society, 1750–1900* (Cambridge: Cambridge University Press, 1984), 227.

44   See Frédéric Le Play, "Tailleur d'habits de Paris," in *Les Ouvriers européens*, 6 vols. (Tours: Alfred Mame et fils, 1878–79), 6:423.

45   In a letter to Eugene Boudin, dated 2 February 1867, Dubourg in fact uses this term to describe the clothing of similar luxury and elegance in *Les Femmes au Jardin* (1866–67, Musée d'Orsay, W. 67): "...ce sont des femmes en grande toilette cueillant des fleurs dans un jardin, toile commencée sur nature et en plein air." In G. Jean-Aubry, *Eugéne Boudin: d'après des documents inédits* (Paris: Bernheim-Jeune, 1922), 64; also cited in Daniel Wildenstein, *Claude Monet, biographie et catalogue raisonné: Peintures*, 3 vols. (Paris-Lausanne, La Bibliothèque des Arts, 1974–1979), 1:444, no. 13. Fragments of Monet's *Déjeneur sur l'herbe* are housed in the Musée d'Orsay, Paris; the oil sketch is in the Pushkin Museum, Moscow.

46   Perrot, *Les Dessus et les dessous*, surveys some sixty of these manuals. See also Heinrich Heckendorn, *Wandel des Anstands im franzosischen und im deutsche Sprachgebiet* (Bern: Herbert Lang, 1970); Theodore Zeldin, *France 1848–1945: Taste and Corruption* (Oxford: Oxford University Press, 1980), 318–32; and Norbert Elias, *The History of Manners* (New York: Pantheon, 1981).

47   Gustave Courbet, *Les Demoiselles de village* [Young Ladies from the Village], 1851 (Fig. 5); idem., *Les Cribleuses de blé*, 1855, 51 x 65 inches, Musée de Beaux-Arts, Nantes; and idem., *Les Demoiselles au bord de la Seine (été)*, 1856–57, oil on canvas, 68 x 78 inches, Musée du Petit Palais, Paris. The first series was composed of *Les casseurs de pierre* (1849), *Un enterrement à Ornans* (1849–50), and *Les paysans de Flagey, revenant de la foire, Ornans* (1850, 1855). See Clark, *Image of the People* for further information on the series.

48   See Patricia Manardi, "Gustave Courbet's Second Scandal: *Les Demoiselles de Village*," *Arts Magazine* 53:5 (January 1979), 95–103.

49   See Perrot, *Les Dessus et les dessous*.

50   Exclaims A. J. Du Pays, "Salon de 1857 (Sixième article)," *L'Illustration, Journal Universel* 30: 753 (1 August 1857), 71:

> L'une de ces demoiselles est plutôt vautrée que couchée, dans un abandon de mauvais gout. Ses bras nus sont jetés au hasard et ses mains sont serrées dans des gants jaunes étroitement coutonnés. Elle s'est fait un oreiller d'une partie de son cachemire, dont l'ature moitié, en echarpe sur son corps, ne dissimule pas l'absence de formes, que présente une masse de volants de gaze venant aboutir à un corsage roide, tendu, et aussi informe que le reste....C'est un scandale que cette figure!

51   Jules Castagnary, "Manuscrit inedit," in *Courbet raconté par lui-même et ses amis*, ed. Pierre Courthion, 2 vols. (Geneva: Pierre Cailler, 1958), 1:130, as cited by Manardi, "Gustave Courbet's Second Scandal," 97.

52   Charles Blanc, *L'art dans la parure et dans le vêtement* (1875), cited from the English translation, *Art in Ornament and Dress* (London: Chapman & Hall, 1877), 272–74. A sequel to the *Grammaire des arts du dessin*, the book on clothing was based on lectures delivered at the Institut de France in 1872 and on articles published in serial form in the Gazette des Beaux-Arts from 1870 to 1874 under the series title "Grammaire des arts décoratifs pour faire suite à la grammaire des arts du dessin."

53   Blanc, *Art and Ornament in Dress*, 274.

54   See, for example, Edgar Degas, *Young Woman in Street Costume*, ca. 1867–72, brush drawing in transparent black wash and opaque black, white body color on rose-beige paper, 13 x 10 inches, The Harvard University Art Museums, Cambridge, Mass., bequest of Meta and Paul J. Sachs, 1965.260. See also Paul Valéry, "Degas, Dance Drawing" in *Degas, Manet, Morisot*, trans. David Paul, Bollingen Series 45 (New York: Pantheon, 1960), 54. He observes that:

> His [Degas's] passion was to reconstruct the body of the female animal as the specialized slave of the dance, the laundry...or the streets; and the more or less distorted bodies whose articulated structure he always arranges in very precarious attitudes (tying a ballet shoe, or driving the iron over the cloth with both fists) make the whole structural mechanism of a living being seem to grimace like a face.

55   Edgar Degas, *Portraits in a Frieze*, inscribed "Portraits in a frieze to decorate an apartment," 1879 (Fig. 7). Degas's notebook for 1859–64 records the project as a "Portrait of a Family in a Frieze: Proportions of the figures barely one meter. There could be two compositions, one of the family in town, the other in the country." See Theodore Reff, *The Notebooks of Edgar Degas*, 2 vols., 2nd ed. rev. (New York: Hacker Art Books, 1985), bk. 18, 204 (BN, Notebook 1, 123). On the probable connection of this drawing, exhibited at the fifth Impressionist exhibition in 1880, to the *Essai de décoration, détrempe* (decorative scheme in distemper), exhibited at the fourth Impressionist exhibition in 1879, and to other works, see Jean Sutherland Boggs et al., Degas, exhibition catalog, Galeries Nationales du Grand Palais, Paris, National Gallery of Canada, Ottawa, and The Metropolitan Museum of Art, New York (New York: The Metropolitan Museum of Art; and Ottawa: The National Gallery of Canada, 1988), 318–20, nos. 204 and 205.

56   Of the twenty-eight drawings, in addition to twenty-seven panels and three canvases that César M. de Hauke, *Seurat et son oeuvre*, 2 vols. (Paris: Paul Brame and C. M. de Hauke, Arts et Métiers Graphiques, 1961), designates as preparatory studies for *La Grande Jatte*, only one, a relatively detailed drawing (no. 625), depicts a strolling female figure. However, there are at least sixteen drawings of standing female figures alone, in profile, arrested or in movement, variously dated by de Hauke from 1882 to 1883; they may be seen, I believe, as the core element from which the more complex tableau of strollers in *La Grande Jatte* emerged. One (Fig. 8), from ca. 1882 (no. 510), and four from ca. 1884 (nos. 609–612), along with a pen-and-ink drawing of a woman that accentuates the infrastructure of the bustle (Fig. 10), are particularly indicative of the distillation of form realized in the painting.

57   Théophile Gautier, "De la mode" (1858), in *La Peau de tigre*, 358.

58   Blanc, *Ornament and Dress*, 269–270. There is no illustration of male costume in the entire work, no instruction in its mechanics, fabrication or proportion. Prevailing assumptions about the respective roles of men and women in production and consumption are revealed and remain unquestioned in this treatise.

59   Although Seurat's allegiance to Blanc's *Grammaire des arts du dessin* is well known, the probable significance to the artist of Blanc's parallel treatment of the decorative arts has, to my knowledge, never been considered.

60   David Sutter, "Les Phénomènes de la Vision," *L'Art* 20 (1880), 76.

61   Stéphane Mallarmé, *La Dernière mode* (1874; rept. ed., Paris: Ramsay, 1978). See also Jean-Pierre Lecercle, *Mallarmé et la mode* (Le Poiré-sur-Vie, Vendée: Librairie Séguier, n.d.), 59–95.

62   Barthes, *The Fashion System*, 288 n13.

63   Jean Sutter, ed., *The Neo-Impressionists* (Greenwich, Conn.: New York Graphic Society, 1970), 13. Guillaumin also can be cited in this regard, for he worked in a women's clothing shop near the Opéra, owned by his uncle, from 1861 to 1863.

64   Letter to Théodore Duret (28 September 1882), in *Correspondence de Camille Pissarro. Vol. 1: 1865–1885*, ed. Janine Bailly-Herzberg (Paris: Presses Universitaires de France, 1980), 167. On Roubaix, see Reddy, *The Rise of Market Culture*, 96.

65 "Je pense qu'il n'est pas nécessaire que mon fils se parque dans une spécialité, mais ce qu'il connaît le mieux, c'est le commerce d'étoffes pour confection." *Correspondence Pissarro*, 1:167.

66 "Rappelle-toi que c'est un métier en main, cela ne t'empêchera pas, le cas échéant, de faire du commerce un jour, mais pendant que tu es libre, pourquoi ne pas en profiter?" (7 March 1883) *Correspondence Pissarro*, 1:181.

67 See Albert Boime, "The Teaching of the Fine Arts and the Avant-Garde in France During the Second Half of the Nineteenth Century," *Arts Magazine* 60:4 (December 1985), 49–51; and Molly Nesbit, "The Language of Industry," paper delivered at the Davis Center Seminar, 13 February 1987.

68 "*Un Dimanche à la Grande Jatte*, qui semble une fantaisie égyptienne...." Octave Mirbeau, "Exposition de Peinture," *La France* (20 May 1886), as cited by Henri Dorra and John Rewald, *Seurat; l'oeuvre peint; biographie et catalogue critique* (Paris: Les Beaux-Arts, 1959), 158. See also the comments of the anonymous reviewer in "Half-a-dozen Enthusiasts," *The Bat* (London), 25 May 1886, 186: "Of the newcomers, Seurat strikes me as possessing the most talent. His large picture, *Un Dimanche à la Grande-Jatte*, looks like a modernised version of Ancient Egypt"; and of M. Hamel, "L'Exposition des Impressionnistes," *La France Libre*, 27 May 1886, in Dorra and Rewald, Seurat, 159: "Des flâneurs endimanchés sous les ombrages de la *Grande Jatte* prennent l'attitude simplifiée et définitive d'un cortège de pharaons."

69 "Et voilà qu'il s'esclaffe; qu'est-ce que c'est que ces gens raides, ces poupées de bois? Ce déballage de joujoux de Nuremberg;...on comprend ensuite la raideur de la badauderie parisienne, compassée et avachie, et dont la récréation même est poseuses." Henry Fèvre, "L'Exposition des Impressionnistes," *Revue de Demain*, May–June 1886, 149. Compare the description offered by Octave Maus, "Vingtistes Parisiennes," *L'Art moderne*, 27 June 1886, 204: "Les figures sont en bois, naïvement sculptées au tour, comme les petits soldats qui nous viennent d'Allemagne en des boîtes d'esquilles." Cited in Dorra and Rewald, *Seurat*, 160. The caricaturist Bertall had made a habit of comparing the figures Courbet's paintings to wooden toys. Wooden toys were also among the goods promoted by Chéret's posters, which Seurat, of course, collected. See Robert L. Herbert, "Seurat and Jules Chéret," *Art Bulletin* 40:2 (June 1958), 156–58.

70 "Mais d'un autre côté, je partage l'hilarité du public devant les bonshommes en bois qui jouent la foire au pain d'épice dans cette toile. Ils sont là une bande d'etres pétrifiés, immobiles, de mannequins qui ont le tort de fixer

l'attention du public et de le pousser au rire." J. Le Fustec, "Exposition de la Société des Artistes indépendants," *Journal des Artistes*, 22 August 1886, 2.

71   A cartoon from 1886 shows a clerk demonstrating a *nouveauté* that is an umbrella deformed in shape towards the rear, in order to cover the bustle. See "C'est le dernier modèle de nos en cas, protêgeant á la fois et les nouveaux chapeaux et...le reste," *Croquis—Par PAF* [Jules Renouard], woodcuts published in *Le Charivari* 55 (23 May 1886), 3. Bibliothèque Nationale, Paris, fol. Lc2.1328.

72   "Et même la raideur des gens, les formes à l'emporte-pièce contribuent àdonner le son du moderne, le rappel de nos costumes étriqués, collés au corps, la réserve des gestes, le cant britannique par tous imité." Paul Adam, "Peintres Impressionnistes," *La Revue Contemporaine*, April–May 1886, 550.

73   The most useful discussions are Miller, *The Bon Marché*; Néré, *La Crise industrielle*, and Nord, *Paris Shopkeepers*.

74   See for example, "Pardessus de Printemps et d'Été, Modes de Chez Mme. Coussinet, Rue Richer, 43," a woodcut published in *La Mode Illustré* 13, 28 March 1886, 100–101.

75   See "model" no. 469, in *Paris-Toilette: Journal de Modes*, 1 April 1886, published by Daydou Fils. Bibliothèque Nationale, Paris, f°v898.

76   The resemblance between the simplified design in Seurat's painting and those illustrated in *L'Art Dans le Costume*, a publication oriented specifically towards *couturières*, is striking. See the cover of the 15 October 1885 issue, which features young girls, the "Costume en velours uni et vigogne frisée (Croquis 13)" on p. 13 (Fig. 12), which is very nearly identical to the profile view of the woman with the monkey in the right foreground of Seurat's painting, and the "Étude de dessin professionel: Appliqué à la couture" on p. 44, a diagram of the figure for the purpose of making a dress pattern (Fig. 13). *L'Art dans le Costume*, 15 October 1885. Bibliothèque Nationale, Paris, 4°V2586.

77   See Robert L. Herbert, "Seurat's Theories," in Sutter, ed., *The Neo-Impressionists*, 23–46; and idem., "'Parade de cirque' de Seurat et l'esthétique scientifique de Charles Henry," *Revue de l'Art* 50 (1980), 9–23.

78   "Décortiquez ses personnages des puces colorées qui les recouvrent, le dessous est nul; aucune ame, aucune pensée, rien. Un néant dans un corps dont les seuls contours existent. Ainsi que dans son tableau de la *Grande Jatte*, l'armature humaine devient rigide et dure; tout s'immobilise et se fige." Joris-

Karl Huysmans, "Chronique d'art: Les Indépendants," *La Revue indépendante*, 2:2 (April 1887), 54–55.

79   Alfred Paulet, "Les Impressionnistes," *Paris*, 5 June 1886, 2.

80   "Il y a là un jockey couché et ayant perdu visiblement sa jambe à la dernière course de haies, ainsi qu'une jeune femme conduisant un singe en laisse qui sont très 'farce,' dirait le joyeux Trublot du *Cri du Peuple*." Fouquier, "Les Impressionnistes," *Le XIXe siècle*, 16 May 1886, 2. See also Auguste Paulet, "Les Impressionnistes," *Paris*, 5 June 1886, 2; and Jules Christophe, "Georges Seurat," *Les Hommes d'Aujourd'hui* 8:368 (1890), n.p.

81   Christophe, "Georges Seurat," n.p.

82   Ibid. For the controversy about this figure, see Herbert, *Georges Seurat*, 176. The similarity of this couple to a Degas drawing inscribed "une grue" (a prostitute) suggests they were a fairly standardized motif. See Edgar Degas, *A Prostitute* (inscribed "une grue"), pencil, 9 x 13 inches. Reff, *The Notebooks of Edgar Degas*, bk. 29, 7 (Collection of Mr. and Mrs. Eugene Victor Thaw, New York, fol. 4, 1887–90). A similar couple, shown bust-length, advertises Félicien Champsaur's *La Gomme* in a poster by Chéret of 1889, reproduced in *Masters of the Poster 1896–1900* (New York: Images Graphiques, 1977), 225, rept. ed. of the text and illus. found in Roger Marx, *Les Maîtres de l'affiche* (Paris, 1895–1900).

83   Flaubert to Louise Colet, 29 January 1854. *The Letters of Gustave Flaubert 1830–1857*, selected, edited and translated by Francis Steegmuller (Cambridge, Mass.: Harvard-Belknap, 1979), 212.

84   See Herbert Spencer, "Manners and Fashion," *Westminster Review*, April 1854, in *Essays Scientific, Political and Speculative*, 3 vols. (New York: D. Appleton and Co., 1907), 1–51; Gabriel Tarde, *The Laws of Imitation*, trans. from the 2nd ed. by Elsie Clews Parsons (New York: Henry Holt, 1903), a collection of essays published in the 1880s in the *Revue philosophique*; and Georg Simmel, "Fashion" (1904), in Donald N. Levine, ed., *On Individuality and Social Forms* (Chicago-London: University of Chicago Press, 1971). I discuss these theories of fashion in a forthcoming publication.

85   Simmel, "Fashion," 305. It is to Simmel's ideas on fashion that Benjamin seems to have turned, as indicated in his notes to Konvolut B of his *Passagen-Werk*. See his *Gesammelte Schriften*, vol. 5.

86   Gustave Kahn, "Chronique de la littérature et de l'art: Exposition Puvis de Chavannes," *La Revue Indépendante*, January 1888, 142–43, trans. in Norma Broude, ed., *Seurat in Perspective* (Englewood Cliffs, N.J.: Prentice-Hall, 1978), 20.

87   Barthes, *The Fashion System*, 280.

88   Ibid., 287–88.

89   Félix Fénéon's description of these motifs has occasioned a great deal of speculation: "By a pseudo-scientific fantasy, the red parasol, the yellow parasol, and the green stocking are oriented in the directions assigned to red, yellow, and green in Charles Henry's color circle." See his "Le Néo-impressionnisme," *L'Art Moderne*, 15 April 1888, 122.

90   Barthes, *The Fashion System*, 248.

91   Jane Gaines, "Introduction: Fabricating the Female Body," in Jane Gaines and Charlotte Herzog, eds., *Fabrications: Costume and the Female Body* (New York-London: Routledge, 1990), 27.

Abbreviations in illustration captions:

de Hauke: César M. de Hauke, *Seurat et son œuvre*, 2 vols. (Paris: Paul Brame and C. M. de Hauke, Arts et Métiers Graphiques, 1961).

Lemoisne: Paul-André Lemoisne, *Degas et son œuvre*, 4 vols. (Paris: Paul Brame and C. M. de Hauke, Arts et Métiers Graphiques, 1946-49; rpt. New York-London: Garland, 1984).

Fashion in the

AN EIGHT

ERIN MACKIE

Between 1709 and 1714, Joseph Addison (1672–1719) and Richard Steele (1672–1729), acting through the fictive personae of Isaac Bickerstaff and Mr. Spectator, published a series of highly influential essays that, deriving their cultural norms from the solid, paternalistic, and domestic virtues of the middling commercial and professional classes of the day, sought to align their readers' habits of conspicuous consumption with their authors' reformative social vision. Emerging, in part, from the popular genre of the conduct manual, *The Tatler* and *The Spectator* are early, and quite modish, publications that market a new and improved 'lifestyle' by offering commentaries that not only critique the prevailing social condition but also enter into and transform the cityscape. In short, these coffee-stained, double-columned, newspaper half-sheets attempt to refashion the textures of daily life. And since the fabric of this existence is woven out of the audience's relationships to and through commodities, Addison and Steele's pattern for individual and societal self-improvement manipulate as well the *spaces* that these *things* occupy in their contemporaries' mental and material lives.

Iuseum

CENTURY PROJECT

Fashionable things are the objects of intense and serious scrutiny in the two periodicals. In *Tatler* 151, Steele observes of an elderly woman who is not so much a person as a shop: "The Memory of an old Visiting Lady is so filled with Gloves, Silks, and Ribands, that I can look upon it as nothing else but a Toyshop."[1] Eighteenth-century "toyshops" were for adults, not children, and their shelves were abundant with knickknacks and accessories. Clearly, Steele's caller has spent ample time browsing through these venues of gimcracks and gewgaws. Just as clearly—and more significantly—she

FIG. 1 *Horst P. Horst, Cleopatra, 1934, gelatin silver print*

has paid dearly for these adventures, exchanging no less than her mind. The lesson of *Tatler* 151 is that things—gloves, silks, and ribbons in this instance—have the disturbing ability to infiltrate the synaptic fissures of the psyche. All too readily, we see, things can usurp the understanding, thereby reducing and reifying human consciousness. In the head of this old woman (as in the brain of the beau and the heart of the coquette that I will be examining in a moment), the thing holds sway over the psyche, the commodity displaces identity, and the nonsense of fashion colonizes the interior locus of rationality.

Yet this analysis presents only half of my story. A keen interest in fashion may result in a kind of Möbius strip of reasoning that seeks to escape, even as it apprehends, the mind's reification. Addison's two-week project for the cultivation of the "pleasures of the imagination" (*S* 411–21), to cite the most salient example, banks on the reification of the mind's objects in its construction of an alternative, dematerialized realm of aesthetic pleasure wherein sophisticated visualization prevails over the sensual delights of the vulgar marketplace. And a similarly directed fabrication, albeit a less familiar one, is a speculative project for a museum of fashion in *Spectator* 478. Proposed by a certain "A. B.," it illustrates how things that get inside the mind may be managed by the force of a disciplinary logic that aspires to surmount the riddling feminine menace and irrationality of the fashion commodity. The catalysts for this museum of fashion, or as it is designated in this *Spectator* paper, this "repository," are the things that fill A. B.'s head while he is out shopping. Embedded in the histories of both the early museum and the early retail boutique, *Spectator* 478 bears witness to the heavily objectified model of the imagination that accompanies these histories. Here, the museum's conceptual ordering of space enlists fashion in its highly motivated, rational, and historicizing plan; the museum directs fashion away from its ephemeral, trivial, and arbitrary channels. In *The Tatler* and *The Spectator*, the commodity is instrumental to the rationalization of the space of fashion and to the reification of the mental landscape, and both are generated in the early eighteenth century by analogous processes of visual consumption and of fantasy.

Historians of English commerce pinpoint the period 1709–11 as the dawn of developments in consumption and shop-keeping that established techniques for the distribution of the hugely expanded retail trade that that surged throughout the century.[2] In a parallel movement, collections of curiosities like the repositories of the Royal Society and of the East India Company evolved into institutional forms approximating those of the public museum. Early on, argues Robert Altick, the histories of the shop and of the collection/museum merged as retail markets catering to collectors sprang up, initiating the museum trade in rare, precious, and antique objects.[3]

It is not surprising that theories of visual perception were formulated by John Locke (1632–1704; *An Essay concerning Human Understanding*, 1690) and by Sir Isaac Newton (1642–1727; *Opticks*, 1704) and then popularized by Addison at a time when there was a huge influx of things to look at and increasingly sophisticated and accessible institutions for their display. The obsessive concerns of both scientists and of shoppers, after all, are piqued by the tantalizing power of the curious gaze. Because I wish to show that the institution of fashion is related to the institution of the aesthetic, I will be arguing that Mr. Spectator's pursuit of the pleasures of the imagination involves processes of visual appropriation, objectification, and fantasy that structure as well the consuming pleasures he so often satirizes. Like Addison's realm of the imagination, the design for the fashion museum floats in a *specular* space at once fantastic and rational, while being grounded in *speculative* discourses that also sustain more material and commercial institutions—specifically shopping and fashion.

CONSUMING PLEASURES

> Were the Minds of the [female] Sex laid open, we should find
> the chief Idea in one to be a Tippet, in another a Muff, in a
> third a Fan, and in a fourth a Farthingale. (*T* 151)

Fashionable articles are highly prized tokens in the economies that produce social, sexual, and cultural values. Anxious to exercise the taste that signals cultural competence, men and women become avid consumers. Shopping, however, should not be equated simply with consumption; the selection and use of things also *produces* meanings, identities, and relationships. Thus, in keeping with their authors' custodial stance, *The Tatler* and *The Spectator* are concerned with the perils of the fashion marketplace, especially with the psychological degradation to which human beings are subject when they embody too perfectly the fashions, trends, and fripperies of the *beau monde*. On the basis of Addison and Steele's condemnations of the consuming passions, we can see how eighteenth-century men and women placed their hopes, their dreams, and their desires in the new commodification, how their creativity and their potential for transformation became attached to physical objects.[4]

In general, according to the two authors, the problem with investing too greatly in consumption is that it implicates men and women in sexual, social, and cultural networks that produce superficial relationships, debased lives, and vacant thoughts. As they internalize the objects of their consuming passions, people are not only at risk of falsifying their desires and their values in the erroneous pursuit of fashion, but of losing their identities. Locating meaning in things, people strive to become them. So in *Tatler* 151 Steele exposes the lady who loses her mind to her gloves, her silks, and her ribbons. Filled with the stuff of which dreams are manufactured, her mind is no longer human but mercantile. The head of a beau, dissected and inventoried in *Spectator* 275, provides us with a similar storehouse of modish paraphernalia:

> The *Pineal Gland*...smelt very strong of Essence of Orange-
> Flower Water....We observed a large *Antrum* or Cavity in the
> *Sinciput*, that was filled with Ribbons, Lace and Embroidery

....Another...was stuffed with invisible Billet-Doux, Love-Letters, pricked Dances....In another we found a kind of Powder, which set the whole Company a Sneezing, and by the Scent discovered it self to be right Spanish. The several other Cells were stored with Commodities of the same kind, of which it would be tedious to give the Reader an exact Inventory.

The list bears a telling resemblance to the catalogue of another beau's lodgings recorded in *Tatler* 113:

Four Pounds of scented Snuff...a Quart of Orange-Flower Water....Two embroidered Suits...a Dozen Pair Red-Heeled Shoes, Three Pair of Red Silk Stockings....Five Billet-doux.

One brain, anonymous. One apartment, quantified. A brace of indiscriminate stereotypes. Equivalency, lack of individuation, fragmentation, and objectification characterize the beau's commodified identity. These features mark as well the discourses of inventory and of anatomy used to expose and scandalize his dehumanization. The representation of the anatomized, objectified mind suggests a subjectivity with neither integrity nor depth; the 'inside' is consumed by the 'outside,' the psyche displaced by the wares of the vendor. A beau's brain, like his apartment, is a mere compendium of fashionable *things*. In his failure to maintain adequate barriers, either cerebral or architectural, against the trivia and detritus of the world, both the beau's mind and his lodgings are the final resting places for the follies of the *beau monde*. The cause of death? Paralysis by fashion.

So, too, in *Spectator* 281, Addison records the dissection of a coquette's heart, its uppermost chamber encasing "a Flame-coloured Hood" and a tiny portrait of "a little Figure...dressed in a very Fantastick manner" at its innermost core. This "little Idol" is a miniature of the same "Deceased Beau" whose brain we witnessed being anatomized a week earlier in *Spectator* 275. Both flamboyant images—the "Flame-coloured Hood" and the fantastically got-up beau—are equally the *objects* of the coquette's heartfelt affection. All image and no substance, an exceedingly "little" figure notable mainly for his dress, the beau is more mannequin than man. As he figures himself and is figured inside the coquette's heart, he becomes a *visual* commodity: ornamental, superficial, and reified, the perfect simulacrum for desires nourished on fashion.

The inventories of the beau's brain and of the coquette's heart draw, as I have noted, on the discourses of anatomy and of commercial inventory, and both are aspects of a broader parallel development between the two systems in early eighteenth-century England. Scientific repositories (such as the one where the beau's head and the coquette's heart are stored), like commercial shops, were important stages for the organization, display, and distribution of things. The two taxonomic *loci* intersect. Having purchased his repertory of fashionable accessories from London shops, the beau becomes an object suitable for the virtuoso's (as well as the coquette's) collection, fashioning himself as a prize specimen. Too heavy an investment in fashion drains the beau of his humanity and so his life. Under the scalpel of empirical science, his cadaver is as lifeless, indeed as deathly, as the snuff, ribbons, and toilet-water that embalm his brain.

In order for early eighteenth-century things to get inside of a person's head, however, they must first enter via the eyes: imaginative intimacy is inseparable from visual consumption. Heads become toyshops as much by simply looking at things as by buying and using them. Fancy—for things as well as people—is engendered through the eyes, begot and nourished by the fascinated gaze. Both the shopping expedition and the cultivation of the imagination exercise the gaze; and through this, the mind; and through this, the body. Both follow a paradigm of psychosomatic interdependence that informs, as well, contemporary accounts of hysteria (i.e., the vapors).[5] There is a relentless trafficking among the eyes, the imagination, and the body. Because this exchange furnishes men and women with the materials for the transformation of their physical and mental selves, it is a powerful avenue for both abuse and reform. Accordingly, I will be exploring the representation of the gaze and its objects first in accounts of shops and shopping trips, then in *The Spectator*'s plan for the cultivation of a polite imagination. Addison's agenda for reform is centered overtly on the uses and abuses of the *visual* faculty: the outright condemnation of certain consuming pleasures; and the proclamation of an alternative, aesthetic operation of the gaze. Anxious to establish distance between mere things and the human faculties of will and imagination, Mr. Spectator adopts a stance self-consciously aloof from the cultural practices he recognizes as the objects of his attention. But while this stance furnishes him with the intellectual distance and the alternative standard of consumption that he believes are essential to his project, it also involves the reification of the aesthetic operation that he proposes as his viable alternative. Mr. Spectator himself is the eponymous cultural embodiment of this visual faculty.

Along with the artful, seductive display of the commodity comes the promise that pleasure, comfort, and amusement are available for the looking. Display counters and windows were put into shops, and the practices of leisured browsing and window-shopping evolve, full of cheap thrills for the shopper—though, as we will see, those who work in retail were often not amused.

In this period, contests over what constitutes the proper space and practice of shopping take their place beside disputes over the standards of taste and fashion. Advertising displays are often condemned for exceeding the prudence of sober mercantilism. There is something 'feminine,' something erotically meretricious about these displays of things set out to snare the unwary passers-by. The suggestive analogies between the desire for women laid bare before the gaze and for things spread out beneath the eyes of the consumer are quite explicit in the descriptions of contemporary retail practices. In *Tatler* 143, Isaac Bickerstaff, the "Censor of Britain," satirically summons an errant shopkeeper who has put a pair of lady's shoes on display, countering the salesman's salacious advertisement by printing a corrective "ADVERTISEMENT" of his own. Here the sexual fetish and the commodity fetish fuse:

> The Censor having observed, That there are fine wrought
> Ladies' Shoes and Slippers put out to View at a great Shoe-

maker's Shop towards *St. James's* End of *Pall Mall*, which create irregular Thoughts and Desires in the Youth of this Nation;
the said Shopkeeper is required to take in those Eyesores, or
show Cause the next Court-Day why he continues to expose
the same; and he is required to be prepared particularly to
answer to the Slippers with green Lace and blue Heels. [italics
reversed]

In a more serious register, Daniel Defoe (1660–1731) laments the
deterioration of the plain, functional shop into the mirrored, gilded,
modish resort of "women...fops and fools."⁶ Defoe finds no use for
these high-overhead retail shops with their bow windows, mirrors,
plate, crystal, and other extravagant trappings. This flamboyant
paraphernalia is just so much frippery sure to drive away substantial patrons and to attract only those worthless customers "most
taken with shows and outsides" (*Tradesman* 180). Even worse,
some shopkeepers, especially those of little substance, may
attempt to profit from these artificial appearances, the sort of scam
that one associates quite naturally with the French, who "are emi-
nent for making a fine outside, when perhaps within they want nec-
essaries." "Indeed," Defoe remarks, "a gay shop and a mean stock
is something like a Frenchman with his laced ruffles, without a
shirt." The English, Defoe reminds us, should steer clear of the
French mode since they tend to "over-do the French themselves."
In any case, he argues, the point is moot; these effeminate retail
tactics are doomed to failure, destined to bankrupt the modish
shop (*Tradesman* 184–85).

Defoe's condemnation of the fashionable retail outlets that were
gaining such a powerful hold on the pockets and imaginations of
Londoners is direct. More celebratory is the account of the shopping trip related by Mrs. Crackenthorpe, "a Lady that knows every
thing," in her *Female Tatler* for Monday, July 25, 1709.⁷ Like her
male counterpart, Isaac Bickerstaff, Mrs. Crackenthorpe is an
acknowledged arbiter of elegance. When a group of ladies who
have a high "Opinion of [her] *Fancy in Cloaths*" ask her to accom-
pany them to Ludgate Hill, she is happy to oblige. Mrs.
Crackenthorpe experiences shopping as a form of leisurely enter-

tainment, "as agreeable an *Amusement* as a Lady can pass away three or four Hours in." She appreciates the luxury that Defoe abhors. In fact, it is inseparable from the marvelous delights that it proffers: "the *Shops* are perfect *gilded Theatres*" where the staging of the commodity takes place within a realm of fantasy, isolated from the mundane world occupied by those who fail to participate in the pageantry of trade. Here, Mrs. Crackenthorpe becomes queen for a day. The shopkeepers treat her with deference worthy of the most glamorous toast of the town: "[T]he *Mercers* are the Performers in the Opera....the sweetest, fairest, nicest dish'd out Creatures, and by their elegant Address and soft Speeches, you wou'd guess 'em to be *Italians*." Tagged as exotic foreigners, the shopkeepers are cleared of any contamination associated with England's military, commercial, and political rival—not French, confides Mrs. Crackenthorpe in the same breath, but Italian.[8]

Conversely, *Spectator* 336 provides us with the account of a shopping adventure as it is narrated from a radically different perspective—not of the consumer but of a businesswoman who signs herself "Rebecca, the *distress'd*." Like Mrs. Crackenthorpe, Mrs. Rebecca relates a speculative shopping trip, but she paints this activity in darker colors. Mrs. Rebecca objects to "female rakes" who loiter in her china and tea shop, treating it like a "Club," asking for everything and buying nothing. They trivialize her trade and they waste her time. In her distress, she asks *The Spectator* to publish her complaints in order to teach these "idle Ladies of Fashion" that shopkeepers have better things to do "than to cure Folks of the Vapours *gratis*."

Mrs. Rebecca is a victim of fashion, or at least a victim of the fashion victims who invade her shop, pull out her stock, and then leave without spending a farthing. The bothersome patrons are specifically *fashionable* women whose class privileges are apparent from their ailments. Theirs is a *chic* disease, alternately labelled the spleen or the vapors, the disorder of a refined lifestyle and of a popular cult of sensibility that shades easily into affectation and preciosity.[9] In order to relieve their somaticized ennui—their "vapors"—they divert themselves with a kind of consumer hooliganism, "tumbling over [Mrs. Rebecca's] Ware," stirring up a great "Racket and Clatter," and disordering "the whole agreeable Architecture" of her displays. "Under pretence of...diverting the Spleen," they shop. But much to the writer's annoyance, the healing properties of looking are independent of any actual buying:

> These Rakes are your Idle Ladies of Fashion, who having nothing to do, employ themselves in tumbling over my Ware. One of these No-Customers (for by the way they seldom or never buy any thing) calls for a Set of Tea Dishes, another for a Bason, a third for my best Green Tea...this is too dear, that is their Aversion, another thing is charming but not wanted: The Ladies are cur'd of the Spleen, but I am not a Shilling better for it: Lord! (*S* 336)

The cure for these ladies' spleen depends on the way that Mrs. Rebecca's commodities have been fetishized; on their "metaphysical subtleties and theological niceties," their mystical, fantastic, and psychosexual capacities for transcending the sensuous, material body.[10] In their work on economic anthropology, Mary Douglas and Baron Isherwood formulate consumption as "a ritual process" that labors to order our experiences in the world.[11] And, as Mrs. Rebecca's letter to *Spectator* 336 attests, shopping, like the shaman's chants, the priest's prayers, or the witch's incantations, can be equally as effective in dispelling "evil" spirits, "vapors," that, according to contemporary etiology, are caused by a disordering of the passions.[12] The symptoms of disorientation, bodily and emotional instability, and fainting are alleviated in the china and tea shop by a ritual of consumption that is supposed to restore harmony and order to one's constitution. But as with everything "sacred," the "charming" rite of shopping is Janus-faced, its value as white or black magic largely dependent on the side of the counter one happens to be standing on. For the shop-keeper, the shopping ritual of the fashionable female rakes is the equivalent not of exorcism but of demonic possession: "I can compare 'em to nothing but to the Night-Goblins" (*S* 336).

Specular shopping exercises the imaginative faculties and, through these, affects both the body and the spirit. In the initial essay of the series, Addison touts his pleasures of the imagination as a boon to health: "the pleasures of the fancy are more conducive to health than those of the understanding"; "Delightful Scenes...have a kindly Influence on the Body as well as the Mind." Specifically, the exercise of the fancy, like immersion in the rites of consumption, cures the vapors by dispersing "Grief and Melancholly" and setting "the Animal Spirits in pleasing and agreeable Motions" (S 411).

In emphasizing these correspondences, I hope to have made plain the connection between Addison's notion of visual possession and the process of commodity fetishism that it so clearly replicates: both are ways that things get into people's heads. That Addison presents the imaginative acquisition of objects in explicit contradistinction to the acquisition of property speaks of the manner in which the aesthetic faculty is conceived in opposition to the material and economic realms whose operations it actually mirrors. And yet, his plan for the cultivation of the fancy is also a scheme for the acquisition and expenditure of aesthetic capital; stocking the poet's, or the gentleman's, head with a fund of images and metaphors entails the same procedures of consumption and objectification that operate within the imaginations of the old woman, the beau, the coquette, and the female rakes. The gazes of the polite connoisseur, of the modish shopper, and of the commodity abuser alike feed on the images of things—ribbons, snuff, china, landscapes, statues, paintings, and poems.

It is hardly surprising, therefore, that Addison's inquiry into the machinery of looking is inseparable from the discourse of scientific empiricism. Both the retail shop and the public repository are designed for the display of information that is predominantly visual: looking is a means for possession as well as knowledge. It is the visual faculty, after all, that "furnishes the Imagination with its Ideas" (S 411). In so doing, however, it also co-opts the faculty of touch, acquiring very nearly a palpable solidity. "Our Sight...may

be considered as a more delicate and diffusive Kind of Touch,"
theorizes Addison, "that spreads it self over an infinite Multitude
of Bodies" (S 411). The pleasures of the imagination are enjoyed as
the pleasures of property. The "man of Polite Imagination,"
Addison proposes, "often feels a greater Satisfaction in the
Prospect of Fields and Meadows, than another does in the
Possession. It gives him, indeed, a kind of Property in every thing
he sees" (S 411). What begins as a polemical distinction between
material possession and visual meditation ends as the figurative
transformation of the latter into the former, of visual and imaginative consumption into a sort of grasping imperialism. Free of temporal or spatial restrictions, the imagination roams, bringing "into
our reach some of the most remote Parts of the Universe" (S 411).
The English desire for economic mastery—taking in, mapping out,
and divvying up its colonial territories—becomes its aesthetic.

THE FANTASTIC FASHION REPOSITORY

Addison's project guarantees the mind's appropriation of objects,
rather than, as is the case with the beau, the coquette, and the old
woman, the mind's colonization *by* objects. The distinction, a
dialectical one, depends on perceptual self-mastery. In Addison's
view, control comes about through reshaping objects that have been
assigned their qualities via human cognition and then subjecting
these objects to rational criteria. Endowed with properties and tied
to purposes beyond themselves, objects are refashioned in ways
that make them seem less autonomous, all the more one's own.
Addison advocates the careful containment of visual objects, the
rationalist domination of imaginative pleasure, within a space that
is disembodied and aestheticized. His purely mental venue stands
as an alternative to both the shop and the museum collection.

Turning now to my final example of imaginative consumption, I
present in some detail the plan for the sphinx-shaped fashion
repository proposed in a letter to *Spectator* 478. I have argued that
shopping produces fantasies, but in *Spectator* 478 these commodity-

induced fabrications are not so much disorders of the imagination as directions for the management of the things that nourish it. In the sphinx-shaped repository, fashions are incorporated and contained by the architectural project that disciplines them. A purely speculative design, yet one with features both of the fashion emporium and the museum, Steele's blueprint occupies a hybrid and somewhat contradictory space that is contiguous to Addison's realm of imaginative pleasure, the early museum, and the fashionable boutique.

THE SHOPPING TRIP

One day in early September, 1712, two gentlemen go out shopping: one who has a number of purchases to make and the other, his friend, who tags along for company. The latter, a certain "A. B.," writes a letter to *The Spectator* narrating this trip and it is published as no. 478 on Monday, 8 September.[13] A. B. gives only two sentences to the actual shopping trip; for what happens takes place more in his imagination than in the stores, a recollection not of purchases but of projects—the imaginative material for a fantastic repository.

A. B. takes little pleasure in shopping. Indeed, his epistle opens with a description of his embarrassment at his friend's obvious devotion to the task: "He was very nice in his Way, and fond of having every thing shewn, which at first made me very uneasy." A. B. never says exactly why this niceness makes him uncomfortable. Is he uneasy because he thinks that his friend is being troublesome, burdening the shopkeepers with all sorts of unnecessary difficulties? Or could it be that A. B.'s concern is traceable, rather, to some sense, not of his own, but of the anxiety of his friend, whose discriminating niceness may be the sign of uncertainty as well as of discernment?

In either case, the problem is one of making choices; for the exercise of *niceness* becomes more demanding with shifts in the practices of consumption that re-produce our social categories.[14] The transitional moment between the Restoration and the early eighteenth century brings about a major redefinition of the commodity—the replacement of the older standard of "patina" with the newer standard of fashion.[15] Things are esteemed not so much for their continuity with the past, but for their novelty, for their reference to change rather than to tradition. The look into the future starts to resemble progress and the backward glance toward the past, a nostalgic regress. Shopping in the early eighteenth century begins to manifest its modern character as a labor-intensive activity for the harried consumer who now requires a steady supply of information (all too quickly made obsolescent) in order to decipher what symbolic messages are being transmitted by which fashionable purchases.[16] In brief, men and women make consumer decisions that are part material reality and part fantasy, constructing their own physical and spiritual worlds of value and meaning.

A. B.'s apprehension dramatizes this recognition of the economic, social, and even political work that fashion can perform. And yet, his discomfort is replaced in a heartbeat by a kind of rapt fascination: "He was very nice in his Way, and fond of having every thing shewn, which at first made me very uneasy; but as his Humour still continu'd, the things which I had been staring at along with him began to fill my Head, and led me into a Set of amusing Thoughts concerning them." Shifting from the objects before him to the ideas they generate, and thus sliding precipitously from the narrative of his expedition to speculative fantasy, A. B.'s account contains precious little information about the shop and its stock. The material splendor of lovely, palpable things that so enthralls the *Female Tatler*'s Mrs. Crackenthorpe—"Garden-Silks...Italian Silks, Brocades, Tissues, Cloth of Silver, or Cloth of Gold...Mantua Silks...*Geneva* Velvet, *English* Velvet, Velvets Emboss'd"—is strangely missing from A. B.'s narrative. Whereas Mrs. Crackenthorpe's fancy seems to have been generated by the profuse wealth of the retail counter itself, A. B.'s speculations appear to *replace*, to stand in, for the absent goods.

This gives the sense that A. B. is seeking to rationalize his experience of being in the marketplace, seeking to redeem its fallen materialism through the careful exercise of his mind. His transition from shopper to speculative projector takes place through the field of vision: "the things which I had been staring at...began to fill my Head."[17] As a "projector," or promoter of projects for sociocultural improvement, A. B. depends upon the same visual acquisition of goods as does the window-shopper. Things in the shops become a display not just for the potential purchaser, but also for the gentleman philosopher, the middling kind of polite projector within whose ranks we also number Mr. Spectator himself. Fixing his gaze on the commodity, A. B. is consumed not only by the desire to purchase, but also by the desire to expound.

Accordingly, A. B. and his friend begin a "Discourse...upon the use of Fashions" and pursue it until "at last the Subject seem'd so considerable, that it was propos'd to have a Repository builded [sic] for Fashions, as there are Chambers for Medals and other Rarities." Noting "how much Man is govern'd by his Senses, how livelily [sic] he is struck by the Objects which appear to him in an agreeable Manner, how much Cloaths contribute to make us agreeable Objects, and how much we owe it to our selves that we should appear so," they first look at the way fashion works in social relations. Exploitation as well as neglect of fashion may produce misreadings of character: "a Fool in Fine Cloaths shall be suddenly heard with Attention...whereas a Man of Sense appearing with a Dress of Negligence, shall be but coldly received." In social relations, fashion displays an instability, a "Variableness" that also marks its presence in the economic arena, where fashion's demand for novelty generates an accelerated and capriciously shifting production of goods. In the social sphere, fashion-generated instability shows up as the ambivalence of fashion's status-defining capacities: because fashion marks social hierarchies it may also subvert them.

We should not underestimate the anxiety that this potential for instability provoked in early eighteenth-century London, where, because of recent waves of immigration, it was becoming more difficult to know for certain much of anything about one's fellow residents. The capitalization of agriculture and of industry, the emergence of a huge wage-labor market, the escalation of commercial opportunities, and vast improvements in transportation networks: all fed into the rapidly expanding and newly constituted urban metropolis, creating more and more situations in which people "knew" one another only by appearance and thus had to evaluate class and character largely on the basis of dress, manner, and accent—all of which could be counterfeited.[18] Distinctions between legitimate and illegitimate fashion often depend on notions of the counterfeit and the genuine, monetary terms that put in considerable time as epistemological and moral categories. The problem of money, like the problem of clothes, is one of reference: what underwrites the banknote or the suit of clothes becomes crucial to the functioning of both financial and social economies.[19]

Clothes are capable of *forging* identities because people can be so easily deceived by the superficial signs of success and of substance: "how much Man is govern'd by his Senses, how lively he is struck by the Objects which appear to him in an agreeable Manner." Like women, clothes too readily generate empty and perilously attractive signs, seducing men into all sorts of regrettable responses. Taken in by a fool in fine clothes, one may pay more attention to him than to the "Man of Sense appearing with a Dress of Negligence" (*S* 478). A. B. and his colleague offer this evidence not so much to undermine our judgment as to reinforce our sense of the social and psychological gravity of fashion. People should take responsibility for their appearances and, by matching their inner worth to appropriate signs, practice fashion in a manner that reduces the subversive slippage between the sign and its referent. Even the most sober citizen, A. B. and his friend confess, must enter into at least a cautious transaction with fashion if he wishes to live authentically in the world.

Having established these precepts, the two gentlemen proceed next to a discussion of the repository itself: "At last the Subject [of fashion] seem'd so considerable, that it was propos'd to have a

Repository builded [*sic*] for Fashions, as there are Chambers for Medals and other Rarities." This structure, we learn, will take the form of that ancient feminine enigma—the sphinx. The sphinx serves as an emblem of fashion as woman: prolific, speculative and material, both hazardous and life-enhancing, at once irrational and open to regulation. Monstrous, hybrid and feminine, fashion is the sphinx of modernity whose riddles must be solved by the citizens of the market-place.

Decorated in bas-relief with curling locks, ribbons, lace, looking-glasses, powder-puffs, patches, combs, and sword-knots, the sphinx's facade is updated and domesticated with the familiar signs of contemporary eighteenth-century fashion.

> The Building may be shap'd as that which stands among the Pyramids, in the Form of a Woman's Head...there may be an Imitation of Fringe carv'd in the Base, a Sort of Appearance of Lace in the Frize, and a Representation of curling Locks, with Bows of Riban sloping over them...
>
> There is to be a Picture over the Door, with a Looking-Glass and a Dressing-Chair in the Middle of it: Then on one Side are to be seen...Patch-Boxes, Pin-Cushions, and little Bottles; on the other, Powder-Bags, Puffs, Combs, and Brushes; beyond these, Swords with fine Knots, whose Points are hidden, and Fans almost closed, with the Handles downward, are to stand out interchangeably from the Sides, till they meet at the Top, and form a Semi-circle over the rest of the Figures.

The familiar and mundane are grafted onto the exotic and fantastic. Not only is the sphinx-museum an emblem of fashion, but she is also herself *fashionable*, outfitted with all the erotic paraphernalia of modernity. The design for the museum replicates the body-as-fashion that we have seen on display in the anatomies of the beau, the coquette, and the old visiting lady. And, like the psyches of those fashion victims, this corporeal monument to fashion's mastery (both as the mastery of and the mastery over fashion) is packed with things. Like the painted and patched faces of fashionable ladies, the sphinx's face/facade is inscribed with cosmetic artificiality. Only the *face* of the sphinx is human and here that face/facade is rendered as fashion itself. We recognize, then, our own relation to the sphinx in the glass of fashion.

The plan for this museum remains sketchy at best. There is much that we will never know. Was the museum supposed to realize the sphinx's entire body or only the facade? Where would it have been built? One wonders how such a design would alter the London landscape. What would it have looked like to eighteenth-century spectators? To us it seems camp; saturated with the flat parodies of postmodernism, we arrogate to ourselves a kind of ironic superiority over A. B. and his friend. But given the playful, if purposive, tone of the proposal, and the high degree of self-consciousness with which fashion is being monumentalized, is our knowing amusement really so far removed from the responses of its architects and their early-modern audience?

Contemporary fashions serve as both the contents and the package for this house of style; the outside of the building is but a decorative stencil of the interior stocked with specimens. This repository contains its fashions in a form specific to commercial distribution at the time. In early eighteenth-century England, there were no fashion magazines; new styles for women were imported from France via dolls—fashion mannequins. In the repository, the specimens of every known style are arrayed on figurines and then labeled, boxed, and shelved "as regularly as Books in a Library." Organized for easy reference, the entire universe of fashion may be called up to serve the specific purposes chartered by the project. I turn first to the ways this project proposes to use fashion and next to the institutional context of the repository itself.

In order to "gain the Approbation of the Publick" whose interests are central to the project's success, A. B. and his friend draft a series of important resolutions. The first addresses the cosmetic uses of fashion. The repository should be a treasure-house of style where people will be able to consult its holdings in order to discover which fashion might best suit them.[20] Employed as an arbiter of elegance, a "gentleman qualify'd with a competent

Knowledge in Cloaths" will offer his tasteful advice to the museum's visitors.

Secondly, the repository should liberate the English from their reliance on the French (an ongoing campaign waged by the *Tatler* and *Spectator*) by promoting stylistic superiority. Noting that "the Ballance of fashion in *Europe*...now leans upon the side of *France*," A. B. and his friend propose that their repository should set the standards for dress and so give to England the ascendancy in her fashion war with France. It would then "become as common with *Frenchmen* to come to *England* for their finishing stroke of Breeding, as it has been for *Englishmen* to go to *France* for it" (*S* 478). It is as much in England's interest to regulate the balance of fashion as it is to regulate the balance of trade. The two are intertwined, and "balance" in the mouth of an Englishmen clearly means dominance rather than equity.[21]

In pursuing these chauvinistic aims, the repository mimics the aspirations of institutions like the Academie Française and the Royal Society. Accordingly, the gentlemen's third proposal is specifically academic, even scientific: to provide material data for future generations of scholars who would no longer have to depend on texts for their understanding of fashion history. As a site for empirical research, the institute would advance the scientific study of costume. As things stand in 1712, historians still depend on outdated scholastic methods; and, as A. B. notes, "several great Scholars, who might have been otherwise useful to the World, have spent their time in studying to describe the Dresses of the Ancients from dark Hints." Indeed, not only are these "dark Hints" a waste of time but they can be positively misleading; for a purely textual approach causes the scholar to rely on the most fallacious sort of etymological analysis, one that might "perswade the Age to come, that the Farthingal was worn for cheapness, or the Furbeloe for warmth."[22] As a progressive institution, the repository would ensure that the modernity would be better preserved than antiquity.

Likewise, since fashion would thus represent itself, the inaccuracies of historical bias and prejudice would be eliminated. By providing material evidence that past generations pursued fashion just as extravagantly as do the present, the repository would silence any complaints of newfangled degeneracy. Again, the advantage goes to modernity over tradition.

As we can tell from the plans for its design and function, the two major paradigms for the repository are the library and the cabinet of curiosities, or, as A. B. calls them, "Chambers for Medals and other Rarities." The project thus shares with the early museum and with the retail shop the function of housing, arranging, and displaying things. Indeed, the term *repository* in the eighteenth century is a "euphemism" for *shop*, especially for a store dealing in "fancy draperies, haberdasheries, or other special articles."[23] There are broad, and deep, connections between the cabinet collections of fine and curious objects and the retail boutique.[24] As historical products of the development of technology and expansion of trade during the sixteenth and seventeenth centuries, both gather together things from all over the world, operating as visual resorts. The East India Company, for example, had its own repository of curiosities in London and, along with the Royal African Company, was a corporate sponsor of the repository of the Royal Society, a collection of natural history specimens, ethnographic data, art, and technology that is probably the closest model for A. B.'s museum of fashion.[25] Housed at Gresham College from the 1660s until 1712, the Royal Society's repository was one of the earliest institutional collections.[26] More importantly, it would have been especially prominent at this time because a new gallery for the collection had been completed only four or five months earlier. Designed by Sir Christopher Wren (1632–1723), himself a founding member of the Royal Society, it was probably the last project that he ever built.[27]

The erection of the fashion museum ties in with the rise of Britain's commercial and cultural imperialism; fashion serves to construct national as well as personal identity from the loot of empire. But this early museum is by no means concerned exclusively with the remote or even the rare. Its passion, rather, is to collect the entire

ARCHITECTURE: *In Fashion*

world: by *having everything* one is believed to *know everything.* Something like this reasoning appears to motivate the thoughts of Thomas Sprat (1635–1713), the Bishop of Rochester, in his description of how the fellows of the Royal Society "have already drawn together into one Room, the greatest part of all the several kinds of things, that are scatter'd throughout the *Universe.*"[28] Sprat's conception of the repository operates according to the same logic as Addison's faculty of the imagination, bringing together within (at least visual) grasp "the remote parts of the Universe" (*S* 411). In order to fulfill this dream of utter comprehension, how-ever, the collection also gathers within its compass some of the not-so-remote parts of the universe; for in a collection of *everything*, after all, the mundane, the familiar, and the domestic have their rightful places as well. Referring to Sprat's vision (and it remained just that) of the Royal Society's repository, Hunter believes that this scientific aspiration "to construct a universal tax-onomy which would accurately mirror the order of nature" parallels that other impossible dream pursued by a fellow of the Royal Society—the project of John Wilkins (1614–72) for a universal language of real characters.[29]

A. B. and his companion share with Sprat and Wilkins the desire to create a totalizing scheme; they want their repository to mirror the order of fashion by collecting and preserving specimens of every style. The whole universe of style is to be encompassed with-in the sphinx: organized, cataloged, and contained. Through col-lection comes possession comes knowledge comes power. In true Foucauldian manner, the repository controls fashion by establish-ing itself as the clearinghouse for information about fashion— information that determines what fashion *is.* As Douglas Crimp notes in his essay on museums and modernism, along with the asy-lum, the clinic, and the prison, the museum is an institution that disciplines and confines.[30] On the one hand, the architectural identification of the repository with the sphinx alludes to the dark enigma and threat of fashion. On the other hand, the institutional context for the repository's empirical aspirations attests to the scientific confidence that these same dangers can be managed. In the sphinx, fashion is possessed and *known*—its riddles solved and rationalized.

Tensions, however, remain. Even as it contains the sphinxlike mystery and danger of fashion, the museum is contained in and by the sphinx. The systematic ordering of fashion takes place within a feminine, monstrous body. The production of knowledge remains inextricably wrapped up in the riddle that, finally, is its inexplicable origin.[31] The attempt to reduce the fashion system to the linear and progressive system of the historical museum produces contradictions that may complicate our understanding of both fashion and the museum.

As institutions devoted to preservation, historicization, and stability, museums would seem to be diametrically opposed to fashion (focused as it is on fleeting novelty, the present, and change). But, as Richard Altick documents, early modern collections depended, just as fashion did, on the charms of novelty.[32] People were attracted to these assemblages of things, as they were attracted to other fashionable resorts and commodities, because they offered marvelous novelties. Indeed, in the eighteenth century, museums were themselves novel institutions, frequented by the leisured classes and the curious in much the same manner as the newly outfitted retail shops. As an institution dedicated, like today's contemporary art museum, to the regulation of taste and the consecration of particular aesthetic ideologies, the sphinx-shaped museum would not merely preserve, but also produce fashion, thus engaging in a kind of circular self-generation. So the fashion museum, again reflecting one function of museums in general, would take part in the design and production of its own content, of the very objects that it is ostensibly established merely to document. The museum collection's investment in the determination of fashion and of fashionability suggests that the production of the object is inextricable from the production of knowledge about the object. Just as contemporary museums set expectations, for viewer and artist alike, about what art should be, and so model the objects they collect, so the fashion repository, with its in-house consultant, would produce normative standards for style, and thus have a hand in the production of fashion itself.

Does the museum capture fashion in its system or is it captured by fashion's system? Are the two institutions related in ways that are mutually informative? Just as the museum's investment in fashion threatens to disrupt its rationale, so its historicizing, stabilizing order alters the nature of its contents. Buried in the museum, anything that is collected immediately loses its status as fashion; yet, outside the walls of the museum (as within), styles also quickly lose their fashionability. Interment in the dustbins of an ever-accelerating history or interment on the dusty shelves of the museum—both wrench style from the instant between the present and the future that is the twinkling of fashion.

The idea of fashion as a theoretical machine being driven relentlessly forward by the intermeshing gears of obsolescence and novelty is misleading. Its apparent logic is only a cover for what is more often a repetitive cycle of recirculation. In recalling its own past, fashion becomes its own museum of style.[33] The sphinx-shaped repository is a hybrid institution, one that realizes both the investment of museums in novelty and the persistence in fashion of history.

Thanks to Michael McKeon for his comments on earlier versions of this essay and to Paulette Singley, especially for her ideas about the relationships between fashion and the museum.

NOTES

1   Quotations from Joseph Addison and Sir Richard Steele's two serials have been incorporated into the body of my text by using the abbreviations listed below, followed by the number of the appropriate essay:

   T: *The Tatler* (London, 1709–11), ed. Donald F. Bond, 3 vols. (Oxford: Clarendon, 1987)

   S: *The Spectator* (London, 1711–12 and 1714), ed. Donald F. Bond, 5 vols. (Oxford: Clarendon, 1965)

2   See Hoh-Cheung Mui and Lorna H. Mui, *Shops and Shopkeeping in Eighteenth-Century England* (Kingston-Montreal: McGill-Queen's Universiy Press; London: Routledge, 1989), 13–28.

3   See Robert D. Altick, *The Shows of London* (Cambridge, Mass.-London: Harvard University Press-Belknap, 1978), 13.

4   Whether or not investment in consumption always displaces desire from its 'true' object is a question that I leave unanswered, if only to draw attention to the extent to which such a solution is ideologically charged and historically informed. Rather, my concern is with the ideological and historical responses that *The Tatler* and *The Spectator* associated with commodity fetishism in eighteenth-century English society.

5   See John Mullan, *Sentiment and Sociability: The Language of Feeling in the Eighteenth Century* (Oxford: Clarendon, 1988), especially his introduction (1–18) and "Hypochondria and Hysteria: Sensibility and the Physicians" (201–40). In *A Treatise of the Hypochondriack and Hysterick Passions* (London, 1711), Bernard Mandeville (1670–1733) traces the etiology of these diseases to the disruption and, more importantly, to the inadequacy of the internal spirits. Hypochondria is the male version of hysteria and goes by the name of spleen. Hysteria, on the other hand, is synonymous with the vapors and the spleen. Both are nervous disorders that play havoc with the passions and with the imagination. Significantly, the symptoms of hysteria—mood swings, fantastic imaginings, investments in improbable desires, the rising and falling of fainting spells—mimic the contemporary movements of the stock market and are commonly linked to it. See also Addison's portrait of the vaporish Lady Credit in *Spectator* 3, and Sir John Midriff [pseud.], *Observations on the Spleens and Vapors: Containing Remarkable Cases of Persons of Both Sexes, and all Ranks, from the aspiring Director to the humble Bubbler, who have been miserably afflicted...since the Fall of the South-Sea, and other publick Stocks* (London, 1721).

6   Daniel Defoe, *The Complete English Tradesman* (London, 1726; rpt. Gloucester: Alan Sutton, 1987), 184.

7   [Thomas Baker], *The Female Tatler* (London, 1709), n.p.

8   It is important to notice that in being figured as Italian opera performers and as neuter "Creatures," the ambivalent sexual status of these shop clerks is also being called into question. Italian *castrati* were the objects of much fascination and ridicule during the eighteenth century.

9   In *Spectator* 216 the vapors are referred to as "this fashionable reigning Distemper."

10   Karl Marx, *Capital* [1867-94], trans. Ben Fowkes, vol. 1 (London: Pelican-New Left Review, 1976), 163.

11   Mary Douglas and Baron Isherwood, *The World of Goods: Towards an Anthropology of Consumption* (New York: Basic Books, 1979), 65.

12   See *Spectator* 3, and Midriff, *Observations on the Spleens and Vapors*.

13   A mysterious "A. B." also writes to *Tatlers* 84 and 145. In a note to Tatler 84, George A. Aitken, ed., *The Tatler*, 4 vols. (London: Duckworth, 1898) suggests that A. B. may have been Alexander Bayne "an advocate then living in London, and afterwards Professor of Scots Law at Edinburgh." In his notes to *Spectator* 478, Donald F. Bond does not identify A. B. The use of the first two letters of the alphabet as pseudonymous initials is commonplace.

14   Douglas and Isherwood, *The World of Goods*, 68.

15   See Grant McCracken, *Culture and Consumption: New Approaches to the Symbolic Character of Consumer Goods and Activities* (Bloomington: Indiana University Press, 1988), 21.

16   Ibid, 20.

17   The plan for the fashion museum is presented as a project and A. B. as a "projector"—one who comes up with schemes for social, cultural, or financial improvement—what we would call an entrepreneur or promoter. The projector may have been a social type, but, unlike *entrepreneur*, the eighteenth-century word had more serious negative connotations. A projector was a shady dealer, a kind of con artist spinning webs to catch the gullible investor; early stock-brokers and venture capitalists were two prominent species. As a result, the projector was often ridiculed as a kind of visionary idiot, an erector of fantastic schemes like A. B.'s project for the sphinx-shaped fashion repository. The best known, and certainly one of the most sinister satires on the projector, is Jonathan Swift's "A Modest Proposal" (1729), in *Jonathon Swift: Irish Tracts 1728–1733*, vol. 12 of *Collected Works of Jonathon Swift*, ed. Herbert Davis (Oxford: Basil Blackwell, 1964), 107–118.

18   See Richard Sennett, *The Fall of Public Man: On the Social Psychology of Capitalism* (New York: Vintage-Random, 1976), 45–88.

19   Ibid., 67-68. Sennett emphasizes the provisional and theatrical nature of urban fashions. The purpose of street clothes, he argues, "was to make it possible for other people to act as if they knew who you were." The point was not "to be sure of whom you were dealing with, but to be able to behave as if you were sure." Anonymity provides the blank site on which one erects one's identity—spurious or honest. So served by fashion's flair for dressing, anonymity became part and parcel of the growing social mobility in the eighteenth-century city. And although this contingent, slippery side of fashion may have been accepted and even advocated by some (Sennett cites the notoriously worldly Philip Dormer Stanhope, 4th Earl of Chesterfield, 1694–1773), the potential for charlatanism in the urban social scene vexed those who sought a ground for authentic identity and so for stable knowledge.

20   While this use of fashion to flatter one's appearance may seem unremarkable, it is by no means a given practice. People often sacrifice their bodies in pursuit of the most recent mode and much of fashion journalism is presented as a philanthropic project for the salvation of these fashion victims. For example, the August 1992 cover of *Glamour* advertises a "NO LIES GUIDE" informing readers "When to Buck the Beauty Trends."

21   It is impossible to isolate English objections to French fashions from the more global hostility of the English to the French government, their religion, and their commercial and colonial ambitions. Indeed, these prejudices may actually have helped to have shaped English tastes, especially in men's clothing. On a broad register of style, eighteenth-century French costume held closely to the stiff formality of court dress, while English fashion moved toward a more relaxed, comfortable, and 'natural' costume of leisurely country life. This new style of informality influenced manners as well as clothes. *Spectator* 119 approves of this new trend in terms that are certainly anti-Catholic if not explicitly anti-French:

> Conversation, like the Romish Religion, was so encumbered
> with Show and Ceremony that it stood in need of a reformation
> ....The Fashionable World is grown free and easie....Nothing is
> so modish as an agreeable Negligence.

Bad fashion, we see, is the equivalent of a Papist French tyrant whose ceremonial hold has been broken through the restoration of reformed English tastes.

22   The farthingale is the Elizabethan great-grandmother of the hoop. A furbelow is a ruffled trim.

23   Mui and Mui, *Shops and Shopkeeping*, 65.

24   Emily Apter, *Feminizing the Fetish: Psychoanalysis and Narrative Obsession in Turn-of-the-Century France* (Ithaca: Cornell University Press, 1991), 39–64, discusses a similar set of congruences between commercial, scientific, and erotic practices of collection and fetishization in *fin-de-siécle* France. The intertwining of discourses around the cult of the commodity that Apter traces appears to be continuous with the earlier phenomena discussed in this essay.

25   See Michael Hunter, "The Cabinet Institutionalized: The Royal Society's 'Repository' and Its Background," in *The Origins of Museums: The Cabinet of Curiosities in Sixteenth- and Seventeenth-Century Europe*, eds. Oliver Impey and Arthur MacGregor (Oxford: Clarendon, 1985), 10; and Nehemiah Grew, *Musaeum Regalis Societatis, or, a Catalogue & Description of the Natural and Artificial Rarities Belonging to the Royal Society and Preserved at Gresham College* (London, 1681).

26   See Hunter, "The Cabinet Institutionalized," 159–60. Nehemiah Grew catalogs the collection in *Musaeum Regalis*.

27   See J. A. Bennett, "Wren's Last Building?" *Notes and Records of the Royal Society of London 27* (1972–73), 101–18.

28   Thomas Sprat, *The History of the Royal Society* (London, 1667), eds. Jackson I. Cope and Harold Whitmore Jones (St. Louis: Washington University Studies, 1958), 251. In the preface to *Musaeum Regalis*, Nehemiah Grew states that the repository's *raison d'être* is "to facilitate and Improve Knowledge."

29   Hunter, "The Cabinet Institutionalized," 164.

30   Douglas Crimp, "On the Museum's Ruins," in Hal Foster, ed., *The Anti-Aesthetic: Essays on Postmodern Culture* (Port Townsend, Wash.: Bay Press, 1983), 43–56, 45.

31   Ibid., 49. Crimp touches on a related tension in his analysis of the excessive, disorderly, heterogenous body of materials that museums seek to order and control: "the history of museology is a history of all the various attempts to deny the heterogeneity of the museum, to reduce it to a homogeneous system or series."

32   Altick, "The Shows of London," 1–21.

33   This phenomenon is not limited to postmodernist fashion. In the eighteenth century, the appearance of the hoop-skirt is often remarked upon as being a stylistic repetition of the farthingale; while the hoop, in turn, reemerges in the middle of the nineteenth century as the crinoline.

PART TWO
work

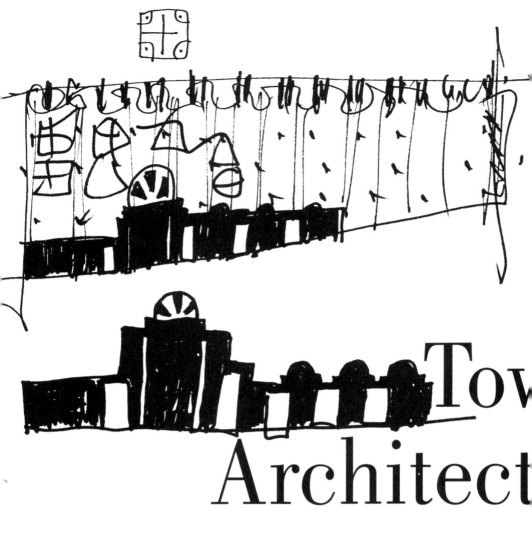

Tow

Architect

SCAFFOLD AND DRAPERY IN THE WO

DEBORAH FAUSCH

The giant floral wallpaper of the Best Products Showroom, the dotted data processing card of the Institute for Scientific Information Headquarters, the checkerboard of the Allen Art Museum, the moiré of the Brant House, the flattened folding and billowing of the Seattle Art Museum (Fig. 1), the draped cloth of the Bard College library (Fig. 2), and as its abruptly cut masonry edges attest, even the Sainsbury Wing of the National Gallery, whose solid, three dimensional, accurately replicated Corinthian pilasters seem so faithfully to extend Wilkin's stolid antithesis of a curtain wall—this compulsive catalog can begin to suggest the intensity of Venturi, Scott Brown and Associates' engagement with the correspondences between fabric and facade.[1]

rds "An e of our Times"

VENTURI, SCOTT BROWN AND ASSOCIATES

To examine the early design elevations for Bard College (Figs. 3, 4, 5) is to comprehend the power of this analogy between curtain wall and clothing, its double edge of metaphor and matter-of-factness. The colorful plaid sketch and grass-skirt studies are at once abstract and literal, even "tectonic," suggesting parallels between the way clothes hang on a body and the way the curtain wall hangs on a frame—loose or close fit, struc-

FIG. 1 *Elevation study, south and west elevation, Seattle Art Museum, Venturi, Scott Brown and Associates, 1985.*

tured or unstructured cut, draping and layering. The choice of abstract or representational pattern and the shifting relationship of ornament to structure reflect an insistence upon a diversity of architectural vocabularies appropriate for different clients and contexts as different clothes are individually tailored for different occasions.

This interest in the detachable surface would seem to be the embodiment of the wall as cloth, the realization of Gottfried Semper's concept of *Bekleidung*.[2] However, unlike Semper's theory, which posits an evolutionary mechanism for the development of the pattern of the surface of the wall—structural in origin, if not in final manifestation—VSBA's architecture articulates the disengagement of the surface both from the structure that holds it in place and from the history of that relationship. This separation is accomplished by means of several characteristic mechanisms: presenting the surface as cut from a larger fabric, as on the Ponte dell'Accademia bridge, whose prefabricated fiberglass panels seem to be lifted out of an infinite sheet of Venetian marble; dividing surfaces composed of structural units into panels that demonstrate their atectonic nature, such as the split keystone of Wu Hall, which straddles two panels and thus divulges its participation in the make-up of the surface; or undercutting apparent support, frustrating the illusion of bearing, as in the entrance to the Sainsbury Wing.[3]

Semper uses the example of ancient sculpture to illustrate his history of style. The form of clothed wooden idols was translated, in his account, through empaestic to stone figures—which he claims were never naked, but always dressed, at least with stucco and/or paint.[4] In a similar way, he argues that the painted surfaces of the Assyrian-Chaldean wall show traces of their evolution from an original demarcation of space with reed fences and later, woven wickerwork, to carpet, paneling, stucco, and finally paint.[5] These skeuomorphs thus contain their own history. They record a progressive dematerialization of an *Urtypus*—a primordial type that is also an *Urtechnik*—whose features survive as formal traditions

Addition to Charles P. Stevenson, Jr. Library, Bard College, Annandale-on-Hudson, New York, Venturi, Scott Brown and Associates, completed 1993. ©Peter Aaron/Esto.

FIG. 2

throughout the succession of changes in their material realization.[6] The result of this evolution is a conceptually straightforward, if historically complex, symbolization of structure in the decorative surfaces of the wall—the history of the facade on the facade. Semper is primarily interested in these traces of technical and material origins in the final product. But as an idealist he insists on the transfiguration of this physical record as well as of the representation of ritual or social meanings. Thus for Semper, true art leaves what he calls the *subject*, or content, behind.[7]

In contrast, a substantial part of Venturi and Scott Brown's theory is devoted to freeing the facade from its engagement with technique in order to fulfill the role of representation—the communication of direct or associative, socially determined meaning through signs or symbols. In *Learning from Las Vegas*, a book whose subject is "The Forgotten Symbolism of Architectural Form," Venturi and Scott Brown return to the site of the original trauma for which modern architecture might be seen as compensation—nineteenth-century eclecticism, with its proliferation of historical styles and literary, religious, or social symbolism.[8] They open the now-famous chapter entitled "Ugly and Ordinary Architecture, or the Decorated Shed" with the declaration: "architecture depends in its perception and creation on past experience and emotional association and...these symbolic and representational elements may often be contradictory to the form, structure, and program with which they combine in the same building."[9] They castigate modern architecture for rejecting "eclecticism and style," as well as historical precedent, and for having "submerged symbolism...[and] promoted expressionism, concentrating on the expression of architectural elements themselves: on the expression of structure and function."[10] In place of this reductive approach, they propose a rhetoric of "communication over space," in which the signifying elements, like Semper's textile dressing, are structurally and conceptually distinct from the building they adorn. Nominating such an architecture the "decorated shed"—"architecture as shelter with symbols on it"—they emphasize the freedom of the facade for "ornamental" signification of the current realities of mass culture and the roadside shopping strip:[11]

> The purest decorated shed would be some form of conventional systems-building that corresponds closely to the space, structure, and program requirements of the architecture, and upon which is laid a contrasting—and, if in the nature of the circumstances, contradictory—decoration.[12]

This separation of structure and space from facade and communication also effects a division between knowledge and experience.

In a 1982 essay entitled "Diversity, Relevance and Representation in Historicism, or *Plus ça Change*...plus a Plea for Pattern all over Architecture with a Postscript on my Mother's House," Venturi makes this commitment to an architecture of communication quite clear:

> The separation of wall and structure through the appliqué of panels on or within a frame is familiar to us in Modern archi-

tecture. When the independent walls or the modular panels were colored or textured (they were seldom patterned), they provided a quasi-ornamental effect otherwise rare in that architecture. But these nonstructural walls in Modern architecture were essentially spatial in function—the marble panels interspersed in the structural grid of the Barcelona Pavilion directed flowing space; the curving walls snaking through the bays of the parliament in Chandigarh enclosed particular space while the modular panels complemented the structural grid in the same building. Instead, I have advocated the use of appliqué as sign, whose function is not basically spatial or structural, but communicative, via symbolism and ornament.[13]

Earlier in this essay, however, Venturi introduces another argument about the nature of the facade, articulating his goals for an architecture that "encourages ornamental surface over articulated form, pattern over texture, and sometimes pattern over all...."[14]

Ornamental pattern is different from historical, vernacular, or pop symbolism in that it can be freer and less consistent and can depend less on association. It could be extremely significant for architecture now and has enormous potential for development....[15]

Pattern-ornament can be abstract, as in the decorative tile or brick surfaces of Moslem architecture—among the supremely beautiful and complex creations in the history of art. It can be representational, as in figured Byzantine mosaics or in the pretty floral wallpapers of Victorian interiors. It can be symbolically architectural, as in the facades of those Italian Romanesque churches whose rows of bas-relief arcades crash into portal, rose window, or moulding, seeming discordant and lyrical at once.[16]

"Pattern over all" has its roots in the modern problematic of the proper architectural expression for the new constructional systems of the nineteenth century—and indeed, Venturi makes explicit his

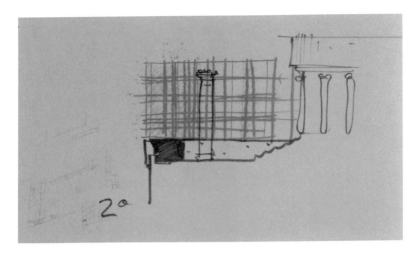

FIG. 3 *Bard College Library addition, elevation study, south elevation, 1989–90.*

FIG. 4 *Bard College Library addition, elevation study, south elevation, December 1990.*

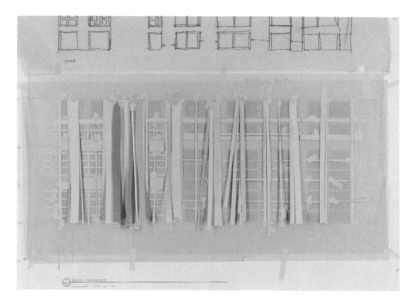

Bard College Library addition, elevation study, south elevation, December 1990. **FIG. 5**

Bard College Library addition, south elevation, 1993. ©Peter Aaron/Esto. **FIG. 6**

sense of connection with these concerns.[17] The architects most deeply involved with these questions, however, were not the modernist heroes of his theoretical tales, Le Corbusier and Alvar Aalto. Rather, it was Otto Wagner whose studied Semperianism was already "transpositioning...formal values from plastic to chromatic, from the three-dimensional to the flat"[18] at the end of the nineteenth century. In *Otto Wagner: Reflections on the Raiment of Modernity*, Harry Francis Mallgrave describes the intellectual milieu within which Wagner's architecture unfolded:

> For the nineteenth century, the *Kunstform*, or artistic dressing, typically did not clad, conceal, or deceive; it, like our clothing, rather mediated between a form's existence and the world and signaled a specific meaning that the designer sought to evoke.[19]

From the formal implications of iron construction—then supplanting masonry for public buildings, with their traditionally monumental programs—Wagner sought to fashion an "aesthetics of the mask," to provide a reconciliation between internal and external, structure and "expression."[20] This struggle intersected with his efforts to work out a new symbolic role for architecture in a society where urban growth and democratic forces were calling into question previously accepted elite systems of architectural signification.[22] Thus the exterior, representational layer of architecture serves— for Wagner as for VSBA—as a means of bridging architectural, structural, and social concerns in a culturally imbedded art of communication.

Wagner's Majolikahaus (1899) and Postsparkasse (1912) represent his exposition of Semper's theory of dressing at its most accomplished. Fritz Neumeyer describes the elegant clothing of the Postsparkasse as follows:

> Like the thin floating garment that clothes the female body in ancient Greek sculpture, revealing as much beauty as it conceals, Wagner's treatment of the structure and construction exploits a similar kind of delicate, sensuous play....Exactly

this principle gives the interior of the Postsparkasse its quality of silklike transparency. The glass veil is lifted up on iron stilts that carefully cut into its skin and gently disappear. Semper's theory of "dressing" (*Bekleidung*) could find no more ingenious interpretation....

Even the aluminum caps attached to the bolt heads in the cladding of the facade—a detail that has provoked art historians to many a subtile and divergent interpretation—can find a better psychological explanation in this way....The cap signifies the suppressed presence of iron, screened by the garment of the building. But like the diaphanous garment, it reveals more than enough to prevent the iron from disappearing. Wagner appropriates it not at the level of construction but as representation. He, in effect, applies the economical, efficient modern *mask*. What he formerly treated monumentally, he now reduces to a minimilist, symbolic statement that no longer depends on mass. This was a victory over mass that was truly modern, like the filigree, wide-span structure of the engineer.[22]

Like the buildings of Venturi, Wagner's mannerist architecture asserts that the surface should not look structural, that is to say, supportive. On the contrary, in these projects the structural characteristics of the surface itself are emphasized by disclosing its cloth-like nature. On the Majolikahaus, the tendrils of Wagner's flower patterns curl over the wall almost regardless of breaks or gaps in the surface caused by openings or structure behind, bearing a striking resemblance to the use of figured patterns on VSBA's Best Products Showroom.

Semper's claim, made in the period before Wagner's "break with the lithic age," is not that the wall *is* a fabric, but that the textile patterns present on the now-solid wall remain as a trace of an earlier cloth construction.[23] Memorialized in paint or pattern, these origins are preserved in the same way as the wood construction details of early wooden Greek temples often are supposed to be elegized in their later stone replicas.[24] But for VSBA and Wagner,

FAUSCH   353

the wall indeed *is* (a metaphorical equivalence) a cloth, and the use of the surface as a substrate for figure or pattern is a mark of structural realism as well as a complex symbolic accommodation.[25] In opposition to the modernist notion of "an elementary creation, that is, an expressive spiritualization of the material...that does not describe but is experienced,"[26] Venturi stresses the "grand contradictions" of structural expression in the modern age:

> Building technology hadn't changed much until recently. In most eras contemporary form and historical symbol could be integral for the whole building; it is only our age that has seen grand contradictions between structure and symbol, or form and symbol.
>
> Modern technical forms and historical symbolic forms rarely harmonize now. Historical symbolism and ornamental pattern must almost inevitably become appliqué. Quoins on the corner of a facade *could* be structural in a Renaissance or Renaissance Revival facade even if they *were* applied; but not now, because we build differently. We see differently now too. We don't *want* harmony between structure and symbol if it is forced or false. If we are at last "Postmodern" enough to accept structural and formal contradiction, we are still "Modern" enough to reject structural and formal "dishonesty." If we don't have to express structure, we don't want to falsify it. *Trompe l'oeil* in architecture is effective for us only so far as it doesn't work.[27]

Trompe l'oeil is a lie. But a lie that reveals itself as such effects the proper relationship between the surface and what lies underneath.

There are of course significant differences in the approaches of these two architects. With its decorative aluminium heads capping the structural steel bolts, Wagner's Postsparkasse makes a great deal of the connections attaching the surface panels to the structure behind. Almost a century later, however, and given VSBA's orientation to an "ordinary" architecture, Venturi's emphasis in on the already-existing conventions of curtain-wall construction, and not the newly developing constructional possibilities of iron. These commonplaces are realities to be acknowledged, not as material for symbolism, but as a preliminary to any symbolism:

> Building systems and their resultant forms should constitute the more universal qualities in our architecture and act as counterpoints to the unique qualities that will be symbolic. The construction method of our building in Iraq, for instance, is concrete frame with precast panels which is standard world-over; yet we designed some of the openings in the precast panels as pointed arches, to conform to the desire of our clients to symbolize national character and express cultural heritage in their architecture.[28]

Thus the beautiful and urbane woven brick skins of the laboratory buildings at Princeton and the University of Pennsylvania limit their display of structure to the odd ornamental detail—a touch of Gothic arch on the former, for instance, to reflect its Ivy League context, or an attenuated allusion to rustication in the latter.[29] Despite these representational elements, and despite the intense attention to detailing in their buildings, for Venturi structure is most salient not as foreground, as event, but rather as the taken-for-granted, the obvious, the unaccented. The structure of the decorated shed—that which is without structural expression—constitutes a late modern vernacular or idiom, "made strange" only in order to show its matter-of-fact employment, in the denouement of modernism's search for an innocent relationship to structure.[30]

Alan Colquhoun has noted the alienating effects of this unmediated exposure of the realities of late capitalist culture, in which structure and expression have no necessary connection.[31] Wagner's message about new construction systems is set within an ameliorating frame of traditional structural and social symbolism. VSBA's use of such elements, on the other side of the modernist divide, can only be read as irony. But in the end, the similarities are more significant than the differences. The idea of "pattern over all" locates the firm's work within the continuum of an extended reflection upon the dissolution of what had once been conceived as an undifferentiated unity, a condensated trinity of symbol, surface, and support. The "inventor" of postmodernism turns out to be fascinated by the role of structure.

Venturi's legacy from Semper—the tradition of the problem of structure versus representation, or the representation of structure—leads ultimately, however, to an absorption in abstraction. The Bard College Library facade is nothing so much as fabric attached to a frame, plaid curtains rippling in a light breeze, both theatrical backdrop and upstaging, a temporary construction set next to a classical temple that is the very emblem of solidity. But paradoxically, this building also pushes the theory of "pattern over all" to its ultimate conclusion—beyond symbolism or communication, beyond the sign architecture of Las Vegas, beyond association, to a representation of the very idea of representation. Emancipated from history, structure, and function, separated from the activities of the interior by an empty space, even the openings in this fabric are determined by the pattern of the facade. The "real" fenestration—that which "looks like windows" and is related to use—is cut into an inner layer, a second, "functional" facade. In this building "pattern over all" is self-referential—a pure display of surface at play.

According to Semper, even the cosmic significance of the Greek deities on the temple facade is "subject," i.e., something to be veiled, like the tectonic history of the forms, in order to free the work from the material, to allow it to become art. In the "pattern over all" of the Bard College Library addition, however, VSBA casts away the subject altogether, constructing a quiescent architecture (Fig. 6). Yet this architecture, which has erased the traces of the history of the facade, reflects upon what it cannot be, its abstraction both a ludic and a tragic gesture.

NOTES

1   The Best Products Showroom (1977), Oxford Valley, Penn.; the ISI Headquarters (1978), Philadelphia, Penn.; the addition to the Allen Art Museum (1973), Oberlin College, Ohio; the Brant House (1970), Greenwich, Conn.; the Seattle Art Museum (1991); the Bard College Library addition (1993), Annandale-on-Hudson, New York; and the Sainsbury Wing of the National Gallery in London (1991).

2   See Gottfried Semper, "The Four Elements of Architecture, A Contribution to the Contemporary Study of Architecture," and "The Textile Art Considered in Itself and in Relation to Architecture," in *The Four Elements of Architecture and Other Writings*, trans. Harry Francis Mallgrave and Wolfgang Herrmann (Cambridge: Cambridge University Press, 1989).

3   The Ponte dell'Accademia proposal (1985), Venice; and Gordon Wu Hall (1980), Butler College, Princeton University. Mark Wigley describes Venturi and Scott Brown's 1967 project for a National Football Hall of Fame as Semperian in its construction of interior space by means of images rather than walls, so that "the images no longer appear to be suspended within space, but in a Semperian sense, are the construction of space itself." Mark Wigley, "The Decorated Gap," *Ottagono* 94 (March 1990), 43. Wigley's conceptualization of the outer, decorative layer of Venturi and Scott Brown's projects as an "independent structure," is of course also "Semperian," and indeed, the interior elevations of Venturi and Scott Brown's project for Philadelphia's Orchestra Hall (1989) would easily double as illustrations of the temporary festival constructions Semper claims were the origin of monumental art: "The festival apparatus, the improvised scaffolding with all the special splendor and frills that indicate more precisely the occasion for the festivity and enhance the glorification of the day—covered with decoration, draped with carpets, dressed with boughs and flowers, adorned with festoons and garlands, fluttering banners and trophies—this is the *motive* of the *permanent* monument, which is intended to recount for coming generations the festive act and the event celebrated." Gottfried Semper, "The Textile Art," 236.

4   Ibid., 258–62. For Semper, as Iain Boyd Whyte points out, style is "the accord of an art object with its genesis, and with all the pre-conditions and circumstances of its becoming." Ibid., 269, cited in Iain Boyd Whyte, "Modernist Dioscuri? Otto Wagner and Hendrik Petrus Berlage," in Harry Francis Mallgrave, *Otto Wagner: Reflections on the Raiment of Modernity* (Santa Monica: The Getty Center for the History of Art and the Humanities, 1993), 171 n53.

5   Gottfried Semper, "Structural Elements of Assyrian-Chaldean Architecture," (Chptr. 10 of *Vergleichende Baulehre*), in Wolfgang Herrmann, *Gottfried Semper: In Search of Architecture* (Cambridge, Mass.: MIT Press, 1984), 205–6. See also Semper, "The Four Elements," 104–7.

6   "Every material conditions its own particular manner of formation by the properties that distinguish it from other materials and that demand a technical treatment appropriate to it. When an artistic motive has been subjected to any kind of material treatment, its primitive type will be modified, having acquired a definite tone as it were. The type no longer rests at its primary stage of development, but has passed through a more or less distinct metamorphosis. When from this secondary or, according to the circumstances, variously graduated modification the motive now comes into a new material transformation (*Stoffwechsel*), the form emerging from it will be a mixed result, one that expresses its primordial type (*Urtypus*) and all stages of modification that preceded the last formation. Assuming a correct course of development, the order of the intermediate links that connect the primitively expressed artistic idea with the various derivations will be discernible." Semper, "The Textile Art," 258–9.

7   "The denial of reality, of the material, is necessary if form is to emerge as a meaningful symbol, as an autonomous creation of man.... The untainted feeling led primitive man to the denial of reality in all early artistic endeavors; the great, true masters of art in every field returned to it—only these men in times of high artistic development also *masked the material of the mask*. This led Phidias to his conception of the two tympana on the Parthenon. Evidently he considered his task, the representation of the double myth and its actors, the deities, *as the subject matter to be treated* (as was the stone in which he formed them), which he veiled as much as possible—thus freeing them of any material and outwardly demonstrative expression of their nonpictorial and religious-symbolic nature. Therefore, his gods confront us, inspire us, individually and collectively, first and above all as expressions of true human beauty and grandeur." Ibid., 257.

8   Robert Venturi, Denise Scott Brown, and Steven Izenour, *Learning from Las Vegas: The Forgotten Symbolism of Architectural Form* (Cambridge, Mass.: MIT Press, 1977 [1972]).

9   Ibid., 87.

10   Ibid., 101–4.

11   Ibid., 8–9, 87–92. As Robert Maxwell points out in the following conversation, although Le Corbusier declared the facade to be free, he did not
understand this freedom as a liberty to be dictated by the urbanistic requirements of the building's context. Neither did he understand it to be free to be
"art," as Semper does, i.e., symbolic of human freedom. Rather, it was free of
the dictates of structure and function, to represent its own freedom, or perhaps
a purist composition. Both "freedom" and "art" take on very different meanings
for these three architects and theorists.

12   Ibid., 100.

13   Robert Venturi, "Diversity, Relevance and Representation in
Historicism, or *Plus ça Change*...plus a Plea for Pattern all over Architecture
with a Postscript on my Mother's House," in Robert Venturi and Denise Scott
Brown, *A View from the Campidoglio: Selected Essays 1953–1984* (New York:
Harper and Row, 1984), 112.

14   Ibid., 108.

15   Ibid., 110.

16   Ibid., 115.

17   "I have never intended to totally reject Modern architecture in words or
work because I do, and I think our architecture should, in many important
ways, evolve out of it, not revolt against it...." Ibid., 115. Venturi and Scott
Brown's definition of the decorated shed also evolves out of modernism; it
assumes a close relationship between plan and function, behind the decorative
facade.

18   Leonardo Benevolo, *History of Modern Architecture*, 2 vols., 3rd rev. ed.
(Cambridge, Mass.: MIT Press, 1977 [1966]), 1:285–6. Mallgrave notes, in the
introduction to *Otto Wagner*, that Wagner was attempting "to make real the
changing relationship of mask and frame (to outfit architecture with a new cut
of clothing, as it were)...." Mallgrave, *Otto Wagner*, 11.

19   Mallgrave, *Otto Wagner*, 7.

20   See Ákos Moravánszky, "The Aesthetics of the Mask: The Critical
Reception of Wagner's *Moderne Architektur* and Architecture in Central
Europe," in Mallgrave, *Otto Wagner*, 199, 205.

21   Wagner's *Modern Architecture* abounds in practical solutions for dealing

with the problems of modernity in Vienna—population growth, the homogenization of democratic society, and speculation in urban land. See especially his fifth chapter, entitled "The Practice of Art," in Otto Wagner, *Modern Architecture: A Guidebook for his Students to this Field of Art* (Santa Monica, The Getty Center for the History of Art and the Humanities, 1988 [1902]), 109ff. See also Fritz Neumeyer, "Iron and Stone: The Architecture of the *Großstadt*," in Mallgrave, *Otto Wagner*, 117.

22   Ibid., 135.

23   Whyte, "Modernist Dioscuri," 174.

24   Although Semper did not accept the theory that the primitive hut is the direct progenitor of the Doric temple, he did believe that the Greek temple had originally been developed in wood and retained many details derived from wood construction. See Herrmann, *Gottfried Semper*, 166ff.

25   On Wagner's realism, see Whyte, "Modernist Dioscuri," as well as J. Duncan Berry, "From Historicism to Architectural Realism: On Some of Wagner's Sources," Harry Francis Mallgrave, "From Realism to *Sachlichkeit*: The Polemics of Architectural Modernity in the 1890s," and Stanford Anderson, "*Sachlichkeit* and Modernity, or Realist Architecture," all in the same volume.

26   Moravánszky, "The Aesthetics of the Mask," 229.

27   Venturi, "Diversity," 111.

28   Ibid., 110–111. In this example, the pointed arches that Venturi says are used as a symbol to convey national identity—a cultural meaning—are in fact also representations of structural elements, although not traces in the way Semper describes. Here they are used in the same way that constructional elements—e.g., columns or quoins—have been used for centuries, to convey class or institutional identity through the display of the wealth required to build in a costly material (which pre-cast concrete, with its high precision requirements, still would have been in Iran in 1981).

29   The Lewis Thomas Laboratories for Molecular Biology (1983), Princeton University; the Clinical Research Building of the School of Medicine at the University of Pennsylvania (1989), Philadelphia, Penn.

30   Venturi, "Diversity," 112.

31   "The contradictions in the buildings of Venturi and Rauch are not, like those of traditional architecture, subject to an overall aesthetic synthesis. They remain deliberately unresolved in a contentious dialectic of popular versus high; banal versus subtle; architecture as mass media versus architect's architecture. They do not, as do other "post-functionalist" buildings, attempt to define an alternative language to that of functionalism. They reveal, but do not overcome, the contradictions latent in the contemporary state of architecture, and this makes it difficult to find a basis for critical discussion of the work." Alan Colquhoun, "Sign and Substance: Reflections on Complexity, Las Vegas, and Oberlin," *Essays in Architectural Criticism: Modern Architecture and Historical Change* (Cambridge, Mass.: MIT Press, 1981), 151.

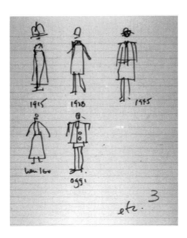

FIG. 1a-c *Robert Venturi, 1990. Sketches of Woman's Dress 1600–1990.*

On December 9, 1990, Robert Venturi and Denise Scott Brown participated in a conversation about fashion and architecture as part of the Mellon Seminars in Architecture at Princeton University, sponsored by the Andrew W. Mellon Foundation for the Visual Arts and Humanities. The following excerpts are from their talk.

CYCLES OF FASHION IN ARCHITECTURE

Robert Venturi (RV): I'd like to place fashion within the context of cycles of taste—evolutions of sensibility—that pertain to the perception of all the arts, not only to fashion and dress—cycles that swing back and forth between subtlety and exaggeration, subtlety and hype. We're within the hype range of the cycle right now.

rication

NVERSATION WITH
BERT VENTURI AND
NISE SCOTT BROWN

For instance, the beat of pop music is loud and dynamic and its tone dissonant; clothing, in the meantime, promotes highly contrasting colors and values and patterns and exaggerated silhouettes—as in padded, extended shoulders and very short skirts. Similarly, the architectural style of Deconstructivism involves little more than an orthodox Modern vocabulary hyped-up through distortions, juxtapositions, and exaggerations of scale; the original vocabulary, you'll remember, was expressed in subtle terms, with subtle details, within a relatively small range of scales: what was called a "human scale" is what prevailed at the time. In a way, Modern theory and philosophy were puritanical, emphasizing directness and harmony—directness concerning structure and form, harmony concerning composition. Decon in architecture employs these same elements, but it hypes them to such an extent that they remind you of a row of Quaker ladies dancing the can-can.

There is another duality that corresponds to this one of hype versus subtlety. It involves deeper issues of sensibility and taste and pertains to universal and plural dimensions within the realms of art and culture. To oversimplify a bit, we might say that the Renaissance ideal was universalist—architects adopted a Classical Roman vocabulary as relevant for all time, for all places. That this style conformed in reality to specific national characteristics during the sixteenth and seventeenth centuries was incidental; and that the French, Italian, and English interpretations of this architecture were in fact not identical was an aberration. Theoretically, ideally, the Renaissance architectural system was appropriate all over: it was universal. Likewise, Modernism in architecture—or, at least, that kind of architecture identified as the International Style—promoted a universal ideal. Industrial vocabulary and processes promised to be appropriate for all over the world. The International Style, starting with Gropius's Fagus Shoe Works, appropriated an industrial vernacular that was to be universally applicable and symbolically ideal.

To illustrate what might be called "cycles of fashion in clothing" that might correspond to "cycles of manner in architecture," both of which derive from changes of sensibility and taste, I sketch some profiles representing women's European fashions. I can begin somewhat arbitrarily with an Elizabethan garment that is hype in its exaggerated silhouette and juxtapositions of patterns. There might be scale contrasts, for example, between details of little bits of pearls sewn into the huge, erect collar and other compositional elements consisting of bold patterns and color ranges. And then there's the wacky hairdo! With a one-hundred-fifty-year jump into the mid-eighteenth century, you find a delicacy of scale and a subtlety of palette, although there is a boldness to the silhouette of Rococo skirts.

Later in the century, during the reign of Louis XVI, there evolved an exaggeration via enormous hairdos and great hats, but the configuration of the profile as a whole is less extreme. During the Neoclassical period, subtlety of effect was stressed: the Empress

Josephine's dresses were severe in silhouette—pastel or white, with little pattern within their fabric. Exceedingly pure and minimalist, this period of fashion would look at home in front of the Villa Savoye. By the 1830s, fashion is almost Elizabethan again: the skirts have widened and sleeves are voluminous. In the 1860s, the skirts are extremely wide, with triangular silhouettes and high waists. And then, during the 1870s, there develops that big, exaggerated behind called the bustle.

Right now, so-called *haute couture* exemplifies exaggeration: big shoulders, short skirts, big ornamental elements, and bold hues or patterns. It can be comprehended as a revival of the fashion of the World War II era, which was also a derivation of the thrift-shop ethos—a kind of symbolism of the second-hand exemplifying the ill-fitting clothes of the waif. Acknowledging some analogy between clothing and Modern architecture, both of the 1920s, 1930s, 1940s, and 1950s, architecture and fashion look wimpy in comparison to today's fashions in architecture and clothing. They look a little thin, undramatic, and weak from our perspective within a context of hype. Because of our sensibility, fifties clothes in old movies and fifties architecture with its "human scale" look wimpy. And "Decon" of the nineties makes plain "Con" of the twenties look puritanical.

MANNERIST CLOTHING AND ARCHITECTURE

RV: Then there's the tradition of what might be called generic clothing involving routine and convention, background and function, as opposed to the highly fluctuating fashion of foreground and frivolity that *haute couture* represents. Consider the clothing that I'm wearing as an example. I could have been wearing exactly this outfit thirty years ago.

Denise Scott Brown (DSB): And you did!

RV: And I did! The necktie and the lapels might have been a little narrower. The advantage of always wearing a "uniform" is you don't have to worry about clothes and image; there's enough else to worry about just being an architect. And this tradition occurs also in women's clothing. Certainly, many of the women sitting in this room are wearing tailored and functional clothing as opposed to *haute couture* or to costume clothing that promotes panache or hype. And this suggests a question concerning appropriate apparel. While it would not be appropriate to wear a costume to work, it would be equally inappropriate to wear blue jeans to a ball or to dinner with the mayor—or would it today? A similar notion of appropriateness concerning architecture seems to have been lost. Many architects succumb to the temptation of designing buildings as costume in order to seem original and to make a statement. This approach proclaims: Down with convention or context or appropriateness, with architecture as background that must last so you don't get tired of it. But we say: Hurray for architecture as background for living; architecture shouldn't be a stage set for acting.

The comparison of costume and architecture points up some negative aspects of architecture today, where we employ journalistic hype to acquire recognition.

Mario Gandelsonas (MG): Returning to how both you and Denise are dressed, one issue that might be useful for discussion is the matter of gender and fashion. For instance, why does Bob sketch women's clothing and not men's? Looking at the historical development of men's fashion might surprise us. Men's clothing is, in many ways, a clothing of resistance, a resistance to everything that men are and are not allowed to wear. A second problem is the idea of time and fashion that you just touched upon. For instance, I am wearing a very old jacket and a very old tie...

RV: So am I.

MG: [pointing to his own clothes] This coat is thrift-shop cashmere, probably forties or fifties; this tie is by a fashion designer, but the outfit sort of plays with working clothing, which you just mentioned in regard to appropriateness, because the coat is not appropriate for the tie; and then, these are just your neutral, appropriate pair of trousers. I was thinking that there's a lot of that kind of play going on in the facades of the National Gallery. That really fascinates me. One part of this is the appropriateness of the front...

RV: Yes, your clothing is more inconsistent than mine, so it's more like Denise's and my architecture. You're more mannerist. I think the reason I showed women's clothing is that there's more contrast within the cycles of change than there is within men's.

MG: What about men in high heels?

RV: I think much of the difference between the clothing of men and women in the past relates to the role of women in the past. Certainly, the women who could afford to wear high fashion didn't do much else but dress up. They could wear corsets that made their waists thirteen inches and if they fainted it didn't matter within the ethos of the leisure class. Cause versus effect came into the picture insofar as women could be more uncomfortable, more constricted in their clothes—not as active as men. Because men's clothing has had to be more functional it's had to be less revolutionary and more evolutionary.

DSB: But men have been peacocks over the ages. Think of the courtier and the court...

RV: Yes, but if you analyze just profiles, the profiles for men's clothing have been more consistent within their evolution.

DSB: What about color?

MG: I agree with Denise. I think it would be interesting to show how, for instance, what Bob calls appropriateness might be a certain resistance in the way we need to dress, a resistance that probably refers to the restrictions, as Denise has described elsewhere, that the public space and the issues of public propriety impose upon the facade of the National Gallery. But moving from the public facade to the secret space of the plan—and I must say that the plans are really insane—only another architect will be able to read the perversions of order, the inappropriate behavior; there you allow yourselves to explore design strategies that are intended for a certain group of people.

ARCHITECTURE IN RESISTANCE TO FASHION

Rodolphe El-Khoury (REK): It would seem that the metaphor of fashion has always been resisted by architects, theorists, and historians of architecture. To qualify an architecture as fashionable is pejorative. Why do you think architects have such a mistrust of fashion and how do you place yourselves within this system of apprehension?

RV: I think the analogies between architecture and fashion are wonderful and compelling, but we also have to acknowledge that architecture is essentially background shelter that has to exist for hundreds of years, while clothes serve primarily to protect the body from the elements and to veil it for the sake of modesty. Clothes are more fragile than buildings and their design can evolve more quickly. I think this is an essential and significant difference despite parallels in evolving sensibility, taste, symbolic gesture, et cetera. Clothing is temporary by its very nature, and architecture, by its very nature, is as permanent as anything human can be in reality. A possible similarity between architecture and fashion may have to do with the cycle of production. Also there is the issue that we change our clothes, whereas architecture is a surrounding constant.

DSB: We've found a good definition of fashion to be "a way of doing things at a time," as Diana Vreeland once observed in *Vogue*. That seems to be able to span architecture, too. I think the notion that architecture should change less often and less quickly than clothing has existed for a long time, although it may be belied by fact. I think that the flurries and eddies we've seen recently are occurring almost as fast in architecture as in clothing. It may also be that the philosophies of Modernism have made architects dislike the notion of fashion. Modernists felt that things should be done for reasons having to do with technology, function, and structure; the idea that you did things because your eye saw in a certain way at a certain time was not especially pleasing to them. The Modernist would say that changes in architecture should result from changes in technology. My feeling is that we shift sensibility before we shift fashion and that these shifts in sensibility tend to go along with social movements more than with technology. Architectural change responds to our seeing something different. When we went to Las Vegas, for instance, we were ready to see something different; and suddenly Las Vegas looked horrifying, but also exciting, because the 1960s were happening and there was revolution in the streets. All of that may be tied into what makes fashion in both clothing and architecture.

Pat Morton (PM): Could you comment on the relationship between seeing something at a certain time and the idea of essence? If the style also concerns the essence of a certain cultural tradition, then in your mother's house, for instance, is essence a universal category even though the house has been modified by a specific context?

DSB: It is also modified by how the particular viewer is feeling at a certain time. We, and others, have used that building as a touchstone, returning to it time and again only to discover another essence. It's reverberative in this way. One can, depending on social or personal conditions at a certain time, see different things in it, just as history is reinterpreted or even reshaped by later events. Every age sees a different essence in Rome or in historical architecture of whatever kind. Some architecture is less interesting to some ages than others. So, the essence of a building or a style could be a rather personal thing, or it could be shared by a school of thought or a group of people or a society.

RV: I think essence is relative. The hut, the temple, the barn, are fairly universal as architectural shelters. When Louis Kahn was the leading architect, the essence was permeated by the heroic and the original. Conversely, my mother's house, but even more so the modest houses we did at the sea shore a little later in the sixties, looked familiar and suggested an elemental kind of architectural shelter. These houses referred to an elemental, familiar, childlike idea of domesticity—what's traditional, what you see in picture books. In not being heroic or original, this architecture reverts to convention, to an elemental convention, whose form and symbol are entirely different from the essence of Kahn.

PLURALISM AND UNIVERSALISM

Deborah Fausch (DF): You've distinguished between a universalist and a pluralist architecture. If there is a duality between the universal as being permanent and the pluralistic as being subject to change, how do you see your work in that respect? By understanding the workings of pluralism, does your work, paradoxically, succeed in imparting a kind of universality or permanence to itself? In other words, I'm asking about your work *as* fashion.

RV: What we were doing in the design of the Sainsbury Wing was adapting a Neoclassical vocabulary that was originally universalist. But it's incidental that we're using this vocabulary; we aren't Classicists. We're using it in an eclectic way as an element of signage —as a particular symbol that was originally a universal symbol. This use of eclecticism, of course, involves its own tradition— a romantic tradition. Our architecture acknowledges that today many cultures are coming together as never before. In one way, heightened systems of communication can work toward promoting one culture. But in another way—when everyone is familiar with everybody else's culture—communication promotes and also glories in the contrasts among them. For this reason, Tokyo today is the equivalent of London in the nineteenth century—a most vital city, a city that adapts to all these combinations. Ironically, the things that are really universal, besides architectural high-design, are fast-food outlets. McDonald's is universal *par excellence*. It's fascinating that Modernist universality won out in commercial and pop culture more so than in high culture.

DSB: It's also somewhat ironic that the Classical architecture that we're calling universal came out of a small peninsula, Italy, where there were perhaps four million people at the time of its inception. We see it as both universal and referring to its time.

THE SAINSBURY WING OF THE NATIONAL GALLERY IN LONDON

RV: I think that the strength of the Sainsbury Wing, and this is also a source of much of the criticism that it evokes, is that it doesn't fit into an ideology. The Modernists reproach it because it's not modern, except for little bits and parts, and the traditionalists or the historicists criticize it because it's not historical enough. It is, indeed, mannerist.

DSB: There are many ways of thinking about the public and the private in this building. The front facade is much more public than those along the sides and the rear. Trying to explain why we wanted the back facade to be so terribly plain, I said to our client, whose clothes came from Savile Row, "Your jacket has lapels on the front, on the back it's beautifully and carefully made but very simple."

Paulette Singley (PS): Comparing the National Gallery with the Seattle Art Museum offers some useful, although slightly reductive, analogies. To begin, the facade of the Seattle Art Museum could be seen as the lacy edge of an undergarment slipping below the hemline or even the embroidered edge of some kind of regional costume. Likewise, the National Gallery, and maybe even the facade of Bard College, is a curtain that has been pulled back to gather on one edge of the facade.

RV: A great analogy.

Robert Maxwell (RM): What is the architectural equivalent of blue jeans?

RV: We're doing work for the Philadelphia Orchestra. They have a very low budget, and we can "do" low-budget; indeed we do low-budget all the time. But you can't do low-budget pretending that it's tuxedo when it's jeans. Again, that involves appropriateness. Blue jeans are the houses in Nantucket; they're convention. Blue jeans are highly related to convention.

DSB: Or the back of the National Gallery.

RV: Blue jeans are fabulous; blue-jean architecture is exciting. We're all afraid of it because it's not heroic and original. We're afraid we're not being original artists if we exemplify it.

DSB: It must be as carefully detailed as the stuff on the front, but it mustn't look as if it has been.

RM: Designer jeans.

RV: I'm afraid we do do designer jeans.

GENDER AND ARCHITECTURE

Mark Linder (ML): Returning to Mario's question regarding gender, it's always seemed to me that there's something about your work—perhaps it's part of the nature of collaboration and perhaps not—that draws upon seemingly excluded terms, excluded symbols. So it doesn't surprise me at all that you would talk about fashion through women's clothing as opposed to through men's clothing. We might distinguish between fashion and style. The word *style* tends to be the masculine code word for *fashion*. I'm elaborating on this difference because it occurred to me during the discussion of men's and women's fashion that you could understand those little Victorian columns on the Sainsbury Wing as a kind of gender reference. Those columns have always perplexed me; they're the hardest thing to understand about the building.

Using Paulette's metaphor of pulling back the skirts—and thinking about Wilkins as a feminine stylist—you're sort of pulling back the clothes to reveal Victoria's undergarments.

DSB: Victoria's Secrets? (laughing) I couldn't resist!

Zvi Efrat (ZE): Your built and written work has positioned itself distinctively in relation to an economy and industry of taste. And yet, it has rarely been judged as tasteful. Your hallmark embracing and staging of the ordinary, at times of the ugly, seems to calculate that an inevitable and delightful surplus will present itself to you, as the reluctant tastemaker, to perpetuate the flow of architectural fashion.

RV: I think a lot of modern art has done that: exemplifying the ordinary or making art that is ugly—not lyrical, but realist. But architecture didn't want to connect with this. Gordon Bunshaft called our designs ugly and ordinary. We took that as a compliment. Yes, we do ugly and ordinary; there is room for ugly and ordinary as well as heroic and original. So, in one sense we are connected with that twentieth-century sensibility of taking the ordinary and making it not ordinary—that is, with the sensibility of Pop art.

DSB: Or you achieve a higher order of beauty. You resolve at another level. The beauty is agonized, and the beauty could well be agonized because the society is agonized. The expression of the agony of this kind of society might well be an agonized beauty. Even a very beautiful person in certain lights looks almost ugly.

PS: I see a relationship, although perhaps a convoluted one, between Zvi's question of ugliness and Mark's analysis of gender. In plan, your buildings often have an uncomfortable size, even ungainly or ugly; while the subtle adjustments and delicate patterns of the elevations often belie this awkwardness. This kind of tension between big and small scales, between the ugly and the beautiful, might also be interpreted as a confusion of gender stereotypes, wherein the building is seen as a form of cross-dressing that fluctuates back and forth between the image of a stout man wearing his mother's dress or a matron in dungarees.

RV: You won't remember how exciting it was when Corb created *beton brut*: he did heavy buildings—he did La Tourette! It was astounding because our sensibility was based on the Villa Savoye, where the more delicate and minimal your structure the more elegant it was. But here Corb made things heavier than they needed to be! Of course, late Kahn came out of that sensibility. *We* feel the need to combine the heavy and the bulky with the delicate and the subtle; and, of course, the National Gallery is a Miesian structure underneath: we made those columns bigger than they needed to be. Aesthetically, there is the need for the big and the little, and the bulky and the delicate.

RM: I'd like to ask Denise a question about something I think you said about assimilation of ideas as part of architectural style. Around 1920 or thereabouts, Corbusier proclaimed the five points of architecture, the free plan, the free facade...and now it seems that we've got the free facade, but that it took some time. Would you agree with that? Would you say that this is part of the delay during which an idea is assimilated? Why did the horizontal window suddenly enter the story when he was proclaiming the free facade?

DSB: You know, the facade of the National Gallery is not free; the facade is very much dictated. It's just dictated by another set of variables than those that dictate the inside.

RM: Free to be dictated by those variables?

RV: Free formalistically, not programmatically.

DSB: The facade is dictated by the urban space, and it is constrained by the parameters that it sets itself. It works out a formula, an algorithm, for that facade. It isn't idiosyncratic.

RV: I think what you've said, not to be pretentious, is that the facade is freer than anything Corbusier did; even though he invented the free facade. Ironically, the inventor often looks timid.

DF: I'd like to conclude by asking Denise a specific question regarding the influence that your explorations in the decorative arts has had upon your architectural design process and its relationship to fashion—in particular, the metaphor of architecture as clothing. We're all familiar with the *Grandmother* and the *Notebook* patterns in relation to the use of overall pattern on your facades. Might you expand upon this, say, with the patterns and textures of Japanese textile design and its influence on your architecture?

DSB: This question could be the subject of a book in itself and its essence is hard to grasp in a sentence. Perhaps for now we can say that our Best Products floral cladding was derived from wallpaper and that the fantastic pattern fragments in Tokyo architecture and urbanism put us in mind of the clashing patterns on a silk kimono and also of the depictions of these patterns in Japanese woodcuts.

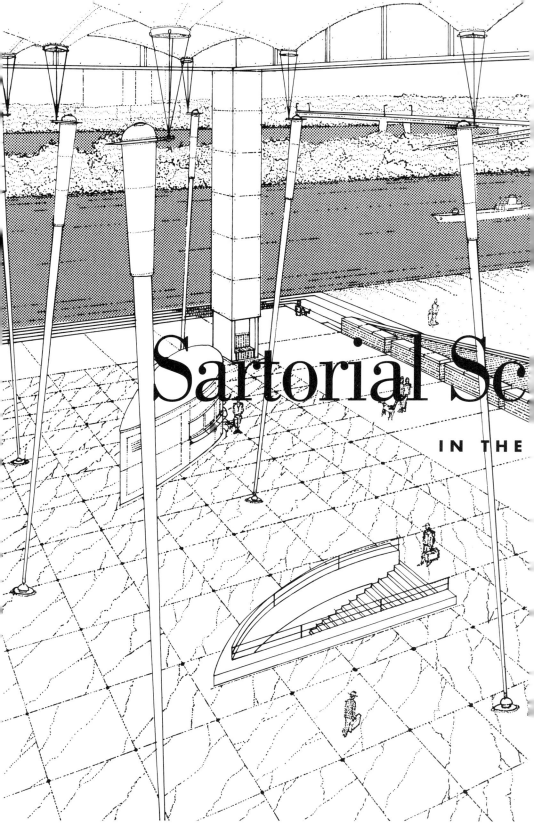

Sartorial Sc

IN THE

RODOLPHE EL-KHOURY

The city of Vienna wants to develop the railroad yard of the Nordbahnhof, *an area of about 90 hectares (220 acres) left vacant with the relocation of the station. Wishing to explore the immense possibilities of the site, the mayor of Vienna called for Machado and Silvetti Associates among an international group of urban designers and contracted them as consultants. For the initial design stage, an eight person team from Machado and Silvetti Associates set up an office in Vienna (at the Remise, an old repair building on the site) during September 1991. Following the preliminary approval by city authorities, the project was developed in Boston and resubmitted in January 1992 to the Office of Physical Planning in Vienna. The city intends to act based on these recommendations.* [1]

To describe—and justify—this design proposal for the site of the Nordbahnhofgelände is to reconstruct a history of an empirical process which constantly readjusts the conception of the whole to the conditions of its parts and, conversely, recasts the particular in view of the whole—an endless bricolage terminated only by the arbitrariness of a deadline. Such a diachronic account of the project's creation should demonstrate the transformation of partis, ready-made layouts or pre-conceived notions of all kinds—inevitable and necessary prejudices—as they are gradually assimilated into the complexities of the site. It should demonstrate the site-specificity of a design strategy which responds to particular conditions and is unlikely to be rehearsed elsewhere *tel quel*. It should, furthermore, convey our skepticism toward pre-packaged ideologies and formulaic approaches to urban design, whether traditional or modern, as well as our disdain for the *Zeitgeist* arguments (electronic age, global village, postmodern sublime, etc...) being brandished with a renewed sense of urgency in the current reconstruction of a cosmopolitan Vienna.

ography

ESE URBAN FABRIC

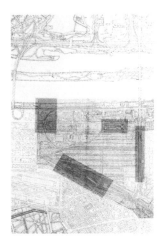

FIG. 1 *Existing conditions: nodes and circulatory armature of proposal*

FIG. 2 *First proposal: adjusted circulatory armature with grid infill*

Our desire to impress upon the site a particular character, an image or recognizable figure, was balanced at the outset with an equal commitment to its optimal integration within the existing urban fabric. The initial design strategy thus aimed to reconcile or productively superimpose these contrasting but not necessarily contradictory premises. The heterogeneity of the immediate context and the varied conditions of its edges (Nordbahnstrasse, Handelskai, and Innstrasse, Fig. 1) disqualified any singular totalizing vision of the site; "particular character" gave way to "characteristic parts" and "strategy" to "tactics" or "*tâtonnement*." A patchwork of different urban fragments and fabrics individually derived from specific nodes or edge conditions, held together by an infrastructural and loosely figurative armature, thus gradually developed (Fig. 2).

This infrastructural armature, consisting primarily of two boulevards that intersect in a formal roundabout, extends and completes existing lines and patterns of traffic in surrounding neighborhoods while emulating the layout of a baroque Praterstern. And as an ideal figure is negotiated against the shapeless and accidental contingencies of context, geometrical perfection yields to subtle distortion, optical deception and illusion: truth is discarded for rhetoric (Fig. 3). One of the proposed boulevards (Flohmarkt Allée) extends diagonally across the site to meet with Instrasse and Vorgartenstrasse

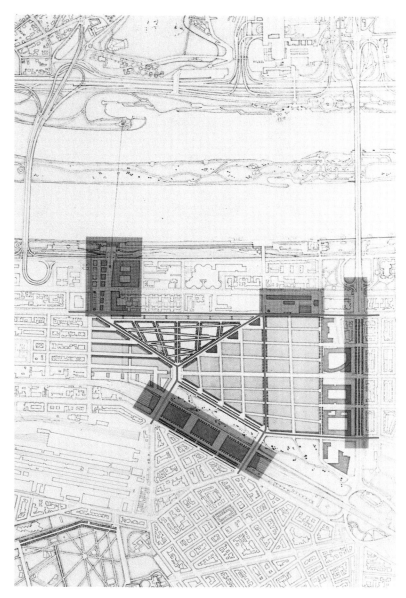

Final proposal. December, 1991: adjusted circulatory armature with grid infill   **FIG. 3**

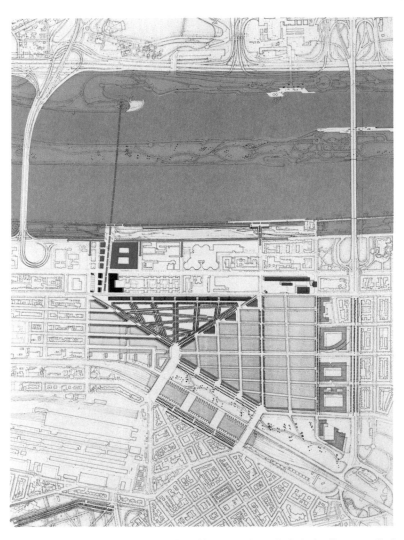

FIG. 4 *The connection between the 'old' city and Nordbahnhof will occur off of Nordbahnstrasse with passages under the railroad tracks (we found that tunnels would work more realistically, for pedestrians and vehicles, than bridges, given the height of the tracks, ten feet over street level) from east to west, on Lassallestrasse, Am Tabor, Taborstrasse, and Innstrasse. Parallel to the Nordbahnstrasse the 'railway infrastructure' will be framed by an 'open market' program (Flohmarkt), urbanizing the adjoining border between Leopoldstadt and Nordbahnhof. The north face of the 'Flohmarkt' fronts onto an open park and boulevard, connecting the Praterstem to the Trichtergarten.*

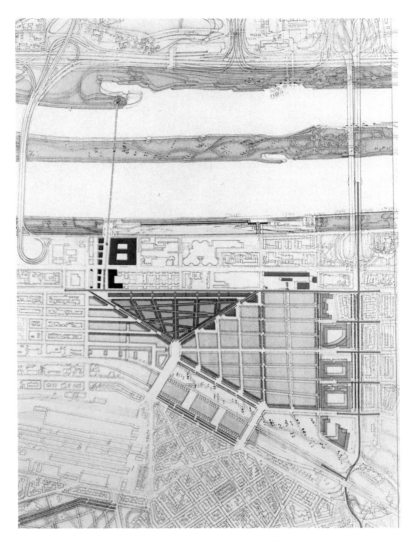

Lassallestrasse is the main thoroughfare connecting the city center to **FIG. 5**
its peripheries. It runs north-south while permitting east-west connections
between the Stuwerviertel and Nordbahnhof districts. Of these connections,
the main public access will occur on Vorgartenstrasse, a principal road
that links Olimpiaplatz to the Heiligenplatz at a broader scale. Three
major programs of this site will be housed on Vorgartenstrasse: the Remise
(a cultural center), an 'exemplary' piece of public housing, and the beginning
of a public sequence towards the Danube.

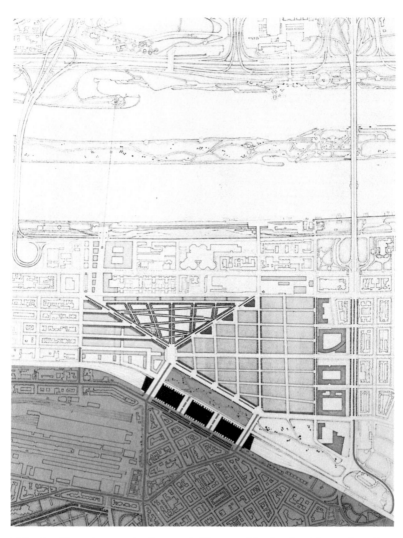

FIG. 6 *The main connection between the Vienna and the Danube will occur through an urban sequence beginning on Vorgartenstrasse and terminating on a public balcony overlooking the waterfront. The aim of this sequence is to filter the public slowly and imperceptibly towards the balcony, overcoming three obstacles that at present, block the city's relationship to the river: the roadway, the railway, and retaining embankment walls. The urban sequence will house a mixed program of commercial, retail, and housing elements. The Donaubalkon descends to a riverfront walk connecting all the way back to Lassallestrasse to the east.*

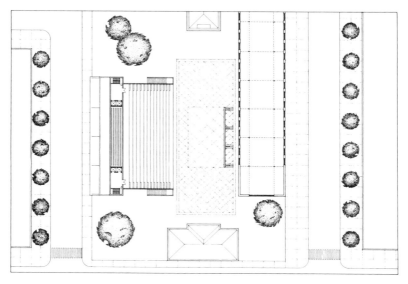

Remiseplatz Outdoor Theater, section and plan details **FIG. 7**

where a pedestrian sequence of public spaces (the Donau Galleries) terminate with the Donaubalkon and a funicular ride across the river (Figs. 10–12); the other boulevard extends Taborstrasse—a street that promises an even more prominent status with the anticipated development of the adjacent railroad yards—through a tunnel under the train tracks, across the new roundabout, and up to the intersection of Vorgartenstrasse and Haussteinstrasse. And from there, against the Remiseplatz (Figs. 7–9), the extension northward of Trichetergarten Allée Ost leads to the riverfront in a pedestrian promenade.

Analogical thinking would liken this infrastructural armature to a colossal suture stretched across the scar of the urban body, bracing regenerated tissue and implanted organs. And in the more

MACHADO AND SILVETTI 383

pertinent—if no less self-indulgent—Semperian language of weaving, or in the Loosian discourse on fashion, the lines of the boulevards would become seams extended between the disparate patches as well as the stitching device that brings together their clashing fabrics and secures the ornamental "appliqué."

FIG. 8 *View of Remiseplatz information tower*

Needless to say, urban design and fashion are concerned with radically different objects; a garment (even a Fath or a Balanciaga) can hardly compare to the nature and complexity of a city, and the *longue durée* of urban histories seems totally alien to the vicissitudes of fashion. We nevertheless retain this comparison for its spatial (fashion as tailoring, i.e., construction of the garment) rather than its temporal dimension (fashion as a cult of the new) and value its ability to actively inflect and suggestively characterize the design process as a *craft*—i.e., an empirically based artistic practice that is distinguishable from both theory and ideology ("fashion" from the Latin *factio*, meaning the act of making). Comparing fashion to urban design should furthermore emphasize the primacy of the perceptible and the superficial in the production and experience of "urbanity" (the etymology of "fashion" also leads to *facies*, face, visible characteristics and appearance). We thereby suggest that "urbanity" is an *effect* that is staged for the pleasure of the senses; a matter of surface and phenomena rather than that of some underlying order or formal structure.

FIG. 9 *View of outdoor cinema at Remiseplatz*

Seams and stitches indeed play a critical role in shaping the character and intelligibility of the site. Violently slashing against the pattern of rectangular blocks, a diagonal cut should create oddly-shaped residual spaces at each intersection—a common condition

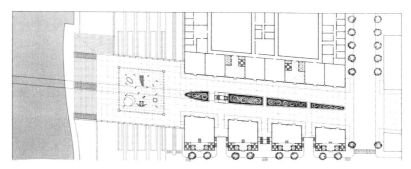

Donaubalkon with mixed-use development **FIG. 10**

in American cities.[2] However, the grid pattern was here manipulated, distorted and finely adjusted to the diagonal seam so as to orchestrate these otherwise accidental oddities into scenographic moments. The device is a familiar one, quite a commonplace in baroque stage design: the juxtaposition of multiple perspectival frameworks within a single frame.

An unprecedented effect is thus created with the succession of scenographic stitches along the seams of the site. We like to think of this serial repetition of the picturesque on the fast boulevard as a paradoxical intersection of Wagner's styled functionalism with Sitte's theatrical tailoring—yet another staging of the fortuitous meeting of the umbrella and the sewing machine upon the operating table (Figs. 13–15).

View of Donaubalkon **FIG. 11**
from Handelskai

View of Donaubalkon **FIG. 12**
from the funicular

An adequate adjustment and alignment of the opposite pattern across the diagonal seam is, of course, required for the scenographies to be properly experienced, since the tableaux are most effective when frontally viewed; hence the configuration of the promenade in the garden and the tunnels under the railroad tracks. The staging of these picturesque moments thus amounts to a process of small readjustments in the structure of all meeting fabrics and fragments, a fine tuning of alignments, patterns and biases that exploits the violent ruptures of seams for costumed and meaningful effects (Fig. 3). If we may again appeal to the fashion paradigm, we could compare this process to the craft of the "couturier," composing clashing patterns and textures of elastic fabrics across the seam.

Here again, in the distortion of regular figures and grids, we accept and cultivate the contamination of the rational with the empirical, the ideal with the contingent, particular, and "real." For irregularities and deformations are not the sites of compromise here, but rather the agents of meaning.

Among the elements thus tailored and assembled, the Donaubalkon, which gives shape to the much desired connection to the river, deserves a more detailed account (Figs. 10–12) We set up the Donaubalkon as the culminating event in an urban procession which originates as far away as the Lust Haus and concludes only across the river with a funicular ride. In this sequence of events, we seek to reframe the river as an integral element of the urban landscape. Characteristic activities of urban life (commerce, leisure and transportation) are thus pulled to the waterfront and staged as a dramatic ensemble under a monumental canopy, against the river as background. In this *mise-en-scène* of urbanity, rushing crowds of train and ferry travelers are played-off against more casual *flâneurs* amidst a wind-driven ballet of suspended columns. The cable car is featured prominently in the scene; it glides above the busy stage between the columnar straps of a diaphanous canvas (our version of sexy lingerie) and across the river so as to enhance the scenographic assimilation of the Danube with a more physical embrace.

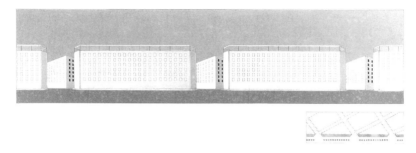

Flohmarkt Allée **FIG. 13**

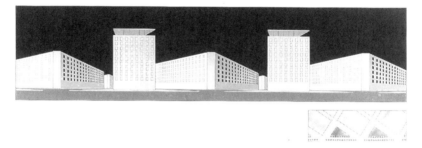

Trichtergarten Allée Ost **FIG. 14**

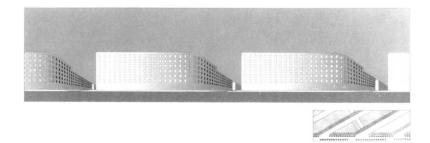

Trichtergarten Allée Westen **FIG. 15**

MACHADO AND SILVETTI 387

In closing, we succumb again to the seduction of metaphor and, casting the garment aside, return to the body—a familiar topos in the discourse of urbanism and the initial site of our analogy. We shall not appeal to the classical morphology of the Vitruvian man nor to the organization of a modern anatomy. We rather invoke Frankenstein's monster as a paradigm for the "seamful" urban body. Here again we dwell on the surface, on the monster's characteristic facial sutures, which register the artifice of imitation. The seam lines are also the characteristic features of our urban proposal; they reflect the inadequacy and impossibility of a seamless simulation of organic growth, and reject the more disjunctive prosthetics of collage. What we propose is not life itself but a flawed imitation that draws an uncanny vitality from the beauty of scars.

The author is a member of the Machado and Silvetti design team in Vienna.

NOTES

1   Design team—*designers:* Rodolfo Machado, Jorge Silvetti; *project coordinator:* Nader Tehrani; *Vienna design team:* Rodolphe El-Khoury, Vedran Glavina, Christopher Kirwan, Carsten Kiselowsky, Jaime Lopes Valdes, Adolfo Perez-Leiva, Giovanni Prestileo, Stephanie Schafroth, Samuel Trimble; *Boston design team:* Ann Catherine Bambrick, Dominique Desmet, Christopher Keane, Mark Schatz, Francisco Thébaud.

2   We do not propose any particular building types or block configurations to implement the new city fabrics while the socioeconomic scenario for their development remain undefined. The new fabric is too large an area to be undertaken as a single "Housing Project." We thus leave it to develop as "city matter," to evolve from more seemingly spontaneous operations. It is thus important to note that the elevations are rendered to give a sense of scale rather than of iconography.

Diller +

UNSEEMLINE

ZVI EFRAT

> For have not I too a compact all-enclosing Skin, whiter or
> dingier? Am I a botched mass of tailors' and cobblers' shreds,
> then; or a tightly-articulated, homogeneous little Figure, auto-
> matic, nay alive?

Thomas Carlyle, *Sartor Resartus* [1]

When does Fashion begin? Let us hypothesize boldly: since Fashion is change, systemic or arbitrary, it could not have begun *ex-mutatio*, in change, in mere rejection of a previous fashion; it must have begun, then, *ex-renuntio*, in the renouncement/announcement of change itself, in self-renunciation, in the studied display of plain-ness, deficiency and absolution.

ofidio's D Press

THE FASHIONABLE

In the annals of sartorial fashion the white dress shirt is described as an essentially immutable article, originating in the social upheaval of the French Revolution and documenting a shift in vestimentary behavior from class-related idio-syncracy to simplifica-tion, uniformity and occupational distinctions. Coincidentally, the rise of the machine, generically referred to as the Industrial Revolution, renders the old exuberant styles inapplicable and demands the representation of reproducibility in clothing. Vestimentary regimes, it is implied in these accounts, are purely contextual, affirmative and progressive.

FIG. 1 *From Ralph M. Barnes,* Motion and Time Study *(New York: John Wiley & Sons, 1937), 192. Courtesy of Factory Management and Maintenance.*

They absorb, mirror, at best interpret social, political and technological change, and in so doing are presumed fully explicable.

I would like to overstate the moment of the white dress shirt as the very genesis of a new order of representation, the fashion system as we know it, arguing that the new taste for albinism in clothing during the last decades of the eighteenth century cannot be explained solely as reflective of sociopolitical reality nor as simple mimesis of the characteristics of the machine, but must be considered as well in relation to 1) the historical imaginary associated with the French Revolution, and 2) the always equivocal *in*vestments of the modern body with the machine. Let us consider these supplementary conditions in some detail: first, the notion of *revolution*, which came to denote radical change, was conceived in the eighteenth century as a full-cycle *return*, a specific revolution *to* classical Greece and Rome, imagined in archaeological white. The new austerity of dress, therefore, reflected not only a progressive machine-age look, embodied in the black coat or the tubular hat, but also a retrogressive, antiquarian one, embodied in the white dress shirt. If architectural tastes of the time are of any analogical relevance— and so most scholars of fashion insist, Roland Barthes notwithstanding—antiquarianism is of the greater import. Furthermore, this first instance of sartorial classicism is also the beginning of sartorial atavism, the first apposition of the sanitary machine and immaculate primitive, which will inform virtually all subsequent trends in clothing throughout and beyond modernism. Before the French Revolution vestimentary regimes were contextual, successive and linear; they were not revolutionary—neither looking back nor decisively cast off the past. Without such double-sensed *revolution* we can hardly speak of Fashion.

Second, the emergence of "the cult of abstract man" as Marx astutely called it, was indeed gender specific—referring exclusively to the male body's abstraction and to abstraction as manly—and entailed charging the female body with bearing the man's loss. The psychologist J. C. Flugel was the first to identify clothing's internal split as a founding moment, considering it, however, to be women's great victory. In *The Psychology of Clothes* (1930), he writes:

> At about that time [the end of the eighteenth century] there
> occurred one of the most remarkable events in the whole his-
> tory of dress, one under the influence of which we are still liv-
> ing, one, moreover, which has attracted far less attention than
> it deserves: men gave up their right to all the brighter, gayer,
> more elaborate, and more varied forms of ornamentation, leav-
> ing these entirely to the use of women, and thereby making
> their own tailoring the most austere and ascetic of the arts.
> Sartorially, this event has surely the right to be considered as
> *"The Great Masculine Renunciation."* Man abandoned his
> claim to be considered beautiful. He henceforth aimed at
> being only useful (emphasis added).[2]

Flugel's stated mission is to reduce the displacement of male
libido from body to clothes, to free men from the "quasi-neurotic
asceticism" of their dress (which coincides with women's growing
emancipation from various forms of corsetry and tight-lacing), and
to close the distance between the principle of utility and the pleasure principle. However, while his analysis plays up the *use* of
ornament for women, it underplays both the use of the same ornament for men, that is, the fetishistic and scopophilic underpinning
of the division, *and* the eccentricity or potential narcissistic *pleasure* in self-renunciation. The Feminine, contrary to Flugel's opinion, had not suddenly been privileged as the Beautiful. In fact, it
had been divested of the implication of organic beauty and had
begun to represent solely the horror of arbitrary change, the mon-
strously erratic alteration of familiar form. It was in relation to this
heightened threat to the body's—and by extension society's—equi-
librium that the historical figure of the Dandy emerged, dressed in
flamboyantly "efficient" clothes.

Beau Brummell is said to have been the protagonist, if not the orig-
inator, of Dandyism, a social doctrine of gentility based on a theory
of "good form." Brummell's fetish was crisp, clean linen: the white
shirt as a whole, a detachable demi-shirt ("dickey" as it was called
in Victorian England), or at least a cravat. Social gentility dictated

the symbolic display of *undergarments*, as white linen was considered until the late nineteenth century (Fig. 2). Good form meant a pronounced surface cathexis and a clear demarcation of parts. The white layer between skin and overgarment intolerantly exposed stains, wrinkles or deformities, and served as a sanitary frame, always extending a little beyond the edges of the overgarment at the wrists and neck. The collar and cuffs, at the junctures of the torso's good form and the more expressive organs, were subjected to the most rigorous boiling, starching, ironing and polishing.

FIG. 2   *Combination garments helped to "keep up appearances." Shirt and waistcoat by John Smith, Cheapside City, 1849. From Sarah Levitt,* Victorians Unbuttoned: Registered Designs for Clothing, their Makers and Wearers, 1839–1900 *(London: George Allen & Unwin, 1986), 22.*

The pristine stiff shirt, an *armor* warding off sensuousness and containing the body's atrophy, was industrial man's annunciation of frailty, *dys*functionalism, and (fear of) loss of physical boundaries. Thus the formal, egological and social eccentricities of the Dandy both set up the foundations of the "aesthetic of efficiency" and point at the origin of Fashion in the avowal/disavowal of industrialism. In the historical moment when men constricted themselves to a virile mechanist frame, they also endowed themselves with a celibate vitalist force, an exaggerated (self)love that hampered the productive/reproductive operation of the machine.

In this light, see *BAD Press*: an installation of fourteen—or endlessly more—white dress shirts in states of acute plication. Five of the shirts are reproduced here, against whiter background, as presented in their exhibition catalog. Note the allegorical attitude of the installation, the close-bodied comportment of the shirts, their catatonic torment and antiquarian allusion. Such a mimetic attitude signals a predilection for the figural and fictional over the philosophical and historical. Note the architectural efficiency of the installation: its reliance on episodic structure or linear plexus, on technological minimums and on technical (uni)formality, to "reproduce difference" or "exacerbate form." Consider, therefore, the number of figures published here arbitrary. Consider as well the negligible gap between the installation's presence in the gallery and its reproduced form. Its ambiguity as object/image, so skillfully built into the frontality of the shirts themselves, and their conspicuously haptic presentation, blur ascribed distinctions of "production"/"consumption" in the mediatory flow of "distribution" and drain in advance any longing for authentic space, any pretense of a time better than now. This ambiguity is, indeed, a fundamental provision of *fashion* as a system of representation; the best indication of the installation's complacency within this system. The questions to be asked here are: what, if any, are the political and critical ramifications of such a position? Can the fashionable be thought of as having an impetus other than the vain perpetuation of need? Does it encrypt a predicament in its compliant surfaces?

Let us turn to Roland Barthes's *The Fashion System*[3] for the most ardent and self-reflexive attempt to seize the fashionable outside the virtuous guidelines of the social sciences.

The Fashion System was devised in 1957 as the ultimate showcase of applied semiology, then "still an entirely prospective discipline."[4] The body of his text is a study of the structures, codes, variants, matrices and ensembles of the "written garment" as they float and engage in a close tautological space. We should point out that by postulating clothes as structurally decipherable signs in a closed system, he studiously avoids their possible deployment as more opaque embodiments or surrogates operating between or on the soft margins of existing systems. Indeed, when Barthes, following Hegel's assertion that the body itself cannot signify, does consider clothes as a "spectacularly empirical version of the body," he notes that "more and more, the event threatens the structure"—an inadmissible threat to Barthes's regulatory precepts.[5] However, the fashion *system* and the vestimentary *metaphor* have their way with their operator and his mode of operation; the internal duration and timing of return. By the time Barthes finally completes his exhaustive study in 1963, he realizes with the certainty of the *arbiter elegantiarum* of his time that it is "already dated," and needs therefore a provisional reframing. As his retrospective Foreword reflects, the initial promise of underpinning fashion theoretically or of launching semiology analogically ends up, by force of changing intellectual fashions, being "*already* a certain history of semiology."[6] It is only when Barthes allows his own venture to be drawn into this insatiable *system*—when he admits this brief pleasure— that he can finally position himself outside fashion, claim a small victory over his slippery subject. Most appropriately, he does not disown or modify the dated Saussurian body of his text, but outfits it instead with contingent Foreword, Conclusion and Appendices, aligned already with the latest intellectual currents. *The Fashion System*, therefore, is not at all a history of semiology but rather a documentation of a shift in intellectual tastes taking place between 1957 and 1963; it is text *and passe-partout*, body *and* auxiliary organs, already a poststructuralist seamiology.

In the Conclusion to the *The Fashion System*, the "infinite metaphor" of clothing, initially intended to define theory from without, to keep it productive and exploratory, becomes one with its machine. The internal economy of fashion, its endless play of substitutions, implicates Theory in the spectacle of reproduction and simulation and folds it back onto its ground of formal logic.

> Fashion thus proposes this precious paradox of a *semantic system whose only goal is to disappoint the meaning it luxuriantly elaborates*: the system then abandons the meaning yet does so without giving up any of the spectacle of signification. This reflexive activity has a mental model: formal logic. Like logic,

> Fashion is defined by the infinite variation of a single tauto-
> logy; like logic, Fashion seeks equivalences, validities, not
> truths; and like logic, Fashion is stripped of content, but not of
> meaning. A kind of machine for maintaining meaning without
> ever fixing it, it is forever a disappointed meaning, but it is
> nevertheless a meaning: without content, it then becomes the
> spectacle human beings grant themselves of their power to
> make the insignificant signify; Fashion then appears as the
> general act of signification.[7]

This outline of the fashion-machine could well be construed as
compatible with Marxist idiom, if only it had a reprimanding conclusion—if only it did not insist on the lack of truth and the truth
of lack as constitutive and enterprising. Without such a conclusion
or internal truth, Barthes' *Fashion System* remains a fancy of "mis-
production," a "bachelor meta-machine" like those into which so
many recent artistic, literary, and eventually architectural fashions
are plugged.

According to Barthes, the formal logic of fashion is supported by a
unique temporal construct which he calls *achrony*, "a time which
does not exist" in which the "past is shameful and the present constantly "eaten up" by the fashion being heralded."[8] Achrony, as
opposed to both diachrony (history) and anachrony (historicism),
suggests an encroachment on or haunting of the present by an
entombed past that saps all vitality or authenticity with its avid
citation marks. Such a "vampiric" ploy could be detected in *BAD
Press*.

In the exegetic text that accompanies the installation, Diller +
Scofidio refer to scientific management as "the practice of rationalizing and standardizing human motion for increased productivity in
the factory." They suggest that this practice fostered a false simili-
tude among the paradigms of *least effort, optimum yield* and *optical
hygiene* that engrossed the household and registered on the surfaces of the body. In response, their aberrant folding, a gesture of
postindustrial *dys*functionalism, undertakes to "release [ironing]

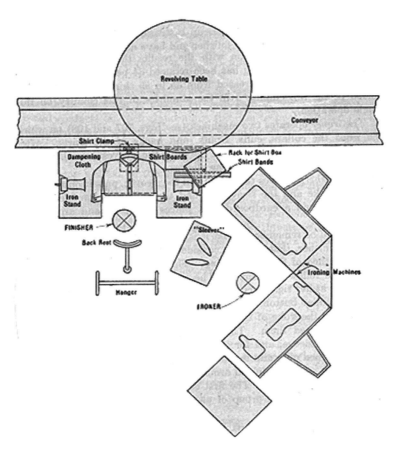

FIG. 3 *Study for maximizing the efficiency of the work place showing the arrangement of the ironer and the finisher's table, circa 1935. From Barnes,* Motion and Time Study, *193.*

from the aesthetic of efficiency altogether." So a "shameful past" of scientific management—and utilitarianism in general—is clearly allocated, reworked and decisively exorcised. That is, if we find absolution a plausible motive. If we don't, the clarity and seemliness of the text only intensify the abyssal "transparency" of the installation itself. After all, the title, strict methodology, inert display and sterile look of the installation, satisfying as they are, do not corroborate the euphoric notion of "release" and seem instead to *paraphrase* utilitarianism's innate coprophobia. The "aesthetic of efficiency," we may conjecture, is not belatedly defiled in *BAD Press*; quite the opposite, it is exhumed as imperative groundwork for the "aesthetic of excess." At issue, then, is the immediate present—that of mutant folding—within which the installation operates clandestinely by connecting to and at the same time cutting itself off from an orthopedic past now pertinent only as irony.

Let us briefly re-activate this past in its moment of most extreme pleasure before assessing its medusian effect on the present.

The main task of scientific management, or "enlightened Taylorism" as it was called during the 1910s and 1920s, was not to measure, but to *visualize* the body at work in curvilinear graphs and pleasing patterns *recorded* by such ghostly agents as micromotion cameras, autoteletime machines, chronocyclographs and wire-models—all "flexible, light, inexpensive, durable" and "adaptable to any type of work and to any type of *observer or self-observation*" (emphasis added).[9]

But with the collapse of the economy in 1930s America, the abstracted "truth" of efficiency ceased to provide credible evidence for the industrialist or sufficient incentive for the worker. The popular media, an industry that still worked, was summoned to spectacularize and ritualize work. Scientific management found its apotheosis in the Hollywood musical, and ironing, a type-activity for scientific study (Fig. 3) was soon re-enacted on the screen.

The musical's "specialty numbers" or "production numbers" had little diegetic content of their own other than the blunt analogy between *chorus-line girls* and *assembly-line workers*. They were conceived as elaborate ruptures in profilmic space. The distinct optical conventions of these numbers—vertical top-shots, exaggerated camera movement, jump-cuts and non-perspectival sets—protested the hegemony of the cinema's deep horizontal gaze and promoted instead "pure" motion, "pure" optics, and an incessantly deterritorialized subject.

FIG. 4   *film stills from "The Girl at the Ironing Board," in Busby Berkeley's* Dames, *Warner brothers, 1934*

FIG. 5   *film stills from "The Girl at the Ironing Board," in Busby Berkeley's* Dames, *Warner brothers, 1934*

film stills from "The Girl at the Ironing Board," in Busby Berkeley's Dames, **FIG. 6**
Warner brothers, 1934

Dames (1934) is "the landmark musical that has it all."[10] Busby Berkeley's four production numbers in the film display the full range of trick technology and male fantasies from fairly innocuous voyeurism in "I Only Have Eyes for You," to sadistic mutilation in "What Do You Go For." Of particular interest is the film's first number, "The Girl at The Ironing Board," which still upholds the optical conventions of cinema. This number "vindicates" the ensuing cycle of abstraction and punishment of the female body in a hilarious necromantic inversion. The routine work at the ironing-board becomes hallucinatory, escalating into a *danse-macabre* of ironing-girls with stiffened men's whites (Figs. 4–6).

In the aftermath of the exstatic dance of *Dames*, of motion as symbolic discourse, Diller + Scofidio leave us with a series of stills. The contorted shirts of *BAD Press* present an impasse, the impossibility of the body to act, to make, to project itself beyond its boundaries. The spectacle of efficiency is wrested from the transitory media and installed in the contemplative order of the bas-relief object's auratic image. In this order, *BAD Press*'s manifold allusions—to eccentric collections and clothes-fetishism, to technobodies and industrial hygiene, to domestic labor and sartorial strictures, to motion studies and ergonomics—are "disappointed meanings luxuriantly elaborated," desires distilled from discourses and internalized as the installation's own lack of proper subject and object. This internal and systemic lack, to reiterate Barthes's point, defines its position in fashion; a position which, on one hand, rejects the eccentricity of being off-discourse or out-of-date, and on the other, trivializes the frantic production of change and wears away the inner linings of the new fetish. Let us outline in conclusion the correlation of *BAD Press* to the newest of them.

The well-coordinated return of the *fold* as a topos to architecture, via philosophy, is undoubtedly the most extravagant instance to date of fashion's musings in this discipline. In brief, the fold was reborn fully formed as at once praxis at all scales, theory at utmost pliancy, and historicism at its most self-ironic.[11] For poststructuralist architectural discourse (to avoid the pitfalls of more spe-cific labels), the fold is an exceptionally potent medium or trope. First, because it consolidates the favored deconstructivist ambiguities of structure/ frame/skin/drape. Second, because it allegedly stands for whatever is culturally associated with the feminine or the marginalized. And finally, because it offers itself as at once an *effect* (a crease, an inscription) of a direct operation on the object, the *operation* itself (folding), and the implied *reversibility* of the operation (unfolding). In this, it fills a gap between the Heideggerian two-foldedness of con-cealment/unconcealment, enframing/unframing, structure/event, motion/stasis, animism/automatism; and the Deleuzian "blind-fold-edness" of rhizomic growth, irregular flow, chance, mutability, inter-connectedness, and continuity between surface and structure.

In *BAD Press*, enough of these conditions of the fold are technically reaffirmed to indicate a full awareness of a new architectural fashion. But, divested of their philosophical garments and presup-posed gender, these conditions become caustic footnotes to the return of the fold and to the workings of Fashion in general. The critical distance of *BAD Press* from what is already termed the New Baroque could be summarized in three interrelated antitheses. First, folding here negates the notion of unfolding. It does not pos-tulate an epic field of action, or an abstract-expressionist skin, or a layered motion picture, but a parataxis of disconnected desires and ungainly actions. Second, folding here is not theoretical and certainly not conciliatory, as the new fold promotes itself to be. *BAD Press*'s fictional and punitive disposition forces us back home. It finds a precise portrayal in Elaine Scarry's *The Body in Pain*:

> Even fictional representations of torture like Kafka's "In the Penal Colony," where the lethal apparatus is an enlarged sewing machine, record the fact that the unmaking of civilization inevitably requires a return to and mutilation of the domestic, the ground of all making.[12]

Finally, and most poignantly, there is nothing "soft," "pliable," "weak," not even slippery, about *BAD Press*. Its folding s(t)imulates a grotesque lasting stiffness. Architecture does not masquerade here as feminine. It is *dis*organized and *mis*directed in its hard phallic crust.

NOTES

1   Thomas Carlyle, *Sartor Resartus, The Life and Opinions of Herr Teufelsdrockh* (London: Chapman and Hall, 1896), 44.

2   J. C. Flugel, *The Psychology of Fashion* (London: Hogarth Press, 1930), 117.

3   Roland Barthes, *The Fashion System*, translated by Matthew Ward and Richard Howard (Berkeley: University of California, 1990). Originally published as *Systeme de la Mode* (Paris: Editions de Seuil, 1957).

4   Ibid., ix.

5   Ibid., 259.

6   Ibid., ix.

7   Ibid., 288.

8   Ibid., 289.

9   Frank B. Gilbreth and Lillian M. Gilbreth, *Applied Motion Study, A Collection of Papers* (Easton: Hive Publishing Company, 1973 [c. 1912–16]), 71.

10   See Lucy Fisher's excellent study, "The Image of Woman as Image: The Optical Politics of 'Dames,'" and Mark Roth, "Some Warner's Musicals and the Spirit of The New Deal," both in Rick Altman, ed., *Genre: The Musical* (London: Routledge and Kegan Paul, 1981). See also Rick Altman, *The American Film Musical* (Bloomington: Indiana University Press, 1987), and Jane Feuer, *The Hollywood Musical* (Bloomington: Indiana University Press, 1982).

11   For an account of the return of the fold as architectural fashion, see *Architectural Design* 102 (*Folding in Architecture*), 1993.

12   Elaine Scarry, *The Body in Pain, The Making and Unmaking of the World* (Oxford: Oxford University Press, 1985), 45.

DILLER + SCOFIDIO

Scientific management, the practice of rationalizing and standardizing the motion of the working body, conceived to expand industrial productivity, was applied to housework in the early years of the twentieth century. Time-motion studies, developed to dissect every action of the factory laborer with the intention of designing ideal shapes of movement—and, ultimately, the ideal laborer—were imported into the home to scrutinize every movement exerted in housekeeping to produce the ideal housewife. The body of the housewife was interpreted as a dynamic force: with unlimited capacity for work, her only enemy was fatigue. And fatigue, in broader terms, undermined the moral imperative of the new social reform: the reclamation of waste as usable potential.

The application of labor-saving techniques from scientific management, in conjunction with the introduction of new household appliances, "electric servants," sought to conserve the physical expenditure of the housewife. The time and energy saved, according to the rhetoric of "efficiency," would release the woman from the home and thus enable her to join the paid labor force. This strategy, however, did not fulfill its liberating promise. The drive for efficiency was often taken as an objective in itself. Ironically, it condemned the housewife to an increased work load as the expectations and standards of cleanliness in the home rose to compulsive states. Accordingly, and magnified with the discovery of the household germ, the design of the domestic interior succumbed to a paranoid hygiene—a program collapsing the dust and germ-breeding intricacies of nineteenth-century space into pure surface under continuous disciplinary surveillance.

As housework slowly becomes de-gendered, most domestic conventions remain unchallenged. Housework's main activities of managing dirt and restoring daily order continue to be subject to the economic ethos of industry. The task of ironing, for example, is

governed by minimums. A minimum of effort is used to reshape the shirt through a minimum of flat facets into a two-dimensional, repetitive unit that will consume a minimum of space. The standardized ironing pattern of a man's shirt habitually returns the shirt to a flat, rectangular form which fits economically into orthogonal systems of storage— at the site of manufacture, the factory-pressed shirt is stacked and packed into rectangular cartons, loaded as cubic volume onto trucks, and transported to retail space, where the shirt's rectangular form is reinforced in orthogonal display cases, and sustained after purchase—in the home on closet shelves or in dresser drawers, and perpetuated in the departure from home in suitcases. The shirt is disciplined at every stage to conform to an unspoken social contract.

When worn, the residue of the orthogonal logic of efficiency is registered on the surface of the body. The parallel creases and crisp, square corners of a clean, pressed shirt are sought-after emblems of refinement. This by-product of efficiency has become a new object of its desire.

But what if the task of ironing could free itself from the aesthetics of efficiency altogether? Perhaps housework could more aptly represent the postindustrial family by trading the image of the functional for new imperatives of the dysfunctional.

Project Assistance: Brendan Cotter, John Bachus, David Lindberg

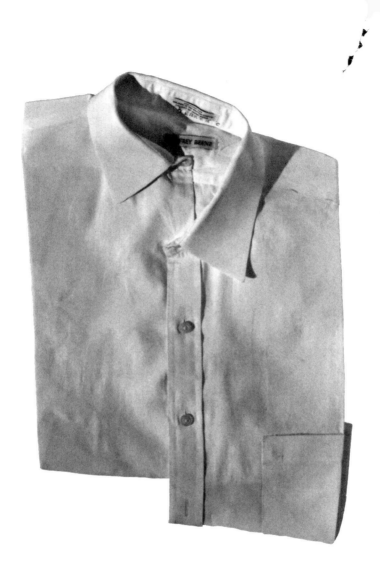

DILLER + SCOFIDIO 407

Project Assistance: Brendan Cotter, John Bachus, David Lindberg

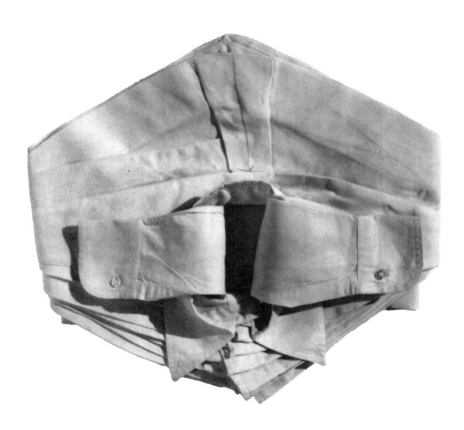

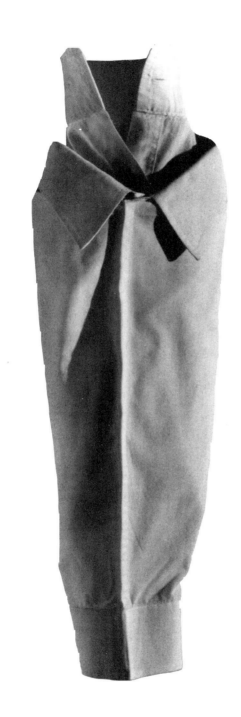

Authors' Biographies

DILLER + SCOFIDIO

Diller + Scofidio is a New York-based collaborative team involved in cross-disciplinary work that incorporates architecture with the performing and visual arts. Elizabeth Diller is assistant professor of architecture at Princeton University. Ricardo Scofidio is professor of architecture at Cooper Union.

ZVI EFRAT

Zvi Efrat received his architecture degree from Pratt Institute in New York and a master's degree in cinema studies from New York University. He has practiced architecture in New York City, and is currently teaching film and architecture at Tel Aviv University. He is the architecture editor of an Israeli art magazine named Studio.

RODOLPHE EL-KHOURY

Rodolphe El-Khoury received his bachelor's in architecture from the Rhode Island School of Design and an master's from the MIT Program in History, Theory and Criticism. He began his professional practice with a Boston firm and subsequently set up Office dA (Office for design and Architecture) with Nader Tehrani. He has held teaching positions at The Boston Architectural Center, Louisiana State University, and Columbia University. He is currently a Ph.D. candidate at Princeton University, and teaches at the Harvard Graduate School of Design.

DEBORAH FAUSCH

Deborah Fausch is a professor of architectural theory and history at Parsons School of Design in New York, and has practiced architecture in New York and Minnesota. She received a bachelor's in English and physics from Carleton College, and a Bachelor of architecture from the University of Minnesota. She is a Ph.D. candidate in architecture at Princeton University. Her publications include "The Knowledge of the Body and the Presence of History," forthcoming in the *Yale Journal of Architecture and Feminism.*

LEILA KINNEY

Leila Kinney teaches art history in the History, Theory and Criticism section of the department of architecture at MIT. Her writing on nineteenth-century French painting has been published in *The Art Journal* and *Assemblage* and she is working on a study of theorists of fashion from Balzac to Barthes.

MACHADO AND SILVETTI

Machado and Silvetti Associates, Inc., is a planning and design firm known for distinctive urban spaces and works of architecture within the United States and abroad. Jorge Silvetti and Rodolfo Machado have practiced together since 1974. Both are currently professors at the Harvard University Graduate School of Design. The firm's work has been published in all major international professional magazines, as well as major newspapers; and exhibited in the U.S., Europe, and Latin America. Among other awards, the firm has received eight *Progressive Architecture* Awards and Citations and two Boston Society of Architects Awards, as well as Design Awards in Argentina, France, Germany, and Italy.

ERIN MACKIE

Erin Mackie teaches in the English department at Washington University in St. Louis, Mo. She has just completed a dissertation on the treatment of fashion in *The Tatler* and *The Spectator* for her degree from Princeton University.

MARY MCLEOD

Mary McLeod is an associate professor of architecture at Columbia University, where she currently teaches architectural history and studio. She has also taught at Harvard University, University of

Miami, University of Kentucky, and the Institute for Architecture and Urban Studies. She is co-editor of *Architecture Criticism Ideology* and *Architectu-re-production* (both from Princeton Architectural Press). Her articles have appeared in *Assemblage*, *Oppositions*, *The Art Journal*, *AA Files*, *Lotus*, *Places*, and *Design Book Review*.

PAULETTE SINGLEY

Paulette Singley is an assistant professor at Iowa State University's School of Architecture. She received a bachelor's in architecture from the University of Southern California and a master's in architectural history and urbanism from Cornell University. She is completing her doctorate in architectural history and theory at Princeton University, and is the recipient of received a Samuel H. Kress Foundation Grant to complete research in Italy for her dissertation, entitled "The Seduction of Archaeology and Exile in Gabriele D'Annunzio's Villa, Il Vittoriale degli Italiani." She has practised in several architectural firms, most notably Venturi Scott Brown and Associates. Published works are "Living in a Glass Prism: The Female Figure in Ludwig Mies van der Rohe's Domestic Speculum," in *Critical Matrix* (1992); and "The Anamorphic Phallus within Ledoux's Dismembered City of Chaux," in the *Journal of Architectural Education* (1993).

VENTURI SCOTT BROWN

Robert Venturi and Denise Scott Brown are world-renowned architects and planners noted for their designs for institutions and their sensitivity to the American context.

VAL K. WARKE

Val K. Warke received a bachelors in architecture from Cornell University and an master's in architecture from the Harvard University Graduate School of Design and has, coincidentally, taught architectural design and theory at these same two schools.

His articles of criticism and theory have appeared in *The Harvard Architecture Review*, *The Cornell Journal of Architecture*, *The Architectural Review*, *Thom Mayne Sixth Street House*, and *Assemblage*, among others. He is currently an associate professor at Cornell (having been promoted from department chair) and practices architecture in partnership with Andrea Simitch.

MARK WIGLEY

Mark Wigley teaches architecture at Princeton University. He is the author of *The Architecture of Deconstruction: Derrida's Haunt* (MIT Press, 1993) and the editor of *Assemblage 20, Violence Space*.